RECONCILIATION AND JUSTIFICATION

The Sacrament and Its Theology

KENAN B. OSBORNE, O.F.M.

PAULIST PRESS
New York/Mahwah

Library of Congress Cataloging-in-Publication Data

Osborne, Kenan B.
    Reconciliation and justification: the sacrament and its theology
/ Kenan B. Osborne.
        p.   cm.
    Includes bibliographical references.
    ISBN 0-8091-3143-9
    1. Penance—History.   2. Reconciliation—Religious aspects—
Christianity—History of doctrines.   3. Reconciliation—Religious
aspects—Catholic Church—History of doctrines.   4. Justification—
History of doctrines.   5. Catholic Church—Doctrines—History.
I. Title.
BV840.083   1990
234'.166'09—dc20   89-48584
                                                                         CIP

Published by Paulist Press
997 Macarthur Boulevard
Mahwah, New Jersey 07430

Printed and bound in the
United States of America

Contents

1

Reconciliation and Justification:
Their Interrelationship

The first occasion, in which the bishops at the Council of Trent began their discussion on the sacrament of reconciliation, took place during their deliberation on the issue of justification. Without any doubt the bishops realized that the theology of justification involved the theology of the sacrament of reconciliation and vice versa. This interconnection, which these bishops at least to some degree articulated, indicates that one cannot speak theologically about the sacrament of reconciliation without presupposing or simultaneously discussing a theology of justification.

In a similar way of thinking, the critique made by the reformation theologians had focused on the then-current practices and the then-current theological understandings of penance and confession, and the ways in which these practices and these theologies reflected a Christian theology of justification. In many ways, the basic reformation statements on justification, which comes only through faith in Jesus Christ, concentrated on the sacrament of penance, in which justification from sin, so it was commonly argued, occurred through the confession of sin and priestly absolution.[1] E. Gritsch, in his discussion on the origins of justification in Lutheran teaching, notes:

> Neither the sacrament of penance, centered in the monastic demand to mortify the flesh, nor Scholastic theology, as presented especially by Peter Lombard, had helped Luther find the gracious God he sought. John Staupitz, the vicar-general of the Augustinian Hermits and Luther's father confessor, forced

1

Luther to come to terms with himself by requiring him to study Scripture in order to teach it.[2]

There is no doubt that reformation theologians generally perceived the theological interrelationship between the sacrament of reconciliation, on the one hand, and justification, on the other, so that their critique of the sacrament of penance depended on their analysis of justification. One cannot understand what the reformation theologians said concerning the sacrament of penance, without understanding what they said about justification.

These two currents of sixteenth century theology, one from the Roman Catholic approach and the other from the reformation approach, have been eminently influential in both churches from the sixteenth century down to our own. A theological understanding of justification underlies not only the sacrament of penance, but the entire sacramental structure of both churches. Moreover, a theological understanding of justification plays a major role in the theological understanding of the ministerial structures of both churches as well, and in both churches official ministers administer the sacraments. Thus, from the sixteenth century onward, the way in which a theology of justification was presented by either the Roman Catholic or the Protestant positions influenced the theological stance and discussion on the sacrament of penance. Since little accord took place on the issue of justification between these two Christian groups during those four hundred years, little accord on a theology of the sacrament of penance could be hoped for. Since Vatican II, however, greater *rapprochement* on this issue of justification has taken place, with the result that a new and ecumenical study of the sacrament of penance is now possible.

It will, therefore, be the interrelationship of these two aspects of Christian life: justification through Jesus alone, on the one hand, and the sacrament or ritual of penance, on the other, which will thread through this entire volume. The main emphasis will, however, be on the theology of the sacrament of penance, but at every stage of the discussion due attention will be given to the theology of justification.

In the Roman Catholic Church, on December 2, 1973, the new Rite of Penance was promulgated. Almost immediately scholars prepared important theological and liturgical commentaries on this new ritual. Pastoral studies and presentations also became part of parish life.[3] In most all of these, the focus was rather exclusively on the new ritual: its meaning, its structure, its spirituality, its strong points and its weak points. Some of the more elaborate commentaries and studies included as well a history of the sacrament of penance, in conjunction with their commentary. None of these commentaries and presentations, however, took up, in any detailed and deliberate way, the issue of justification, so as to indicate the fundamental interconnection between a theology of justification on the one hand and its theological basis of this new rite of penance on the other. As time went on, it has become more and more evident, however, that this is a fundamental need. The new Rite of Penance is clearly an improvement over the former ritual in the Roman Catholic Church; nonetheless, many of its limitations stem precisely from its lack of catechetical and theological integration into the theological aspects of justification.

Every sacrament is, in its own way, a moment of reconciliation: holy baptism and confirmation as sacraments of initiation bring one the healing grace of God's love for us in Jesus; the eucharist celebrates and makes Jesus, who healed the sick and forgave sinners, present to the gathered community; marriage brings strengthening grace to the love-relationship between a husband and a wife; holy orders brings the ministry of Jesus' healing into each local Christian community; anointing of the sick is a special sacrament of Christian healing for those who are infirm. Every Christian sacrament is rightfully a sacrament of reconciliation, whether one's church acknowledges two sacramental rituals (baptism and eucharist) or seven sacramental rituals. All such sacraments must be seen as sacraments of reconciliation. The sacrament of penance is, therefore, but one expression of Christian reconciliation, and by no means can it be presented as either the only sacrament of reconciliation or the most important sacrament of reconciliation.

This relativization of the sacrament of penance as a moment of reconciliation has been endorsed by Vatican II. The documents of Vatican II clearly attest to the church itself as a basic or fundamental sacrament. The church community, as a basic sacrament, is itself, then, a major sacrament of reconciliation. M.-J. Le Guillou notes: "In the same way that Christ is the sacrament of God for the world, so too the Church is the sacrament of Christ for the world."[4] If Jesus is the sacrament of God's reconciling love for all men and women, then the church in itself, not merely in one of its ritual moments, is a sacrament of reconciliation. Indeed, the church is a basic or foundational sacrament of reconciliation and, consequently, an even "more basic" sacrament of reconciliation than either penance or the eucharist.

A further indication of this relativized place of the sacrament of penance within a total theology of reconciliation is to be found in contemporary Roman Catholic sacramental theology, in which the most fundamental or primordial sacrament is the very humanity of Jesus.

Although the documents of Vatican II never speak of Jesus, in his humanness, as a sacrament, the conciliar statements on the church as a basic sacrament make no sense except on the premise that Jesus is himself, in his human nature, the primordial sacrament. The Christian community from its beginnings down to the present acclaims that Jesus is the Lord and savior. In Jesus alone is there salvation, reconciliation, or justification. Jesus, in his human condition, then, is the primordial sacrament of reconciliation. All other sacraments of reconciliation are meaningful only in and through this primordial sacrament, Jesus himself. Whenever a Christian hears the term "sacrament of reconciliation," the first correlative thought should be Jesus, not a ritual, not even the church. Jesus is the most fundamental sacrament of reconciliation.

Jesus is also the revelation and source of all justification. It is this convergence of both reconciliation and justification in Jesus that is the starting point for both a theology of justification (Jesus, the savior of all) and a theology for a sacrament of penance (Jesus, the primordial sacrament of reconciliation). Accordingly, the point of departure is not:

a. a definition of sacrament;
b. a definition of justification;
c. a study of the history of the sacrament of penance;
d. a study of the history of the theology of justification;
e. a study of the rituals of penance.

The above issues are all of vital importance, but the more fundamental issue is christological. In Roman Catholic theology it is acceptable today to speak of Jesus as the primordial sacrament, but often this is done in a fairly general way. Jesus, in his humanity, is described as the primordial or fundamental sacrament, but since primordiality means that all other Christian sacraments are unintelligible and meaningless unless they are intrinsically connected with this sacramentality of Jesus, the interrelatedness of Jesus to each sacrament (church, baptism, eucharist, etc.) must be more profoundly and carefully spelled out. In other words, Jesus in his human condition must be presented as the basic baptismal sacrament, as the basic eucharistic sacrament, as the basic matrimonial sacrament, as the basic reconciliation sacrament, etc.[5]

When we come to the issue of justification, we should note first of all that justification is but one way to speak of the mystery of salvation. There are many theological expressions which also describe, in one way or another, some facet of this mystery, all of which have a certain legitimacy:

reconciliation	illumination
justification	purification
salvation	divinization
sanctification	atonement
expiation	redemption
satisfaction	regeneration
forgiveness of sin	liberation
healing	freedom

In various Christian traditions, one or other of these terms have taken on a central role. In the Protestant traditions, "justification" has been the preferred term. In the Roman Catholic tradition, from the medieval period on, "redemption" has been the more common term. In the Orthodox traditions, the term "divinization" has centralized the mystery of Jesus. In the sixteenth century, the reformation theologians began to distinguish "justification" as an act of God, external to human endeavor, by which God declared a man or woman righteous, from "sanctification" as an internal, human process through which a man or woman undergoes a spiritual renewal. In this view, justification and sanctification are concomitant, but logically they are considered different. Not all theologians, however, agree with this view, as we shall see in later chapters.

Karl Rahner speaks of a variety of terminology for this central mystery: a negative terminology, such as "redemption," and a positive terminology, such as "reconciliation" or "restoration"; a liturgical terminology, such as "expiation" or "the shedding of blood," and a juridical terminology, such as "ransom." There is, he adds, a more generic term: "salvation." There are also terms, in his view, which describe the effects of Jesus' saving work: "liberation, new creation, rebirth, justification, possession of the Spirit, son/daughtership, resurrection, vision of God, eternal life."[6]

A. E. McGrath in his history of the Christian doctrine of justification advises us to make a distinction between the concept of justification and the doctrine of justification.

> The *concept* of justification is one of many employed within the Old and New Testaments, particularly the Pauline corpus, to describe God's saving action towards his people. It cannot lay claim to exhaust, nor adequately characterise in itself, the richness of the biblical understanding of salvation. The *doctrine* of justification has come to develop a meaning quite independent

of its biblical origins, and concerns the *means by which man's relationship to God is established.*[7]

McGrath goes on to state that in the western church the term "justification" came to be applied more and more to the doctrine of salvation, bearing thereby a meaning within dogmatic theology which is quite independent of its Pauline origins.

That it was justification, rather than some other soteriological metaphor which was singled out in this manner, may be regarded as an accident of history, linked to several developments.[8]

These developments include: (a) the interest in Pauline thought in the theological renaissance of the twelfth century; (b) the high regard for classical jurisprudence within the western church; (c) the semantic relationship between *iustitia* and *iustificatio* which allowed medieval theologians a means to describe God's forgiveness of sin; (d) Luther's emphasis on the phrase "God is just," and its connection with justification; (e) Trent's discussion of salvation using the same word, justification.[9]

It is evident that in the history of the Christian church this central mystery of our faith has been nuanced differently through the use of various names. However, it is not simply the variety of names which one should consider, but even more importantly the underlying theological positions. All of these words—justification, salvation, reconciliation, etc. —have a christological center, namely: there is no salvation outside of Jesus Christ. The New Testament is quite clear on this:

Jesus died for sinners	Rom 5:6: "We were still helpless when at his appointed moment Christ died for sinful men."
Jesus died for us/you	Rom 5:8: "But what proves that God loves us is that Christ died for us while we were still sinners."
	1 Cor 1:13: "Was it Paul that was crucified for you?"
	1 Cor 11:24: "This is my body which is for you."
	2 Cor 5:21: "For our sake God made the sinless one into sin."

Gal 3:13: "Christ redeemed us from the curse of the law by being cursed for our sake."

Eph 5:2: "And follow Christ by loving as he loved you, giving himself up in our place as a fragrant offering and a sacrifice to God."

Tit 2:14: "He sacrificed himself for us in order to set us free from all wickedness and to purify a people so that it could be his very own and would have no ambition except to do good."

1 Pet 2:21: "This, in fact, is what you were called to do, because Christ suffered for you and left an example for you to follow."

1 Jn 3:16: "This has taught us love—that he gave up his life for us."

1 Thes 5:10: "God never meant us to experience the retribution, but to win salvation through our Lord Jesus Christ, who died for us, so that, alive or dead, we should still live united to him."

Jesus died for me	Gal 2:20: "I live in faith: faith in the Son of God who loved me and who sacrificed himself for my sake."
Jesus died for someone	Rom 14:15: "You are certainly not free to eat what you like if that means the downfall of someone for whom Christ died."
	1 Cor 8:11: "In this way your knowledge could become the ruin of someone weak, of a brother for whom Christ died."
Jesus died for many	Mk 14:24: "This is my blood, the blood of the covenant, which is to be poured out for many."

Mk 10:45: "For the Son of Man himself did not come to be served but to serve, and to give his life as a ransom for many."

Jn 17:19: "And for their sake I consecrate myself, so that they too may be consecrated in truth."

Jesus died for the just

1 Pet 3:18: "Why Christ himself, innocent though he was, had died once for sins, died for the guilty, to lead to God."

Jesus died for all

Rom 8:32: "Since God did not spare his own Son, but gave him to benefit us all, we may be certain, after such a gift, that he will not refuse anything he can give."

2 Cor 5:14: "And this is because the love of Christ overwhelmed us when we reflect that if one man has died for all, then all men should be dead; and the reason he died for all was so that living men should live no longer for themselves, but for him who died and was raised to life for them."

Heb 2:9: "By God's grace he had to experience death for all mankind."

1 Tim 2:6: "For there is only one God, and there is only one mediator between God and mankind, himself a man, Christ Jesus, who sacrificed himself as a ransom for them all."

Jesus died for the church

Eph 5:25: "Husbands should love their wives just as Christ loved the church and sacrificed himself for her."

Jesus died for sin

1 Cor 15:3: "Well, then, in the first place I taught you what I had been taught myself, namely, that Christ died for our sins."

Gal 1:4: "We wish you the grace and peace of God our Father and of the Lord Jesus Christ, who in order to rescue us from this present wicked world sacrificed himself for our sins."

Heb 10:12: "He, on the other hand, has offered one single sacrifice for sins, and then has taken his place for ever at the right hand of God."

1 Pet 3:18: "Why Christ himself, innocent though he was, died once for sins."

Rom 8:3: "And in that body God condemned sin."

1 Jn 2:2: "He is the sacrifice that takes our sins away."

1 Jn 4:10: ". . . God's love for us when he sent his Son to be the sacrifice that takes our sins away."

Rom 4:25: "Our faith too will be considered if we believe in him who raised Jesus our Lord from the dead, Jesus who was put to death for our sins and raised to life to justify us."

Jesus died for many

Mt 26:28: "For this is my blood, the blood of the covenant, which is to be poured out for many for the forgiveness of sins."

Jesus died for the world

Jn 6:51: "And the bread that I shall give is my flesh for the life of the world."

Jesus died for his sheep

Jn 10:11: "The good shepherd is one who lays down his life for his sheep."

Jn 10:15: "And I know the Father; and I lay down my life for my sheep."

Jesus died for the nation	Jn 11:31: "It was as high priest that he made this prophecy that Jesus was to die for the nation."
	Jn 18:14: "It was Caiaphas who had suggested to the Jews: It is better for one man to die for the people."
Jesus died for friends	Jn 15:13: "A man can have no greater love than to lay down his life for his friends."

This is a powerful array of New Testament citations on this issue of Jesus and salvation, and although a mere listing of New Testament passages is, by itself, inadequate to "prove" a particular position, the almost incessant repetition of a given idea is indicative of something central to the gospel message. Whether the words used are: for us, for many, for all, or for some other group, the constant belief of the Christian community, down through the centuries, has been: Jesus died for all, that is, Jesus is the savior of all. There is no other savior. There is no other means of salvation for anyone except in and through Jesus.

This central belief of the Christian community raises *external* questions, that is, about other world religions and their relationship to Jesus and to Christianity. This complex issue cannot be addressed in this present volume. This particular *external* question, however, is clearly one of the most profound questions which a full-blown christology must confront, particularly in today's religiously pluralistic world.

However, this central belief has also presented a series of questions *internal* to the Christian community as well, questions which galvanized the reformation theologians. If Jesus alone is the savior of the world, if (in their terminology) the death of Jesus is once and for all and totally expiatory for the sins of all men and women, in what way can such sacraments as baptism, eucharist and penance be related to this once-and-for-all justification? How is the process of contrition, confession, absolution and satisfaction related to this once-and-for-all justification in Jesus? Any Christian ritual, sacrament, prayer, good work, etc., which compromises the full efficacy of Jesus' salvific work, cannot be regarded as compatible to this central message of the Christian faith. The word or name "justification" is not the issue. As noted above, other names might be used with equal validity. Rather the issue is: *the full efficacy of Jesus' saving act.* However one might name this central issue will always remain secondary. What the name denotes and refers to, namely, Jesus' full efficacy for the salvation of sinners, is absolutely primary.

R. Bertram in his analysis of this issue tells us: "The divine rescue [from sin] depends . . . fully upon human history, both Jesus' history and also the history of his followers. . . . How, then, in face of such historical contingency, can Christian teaching do justice also to the unconditionality of the divine grace in Jesus Christ? For the Lutheran Confessors the only biblical and Catholic way to be faithful to both concerns was to insist upon not only the SOLA *fide* but the IUSTITIA *fidei*."[10] He adds, however, that the issue is not simply one of christology or of grace, but includes as the *praecipuus locus doctrinae christianae* (the main item of Christian doctrine) the way in which sinners are justified by their faith.[11]

There is, however, a second and complementary aspect in this theology of justification which is likewise at the heart of the reformation critique. It is, actually, an aspect which one can trace from the writings of Paul, through Pelagius and Augustine, to the medieval and reformation periods. This issue is also central to the theology of justification, namely, the absolute gratuity of God's grace. Any Christian ritual, sacrament, prayer, good work, etc., which compromises the absolute gratuity of God's grace, is incompatible with Christian faith.

In the following pages I will abbreviate these two issues by calling them "justification." Under this term, *justification,* I wish to include (1) the complete efficacy of Jesus' salvific action vis-à-vis the sinner, and (2) the absolute gratuity of God's forgiving grace, again vis-à-vis the sinner.

As one readily sees, these two fundamental issues raise profound questions which involve in some way or other the theology and practice of the sacrament of penance. As he begins to introduce the history of the Tridentine decree on justification, H. Jedin distinguishes seven groups of questions on the issue of justification which the bishops at Trent considered, with the *caveat* that "such a deployment of the one problem exposes us to the risk of being accused of superficiality and over-simplification."[12] The seven groups of questions, which Jedin enumerates, focus on the following:

1. The absolute gratuitousness of justification was and always remained the basic concern of Luther. If this is so, is there a possibility of a person disposing himself or herself for justification?
2. Does justification consist essentially and exclusively in the remission of sin, or does it include one's intrinsic sanctification by a created grace?

3. Can the sinner participate in Christ's merits by faith alone or are good works likewise required?
4. Is the human will passive in the process of justification or does it actively concur with grace?
5. In what sense can the good works of the justified be described as "merit"?
6. What is the connection between justification and the sacraments of baptism, eucharist and penance?
7. How does justification, as a personal experience, start and progress?[13]

In these questions we see that conversion, penance, contrition, sorrow for sin, admission of sin, works of satisfaction, the administration of absolution by the priest—all have a connection with this "process of justification." But how can these various aspects of the sacrament of penance be theologically presented in a way which does not compromise (a) the complete efficacy of Jesus' salvific action and (b) the absolute gratuity of God's forgiving grace?

In the pages which follow, we will explore this interrelationship, focusing primarily on the sacrament of penance and secondarily on the issue of justification. The method will be basically chronological and historical. In chapter two we will consider Jesus himself: his message and his works, and their relationship to reconciliation and justification. In chapter three, we will consider the death of Jesus in its context of reconciliation and justification. As we shall see, there is no single theological way to interpret the death of Jesus nor can his death be isolated from his life and his resurrection.[14] We have been saved not simply by the death of Jesus, but by the life, death and resurrection of Jesus.

In the subsequent chapters we will trace the way in which this divine mystery of human salvation through the sacrament of penance has been theologically expressed and historically practiced. In chapter four we will turn our attention to the patristic period. In chapter five we will consider the Celtic penitential movement and its effect on early medieval theology. In chapter six we will study the practice and theology for the sacrament of penance in the high medieval period, as also the theology of justification which these scholastic theologians developed. In chapter seven we will survey the theology of justification and the critique of the sacrament of penance which the reformation theologians developed. In chapter eight we will consider in great detail the response which the Roman Catholic Church made to this critique at the Council of Trent. In chapter nine we will briefly consider the post-Tridentine Roman Catholic theology and the post-reformation Protestant theology on the issues of justification and of the sacrament of penance before moving on to analyze the work accomplished on this matter at Vatican II and in the post-Vatican II official renewal of the sacrament of penance. Finally, in chapter ten we will consider the wide-ranging issues which can be considered the unfinished agenda of Vatican II. In this final chapter we will address some central theological and pastoral issues facing the Roman Catholic Church today, issues such as first penance, general absolution, and the frequency of confession. We will also consider the ecumenical ramifications of this sacrament of reconciliation in today's inter-church discussions.

At each stage we will look both at the theology of justification and at the theology and practice of the sacrament of reconciliation, indicating the ways in which an understanding of justification underlies and shapes both the theory and the practice of sacramental reconciliation. To accomplish this, it will be necessary to retain an historical or chronological grid, indicating step by step the development of the sacrament of penance on the one hand, and on the other the development of a theological understanding of justification. In recent years there have been many excellent studies on the history of the sacrament of reconciliation, and these historical findings will be generously used throughout the ensuing chapters. Indeed, without this vast and solid historical research a theological presentation of the sacrament of reconciliation is in today's church an impossible task.[15] A history of the theology of justification is only currently being assembled, but there have already been some highly significant and substantive works on this issue which can readily serve as a solid foundation.[16] History, it must be admitted, both helps and complicates issues. It helps issues, since history provides the way, the reasons, the stages by which these issues have developed. It complicates the situation, since history often alters or even destroys a set of currently-prevailing ideas on a given issue. The use of history also complicates the discussion of an issue, since the more one studies its history, the more one wants to nuance one's descriptions. For both the issue of the sacrament of reconciliation and the issue of justification, these constructive and destructive factors are at play. The more one studies the history of the sacrament of penance, the more one realizes that there have been significant and major changes both in theology and in practice, changes which cannot trace themselves back to the apostles. Moreover, the more one studies the history of the sacrament of penance, the more one wants to nuance one's judgments about each and every particular time. Unalterable positions and statements need careful rethinking and rewording at every stage of development. Even with these *caveats,* let us begin our analysis.

SUMMARY OF CHAPTER ONE

1. The issues in justification and the issues in the sacrament of penance are interdependent. This interdependence is evident both in the writings of the reformation theologians and in the deliberations of the Council of Trent.
2. The renewal of the rite of reconciliation, mandated by the Second Vatican Council did not, unfortunately, address the issues regarding justification. Rather, the entire emphasis remained on the ritual of penance. This lack of such an interrelationship remains a weakness in the theological foundation for this renewal.
3. The ritual or sacrament of penance is only one instance of the Christian theology of reconciliation. Every Christian sacrament involves reconciliation. In a more profound way, the church itself is a basic sacrament of reconciliation, and in the most primordial way Jesus, in his humanity, is the foundational sacrament of reconciliation. This relativization of the sacrament of penance is essential for any solid theological and pastoral understanding of its place in the Christian community.
4. Justification is but one of the many names given to the central message of the Christian gospel. Consequently, from a theological point of view justification will only make sense when it is considered in conjunction with other terms descriptive of this central message, e.g. divinization, salvation, expiation, etc.
5. The centrality of Jesus as the "savior of the world" lies at the core of both justification and reconciliation. This centrality of Jesus includes (a) the full efficacy of Jesus' saving act, and (b) the absolute gratuity of God's grace. Any theology of justification or any theology of the sacrament of penance which compromises this centrality of Jesus and this gratuity of God's grace is incompatible with Christian faith.

2

Jesus: The Primordial
Sacrament of Reconciliation

Every page of the New Testament speaks of reconciliation. The words of Jesus, his actions, his cures—all betoken reconciliation. From the New Testament period onward, the Christian tradition has understood the message of Jesus as a message of reconciliation. In an unbroken way this same tradition has understood the death of Jesus, both as a powerful statement about reconciliation and also as the universal means for reconciliation. Jesus, we hear in the pages of the New Testament, died for all; his death was a ransom for many. Moreover in the letter to the Romans, Paul includes the resurrection of Jesus as part of the sacred event which has brought about the reconciliation of all men and women (Rom 4:25). The sending of the Spirit at Pentecost is no less a moment in this event of reconciliation. It is an essential part of the paschal mystery. The history of the early church, as we find reflected in the Acts of the Apostles, the letters of Paul, the four gospels and the other writings of the New Testament, indicate that the central message of the early disciples of Jesus was a message of reconciliation. Reconciliation is omni-present throughout the New Testament:

	☐ The meaning of Jesus' birth
	☐ The message of Jesus' life
	☐ The meaning of Jesus' life
One finds reconciliation	☐ The meaning of Jesus' death
central to:	☐ The meaning of Jesus' resurrection
	☐ The sending of the Holy Spirit
	☐ The preaching of the apostolic church
	☐ The meaning of the apostolic church

15

For a Christian, then, reconciliation is synonymous with the gospel message itself and forms an essential part of gospel living. In other words, Christian life as such is a life in and through reconciliation. Were one to remove every aspect of reconciliation from the life of a Christian, then there would be no Christian life at all. This omni-presence of reconciliation in the warp and woof of Christian life forewarns us that a single event of reconciliation, such as the sacrament of reconciliation, in no way encompasses the Christian understanding of reconciliation, or that without the sacramental ritual of reconciliation there would be no reconciliation in the church. Rather, the opposite is true. The sacrament of reconciliation makes sense only when one understands it against this wider and *more important* background of Christian reconciliation. The sacrament of reconciliation is only one of many moments of reconciliation in the Christian community, and it is not even the most important moment of Christian reconciliation.

These reflections help us to grasp the method we should use to study the sacrament of reconciliation. We can formulate this theological method as follows:

- [ ] First, one begins with Jesus himself and sees in both Jesus' message and in his total life-death-resurrection the full and most important meaning of reconciliation. Jesus is in the fullest sense of the term: the sacrament of reconciliation.
- [ ] Second, and only at a secondary level, would we then consider the church, the community of Christians, as a *locus* of reconciliation. The term "church" in this context is by no means restricted either to a hierarchy or to a hierarchical act. Rather, it is the total church which everyone, whether ordained or not-ordained, experiences on a day to day level both in oneself and in one's relationships with others. The living out of one's baptismal-eucharistic life is the *locus* of reconciliation as far as the church is concerned. At this stage, one has clearly exceeded any boundaries posed by a particularized sacramental action of reconciliation. In this sense the church is in a relativized way the fundamental sacrament of reconciliation.
- [ ] Third, and only at this third stratum, should we consider a particularized sacrament of reconciliation, such as baptism, eucharist or, in our present discussion, penance. The ritual of penance is a sacrament of reconciliation, but by no means the major sacrament of reconciliation.

This methodology follows the contemporary theological approach to all sacraments: (a) Jesus is the original or primordial sacrament; (b) the church is a basic or fundamental sacrament; (c) individual sacraments have their meaning only in virtue of these two fundamental sacraments: Jesus and the church. In this approach, Jesus is the most important sacrament of reconciliation. The church, as a sacrament of reconciliation, is important but relativized vis-à-vis Jesus. Even more relativized are such sacraments of reconciliation as baptism, eucharist, penance, and anointing of the sick. They are relativized, in meaning, in importance, in practice, to both the church and to Jesus. Accordingly, this chapter is divided into the following themes:

1. The classical New Testament passages on the power to forgive sin.
2. The apostolic church's application of this power over sin.
3. Jesus, the sacrament of God's grace of reconciliation.

1. THE CLASSICAL NEW TESTAMENT PASSAGES

In the manuals of theology, as well as other theological treatises, it had been rather commonplace to consider three particular New Testament passages, which dealt with the power of the keys, as the basis for an institution of the sacrament of penance, namely:

☐ Matthew 16:16
☐ Matthew 18:18
☐ John 20:22–23

In this classical or traditional approach, the power to forgive sins is seen as promised in Matthew 16:16:

I will give you the keys of the kingdom of heaven: whatever you bind on earth shall be considered bound in heaven; whatever you loose on earth shall be considered loosed in heaven.

The future tense in the text, that is, "will" and "shall," indicates, so it was argued, the promise aspect. In Matthew 18:18, this same power, which had been promised, was granted or conferred on the apostles:

I tell you solemnly, whatever you bind on earth shall be considered bound in heaven; whatever you loose on earth shall be considered loosed in heaven.

In John 20:22–23, we have an additional text corroborating this bestowal of penitential power:

> After this he breathed on them and said: Receive the Holy Spirit. For those whose sins you forgive they are forgiven; for those whose sins you retain, they are retained.

Contemporary Roman Catholic and Protestant New Testament scholarship, however, warns us against any simplistic or fundamentalist approach to the interpretation of these three passages. In his *Commentary on the Gospel of John,* R. Brown, apropos to the Johannine passages, writes:

> In summary, we doubt that there is sufficient evidence to confine the power of forgiving and holding sin in John xx, 23, to a specific exercise of power in the Christian community, whether that be admission to Baptism or forgiveness in Penance. These are but partial manifestations of a much larger power, namely, the power to isolate, repel, and negate evil and sin, a power given to Jesus in his mission by the Father and given in turn by Jesus through the Spirit to those whom he commissions.[1]

Prior to this statement, Brown had analyzed in detail all of those biblical exegetes who saw in the Johannine passage a reference either to the sacrament of baptism (and there are a number of exegetes who have interpreted the Johannine passage in this way), or to the sacrament of penance (and there are a number of exegetes, primarily Roman Catholic, who had interpreted the passage in this way). Brown then surveys contemporary biblical scholarship, both Roman Catholic and Protestant, a scholarship which reaches the conclusion that neither the text nor the context of John 20:22–23 allows such a constricted view. Rather, John is describing the power in Christian life generally which isolates, repels and negates sin. Such a power has not only been entrusted to the hierarchy but to all whom Jesus has commissioned. In other words, it is a power which is essentially a part of the gospel life wherever this gospel life is found.

A. BROWN'S SUMMARY OF THE BAPTISMAL INTERPRETATION

That reconciliation is accomplished in a very special way in the church through baptism has been proclaimed century after century in the Nicene Creed, which states: "We acknowledge one baptism for the remission of sins." Every study of baptism indicates that not only in the patristic church, but also in our contemporary church, with its Rite of Christian Initiation of Adults (RCIA), baptism is a process radically moving a person from sin to grace, which is precisely a description of reconciliation. In Acts 2:14–36, we have Peter's speech after the Pentecost event. At the end of this speech, the people were cut to the quick and asked what they should do. Peter replies: "You must repent and every one of you must be baptized in the name of Jesus Christ for the forgiveness of your sins." Baptism and reconciliation are clearly united.

John the Deacon, at a later date (c. 825), described the remission of sin in the life of a baptismal catechumen as follows:

> *Catechesis* is the Greek word for instruction. He is instructed through the Church's ministry, by the blessing of one's laying his hand upon his head, that he may know who he is and who he shall be; in other words, that from being one of the damned he becomes holy, from unrighteousness he appears righteous, and finally from being a servant he becomes a son.[2]

The entire shape of baptism from apostolic times down to the twelfth century clearly indicates that reconciliation and holy baptism are essentially connected. Still, the power to remit sins mentioned in John 20:22–23, though evident in baptism, is not limited to baptism. The power to reconcile goes far beyond the sacrament of baptism.[3]

B. BROWN'S SUMMARY OF THE PENANCE INTERPRETATION
Brown continues his explanation of this power:

> It is an effective, not merely a declaratory, power against sin, a power that touches new and old followers of Christ, a power that challenges those who refuse to believe. John does not tell us how or by whom this power was exercised. (In Matthew's community the power over sin, expressed in the binding-loosing sayings, must have been exercised in formal decisions about what was sinful and/or in excommunication.)[4]

To read exclusively or even primarily into the text or context of this Johannine passage the later sacrament of reconciliation would be a case of *eisegesis* (a reading *into* the text) rather than a case of *exegesis* (a reading *out of* the text). This wider understanding of both the text and the context of the Johannine material does not mean, however, that the sacrament of penance, which developed at a later stage in church history, contradicts the meaning of this Johannine account. Rather, this later sacramental ritual of penance should be seen as one of the ways in which the church, through pastoral need and under the guidance of the Spirit, exercised this power of isolating, repelling and negating sin. Brown touches on this later development:

> In the course of time this power has had many different mani-
> festations, as the various Christian communities legitimately
> specified both the manner and agency of its exercise. Perhaps,
> John's failure to specify may serve as a Christian guideline:
> exegetically one can call upon John xx, 23 for assurance that the
> power of forgiveness has been granted; but one cannot call upon
> this text as a proof that the way in which a particular commu-
> nity exercises this power is not true to Scripture.[5]

These passages from Brown might be considered, however, as a new and therefore suspect interpretation of the Johannine passage. However, it must be noted that Brown himself has drawn together, in this section of his commentary, not merely his own view, but the views of the most eminent Catholic and Protestant scholars. Brown is presenting a position, which is maintained by the best of contemporary scholarship. Still, even with this phalanx of contemporary biblical scholarship, some might still be doubtful of Brown's conclusions. After all, during many centuries, this passage from John had been interpreted by reliable Catholic scholars as indicative of an "institution" of the "sacrament of penance."

C. THE SUMMARY BY BEDA RIGAUX

Almost at the same time, in which Brown in the United States was working on his Johannine commentary, Beda Rigaux in Europe was preparing an article, quite independently from Brown, which dealt with these same three classical passages from the New Testament on the power to remit sin. His article, " 'Lier et délier': Les ministères de réconciliation dans l'Église de temps apostoliques," is by no means an attempt to de-velop a new hypothesis, but rather to line up in an orderly fashion what contemporary Catholic scholars were and are saying about Matthew 16:16; 18:18; John 20:22–23. Rigaux carefully synopsizes each of the authors and does this in a comprehensive way.[6] At the end of this cata-loguing and analyzing, he draws together a summary statement:

> Thus the Church and its representatives bound and loosed, re-
> mitted and retained. It does not seem that in our gospels an
> institution of the sacrament of penance is directly stated. It is
> fitting, indeed, to note that the post-apostolic Church has not

falsified the tenor of these texts in its interpretation of the penitentiary discipline. They (the texts) contain it (the interpretation) *in nuce,* in the totality of their profundity and the amplitude of their extension.[7]

These three classical texts from the New Testament, dealing with the remission of sin, should be seen, then, both textually and contextually, as referring to that all-pervasive power in the Christian community which moves one from sin to holiness. Christian life, in all its aspects, includes a binding and loosing from sin, a forgiving of sin. Christian life in all its aspects includes reconciliation. This is the reason why Christian communities have seen and have named the heart of the Christian life by various terms: reconciliation, redemption, justification, sanctification. No one of these terms fully encompasses the totality of this central Christian mystery of our faith. Each term highlights an important aspect of this mystery, but does not exhaust its meaning. There is no sanctification—a term central to eastern Christian theology—without redemption—a term central to western Christian theology, and vice versa. Moreover there is no justification—a term central to Protestant Christian theology—without redemption and sanctification and vice versa. Reconciliation, a term which has received new impetus from the renewal of Vatican II, itself is unintelligible without the aspects of justification, redemption and sanctification.

D. THE SUMMARY BY ADRIEN NOCENT
Adrien Nocent follows the same pattern as Brown and Rigaux, as he traces the liturgy of the sacrament of penance.[8] Nocent studies the New Testament from the standpoint of sin and reconciliation, both of which he notes are omni-present in the New Testament writings. Only against this comprehensive view of reconciliation does Nocent then take up the issue of the three classical passages.

I. Matthew
For the passages in Matthew, Nocent states that there have been three different interpretations over the centuries:[9]

1. *The juridical interpretation:* in this interpretation one understands that supreme and universal power over sin in the church has been given to Peter and to the apostolic college. This is, he notes, an older interpretation which has both Catholic and Protestant supporters. "Today, however," Nocent adds, "it is no longer acceptable."[10]

2. *The ecclesiological interpretation:* in this interpretation the focus is not on the sacrament of penance. Throughout the eighteenth chapter of

Matthew the entire Christian community is addressed. Vv. 1–4 present to all of Jesus' disciples a criterion to judge who is the greatest in God's kingdom. Vv. 5–10 describe for all Jesus' followers those who cause evil and scandal. Vv. 12–14 describe the mercy of God to the sinner and the sending of God's own Son. Vv. 15–18 indicate the process for correction. In all of these verses, the audience is clearly the disciples of Jesus, generally. To restrict v. 18, with its binding and loosing, to Peter and the other apostles, is unwarranted either by the text or by the context. The Christian community as such is meant to be a sacrament of God's merciful love, and it does this in three stages:

a. There is first of all a private correction between the two individual Christians who are at odds.
b. If the wrongful Christian refuses this private correction then another correction should be made, but this time with an additional Christian witness, a third party.
c. If this too is ineffective, then the issue should be brought before the entire Christian community. If the wrongful Christian remains obstinate, then the community as such "excommunicates" the individual, considering him/her as a pagan or publican.

Nocent states that in this view it is the community which excommunicates. Only after mention is made of this "excommunication" do the words binding and loosing appear. "Still," Nocent adds, "the question to consider is to whom such power has been committed. The answer is delicate, but the problem, which has had its own particular repercussions on understanding the penitential discipline, can also affect the sacramental liturgy."[11] Certainly, Peter and the apostolic college have, in their service to the church, such a power of binding and loosing. The context however, according to Nocent, indicates that the community also has such a power. Two observations, he notes, are in order:

a. The power given to Peter and the apostolic college is not an absolute power, an unrelated power. Rather, it is intimately united to the power of the Christian community itself. The exercise of this power over sin by Peter or by any of the apostles must be related to the community; vice versa the community itself has a relative power, since it cannot act independently of its leadership.
b. The context of Matthew 18 indicates that there is need for "penitential space," a time in which the process of reconciliation can

take place. A later Christian generation formed such a penitential space in the "order of penitents" and even later, though somewhat abridged, through the process of individual and frequent sacramental penance. Matthew 18, then, indicates, according to Nocent that in the Christian life there must be both a time and place—a "space"—for reconciliation.

3. *The demonological interpretation:* in this interpretation a person is released from Satan's power. The power of Satan is a theme which one finds again and again throughout the gospels. The healings of Jesus, in particular, evidence this power over Satan. In the Christian liturgy, as it developed over the centuries, we find this interpretation particularly evident in the sacrament of baptism with its many exorcisms, in the establishment of an order of exorcism, in the sacrament of penance with its lengthy asceticism, and in the sacrament of the anointing of the sick with its prayers to restrain the power of Satan. Both Catholic and Protestant biblical scholars have seen in these two texts from Matthew's gospel (16:16; 18:18) a binding and loosing over Satan himself. Clearly, this interpretation has played an extensive role in the way that the life and liturgy of the Christian church has defined itself. In this view, the "binding and loosing" of Satan's power far exceeds any particularized sacrament (baptism, penance, etc.), and is not restricted to a hierarchical group. The Christian community, in many ways, exercises a power over Satan.

II. John

As far as the Johannine passage (20:22–23) Nocent states that the history of the church has emphasized two differing views:[12]

1. *The juridical, medieval interpretation,* which understands the loosing of sin as the pardoning of sin by God but in and through the context of the church. The binding of sin is seen as the refusal of absolution with the requirement that the penitent truly repents and returns to the church for absolution.
2. *The ecclesial interpretation* sees the forgiving of sin as a forgiving of the offense against the church: "whose sins you shall forgive," which at the same time indicates that God has forgiven the sinner as well: "they will be forgiven." Binding of sin does not, in this perspective, mean the refusal of absolution, but the binding of a penitent to a gospel way of life, which will lead one to conversion and forgiveness of sin.

E. CONCLUSION

From all that Brown, Rigaux, and Nocent—and through them so many other scholars as well—have drawn together on these three classical New Testament passages concerning the remission of sin, we can conclude that they cannot be automatically taken to refer to an institution of a sacrament of penance. Indeed, to interpret these passages in such a way today goes contrary to all that contemporary biblical scholarship offers. Rather, these passages refer to a much broader power in the Christian community to isolate, repel and negate sin. This power is found throughout Christian life, and the sacrament of penance (which begins to appear in the second century) is but one manifestation of such power and by no means the most important manifestation of such power. Moreover, one cannot say that these passages refer to a power given exclusively or primarily to Peter and the apostolic college. That Peter and the other apostles, in virtue of their position as early church leaders, shared in this power over sin is indisputable, but that they were *exclusively* given such power cannot be maintained either from the texts themselves or from their context. Rather, wherever one finds Christian leadership, one finds the power to isolate, repel and negate sin. Indeed, this power, as a constitutive part of the gospel itself, is evident wherever the gospel life manifests itself.[13]

2. THE APPLICATION OF THIS POWER OVER SIN

Even though every part of the New Testament speaks of reconciliation, and even though the three texts mentioned above speak strongly about the power in Christian life to negate sin, the apostolic church, at times, did not find the application of this power easy to square with concrete problems.

For instance, it was only after long and apparently heated discussions that the apostolic community began to understand how Jesus' liberating message of reconciliation was applicable to the Jews who comprised that community. B. F. Meyer describes at great length this early controversy between the *hebraioi,* i.e. the native Palestinian Jewish followers of Jesus, and the *hellenistai,* i.e. the Jews for Jesus who came from the diaspora of the Greeks. The *hebraioi* saw themselves as the true Israel, the first fruits of the messianic salvation, a community not built in place *of* Zion but precisely *on* Zion. "It was precisely in fulfillment of the scriptures that the Easter community of Jerusalem became the point of assembly for the dispersed of Israel."[14] These "*hebraioi,* gathered around Cephas and the twelve, accordingly knew themselves as that sanctuary which Jesus was to build 'in three days'."[15] The *hebraioi* believed that "the regime of the Torah remained intact as in Jesus' day."[16] The *hebraioi* felt that they had truly understood the meaning of the life, death and resurrection of Jesus, and had found this meaning precisely in the fact that they were the elect of God, the true heirs of the Jewish faith. God had reconciled himself with Israel, precisely in and through this group of Jews who had come to believe in Jesus as Lord.

On the other hand the *hellenistai* saw things somewhat differently. These men and women were different from the *hebraioi* through a difference in language, through a difference in biblical translations and texts, through a difference in styles of synagogue worship and exegetical traditions, and through the difference of culture.[17] For the *hellenistai* the Torah had come to an end and was no longer binding. The Jerusalem *hellenistai* differed from the Jerusalem *hebraioi* on two points: "their hostility to temple and Torah (Acts 6:14) and their openness to proselytizing Samaritans (Acts 7:5) and Gentiles (Acts 11:20)."[18] Because of these differing views, the first issue the early Jesus community faced was this: Were such persons as Samaritans and Gentiles even worthy of the message of Jesus? If they were, then the second question became acute: Did such Samaritans and Gentiles, or even the Jewish community itself, have to follow the regulations of the Torah?

According to Luke, we have in the account of Peter and the pagan Cornelius (Acts 10) the first instance of the Jesus community going beyond the Jewish world. Luke clearly emphasizes that it was Peter, not Paul, who was the first to "go among the Gentiles," thus providing the mission to the Gentiles with a legitimizing, apostolic character. Luke also emphasizes that God himself had to make this known to Peter through Peter's dream and the dream's interpretation. Only on the basis of these two factors—(a) a divine revelation; (b) made to Peter, the main leader of the twelve—did the early followers of Jesus begin to feel free, in Luke's presentation, to extend the message of reconciliation to non-Jews. However, beneath this Lukan account of Petrine legitimacy, we see the issues caused by the differences between *hebraioi* and *hellenistai*.

Even when such non-Jews were accepted as followers of Jesus, were they bound by the laws of Moses, the Torah, especially the law of circumcision? The *hebraioi* thought that the converted non-Jews were indeed bound to such a law, and consequently to disregard and thereby break Moses' law made them sinners, incapable of fellowship with Jesus, and outside of the salvation Jesus had acquired. In two different passages from Acts we catch a glimpse of the long debates and arguments which went on in the early Christian community over this issue of non-Jewish converts and their obligation to comply with the Mosaic law: Acts 15:1–35 and Acts 21:24–25. From these passages we see that the final

93-1481

decision (Acts 15:29) was this: the non-Jews, who have been baptized, should refrain:

☐ from food sacrificed to idols
☐ from blood
☐ from the meat of strangled animals
☐ from fornication

If baptized Jews or baptized non-Jews did such things, their actions were seen, by *hebraioi,* as incompatible with Christian behavior. In their eyes, those who ate such foods or who committed fornication suffered, in some form or another, severance from the Jesus community. To be readmitted, such sinners needed to be reconciled. We do not, however, have any clear picture of the way in which such a reconciliation would take place. Rather, we know that there was opposition even to this decision. The *hellenistai,* and among them would be Paul himself, believed that "the 'true' propitiatory was the crucified Christ. In the perspective of this text [Rom. 3:25-26] the forgiveness of sins had awaited the climactic, definitive, unrepeatable *yom kippur* of Golgotha. Once given this reality, temple and Torah could claim no independent significance."[19] The Torah, in the view of these *hellenistai* and expressed most strongly by Paul, had never meant to mediate the one thing necessary: righteousness in the sight of God. Only the life, death and resurrection mediated this justification.

In this division of the early Jesus community, between *hebraioi* and *hellenistai,* we see in a very focused way that the issue of justification— i.e. are we justified through the Torah or through Jesus?—lies at the heart of the matter, and that an understanding of reconciliation depends on the way in which one understands the meaning of justification. What we see in all these passages is a struggle to understand how comprehensive Jesus' message of reconciliation truly is. *That* the early community had difficulty in applying this reconciling message to some concrete situations is clear; *how* such eventual reconciliation was performed is not clear.

The requirement of circumcision also caused a deep schism within the apostolic community. We find Paul frequently combating the "judaizers," i.e. those followers of Jesus (*hebraioi?*) who insisted on circumcision. The uncircumcised, in the opinion of this group, had to be excluded from the community (cf. e.g. Gal 5:2-6; Rom 15ff). Paul's argument, however, was this: If we are still bound by circumcision, then reconciliation in Christ is not a gift of grace. Must we ourselves first do something (i.e. be circumcised) and only then can Jesus bring us salvation? Or is not God's salvation first of all and above all his doing, and therefore a gift? In this debate over circumcision, we see the beginning of the century-old argument regarding faith and good works, an argument which lay at the core of the Protestant reformation. We also see the roots for the debate between Augustine and Pelagius on the gratuity of God's grace and the role of free will. If we see this early community of Jesus struggling over these issues, we should not be surprised when time and time again subsequent Christian communities, our own included, have had to struggle over the same basic issues. No Christian community has found it easy to apply, in the concrete, the message of justification and reconciliation which Jesus has given us.

Another instance which indicates a hesitation over the scope of reconciliation in this apostolic church is found in 1 Corinthians 5:1–13. This is the case of the incestuous man. Biblical scholars, down through the centuries and even today, might argue over the precise sin of the person involved, but that the passage in this letter indicates some form of separation from the community is not debated. The passage ends: "You must drive out this evildoer from among you." The sinner is "outside." Just before stating this, Paul had said: "Of those who are inside, you can surely be the judges. But of those who are outside, God is the judge" (15:12). Who is "outside" reconciliation and who is "inside" reconciliation? Who can determine this outside-inside situation? God alone? The Jesus community? Only the leaders of the community? The first letter to the Corinthians offers us no clear answers to such questions.

Written some thirty years after Paul, the pastoral letters offer us an insight into another period of early Christian life. In 1 Timothy 1:19–20, we read of a separation from the community for Hymnaeus and Alexander. In the book of Revelation each local church is asked to consider its sinful ways and be reconciled (Rev 2:1–3:22). The sinfulness of the churches is stated; the call to reconciliation is also stated; the way in which such reconciliation might take place is not stated. Nonetheless, it is evident that the author as well as the communities addressed believed that in Jesus there was a power to isolate, repel and negate sin, a power we call reconciliation. In 2 Timothy 2:25–26, Titus 3:9–11, James 5:16–20 and 1 John 5:17 we find similar indications: a sinfulness on the part of individuals which implies severance from the Christian community and a call to reconciliation.

In all of these instances we have only a small window which allows us some glimpse into the life of the apostolic community, as it wrestled with concrete situations of sin and reconciliation. Many details, even important ones, are not mentioned. However, it is clear that the community believed that in and through Jesus there was power to isolate, repel and negate sin, a power of binding and loosing. The apostolic church clearly attests to their belief *that* such power existed in the Jesus community. *How* such power was activated is not described. To claim that there was a "sacrament of reconciliation" at this point of time goes far beyond both texts and contexts. Rather, we find the church struggling with the issue of post-baptismal sin. B. Poschmann, after surveying this same New Testament material, remarks: "Much is lacking for a complete picture of penitential doctrine and practice."[20] J. Favazza, in *The Order Of Penitents,* surveys the New Testament material and concludes:

> In the New Testament witness to penitential procedures, no uniform discipline is practiced by the Church toward postbaptismal offenses. The apostles knew only that the Church must somehow continue the mission of Jesus, who forgave sins.[21]

Favazza then proceeds to mention some aspects of reconciliation mentioned by various authors of the New Testament which will continue to play a role in the forgiveness of post-baptismal sin: prayer, good works, mutual confession of sin, some sort of isolation of the sinner from the community, the role of the community throughout the process of reconciliation.[22] However, from the New Testament data not only the practice of reconciliation, i.e. the rituals (if any) used by the church for reconciliation, but also many aspects of the very doctrines of justification and reconciliation remain unclear.

3. JESUS, THE RECONCILIATION OF GOD

If one merely combed the New Testament for passages which deal with the early church's handling of difficult situations involving sinners, one would have a very incomplete understanding of reconciliation in the Christian community. The few instances, mentioned above, barely touch the surface, but even a full cataloguing of such instances would not offer us a gospel presentation of reconciliation. Instead, one must begin with Jesus himself, for it is precisely Jesus, in his humanity, who is the sacrament of reconciliation. Indeed, Jesus himself is *the primordial sacrament of reconciliation.*

Such a position means that the only genuine understanding of reconciliation is in and through christology. Christology precedes and substantiates both ecclesiology and sacramental theology. To begin a study on the sacrament of reconciliation with the classical texts referred to above or with the various incomplete pictures of the early church struggling with post-baptismal sin is to start not only in the middle of things, but to start falsely. Jesus alone is the point of departure.

In christology, however, there are two aspects about Jesus and reconciliation which need our attention:

1. *The message of Jesus:* Jesus preached a message of reconciliation.
2. *The life-death-resurrection of Jesus:* Jesus' entire existence, which includes his life, his death and his risen life, proclaims reconciliation.

Both in what he said and in what he was is Jesus the sacrament of reconciliation. We will consider in the remainder of this chapter the message of Jesus, that is, what Jesus himself preached. In the next chapter we will consider the life, death and resurrection of Jesus as the salvation event.

According to J. Jeremias, Jesus' preaching focused on four themes:[23]

1. The return of the quenched Spirit.
2. Overcoming the rule of Satan.
3. The dawn of the reign of God.
4. Good news for the poor.

Scholars may differ and have differed with many details of Jeremias' approach. Still, such themes as the reign or kingdom of God, the message of salvation to the poor, the overcoming of Satan, and the renewed presence of the Spirit constitute in one way or another, according to almost all biblical scholars, the message of Jesus' preaching. J. H. Charlesworth, in his volume *Jesus Within Judaism,* has gathered together a great deal of material on christology, to which he gives the general name "Jesus research."[24] This recent spate of material on the socio-historical Palestine of Jesus' day, together with its variety of religious movements, has far surpassed Jeremias' attempts to understand the Aramaic Jesus. Nonetheless, Charlesworth expresses his great indebtedness to Jeremias, and precisely to Jeremias' volume on *New Testament Theology: The Proclamation of Jesus,*[25] in which these four themes are categorically described.

Let us consider each of these themes, although not in the sequence which Jeremias uses, but rather in the sequence of apparent importance.

A. THE KINGDOM OF GOD

It is certainly the consensus of New Testament scholars, both Catholic and Protestant, that the central message of Jesus' preaching was the kingdom of God (no. 3 above). No rabbi prior to Jesus, nor even the Essenes, had spoken so often and so clearly about the kingdom of God.

When Jesus says "The kingdom of heaven," this is but a Jewish way of saying the kingdom of God, since Jewish people at the time of Jesus made great efforts to avoid saying God (Yahweh) and so they would use a roundabout expression, such as "kingdom of heaven." The two phrases "the kingdom of God" and "the kingdom of heaven" mean the same thing.

In the New Testament, however, we nowhere find a definition of this kingdom. In the parables, we hear that Jesus said again and again:

The kingdom of heaven is . . .

- ☐ like a mustard seed
- ☐ like wise and foolish virgins
- ☐ like a king who left the administration of his money to three servants
- ☐ like a treasure hidden in the field
- ☐ like a man going out to sow his seed
- ☐ like yeast which a woman mixed into the dough

Image upon image reveals to us what this kingdom of God is all about, not in the form of a definition, but in the multifaceted form of images. Moreover, Jesus says that this kingdom is not only something in the distant future, but that it is in existence right now, like the yeast already working in the bread-dough, like the seed already sprouting in the ground. For this reason, biblical scholars say that the kingdom which Jesus preached is a kingdom, an end-time rule of God, which is already evident in our world.

> Like the Essenes, Jesus' theology was categorically eschatological. He preached a somewhat more imminent eschatology, but one should talk about the difference between the Essenes and Jesus in such a way that Jesus' eschatology was more realizing in terms of degree, not kind. . . . Furthermore, Jesus differed from the Essenes regarding the nature of the future, the understanding of the approaching Kingdom of God, and most significantly on how one must prepare for its coming.[26]

It may be difficult to ascertain exactly what the relationship between the "already" and the "not yet" of this rule of God might be, but if one overstresses the future aspect of this kingdom which Jesus preached and makes it simply the goal which we might have after our death, then the true meaning of the kingdom is missed. On the other hand, if one overstresses the kingdom of this world, making it almost another earthly paradise or a political kingdom, then one also loses the true meaning of Jesus' words. In spite of this delicate balance and the difficulties it might entail, contemporary biblical scholarship sees the central message of Jesus in his presentation of God's kingdom.

If the kingdom of God has, in some degree at least, already begun, if God's dominion has already begun to take effect in our lives as we submit to God's loving presence and power within us, then reconciliation has likewise begun. To preach the kingdom of God is to preach reconciliation. The kingdom means that God is present to us in a loving and forgiving way, and we are present to God in a loving and forgiven way. The power of God's presence or of God's kingdom is a power of both love and forgiveness. It is a power of reconciliation. Wherever this kingdom of God might be, there too is reconciliation. *Ubi regnum, ibi reconciliatio.*

B. EVIL IS OVERCOME

What one says about the kingdom of God has a flip-side as well: namely, evil (Satan and sin) is overcome. If the kingdom of God has begun, even on this earth, then the power of sin has also begun to wane, even on this earth. At the time of Jesus, in the popular Jewish belief, Satan was considered the leader, the commander-in-chief, of all demonic forces. With the approach of the kingdom of God, this commander-in-chief was vanquished. With the destruction of the leader, the force which he represents is also destroyed. Behind this imaginative and mythic language of armies, forces, commanders-in-chief, there is a powerful message which can only be considered "good news." This powerful message tells us that evil, in any and all of its forms, is not the final answer. Rather, God's loving and forgiving presence remains the only final answer. Sin is, in principle and in fact, destroyed. Sinners are, in principle and in fact, forgiven. To say that Satan's power of destruction is overcome is itself a message of reconciliation. From a positive approach, Jesus announced the coming of God's kingdom; from a negative approach, Jesus announced the destruction of Satan. These two themes are the two sides of the same coin. Both individually and together they announce reconciliation.

The prayers of Palestinian Judaism, which were written roughly around the time of Jesus, portray a deep sense of sin and a profound confidence in God's mercy.[27] Rightly, the stereotyped view that the Jews at Jesus' time were legalistic, rigid, self-righteous, has been shattered through contemporary scholarship of the pseudepigrapha, apocalyptic literature, and the Nag Hammadi codices and the Dead Sea scrolls. Many Jews at the time of Jesus thoroughly believed that only God could forgive sin and that God would forgive sin generously. Many Jews at the time of Jesus believed that sin was a dreadful evil, socially and personally. Jesus' message on the overcoming of evil echoed much of the Jewish belief of his own day. Jesus' insistence on the closeness of the kingdom only emphasized the need for conversion of life, acknowledgement of sin, and total trust in the reconciling and covenantal love of God.[28]

C. THE RETURN OF THE HOLY SPIRIT

It was also the popular belief among the Jewish people at the time of Jesus that the Holy Spirit had been taken away from the Jewish nation. This had occurred at the Babylonian captivity. From that time on there were no more prophets. Zechariah, Malachi and Haggai were among the last of the writing prophets. However, when the messianic kingdom would come, so the Jews believed, then God's Holy Spirit would return. In the life and teaching of Jesus, we see that the Holy Spirit had indeed returned. Reconciliation in the Spirit had been accomplished. We find this in the infancy narratives of both Matthew and Luke. Without the presence of the Holy Spirit, these infancy narratives make no sense. The conception of Jesus and the birth of Jesus take place in and through the power of the Spirit. At the very first moment of Jesus' existence, God's Holy Spirit was present. Because of this presence of the Spirit, according to both Matthew and Luke, Jesus, from the first moment of his life, was truly God and truly human. Even a form of pre-natal adoptionism is excluded by this presence and power of God's Spirit in Jesus.

In Mark's gospel we find that the Holy Spirit is present from the very beginning of Jesus' public life. At the baptism of Jesus, Mark notes, the Spirit descended on him. This opening of the heavens is a sign of reconciliation. So, too, in John's gospel, the Holy Spirit is already present to the Word made flesh. When John treats of Jesus' baptism, he mentions that John the Baptist had seen the Holy Spirit descending on Jesus and *remaining* with him. Jesus and the Holy Spirit are inseparable. In this way of speaking, all four gospels emphasize the divine nature of Jesus, but they also indicate that reconciliation belongs to the very being of the incarnate Lord.

If the Holy Spirit has "reentered" our world (as the Jewish people would have described it), then the end-time, the messianic time, has begun. This end-time is a time of reconciliation. The presence of the Holy Spirit is primarily a reconciling presence. The heavens opened; the Spirit descended. Heaven and earth are once again reconciled. Throughout the life of Jesus the presence of the Holy Spirit indicated reconciliation. Jesus healed in the power of the Spirit, and healing from illness meant a presence of the forgiving power of sin. Jesus without the Spirit of God would be no Jesus at all. With the Spirit of God, Jesus is the very presence of God, the very presence of God's reconciling power.

D. JESUS PREACHED SALVATION TO THE POOR

If any of the major themes of Jesus' message indicated reconciliation, his preaching to the poor, the anawim, the marginated, surely indicated God's forgiving love. These anawim were often materially poor. They had almost nothing. They lived almost totally by charity. However, other anawim did have some material things, perhaps even a rather large amount of material goods. Still, in the eyes of the Jewish authorities, they had no power. This lack of power seems to be at the core of what anawim really meant. The New Testament does not present us with a mystique of poverty; rather, it urges us to share with our brothers and sisters, so that no one will be poor.

According to Jeremias a man like Zacchaeus was part of this anawim-group: he had money, a home, and many comforts. But he was "excommunicated," since he was part of the Roman tax-system. Because he was excommunicated, he had no "clout" with the Jewish authorities and therefore none with the prominent Jewish people either. Lepers were also anawim, outcasts from Jewish society, with no power at all. Sinners were equally alienated. The Jewish leadership—the leading scribes, Pharisees, and the high priestly circle—had rejected all of these. All of these people remained powerless within the religio-social community in Palestine.[29]

Jesus, for his part, deliberately went among these outcasts, these sinners, these anawim. He preached to them a message of forgiveness. In doing this, Jesus was publicly undermining the authority of the Jewish leadership. This leadership had condemned these "outcasts." Jesus, however, promised them salvation and forgiveness. It was this aspect of Jesus' message, above all, which triggered the process that ended in his death. Jesus' message of such prodigal forgiveness, such far-reaching reconciliation, clashed with everything the Jewish leadership of that time maintained. It was not simply a message of reconciliation which triggered this struggle to death; rather, it was the prodigality of such reconciliation that divided Jesus and the Jewish leadership in such a fatal way. The crux of Jesus' preaching (and this in a very literal sense) was the seventy-times-seven-times forgiveness of God. In the face of sin, God's love and mercy knew no limit. If Jesus enjoined us to walk the extra mile, how many additional miles would God himself go? If Jesus enjoined us to forgive our brothers and sisters, how much greater is the forgiveness of God? If Jesus told us to forgive our enemies, how much greater is God's forgiveness of his enemies, sinners? Jesus proclaimed a message of apparently unlimited reconciliation. This kind of message contradicted the main-stream leadership among the Jewish people of that time.

E. P. Sanders notes that Jesus' message that God's love was extended to sinners would not have been offensive to first century Jews, but Charlesworth, and I think rightly, disagrees with this judgment. Charlesworth writes:

> This statement [i.e. that of Sanders] needs to be carefully ar-gued. There was no "normative Judaism" in the first century. In first-century Palestine many—and not just some—Jews would have been offended by Jesus' inclusion of sinners, such as pros-titutes and tax-collectors, into his group. Certainly the pious Jews still living near Qumran, the Sadducees and other priests administering sacrifices in the Temple cult, the zealous ones (the forerunners of the Zealots), the strict Pharisees and even the conservative "people of the land" would have found Jesus' message of God's call to sinners to be offensive. Jesus attempted to shatter the boundaries that had been constructed by many Jewish groups to separate the pure from the impure and the righteous from the unrighteous. His movement attacked a con-cept of purification that was elevated after Herod increased the grandeur of the temple.[30]

Such words as "offensive" and "attacked" are important for an understanding of Jesus' message and person. If Jesus refused to claim the title "Messiah," if Jesus showed himself quite restrained vis-à-vis the political oppression by the Romans, and if Jesus reechoed much that one finds in first century Palestinian Judaism, how can one explain his rejec-tion by the Jewish leadership and his eventual crucifixion? Jesus' message has been rightly called: gospel or good news. But it must also have in it something devastating or "bad news." The words "offensive" and "at-tack" indicate that in the very message of Jesus, which many Jews called "good," there was also a negative response by some Jews of Jesus' time. The issue of offense was certainly Jesus' prodigal reconciliation, but even this prodigality of God's forgiveness would not be enough to engender the fatal animosity indicated by the gospels. The offense created by Jesus' preaching came because Jesus used this theme *in a public way,* i.e. he publicly rebuked certain key leaders of the Jewish world. Not only was the theme of such prodigal forgiveness on the part of God offensive to these Jewish leaders, and considered by them as an attack on their reli-gious and political authority, but also the way that Jesus publicly under-mined these leaders' religious and political authority, precisely in and through this theme, caused both their offense and their attack against Jesus. Even the clearing of the temple by Jesus must be seen against this background of his public indictment of these leaders and their limited view of God's mercy.

The message of Jesus, on any of these themes, cannot be heard by itself. Perhaps Jeremias does not adequately integrate this message of Jesus into its Jewish heritage, for in the kerygma of Jesus one hears and must hear the kerygma of God, which comes echoing through every page of the Old Testament. There is a powerful historicity to the message of Jesus, inasmuch as Jesus' message gathers together the prophets and the law, the wisdom literature and the historical data of the Old Testament. The New Testament presents Jesus in historical, scriptural terms. Jesus, in his message, was bringing to realization what had been promised. The purpose of the kerygma of Jesus (and, as we shall see, the kerygma of the cross and the resurrection) was "to bring Israel into its appointed destiny as eschatological people. In accord with this purpose, the kerygma highlighted God's promises to Israel by announcing their fulfillment."[31] In the message of Jesus, therefore, we need to hear the coming-to-realization of what had been foreshadowed, the coming to completion of time, sin, suffering and the entire drama of history. The message of Jesus presented the nation with a kerygma rooted in the scriptures and deliberately reminiscent of the message of the Deutero-Isaian herald (Is 52:7; 60:6; 60:1), reminiscent of the other prophets as well and of the psalms. The message of Jesus concerning God's justification (salvation) and reconciliation is none other than that same message of God which had appeared in preliminary form throughout the entire Old Testament. The Jewish rootage, historically and intellectually, of Jesus' message on the kingdom, on the overcoming of evil, on the presence of the Spirit, on the forgiveness of the anawim, gives the necessary context of his message and underscores once again why this message of Jesus became an offense, a "bad news," to certain Jewish leaders of his time. It provides the clue to his rejection by these leaders, a rejection which began the process of arrest, trial, condemnation and death.

Whether one focuses on Jesus' theme of kingdom, or on the destruction of Satan, or on the presence of the Spirit, or on the forgiveness of the anawim, the binding thread in this message is clearly justification and reconciliation. The entire gospel message is based on this theme. The heart of Jesus' message is clearly justification and reconciliation, taken in this large perspective. In the gospels, particularly in the synoptics, one does not find, of course, a direct teaching that (a) Jesus alone is the savior, or (b) grace is absolutely gratuitous. Jesus did not make the claim of divinity or the claim of messiahship the direct theme of his message.

Indirectly, however, each in its own way, the four gospels proclaim the divinity and messiahship of Jesus, but to express this the gospel authors realized that the death and resurrection of Jesus, and not just his message, are essential.

In the actual preaching of Jesus we nowhere find that one can attain salvation (justification, deification) by one's own efforts. This forgiveness and reconciliation is a gratuitous gift from God, not a forgiveness which we of ourselves can "merit" or gain through "good works." In fact, the gospels indicate again and again that good works, by themselves, do not lead to justification. The parable of the two men who went up to the temple to pray is a powerful exemplification of this aspect of Jesus' message. Although one could say that Jesus is the primordial sacrament of reconciliation because his message focused on this theme, it would really be only the message of Jesus that sacramentalizes God's forgiving love, not Jesus himself. Jesus would be the prophet or spokesman of God. His words might be a sacrament, but he himself would not really be the sacrament of God's reconciling love. For this reason we must consider Jesus himself, his very being, and not simply his message, so that the fullness of Jesus as sacrament of reconciliation is adequately expressed. This is the theme of the following chapter.

SUMMARY OF CHAPTER TWO

In this chapter we have considered the following points:

1. The New Testament speaks of reconciliation on every page. This omni-presence of reconciliation is the basis for a theology of sacramental reconciliation.
2. Reconciliation in the Christian community cannot be limited to any particular sacrament of reconciliation, such as baptism, eucharist, penance or the anointing of the sick. Rather, reconciliation is an essential part of gospel living.
3. Jesus, in his humanity, is the basic or fundamental sacrament of reconciliation.
4. Prior to understanding the sacrament of penance, it is also necessary to understand and experience the church as a basic sacrament of reconciliation.
5. The classical passages on the power to forgive sin cannot be interpreted as an "institution" of a sacrament of penance. Nor can these passages be interpreted as applying only to the hierarchy. These three passages refer to the power to isolate, repel and negate

sin, a power which Christians found in every aspect of their life, not simply in its leadership.

6. The apostolic church, as we see in the New Testament itself, had to struggle to apply this power of forgiveness to all areas of post-baptismal sin. In the New Testament we do find here and there some instances of separation from the community for those who committed serious post-baptismal sin.

7. We have no indication in the New Testament of a sacramental ritual of reconciliation.

8. Jesus, as the primordial sacrament of reconciliation must be considered from two aspects: (a) from his message of reconciliation; (b) from his life-death-resurrection.

9. The part of Jesus' message which is called "preaching the good news to the poor" indicates the prodigal extent of God's reconciliation. It was precisely this aspect of Jesus' teaching and his preaching this message in a public way which caused the Jewish leadership to turn against him in such a decisive way.

3

The Life, Death, and
Resurrection of Jesus

Not only did Jesus preach limitless reconciliation, but his very life was a sign of unbounded and unbounding forgiveness. In a special way, his death from earliest Christian times has been understood as reconciling and saving. However, the resurrection of Jesus has likewise been an essential part of the paschal mystery, the saving event in Jesus. In the *Praenotanda* of the new ritual of reconciliation, we read that Jesus both preached reconciliation and that his very death and resurrection were themselves reconciliation:

> Jesus began his work on earth by preaching repentance.
>
> Jesus not only exhorted men and women to repentance . . . but he also welcomed sinners and reconciled them with the Father.
>
> By healing the sick he signified the power to forgive sins.
>
> Finally, he himself died for our sins and rose again for our justification.[1]

It would take an entire volume on christology to develop a comprehensive understanding of this paschal mystery in Jesus' life, death and resurrection. In this chapter we will consider only some of the key points in this mystery of our salvation, which have direct application to both justification and to the sacrament of reconciliation. Because the sacrament of penance is one of the ways in which the church has celebrated the mystery of our salvation, the connection between the death and resurrection of Jesus with this sacrament is theologically and pastorally important. Because the salvific significance of Jesus' death and resurrection in western theology has been called justification, the connection between the paschal mystery and justification is likewise theologically and pastorally vital.

> Historical research in recent generations has greatly increased our awareness of the degree to which the debate over justification in the sixteenth century was conditioned by a specifically Western and Augustinian understanding of the context of salvation which, in reliance on St. Paul, stressed the scriptural theme of *iustitia*, of righteousness. Eastern theologians, on the other hand, generally saw salvation within the framework of a cosmic process in which humanity occupies a place of honor. Combining biblical allusions to divinization with an ascetically oriented, Neoplatonic understanding of the ascent of the soul, Eastern theologians described human salvation in terms of a return to God of a creation that had gone forth from God.[2]

Since the sacrament of penance in the west developed under the influence of the western approach to salvation and justification, the eastern approach will not be specifically treated in this chapter, except in a passing way. Nonetheless, the above citation makes us aware that the ordinary western approach to justification, whether Roman Catholic, Protestant or Anglican, is but one approach to the meaning of salvation. The eastern churches have developed other theologies on deification or salvation.

Nonetheless, one can say that the way in which one theologizes on justification will have repercussions on the way in which one theologically considers both the death and the resurrection of Jesus. Vice versa, the way in which one theologizes on the death and resurrection of Jesus will shape the way one theologizes on justification. Since the western approach to justification is but one approach to this mystery of our faith, its theological connections to a theology of Jesus' death and resurrection are also only one way of considering this relationship between Jesus' death and resurrection, on the one hand, and justification, on the other.

In this western framework, the emphasis in a theology of salvation has been at times somewhat exclusively focused on the death of Jesus. In fact, this focus on the death of Jesus as the central event of justification has been so overwhelming that the salvific aspects both of Jesus' resurrection and of his life have been neglected. Kähler's remark that Mark's gospel is a passion-narrative with a long introduction has, as Schillebeeckx remarks, a kernel of truth, but misses the finer details.[3] Moreover, the liturgy of the church has often implied that salvation has come to us through the death of Jesus, without any liturgical reference to Jesus' resurrection or to his life. In the *Exultet* of the Easter vigil we read, for instance:

> O truly necessary sin of Adam which was blotted out by the death of Christ!

And in the Good Friday liturgy, which was normative just prior to the post-Vatican-II renewal, the first prayer of the assembly reads:

> O God, by the passion of Christ your Son our Lord, you have cancelled the legacy of death due to the old sin.

And in the procession antiphon in that same liturgy for Good Friday we hear:

> We adore you, O Christ, and we bless you, because by your holy Cross you have redeemed the world.

And in the final prayer of this same service:

> Almighty and merciful God you have restored us by the blessed passion and death of Christ your Son.

The *Baltimore Catechism,* in turn, asked the question: "What is meant by the Redemption?" and the answer was crisply presented:

> By the Redemption is meant that Jesus Christ, as the redeemer of the whole human race, offered His sufferings and death to God as a fitting sacrifice in satisfaction for the sins of men, and regained for them the right to be children of God and heirs of heaven.[4]

In each of these instances the concentration on the death of Jesus as the one event in which the salvation of the world took place has often crowded out a redemptive significance to the life and resurrection of Jesus. Everything seems to be concentrated in the single event of Jesus' dying. Contemporary theology as well as pastoral and liturgical practice, both Protestant and Catholic, however, has moved away from this almost exclusive concentration on Jesus' death, and has begun to take into account the salvific value of the total Jesus: his life, his death and his resurrection.

In the preceding chapter we considered the message of Jesus with a brief allusion to his healing miracles. In some ways, that chapter has already indicated that the import of Jesus' life certainly included in a central way the reality of reconciliation. Reconciliation is basic to his public ministry, to the message he preached, and to the meaning of his healing miracles. In this present chapter, then, let us consider, at least in a summary way, the theological and salvific import of (1) his death, and (2) his resurrection. In both instances let us focus on the New Testament data, rather than on later theological interpretations.

1. SALVATION, THE DEATH OF JESUS, AND THE NEW TESTAMENT

We find this new emphasis, for instance, in the way contemporary biblical scholars interpret the Pauline material. N. Flanagan gathers together the various terms which Paul uses in his letters to express the multidimensionality of Jesus' saving work:[5]

Expiation	Rom 3:25
Sacrifice	1 Cor 5:7; Eph 5:2
Sanctification	1 Cor 1:30
Liberation	Gal 5:1, 13
Redemption	Gal 4:5
Reconciliation	2 Cor 5:17–21; Rom 5:10–11
Salvation	Rom 1:16
Justification	Rom 3:21–28
New Creation	Gal 6:15; 2 Cor 5:17
Adoption	Rom 8:15; Gal 4:5
Transformation	1 Cor 3:18; Rom 9:29

In Paul we find that there is a plethora of metaphors and descriptions of the saving event. "No single one of them nor all together," Flanagan adds, "can describe in its completeness the blessing that Jesus has brought to humanity."[6] Or as Fitzmyer writes: "The nuance of 'mystery' added to Paul's understanding of the gospel opens up the broad perspective in which it must really be considered. He [Paul] saw the gospel only as part of the magnificent plan, itself gratuitously conceived by the Father for the salvation of men, which was revealed and realized in Christ Jesus."[7] The passion, death and resurrection of Jesus were, for Paul, decisive moments in this divine plan, but not the only moments. It is clear that in Paul, the death of Jesus was unintelligible except in conjunction with the resurrection. That Paul was consistent in presenting this connected view is not all that certain, according to contemporary biblical scholars. D. Stanley noted some years ago that Paul's soteriology gradually evolved under the impact of his own personal experiences.[8] From an eschatological perspective on Jesus' death, Paul moved to its impact on Christian life not merely in the eschaton, but in the present existential situation, and finally, in his last epistles, to an inner connection of death and resurrection. E. Käsemann concurs in this approach to the Pauline material. The term "cross," Käsemann notes, is not confined to a one-time historical event, statically embedded in the past. Nor is the cross idealized, a sort of utopian dream in which the one who might lose his or her life would eventually find it. There is clearly an historical mooring in the Golgotha event which can never be erased; but Jesus as the crucified is not a past event. Rather, Jesus is eschatologically present, both already and not yet, in the very life of the Christian. Nor, Käsemann adds, is the resurrection of Jesus simply an after-thought. "The resurrection is here [in Paul] a chapter in the theology of the cross, not its surpassing counterpart."[9]

Schillebeeckx, in his book, *Jesus,* summarizes some of the major contemporary biblical scholarship: "In early Christianity there were three complexes of tradition, existing side by side, in which Jesus' death is variously interpreted, three blocks of tradition all of which appear to be very old, but with no very cogent grounds for assigning any chronological order to them."[10]

These three strands of early tradition are:

A. JESUS WAS THE ESCHATOLOGICAL PROPHET-MARTYR

In this view, Jesus was seen as a latter-day Jewish prophet, who was sent by God but rejected by Israel. The idea that Israel kills its prophets is found in many places in the New Testament, but the idea itself is a pre-Christian one, stemming from an earlier Jewish tradition. The history of Judaism in the Old Testament recounts few prophets being rejected and killed by Israel (cf. Neh 9:26; Ezr 1:10–11; 2 Kgs 17:7–20; add to this Dan 7:20 and 25, and 1 Macc 1:44–49). Nonetheless, there was enough of a tradition, emphasized to some degree in the rabbinical and apocalyptical material, that Israel had rejected the God-given prophets, so that the early Jewish followers of Jesus could relate Jesus to this rejection and death of a prophet theme. Jesus attempted to call Israel back to the true law of God, but his opponents saw in Jesus a new "gainsayer," similar to the one who had caused the angels to sin, and had on so many occasions hardened the hearts of the Israelites. Rather than an acceptable prophet, Jesus was considered by them as a despicable agent of evil who had to be put to death.[11] This view of Jesus as a latter-day prophet, whose death was a martyrdom, provides an interpretation in which "no significance is attributed to Jesus' death itself," but his death "gives expression to the fact that Jesus' person and ministry and prophetic career is itself the 'light of the world.' "[12] Schillebeeckx tends to associate this view particularly with Mark's gospel.

B. JESUS' DEATH IS PART OF THE DIVINE PLAN OF SALVATION

In this view the death of Jesus is anchored in the scheme of salvation history. The suffering and death of Jesus are part of the salvific economy, God's plan of salvation. In a number of places in the New Testament one finds the term: it is necessary (*dei:* it had to happen this way). J. Roloff, H.-E. Tödt, W. Popkes and F. Hahn further subdivide this destiny-approach to the death of Jesus into: (1) Jesus is the passive figure, standing between two active subjects—on the one hand, the Jews and on the other God himself; (2) Jesus as the Son of Man does not stand between two opposing sides, but God, who is the sole initiator, hands over the Son of Man to the sons of men.[13]

D. Senior begins his summary-analysis of the death of Jesus in Matthew with the same idea: "Jesus is the obedient Son of God who fulfills the Scriptures and is faithful to God's will unto death."[14] The gospel of Matthew

> presents the death of Jesus as inevitable, foreseen, and accepted. While human forces move to quench the life of Jesus, on another level that death is absorbed into the mysterious redemptive plan of God and transformed into a life-giving force. It is on this level that the Gospel portrays Jesus as the Son of Man committed to going to Jerusalem and offering his life in ransom for the many. Acceptance of death becomes for the Matthean Jesus the acceptance of God's will to save humanity.[15]

Jesus' death is never seen as absurd or irrelevant. In fact his death called for an interpretation, and it is this idea: "It was necessary . . ." which in many ways gave rise to the early Christian struggle to interpret the death of Jesus. The suffering servant passages in Isaiah helped in developing the cogency of this interpretation, as well as the many passages in the psalms in which the righteous one, though beset by suffering and even death, finds justification in God. The "Son of Man" in Daniel also played a role and perhaps the story of Susanna, the righteous woman. It would seem that the Wisdom literature, the eschatological literature and the apocalyptic literature all contributed in fleshing out this understanding of Jesus' death.[16] "For Matthew the death of Jesus is not only the final revelation of his identity but the most powerful expression of his redemptive mission."[17]

C. THE DEATH OF JESUS IS AN ATONING DEATH

The long list in chapter one of the many New Testament passages which state that Jesus died for someone, i.e. the *hyper* passages, indicates here and there the theme of atonement. This way of describing Jesus' death is, however, not part of the earliest stratum of the New Testament, but begins to appear as later reflection on the significance of Jesus' death took place within the early Christian community. Still, one should not call this interpretation a "secondary" understanding; it stands beside the other two traditions, neither in a secondary role, nor in a privileged role. Reflection on Isaiah 53, the suffering servant, certainly contributed to the deepening of this view of Jesus' death.[18] The many formulae used to describe this atoning death—an atonement for the sinfulness of others—cannot be seen as a secondary deduction from other interpretations of Jesus' death. Rather they are a very old and self-contained complex stemming from pre-Christian, Jewish traditions, and developed by early Jewish-Christians.[19]

W. Kasper in his book on Jesus devotes only a few pages to the death of Jesus. These slim pages, however, are dominated by the author's defense of the atoning aspect of Jesus' death against its critics. Criticism of an atonement interpretation of the death of Jesus was begun by W. Wrede and continued by R. Bultmann and W. Marxen. Already, Pius X, in *Lamentabili* (D. 3438), had condemned the view that Jesus had no sense of his death as a saving event and that the idea was actually an invention of Paul. H. Kessler and A. Vögtle are also cited by Kasper as contemporary Catholics who tend to espouse this view.[20] Kasper, unlike Schillebeeckx, does not develop the various New Testament traditions on the significance of Jesus' death. As a result his presentation lacks a certain completeness and accuracy. However, he makes the following insightful statement: "The important question for us is how Jesus himself understood his death? How did he interpret his failure?"[21] To answer this question one must study all the various interpretations of this suffering and death which the New Testament presents and attempt to see them in their form-histories and tradition-histories. Kasper implies that the atonement interpretation of Jesus' suffering and death is the only approach possible and that any criticism of this atonement interpretation has no merit.

J. Sobrino devotes an entire chapter of his book to the death of Jesus, and presents his stance in fourteen theses.[22] Sobrino's first theses state that even in the New Testament there was a tendency on the part of the early followers of Jesus to preserve the scandal of the cross. This is evident from the fact that the death of Jesus as one abandoned by God was mollified (n. 1), even emasculated into a noetic mystery (n. 2).[23] The New Testament notion of the phrase "it was necessary" is used by Sobrino to establish these claims. That the cross of Jesus is, indeed, part of the salvific process is not denied by Sobrino; in fact, he sees this issue as the "positive" aspect in these various interpretations. There is, he claims, a "negative" aspect to these various interpretations, since such a view "draws our attention away from God himself and his relationship to the cross. It tells us *that* God loved us, but it does not say *how* God himself loved us and liberated us."[24]

Sobrino (n. 6) unites the cross of Jesus with the incarnation, but not simply an incarnation in which God enters into the human world. Rather, it is God entering into "a world of sin that is revealed to be a power working against the God of Jesus."[25] In the cross, then, we are asked to see the very reality of God (nn. 7, 8, and 9). Sobrino sees in the cross a complete abandonment of Jesus by God, a complete denial of any human imaging of God, a calling into question of all knowledge of God based on natural theology (nn. 10, 11, and 12).

> On the cross of Jesus God himself is crucified. The Father suffers the death of the Son and takes upon himself all the pain and suffering of history. In this ultimate solidarity with humanity he reveals himself as the God of love, who opens up a hope and a future through the most negative side of history. Thus Christian existence is nothing else but a process of participating in this same process whereby God loves the world and hence in the very life of God.[26]

Sobrino's views are highly concentrated on the cross of Jesus, although his final thesis includes the resurrection. Whether one can substantiate this view of a total abandonment of Jesus by the Father on New Testament data remains quite controversial. Still, Sobrino's efforts, first criticizing the more standard western approaches and then attempting to formulate his own interpretation, indicates that the approach to the cross of Jesus has been and remains a fairly open question within theology. Noteworthy, however, is the fact that Sobrino in no way relinquishes the aspect of reconciliation in his positive theological presentation of the cross of Jesus.

The conclusion which one must draw from all this material is as follows: In the New Testament the death of Jesus clearly presented many questions to the early communities. For some the crucifixion of Jesus was even a scandal or a folly. Various New Testament authors attempted to provide some interpretation to this violent death of the messiah, and their attempts moved in several differing directions. There is no one single interpretation of the death of Jesus in the New Testament data. Nonetheless, all the various Christian interpretations in the New Testament do include a clear relationship between Jesus' death and God's reconciling and justifying love.

This multi-dimensional interpretation of the death of Jesus is borne out by the writings of the earliest church fathers. Aulén has noted:

> The early church had, it is said, no developed doctrine of the Atonement, properly so called. The contributions of the patristic period to theology lie in another direction, being chiefly concerned with Christology and the doctrine of the Trinity; in regard to the Atonement, only hesitating efforts were made along a variety of lines, and the ideas which found expression were usually clothed in a fantastic mythological dress.[27]

J.N.D. Kelly in his volume *Early Christian Doctrines* says the same thing: "The development of the Church's ideas about the saving effects of the incarnation was a slow, long drawn-out process."[28] The fathers, he notes, were convinced of redemption in and through Jesus, but no "final and universally accepted definition of the manner of its achievement" was formulated.

Eventually several theological interpretations developed. In one of them, Jesus was seen as a victor. In the same patristic period, other bishops and theologians stressed the sacrificial aspect of Jesus' death, which eventually (with Anselm) came to be theologically interpreted as the victim theory. Still a third patristic approach can be seen in an interpretation of Jesus' death as revelatory, a theory which reached a certain theological level with Peter Abelard. J. Riviére provides us with an even more nuanced list of such theological interpretations, which one finds in the history of Christian doctrine.[29] J. Pelikan reaffirms this multi-dimensional approach to the redemption in his own analysis of the early church.[30]

Aulén, Kelly, Riviére, and Pelikan all indicate that a theological interpretation of the death of Jesus developed very slowly in the early church and did so along a variety of paths. These authors are simply a few scholars of early church history who present this view; others could be cited as well. Their conclusions about the early church and the interpretation of Jesus' death seem to be exact. If the New Testament had provided a single interpretation of Jesus' death, this variety of patristic interpretations of the death of Jesus would be unthinkable. The fact that such a variety of views among the fathers of the church exists indicates that there was an openness to the interpretation of the Lord's redemptive death throughout the early church period. This also means that such terms as "justification," "redemption," "salvation," etc., did not have any canonized interpretation. Two conclusions seem to follow from this:

1. The variety of interpretations of the death of Jesus (and therefore his life and resurrection as well) warns us that a rigid and monolithic interpretation of New Testament data on the issue of "justification" might easily be too narrow, whether this interpretation be called that of Paul or whether it be labeled "atonement." That all people are "justified" in Jesus (for the eastern churches this would read "divinized in Jesus") is indeed central. The "theology" of such justification is not so easy to identify in any rigid way. The New Testament, including the letters of Paul, does not present us with any full-fledged "theology of justification."

2. The earliest historical development of the sacrament of penance, therefore, was not shaped in any specific way by a "theory" of redemption or a "theory" of justification. As a result we cannot look to the early historical development of this sacrament for a confirmation of any given interpretation of justification or of redemption. Because of this lack of real integration of "justification" and the emergence of a ritual of reconciliation, the eventual patristic ritualizing of reconciliation, with all its preceding and subsequent elements, at times indicated a definite derailment from a solid and acceptable theology of Jesus' salvific life, death and resurrection. The early patristic forms of the sacrament of reconciliation do not manifest a solid theological approach to justification in each and every stage of their development. This is true since the early patristic forms of the sacrament of reconciliation are not carefully integrated into a New Testament theology of the life, death and resurrection of Jesus. The patristic stress on the area of "good works" is, of course, the achilles heel.

2. SALVATION, THE RESURRECTION OF JESUS, AND THE NEW TESTAMENT

In the first half of the twentieth century biblical scholars and theologians turned their attention to the resurrection of Jesus in a very strong way. In a bibliographical essay, G. Ghiberti lists 1,510 scholarly books, monographs and articles from the major European languages on the resurrection of Jesus written between 1920 and 1973.[31] On the Protestant side, W. Künneth reminded his readers that Schleiermacher had for decades highly influenced Protestant thought on Jesus' resurrection.[32]

Schleiermacher had written: "The facts of the resurrection and the ascension of Christ . . . cannot be taken as an authentic part of the doctrine of his person."[33] Künneth goes on to cite in this same vein A. Ritschl and H. Stephan. Only with the criticism of Schleiermacher by R. Frank, L. Ihmels and C. Stange did the German Protestant theological thought on the resurrection of Jesus move away from this depreciation into a much more positive valency. M. Kähler, P. Althaus, K. Heim, K. Barth, E. Brunner and F. Gogarten all took up a more positive theological position vis-à-vis the resurrection than that of Schleiermacher.

On the Roman Catholic side, the resurrection of Jesus was generally described in apologetic terms. It was consistently presented as the great proof for the divinity of Jesus. On the popular side of Roman Catholic thought, *The Faith of Millions,* written by John O'Brien, brings out this approach: "Even if there remained any traces of uncertainty in the minds of any of the disciples as to the deity of Jesus after witnessing the numerous miracles he had wrought, surely those vestiges must have been dispelled by the stupendous miracle of the Resurrection."[34] On a scholarly side, A. Tanquerey in his *Manual of Dogmatic Theology* sums up his approach as follows: "If Jesus of Nazareth actually arose from the dead, we must believe that He has been really sent by God in order to teach us the true Religion."[35] Actually it was the publication of F.X. Durwell's *La Résurrection de Jésus, mystère de Salut,* in 1950,[36] which turned the Roman Catholic theological thinking on the resurrection of Jesus into a different approach.

For a long time, this theological thinking remained an academic matter, but with the renewal of the rites after Vatican II, the very phrase "death and resurrection of Jesus" appears more and more frequently in many of the revised liturgical prayers. Whereas former rituals had mentioned only the death of Jesus as the source of our salvation, these newer rituals, more times than not, mention both the death and the resurrection as the source of our salvation. This means that the death of Jesus and his resurrection must be seen as integral to all the terms which we have noted above: redemption, justification, expiation, salvation, sanctification, ransom, etc. None of these terms have an adequate theological interpretation if they only take into account the death of Jesus; each of them must equally encompass the resurrection of Jesus.

F.X. Durwell attempted to explain this interconnection in the following way, although he apologizes for defining the liturgy of heaven in terms that are not scriptural.

But Christ is not fixed in death as in a state following an act; the sacrifice remains actual. Not in the act of happening, of course, but in its final point, the moment of its consummation. Indeed, as Scripture describes it, Christ's glorification can be defined as a permanent act beyond which Christ's existence never passes. Our Lord's redemptive death is also ordered towards the glory in which it is fulfilled, and with which it coincides, as in any change the end of one way of being coincides with the beginning of another. In the ever-actual permanence of his glorification, Christ's death itself thus remains eternal in its actuality, fixed at its final point, at the moment of its perfection.[37]

In this Durwell is clearly arguing that salvation is not a matter of the death of Jesus alone, but essentially involves the resurrection as well. Durwell, of course, is not alone in this, but it was really he who first brought the Roman Catholic theology into the contemporary discussion on the resurrection of Jesus, and thus began the contemporary emphasis in the Catholic world on the justification aspect of Jesus' resurrection. This discussion sees in the resurrection what salvation is all about. Justification is not simply a forgiveness of sin, a making up for evil, a restoration of an original holiness and wholeness. Rather, the resurrection speaks about a new life: risen life. This life is a new way for Jesus in his humanity to be united with God; it is a new way for all humans to be united with God. Justification must include this newness of life, this risen life in God.

The sacraments are moments when this new life breaks through the darkness and limits of our present life. The sacraments of initiation, baptism, (confirmation), and eucharist are not simply initiation into the church, but into the risen Christ, into the newness of risen life. So, too, reconciliation is not simply a reuniting or reconciling of two parties, sundered by sin, but a new way of being united. Reconciliation does not simply restore: the result is a union which eye has not seen, ear has not heard, and which has never entered into the human mind and heart. Viewed in this light, terms such as "expiation," "satisfaction," "atonement," "justification," etc., begin to exhibit their limitations. The Greek term "divinization" has distinct advantages in this process of reconciliation. God, incarnate in Jesus, in the church, in the holy liturgy, is not only a holy presence, but his presence is holy-making. It is not only a presence of the divine, but divine-making presence. God's presence in the sacrament of reconciliation is a holy-making presence, but with a holiness that far exceeds our deepest hopes. God's presence is a divine-making presence which makes either reconciliation or justification too small a word. "Reconciliation" cannot encompass that profound unity, a resurrection unity, which this central mystery of our faith, "salvation in Jesus," truly means and truly is.

A theological expression of resurrection within a theology of "justi-fication," of "redemption," of "salvation," is perhaps like the new wine being put in old wineskins. These and similar terms are the old wineskins and by themselves they cannot adequately contain the true depth and breadth of Christ's saving action. So, too, such terms, when applied to the sacrament of penance, burst at their seams, since the reconciliation of God, which is celebrated in this ritual, far outstrips both the denotation and the connotation of these terms. The sacrament of penance is much more than penance; the sacrament of reconciliation is much more than reconciliation. This sacramental ritual is a sacramental sign of new life—i.e. of risen life. The resurrection of Jesus not only affects our under-standing of "justification," but it also affects our understanding of the "sacrament of penance."

Moreover, since risen life is clearly one of the greatest of all God's gifts, the absolute gratuity of God's grace is even further acknowledged and maintained by this interrelationship of resurrection and the sacra-ment of penance. Since the resurrection is central to the very meaning of Jesus, Jesus, the crucified and risen one, the only and the-once-and-for-all Lord and savior, remains uncompromised by any Pelagian position, when resurrection and the sacrament of penance are interfaced.

The theological elaboration of the resurrection has, for the most part, taken place in fairly contemporary times. Its interrelationship with a theology of justification still needs further study, and its interrelationship with the sacrament of penance has only just begun. Nonetheless, we are in actuality saved by the life, death and resurrection of Jesus. Accord-ingly, if a theology of justification is a theology of such salvation, it must integrate Jesus' life, death and resurrection into the justification process. Moreover, if a theology of the sacrament of penance involves salvation, it, too, must integrate Jesus' life, death and resurrection into the sacra-mental process. As far as the resurrection is concerned, it is this aspect of "new life" which seems to be the most helpful in the elaboration of both tasks.

SUMMARY OF CHAPTER THREE

In this chapter we have considered the following points:

1. Salvation in Jesus has been given to us through the life, death and resurrection of Jesus, not simply through his death. This compre-hensive approach makes us reevaluate the theological meaning of

the death of Jesus, since in the west the theological interpretation of the death of Jesus has often drastically reduced the soteriological or theological meaning of the life and the resurrection of Jesus.

2. In the New Testament, particularly in Paul, there are many terms for "salvation," none of them totally comprehensive. Justification is only one of these terms, as is also redemption or even deification.

3. One New Testament view sees Jesus' death as that of the latter-day prophet, an eschatological confessor-martyr. Another New Testament view sees Jesus' death as part of God's over-arching plan of salvation. Still another New Testament view sees Jesus' death as an atoning death. All three are equally traditional, equally important; none of the three views in the New Testament has a claim to superiority.

4. The fact that the early church continued to interpret Jesus' death in a variety of ways further grounds the position that the New Testament presents us with no normative theoretical interpretation of the death of Jesus.

5. Recent theology, both Protestant and Catholic, has enlarged our view of the theological and soteriological importance of the resurrection of Jesus. The resurrection of Jesus is seen and interpreted as essential to the theology of salvation (justification, deification).

6. Risen life is a new way of life with and in God, unheard of in our present human condition. This new way of being with and in God is the goal of all salvation (justification, deification) and comes to us only in and through the once-and-for-all life, death and resurrection of Jesus. Since it is unheard of, it is totally gratuitous.

4

Justification and Reconciliation in the Patristic Period, 150 to 700 A.D.

When a Vatican commission had been established to prepare a draft for the renewal of the sacrament of penance, and when it early on submitted a draft to the *Concilium ad exsequendam constitutionem de sacra liturgia,* the commission included a brief summary of the history of the sacrament of penance. Although this might appear as a minor detail, it points out that only a few years ago it could not be taken for granted that the history of this sacrament was widely known, even among highly placed ecclesiastics. Indeed, our present knowledge of this history of the sacrament of penance might not be so detailed, had not an anti-Catholic author, H.C. Lea, in 1896, published *A History of Auricular Confession and Indulgences in the Latin Church.*[1] From 1896 to Vatican II (1962–1965) an enormous amount of historical work had taken place, providing details of the history of this sacrament which had not been fully known before.

In this chapter we will consider the emergence of a ritual of reconciliation as we find it documented in the pages of church history. Remarkably, it is not until the middle of the second century that there is clear indication in the available data of such a ritual. Nonetheless, even from the middle of the second century onward there are, at first, only scattered historical data which indicate the way in which the early patristic church through a ritual isolated, repelled and negated sin. At the height of the patristic period, i.e. in the fifth and sixth centuries, one finds a clearer picture both of the theology and of the liturgy of reconciliation in this period of church history.

One must also keep in mind that in the history of this sacrament there has not been an organic development. One generation's practice did not, at times, lead smoothly into the next generation's practice. From the patristic period to the twentieth century, there have been several "official" positions of the church as regards the ritual of this sacrament. As we read and reread this history, we find many stages of "new beginnings" and "slow endings," both in theory and in practice. In this regard, the history of the sacrament of penance differs considerably from the histories of baptism and eucharist. In these latter two sacraments, the history has been far more organic and orthogenetic, whereas the history of the sacrament of penance is far more jagged and disconnected.

This chapter is divided into five sections:

1. The Early Patristic Period: 150–300 A.D.
2. The Earliest Rituals of Reconciliation: 200–500 A.D.
3. Early Church Councils: 300–600 A.D.
4. Three Specific Patristic Rituals
5. Patristic Theology of Justification

1. THE EARLY PATRISTIC PERIOD: 150–300 A.D.

The post-apostolic age up to Hermas (c. 140) provides no identifiable references to any ritualized practice of reconciliation. The *Didache,* Clement of Rome's *Letter to the Corinthians,* the letters of Ignatius of Antioch, the writings of Polycarp of Smyrna, the *Epistola Apostolorum,* and the epistle of Barnabas offer nothing on the theme of the church's ritualized penitential practice of that time. All of these writings, however, mention in some fashion or another the forgiveness of God which Jesus has brought us, and therefore the power in the church to repel, isolate and negate sin. Here and there we find clear indications of post-baptismal sin. Forgiveness and salvation strongly undergird all these writings, but none of them offer us a clue to a "sacramental" ritual of reconciliation.

Moreover, E. Bourque, among many others, notes that in this sub-apostolic period there was a general tendency toward rigorism (*enkratism*), so that, once baptized, the Christian was seen as someone who ought never to sin again.[2] Post-baptismal sin was not something which Christians of that era took for granted. This rigorism helps explain some of the difficulties which the early patristic church encountered in its efforts to apply the power to forgive sin, particularly serious and substantive post-baptismal sin.

A. HERMAS

It is Hermas (c. 140), a lay person apparently connected with the church at Rome, who first clearly mentions the possibility of a penitential rite for serious sins committed after baptism. Whether he had initiated something hitherto unknown in the church, or whether he is propagating something that was already present, is controverted.[3] Nonetheless, it is safe to say that in Hermas' writings we see the following:

  a. After baptism there is one and one only possibility for reconciliation with the church.
  b. This reconciliation is ecclesial and has a public quality about it.[4]

These two ideas—(a) reconciliation can be received once and once only; and (b) this is to be done in a public way—characterize the entire official penitential practice of the Mediterranean church, east and west, from mid-second century to the eleventh century. There is some debate on the origins and the meaning of the regulation that *penitentia secunda* can be received only once in a person's lifetime. Perhaps Hermas is the author of this approach; perhaps it antedates him, but no matter what the result of this controversy might be, it is clear that the influence of Hermas' writings affected the discipline of the church for centuries. In the west, Jerome, Ambrose, Augustine, Pacian, Leo, and Gregory the Great, to name only a few, clearly attest to the unrepeatability of penance. In the east, the Alexandrians, Clement and Origen, echo this discipline of unrepeatability. Other eastern bishops and writers do not mention this discipline of a single *penitentia secunda,* but neither do they mention that *penitentia secunda* might be repeated. It is only through the influence of the Celtic approach to penance, in the early middle ages, that there is a change in this discipline.

One should also note that in both east and west, during the entire patristic period, there was (a) no "confession of devotion" as we find it in later ages, (b) no private confession, such as that of a later age, and (c) no confession of venial sin. *Penitentia secunda* was meant for serious sins only, and it was always ritualized in a public way.

Hermas, however, is not crystal-clear in his presentation. In his writings there is an eschatological urgency: the end of the world is coming soon, and consequently conversion of heart is absolutely necessary to prepare oneself for this finale. On the other hand, Hermas at times comments on the sinlessness of those who have been baptized, so that after baptism there seems to be no room for reconciliation, should one sin. On other occasions, one might argue that he implies a form of post-baptismal reconciliation, and this form of post-baptismal reconciliation has an ecclesial dimension. Hermas, however, gives us no clear picture as regards any ecclesial ritual. Poschmann summarizes his judgment on Hermas' penitential position as follows:[5]

a. There is a saving penance after baptism.
b. Because of the end of the world, such a penance may be the final opportunity.
c. No sinner seems to be excluded.
d. Amendment must be once-and-for-all. Relapse into sin could be fatal.
e. The purpose of post-baptismal penance is a complete reform of the sinner.
f. Post-baptismal penance brings about internal sanctification.
g. Post-baptismal penance is *in the church* as an institution, necessary at times for salvation itself. In all of his works, Poschmann emphasizes the role of the Church as a sort of "constant" in the patristic literature.

In spite of some unclarity in the writings of Hermas, we can say that a public form of reconciliation, which could be received only once in a lifetime, became the "canon law" of the entire church, both east and west, for the next nine centuries. *The Shepherd of Hermas,* as his work is called, seems to include some material from an earlier date, roughly from around the end of the first century. A strong factor in such a dating is the mention of the Roman church leader, Clement. Today, however, the vast majority of patrologists maintain that Hermas lived about the middle of the second century, because of the mention of another Roman church leader, Pius, who lived at the mid-century mark. However, the material on penance, which is in Hermas' *Shepherd,* reflects mid-second century church practice. Such a view is the common approach among contemporary patristic scholars.

The final word on Hermas has not yet been formulated. This is due, in many ways, to the unclarity both of his own writings and the lack of any other corroborative writings, either immediately before or after Hermas. In the same century as Hermas, much of the apocryphal literature of the New Testament, i.e. various apocryphal gospels, acts, and epistles, were written, but they make no mention of any ritual of reconciliation. Nor do we find any mention of a reconciliation ritual in the various acts of the martyrs, dating from about 150 onward to 300 A.D. Early apologists, such as Justin, Aristides of Athens, Tatian, Athenegoras of Athens, and Melito of Sardis, all of whom lived in the last half of the second century, offer no hint of a rite of penance. In some of these writings, it might be noted, the rituals of baptism and even of eucharist are mentioned, but one finds nothing on a ritual of reconciliation for post-baptismal sin.

The so-called second letter of Clement—a letter not written by Clement of Rome, but written shortly after Hermas' time—has a small section, exhorting the baptized to do penance for sins. In many ways, the author of this letter echoes the thinking of Hermas, so that there is the possibility that it is dependent on Hermas for this material of post-baptismal penance.

B. TERTULLIAN

A second early author who wrote on penance was Tertullian (c. 150–230). In *De Poenitentia,* Tertullian speaks of forgiveness of sin after baptism, although at times this is put in a very generic way. Tertullian writes:

> Although the gate of forgiveness has been shut and fastened with the bolt of baptism, he (God) has still allowed some opening to remain. He has stationed in the vestibule a second penitence to open to them that knock.[6]

We find in Tertullian's writings indications of an *exomologesis,* or confession of one's sins (*De oratione* 7, 1–2; *De poenitentia* 8, 9). Prayer, as well, is in Tertullian's view a form of exomologesis (*De poenitentia* 7, 1–2). Moreover, love of one's brother and sister is essential for the forgiveness of sin. At least in his Catholic years, Tertullian clearly perceived that reconciliation of sin was part of the warp and woof of church life, even in the lives of those Christians who after baptism seriously broke with the church and with God. Tertullian emphasizes, however, that such a post-baptismal reconciliation can be received only once in one's lifetime.

In Tertullian's writings, there is a clear theological connection between baptism and reconciliation. We see this connection, for instance, in those passages in which Tertullian insists not only that there should be a confession of one's sin for post-baptismal reconciliation, but that there should also be a requisite confession of God's mercy. This corresponds to:

(a) the renunciation of Satan in the baptismal liturgy;
(b) the profession of one's faith in Jesus also in the baptismal liturgy.

Moreover, just as there was a laying on of hands in baptism, so, too, there is a laying on of hands in reconciliation prior to the reception of eucharist. The baptismal-reconciliation link is clearly stated by Tertullian.

Tertullian nowhere describes the actual ritual of reconciliation; rather, he mentions here and there aspects of reconciliation: exomologesis, the wearing of sackcloth, being sprinkled with ashes, abstention from fine food and drink, continual prayer, kneeling, and to some extent an exclusion from the community.

In the *De Pudicitia,* a work written in his Montanist period (after 207), Tertullian openly says that he has changed his view on reconciliation; he speaks of some "edict" which even today is difficult to identify precisely, in which adulterers were allowed reconciliation. That there was forgiveness of post-baptismal sin in the church is clear in Tertullian; that this includes certain adulterous situations is challenged. This does not mean that such sins cannot be forgiven by God, but it does mean that Tertullian does not consider the church capable of offering outright reconciliation to such sinners. Throughout the discussion, however, one hears echoes of some ecclesial rite of reconciliation (whether approved by Tertullian or not), but nowhere do we find a clear picture of what this ritual might be. *That* such a ritual existed seems clear; *what* it involved is not all that clear.

Tertullian is also a witness to the role of the episkopos in the ritual of reconciliation. By the end of the second century and the beginning of the third century, the role of the episkopos had begun to stabilize. The episkopos became the name for the main liturgical leader in a local community. As such, he was also the main liturgical leader for whatever public ritual of reconciliation a church might have developed. Von Campenhausen had argued that the ritual of public penance did not develop either from general hortatory sermons such as one finds in Hermas, or in the voluntary acts of penance. Rather, it developed from the community's excommunication (to whatever degree) such as we noted above in the discussion of Paul and the Corinthian community. Eventually, the determination of such an "excommunication" depended on the monarchical episkopos, wherever this form of church leadership had set in. Von Campenhausen's argument is no doubt simplified and has not met with general acceptance. Still, it is clear in Tertullian that the episkopos, in this matter of public reconciliation, had a key role to play.

C. THE ALEXANDRIANS: CLEMENT AND ORIGEN

Clement of Alexandria (c. 215) repeats the position of Hermas on the need and possibility of reconciliation for post-baptismal sin: "Accordingly, rich in mercy, he [God] has granted to those among the faithful who have fallen into any transgression another and a second penance" (cf. *Stromateis,* 2, 13). Clement does not describe the ritual for such sinners, although he uses the term *exomologesis* and its cognates rather regularly and in a sort of technical way. In *Quis Dives Salvetur* Clement also attests to the possibility of reconciliation within the church for post-baptismal sin (42). Authors disagree on the issue of separation from the church community in Clement: is it a voluntary or imposed separation? At any rate, if there is a reconciliation with the community after such serious sin and separation, it occurs once in a lifetime only.

Origen (253) often describes baptism as the source of reconciliation. Still, he is well aware that there is post-baptismal sin. Many means are available to remove such sins: martyrdom, almsgiving, charity, fraternal forgiveness, but he also includes in his list the "hard and laborious remission of sin through penance," which includes a confession of sin and tears which wash one's bed (*In Lev. hom.* 2, 4). Origen, however, on other occasions indicates that some post-baptismal sins, such as idolatry, adultery and fornication, are unforgivable through the rituals of the church (*De Orat.* 28), although some authors, such as Latko and Galtier, interpret this passage of Origen as restrictive only for those who remain impenitent in their sins.

Origen is not all that clear regarding the role of the episkopos, but he is clear that the entire church community, not just the episkopos, plays a role in reconciling sinners. Certainly the church community plays a role by prayers, fasting, etc. for the sinner, but in the public ritual of reconciliation, it would *seem* that the episkopos played a leadership role.

Both Clement and Origen clearly indicate that the church forgives in a public way post-baptismal sin. Neither author, however, describes the ritual for such reconciliation. With Clement there is a strong sense of the social dimension of sin, i.e. sin injures the community, not simply the individual. With Origen we see some hesitation about ecclesial reconciliation for certain sinners.

D. THE "TRIA CAPITALIA"

After Hermas and continuing to the Council of Nicaea (and even beyond), the instances of apostasy, adultery and murder, the so called *tria capitalia,* provided both pastoral and theological difficulties to many early patristic churches. Some scholars have held that it was at least the practice in some patristic churches to exclude such sinners from this second "plank" of salvation even on their deathbed.[7] Other scholars maintain that the churches consistently opened the ritual of penance to all sinners.[8] The evidence does not allow for a clear resolution of this problem, but the evidence does strongly show that these three sins caused serious problems for some early churches. For instance, it was in the church at Carthage at the time of Tertullian, and in the church at Rome during the time of Hippolytus (160–236), that the question whether and to what extent there is post-baptismal reconciliation for an adulterer came to the fore. Both Tertullian (as a Montanist) and Hippolytus were against such reconciliation, and their arguments centered around the fact that the practice of the churches had not allowed for this, an argument from "tradition." These positions of both Tertullian and Hippolytus are not presented as new doctrine, and as a result one must admit that at least in some areas of Christian life the admission to reconciliation of publicly known adulterers caused a pastoral and theological problem.[9] Local churches gropingly worked their way to a resolution of these problems, and not always in an orthogentic way.

A different issue, but one with the same dynamics, arose somewhat later in Carthage and Rome.[10] During the persecution of Decius, the issue of the reconciliation of apostates became highly controversial. The major figure in Carthage was the bishop, Cyprian (d. 258), and in Rome the principals are Novatian (d. 260) and Cornelius (d. 253). The Decian persecution was one of the more intense persecutions against the Christians, with the result that many baptized apostatized. This persecution, particularly in North Africa, tended to have periods of intensity and periods of abatement. In the abatement periods, the issue of readmitting the *lapsi* to the church became acute. In Carthage, Cyprian makes mention of those who maintained that the tradition of the church was to exclude them from the rite of reconciliation, and in Rome Novatian claimed that to admit them ran counter to what the church had always done. These Christian leaders did not make up this "tradition." In the minds of a number of Christians at that early date, readmission of apostates was not in accord with church discipline, and this position was considered part of the church's tradition. The conservatism which one finds in such people as Tertullian and Novatian indicates that certain practices and positions had become so indigenous to church life that they were associated, though wrongly, with something essential to the Christian message itself.

The letter of the presbyters of Rome,[11] which was sent to Cyprian in the interim between the martyrdom of the Roman bishop Fabian and the election of Cornelius as the succeeding bishop of Rome, indicates a reserved but slightly open policy of readmission of apostates. Cyprian himself called on the leaders of the North African church not to readmit such sinners until a regional council could be convoked and the issues discussed at greater length. Until that council, however, Cyprian was under great pressure to give a green light to the readmission of the *lapsi.* This pressure was complicated by the so-called *libelli* of the martyr-confessors, i.e. by someone who had suffered severely for the faith but had not been killed and who then provided an apostate with a statement that he or she had been forgiven and was, as a consequence, to be readmitted. Such holy men and women were seen by Christians generally as filled with the Holy Spirit. If the Spirit had not been with them, how could they have endured the sufferings and tortures and not given up their faith? These martyr-confessors were considered the "holy people," the oracles of the Holy Spirit. If Cyprian refused to acknowledge these *libelli,* it would appear that he was rejecting a message from the Holy Spirit. If he acknowledged them, gross confusion would take place, since many of these martyr-confessors were distributing *libelli* with abandon.

The council finally took place at Carthage in 251, and the decision was this: those who were *libellatici* could be reconciled, after adequate penance, by their own bishops; those who had sacrificed, the *sacrificati* and *thurificati,* could be reconciled only at the time of death, provided they had done penance during their lifetime. Apostasy, at this period of church history, was seen in a graded fashion, depending on the degree of *communicatio in sacris* (sharing in a religious rite).[12]

a. The *sacrificati:* these were the most serious offenders, who actually offered sacrifice either to the Roman emperor or to the Roman gods.

b. The *thurificati:* these offered only incense to the emperor or to the gods. This group was not specified in the Council of Carthage, but other churches did use this term.

c. The *libellatici:* these had procured statements from Roman authorities that officially showed that they were no longer Christians, documents which could be gained, at times, simply by paying a price.

d. Those who had received the *Libellus pacis* from a martyr-confessor were not even mentioned at the council in 251. Indirectly this prerogative of the martyrs was nullified. Unless they submitted to the public ritual of penance, such Christians were to be shunned.

Penances, imposed by the church, were graded to match the severity of the crime. For those who had not done penance, reconciliation, even on their deathbed, was not allowed. For the *sacrificati* and *thurificati* penances during one's lifetime were severe; less severe penances were enforced on those who were the *libellatici.* These decisions of the church of North Africa were then sent to Rome, not for confirmation, but for information. At Rome in a council which was held later in that same year these same positions were adopted by the church of Rome for its jurisdictional area. News of these decisions traveled to other parts of the Christian world and gradually similar legislation was enacted for other

Christian jurisdictions as well. From then on, readmission of the apostate, just as the readmission of the adulterer, became more and more acceptable by all the churches, east and west.

Peter of Alexandria (c. 311) in the sections of his lost treatise *On Penance* mentions the various classes of apostates and the penances to be imposed on them. Since his writing, to some degree, has been preserved in the *Canonical Epistle* or collection of laws used by the eastern churches, his views offer us a fairly good window into fourth century eastern church practice as regards a ritual of reconciliation.

There is scant evidence for the readmission of a murderer, but we find that already in the fourth century these too were readmitted to communion with the church.[13] With this resolution of publicly-known adultery, publicly-known apostasy, and publicly-known murder, the so-called *tria capitalia* did not fade from sight in the early church. It seems that at the time of Augustine and Innocent I these three sins were the only sins which needed to be submitted to the public rite of reconciliation, at least in their churches of Rome and North Africa.

In this early patristic period, we find clear indications of a public ritual for post-baptismal sin. We also find hesitation in at least some churches as regards the extent of such ecclesial reconciliation. We do not have any clear picture of the rituals which were used for reconciliation, although we do have, here and there, passing references to components of this reconciliation process. At the time of Cyprian, laying on of hands by the episkopos was certainly a normal part of the ritual in North Africa. Stephen, the episkopos at Rome, in a letter to Cyprian, written in 256, indicated that the laying on of hands was part of the traditional ritual for post-baptismal reconciliation in the vicinity of Rome as well.

2. THE EARLIEST RITUALS OF RECONCILIATION: 200–500 A.D.

Hand in hand with this wrestling with the question of forgiveness of apostasy, adultery and murder, the rituals of reconciliation also began to develop. In Hermas, as we noted above, there was no indication of the ritual which was used for post-baptismal reconciliation, although Hermas implies that there was some ecclesial practice. In Tertullian we have the beginnings of a Latin vocabulary for the theology and ritual of penance. Tertullian used the term *agere penitentiam* as the technical term for the performance of post-baptismal penance. This is generally accompanied by *exomologesis* or confession, not a private confession to a bishop or priest, but a public avowal of one's faith in God's mercy, as also of one's sinful life. Finally, after an unspecified period of doing penance and confessing one's sinfulness, there is a public ritual of reconciliation.

For Tertullian *agere penitentiam* involved:

1. wearing some sort of sordid clothing, e.g. sackcloth and ashes;
2. restriction of diet and on certain days fasting completely;
3. lamentation;
4. prostration before the presbyters;
5. kneeling before the entire Christian community.[14]

The confession of sin (*exomologesis*), however, does not seem to have been a confession of specifics, but rather a generic attestation of God's mercy and of one's sinfulness. As we have seen above in the cases of apostasy, adultery and murder, the situation was already publicly known. In the Latin church, Cyprian is the first person to mention a laying on of hands as the culminating gesture in the actual rite of reconciliation. Still, when he mentions this laying on of hands, he does so in a way which indicates that it is an already established custom, not an innovation.[15]

Cyprian also had to contend with the martyr-confessors who had granted publicly-known sinners a *libellus reconciliationis* or *pacis.* In many instances, this made reentry into the community a prerogative of any baptized person who had suffered for the faith. Cyprian fought against such *libelli,* and in the end established the episkopos as the primary person who supervised post-baptismal reconciliation and officially determined who might be readmitted to the community. This episcopal leadership in reconciliation lasted until presbyteral baptismal and eucharistic leadership had supplanted that of the episkopos, namely after 400 A.D.

In the writings of Origen we find that remission of sin is connected to the eucharist, to prayer, to almsgiving and to the forgiveness of our brothers and sisters. Origen also speaks of sins which lead to death and sins which the church cannot forgive (sins against the Holy Spirit). The entry into the penitential state can be done once only in a Christian's lifetime. During one's time in the status of penitent, the Christian is to a degree excommunicated, but at the end this same Christian is restored to the community.[16] Origen also noted that anyone who had submitted to *penitentia secunda* was barred from entering the clerical state. This injunction was picked up by many early communities, east and west, indicating that there was a punitive aspect to the entire process of reconciliation, a punitive aspect which remained with a person throughout the remainder of his or her life.

Innocent I sent a letter to Decentius, the bishop of Gubbio, in 416. He mentions that Holy Thursday is the day set aside for reconciling penitents, according to the custom in Rome. This allocation of the ritual to Holy Thursday provides us with a window into the early process of ritualizing time. Innocent also states that the penance which a person must do depends on the severity of the sin, and a bishop must use prudent judgment in this matter. In case of imminent death, reconciliation should not be postponed.[17]

Ambrose, in his *De paenitentia* (c. 384), encourages the Christians of Milan to undergo the rite of penance. Evidently Christians did not find this form of reconciliation something beneficial. Many Christians avoided entry into the penitential process. All sins can be forgiven, according to Ambrose, but the ritual of reconciliation is open to Christians only once during their lifetime. F. Homes Dudden summarizes Ambrose's teaching on the ritual of reconciliation under three headings: (1) conversion of heart or contrition, (2) confession of sin, and (3) satisfaction. For Ambrose contrition is essential, and it must be sincere and real. Confession of the most heinous sins is also necessary, since forgiveness of such sins must include the intercession of the whole church. Ambrose particularly emphasized this aspect, since many Christians in and about Milan refrained from such open confession of sin. Satisfaction, for Ambrose, was also requisite, especially tears and prayers, fasting and almsgiving. In his *De Elia* Ambrose says that such works are the "means of making an end of guilt" (n. 37). Indeed, Ambrose continually laid great stress on the efficacy of such works of satisfaction. He even speaks of reward-earning merits and of the superabundant merits of very saintly people being transferred to the credit of others. Ambrose is, however, more practical than theoretical, and even though called a "doctor of the church" he cannot be considered a first-class theologian. In his treatment of grace and sin, of salvation from Jesus and the works of satisfaction, Ambrose leaves many aspects unanswered.[18]

In the writings of Augustine, we find an attempt to categorize sins: those which needed the public ritual of penance and those which did not. The way in which Augustine separates these two classes does not, however, correspond to the contemporary division of mortal and venial. The rite of reconciliation, Augustine tells us, is available once only in a Christian's lifetime, but no sin seems to be excluded, although there is some debate among Augustinian scholars on the kinds of sins which need to be submitted to public penance according to Augustine.[19]

Leo I cautioned against public declarations of sin in the various churches. He did not see any pastoral advantage in such denunciations or proclamations. Even at the time of Leo, however, a special mention of the sin of apostasy seemed necessary. In his writings we also see that sinful bishops, priests and deacons did not enter the order of penitents, but were sent to monasteries for the remainder of their lives. Likewise, once a Christian has received the laying on of hands in the ritual of reconciliation, he is forbidden to enter the military life. At the time of death, Leo notes, reconciliation is not to be denied.[20]

During the fourth to the sixth century, the formation of the order of penitents evolved, similar to the order of catechumens. This development reflects what Tertullian in a rudimentary way had already established. Although various stages of this penitential order developed, no uniform pattern or naming of such stages is evident. In some churches, the penitents were supposed to wear a *cilicium,* a goatskin dress (Synod of Toledo, 401). Elsewhere, one was required to cut one's hair and beard. On the other hand, other churches required that a penitent neither shave nor have one's hair cut. Dionysius of Alexandria (d. 265) is the first to mention the following grades: a "hearer" for three years; a "kneeler" for ten years.[21] Gregory the Thaumaturgos (c. 270) in one place mentions two grades: "standers" and "kneelers." In the so-called canonical letter of Gregory we read:

Canon 7: Those who have enrolled among the barbarians and accompany them in captivity, and, forgetful that they are Pontians and Christians, become so barbarized as even to put to death by the gibbet or by strangulation those of their own race, and to point out to the barbarians their way of escape or their houses, such you must exclude even from [the grade of] *hearer,* until a common decision as to what should be done with them is reached by the saints, and, prior to them, by the Holy Spirit.

Canon 8: With regard to those who have dared to break into the houses of others during the plundering raids of the barbarians. Those who have broken into the houses of others, if they have been brought to trial and convicted, are to be unworthy even of the *hearing;* but if they declare themselves and make restitution, they are to be *fallers* in the ranks of the penitents.

Canon 9: But those who have found in the field or in their own homes something left behind by the barbarians, if they are brought to trial and convicted, they are likewise to be placed among the *fallers;* but if they declare themselves and make restitution, they are to be deemed worthy even of the prayer.

Canon 11: The grade of *mourner* takes place outside the door of the church (oratory); here it is proper for the sinner to stand and to beseech the faithful as they enter to pray for him. That of *hearer* is inside the door, in the narthex; here it is proper for the sinner to stand as long as the catechumens remain, and then to go forth. For he (Gregory) says, when he has heard the Scriptures and the instructions, let him be put forth and not be counted worthy of the prayer. The grade of *faller* is had when he stands within the door of the nave, and goes forth with the catechumens. That of *bystander,* when he takes his stand with the faithful, and does not go forth with the catechumens. Last is that of *participant* in the Holies.[22]

Basil (d. 379) also attests to a preliminary stage of "weeper," who was excluded from entering the church building and simply remained outside, asking for the prayers of the Christians as they went into the church.[23] Generally, this stage of weeper was begun voluntarily, and only when perseverance on the part of the sinner was judged adequate by the bishop was the person admitted clearly into the order of pentitents as a stander, followed later by another determined period as a kneeler. Nonetheless, there was no uniform regulation regarding these stages or their naming throughout the churches, both in the east and in the west. Each local church developed such stages, if they had any at all, in a variety of ways. Sozomen (450) gives the following account of the penitential liturgy in Rome.

There [Rome] the place of those who are in penance is conspicuous: they stand with downcast eyes and with the countenance of mourners. But when the divine liturgy is concluded, without taking part in those things which are lawful to the initiated, they throw themselves prostrate on the ground with wailing and lamentation. Facing them with tears in his eyes, the bishop hurries towards them and likewise falls to the ground. And the whole congregation of the church with loud crying is filled with tears. After this the bishop rises first and raises those who are prostrate; and after he has prayed in a fitting manner for those who are repentant of their sins, he dismisses them. Then each one by himself willingly spends as much time as the bishop has appointed in exercises of hardship either in fasting, or in not bathing, or in abstinence from meats, or in other ways which have been prescribed. On the appointed day, having discharged his penalty after the manner of a debt, he is absolved from his sin, and takes part in the assembly with the people. The bishops of the Romans have guarded this procedure from times long past up to our own day.[24]

An earlier indication of these stages of penance can be seen in the decisions of the Council of Nicaea (325), evidencing the practice of at least some areas of the eastern church.

Canon 11: With regard to those who lapsed without duress, or without confiscation of goods, or peril, or any such reason in the persecution which took place under the tyrant Licinius, the Synod has decided that, even though they were unworthy of benevolent treatment, assistance should nevertheless be given them. As many then of the faithful who sincerely repent shall fill out three years among the hearers, and for seven years shall be fallers; for two additional years they shall have fellowship with the laity in the prayers, without making the offering.

Canon 13: With regard to those who are departing this life, the ancient and canonical law shall even now be safeguarded, to the effect that if anyone is departing he is not to be deprived of the last and most necessary gift for the journey [viaticum]. But if after his reconciliation and reception once more to fellowship, he is again numbered among the living, let him take his stand among those who have fellowship in the prayer only. But in general, with regard to all, whoever they be, who are departing this life, and who ask to partake of the Eucharist, let the bishop after investigation grant it.

Canon 14: With regard to catechumens who have lapsed as well, the holy and great Council has decided that they should be only hearers for three years, and afterwards pray along with the catechumens.[25]

In the eastern church, the practice of dismissing those in the order of penitents after the homily was common, although this was not too common in the western church. Since the time spent in the order of penitents was generally quite long, it should be noted that such Christians who were dismissed after the homily often went years without attending the eucharist on Sunday (or any other day), and there was no thought at all that they had "missed mass" and thereby committed additional serious sins. In fact, in dismissing the penitents, the local church law was forbidding them to assist at the eucharist on Sunday.

Even though there were long periods of penance, often many years, the imposition of the bishop's hand and the reception of the eucharist with the Christian community did not, in many areas, mean the end of the situation. In quite a number of locales a person who went through the penitential rite was required to remain celibate for the remainder of his or her life. The thinking of the church leadership was this: since in baptism one had truly converted to the Lord, this second conversion in reconciliation should give evidence of an even more genuine *metanoia,* and what greater evidence could a person offer than sexual abstinence on a lifelong basis. On this subject, Poschmann writes:

> A person who has once undertaken penance remains forever a Christian of inferior juridical status. He is not to be admitted to the clerical state, and he must submit to restrictions which profoundly affect the conduct of his life. To these belong the prohibition of holding public offices, in particular, of engagement in military service, and, most important of all, abstention from marital intercourse. In other words, the "status of penitent" requires a renunciation of the "life of the world," not different in kind from that of the "religious state." . . . Moreover, the obligations are so strictly interpreted that their infringement is equivalent to a relapse into sin. . . . The existence of the lifelong obligation is established with certainty for the period from the fourth century onwards. There is no hint of them in the source material of the first three centuries, and yet in some respects this is quite rich. . . . It seems that in the Orient they [these lifelong restrictions] simply did not arise.[26]

The length of the time spent in the order of penitent, the rigor of it, and the matter of permanent celibacy created such a state in the church from about 500 onward that the sacrament of reconciliation came more and more to be seen and to be observed as the sacrament of the dying. Christians simply refused to undertake this rigorous program until death seemed imminent. Watkins states that "in the fifth century, penance in time of health was nearly lost in the West as in the East."[27] The sacrament of penance from that time on became a sacrament of the dying.

It was surely not the bishops who urged this postponement; rather, we find in their sermons continual exhortation to the Christians to enter the order of penitent. It appears that the Christian lay people themselves rejected the penitential procedure as it was prescribed by the hierarchy of that time. There may be some comparison between that situation in the sixth, seventh and eighth centuries and what occurred around the middle of the twentieth century, in which once more we find the Christian lay people simply not receiving the sacrament of penance. In the twentieth century, as in the earlier period, it was not the bishops or priests who advocated such a rejection of the sacrament, yet the decline in sacramental confession was rapid and dramatic. In both instances, it was really the lay Christian saying to the church officials: what you ask of us in this matter of reconciliation is not helpful.

From these sources and others not cited in this volume, certain questions regarding this early practice of penance arise. Many of these questions cannot be answered easily; some may never be resolved.

WHO PRESIDED OVER THE RITUAL OF RECONCILIATION?

As far as the person who performed the ritual of reconciliation, it is abundantly clear that in most cases it was the episkopos who laid hands on the penitent. Still, there is some evidence, though not abundant, that presbyters and even deacons were, at times, appointed to this task.[28] By and large, however, during the first six centuries of church history, the admission to the order of penitent and the reconciliation of such penitents was the prerogative of the episkopos.

WAS THERE PRIVATE CONFESSION OF SIN?

There is no doubt that in some few instances, prior to the rite of reconciliation, there was a private confession or discussion of specific sins made to the episkopos. This procedure is clearly attested to in the patristic literature.[27] However, when the discipline of the church required that the sinner do penance, *agere penitentiam,* i.e. enter into the order of penitent, this confession to the bishop never took the place of public penance. In other words, there were not two ways of receiving remission of serious post-baptismal sin: (1) the first through a public process of reconciliation; (2) the second by a private confession of sin to the bishop. The overwhelming evidence indicates that in the early church there was only one sacramental form for reconciliation: namely, the public order of penance. The private confession of sins to a bishop was non-sacramental in its nature, and simply provided one way by which the episkopos determined whether or not the penitent was truly sorry and ready for the "order of penitent." Forgiveness of sin came only in the public rite of reconciliation.

WERE THERE CONFESSIONS OF DEVOTION?

In the early church there is no indication of either private confession or confessions of devotion.[29] The ritual of reconciliation was meant only for those who had seriously and substantively separated themselves from God and from the Christian community. One could say that in this patristic period most Christians never received the "sacrament of penance" during their entire life. Even Caesarius of Arles, who developed a sort of charismatic way of penance for those unable to perform the public penitential discipline, did not have recourse to a second "official" way of penance, namely, a form of private penance. For Caesarius there was only one "official" form of reconciliation: the public form which one could receive once in a lifetime.[30]

WAS THERE A FORM FOR ABSOLUTION?

The formula: "I absolve you from your sins in the name of the Father, and of the Son, and of the Holy Spirit," originated in the medieval period. It was never used in this early period of church history. Its inclusion and requirement for the sacrament of reconciliation stems from a later date. When medieval theologians, canonists and church hierarchy began to see this formula of absolution as a requirement *ad validitatem* (for the valid administration of confession), one can only say that they did so because of church law and discipline, not from any intrinsic factor. In other words, this formula does not go back to Christ, to the apostles, or to the patristic church. As the so-called "form" of this sacrament, it enters the picture only in medieval times. Consequently it can only be seen as a canonically established form which can be changed, since it is clearly an addition.

WERE THERE MORTAL AND VENIAL SINS
IN THE PATRISTIC PERIOD?

During this early patristic period, beginning with Cyprian, through Augustine, but especially in John Cassian, attempts were made to indicate which sins were the "deadly" ones, the *crimina,* thereby requiring the public form of reconciliation, and which sins were the "everyday" sins.[31] No clear pattern emerges in this early church period, and it would be a great misreading of history to see in these early witnesses the same distinctions between those mortal and venial sins, commonly understood and quite theologically precisioned, which one finds from the late medieval period onward. This means that the line, indicating which sins might exclude from eucharistic fellowship and which do not, has been differently drawn at different periods of church history, and even differently drawn by different local churches, even at the same period of church history.

That the ritual of reconciliation in this early church period was a sacrament should not be easily assumed, for it is generally not called a *sacramentum,* although it was an important public act in the church. The first time the rite of reconciliation was called a sacrament appears in the writings of Alger of Lüttich (c. 1121).[32] In the patristic period, however, the heart of the reconciliation process was the internal conversion from sin and a deep-felt movement toward God. This grace of forgiveness was radically rooted in the redemptive life, death and resurrection of Jesus. Fundamentally, and this was stressed again and again, forgiveness was God's action, not the bishop's, not the priest's, not ultimately the church's itself. The climactic moment of this entire penitential process, and the occasion that was maximally liturgized, was the laying on of hands, and it is in this laying on of hands, not in the preliminary confession of sins to a bishop or priest, nor in the more generic confession to the ecclesial community, that (eventually) the "sacramentality" of the penitential process finds its summation, for it is precisely in the laying on of hands that we have the sign of forgiveness, a sign which summarizes the *exomologesis* and the *agere poenitentiam.*

Two other items are important to note: the first is that both sin and conversion were seen, not as a private matter, but as a situation which had social implications. This aspect of the early church has been resumed in the new rite of reconciliation with its emphasis on sin as an offense against God and at the same time as an offense against the community, and reconciliation with its emphasis on reconciliation both with God and with the community. Secondly, the climactic rite of reconciliation, the laying on of hands, took place in a context of prayer and indeed was itself a moment of prayer. Throughout the ritual, it is prayer: the prayer of the penitent, the prayer of the bishop, the prayer of the community, which remains center-stage. This emphasis on prayer is also a substantive part of the new rite of penance.

3. EARLY CHURCH COUNCILS, 300–600 A.D.

A study of early church councils helps us see some issues connected with the rite of reconciliation in the patristic period. Councils generally take up specific issues, and thus we find in such councils only disparate elements. These councils do not offer us a complete picture of reconciliation at this period of early church history.[33]

Three early councils, that of Elvira (306), Epaone (517) and Arles (524), passed legislation regarding a cleric, who had committed adultery. Such clerics were not to enter the "order of penitents." Rather, they were to be sent to a monastery for the remainder of their lives and perpetually deprived of their status as clerics. At these monasteries, they received the eucharist along with the lay people. If they were married, this banishment to a monastery included the break-up of the marriage, and such clerics were obliged to celibacy for the remainder of their lives.

In these three councils there was also legislation against ordaining anyone who had been in the "order of penitents." There was a stigma attached to those who, after baptism, committed so serious a sin that they had been excluded from eucharistic fellowship. This stigma prevented their entry into the ordained state.

The Councils of Tours (461), Vanne (461) and Orlean (511) reaffirmed the practices that those who were "recidivists," i.e. those who after post-baptismal reconciliation fell again into serious sin were to remain in lifelong excommunication, unable to take part in the life of the Christian community. Younger people, these councils cautioned, should not be allowed into the "order of penitents," since the danger of falling back into sin was strong. They should wait for a more mature age. This same admonition is mentioned in the Council of Agde (506).

It is clear, from these statements about younger people, that the early church in no way viewed the rite of post-baptismal reconciliation as a ritual open to children. The rite of post-baptismal reconciliation was seen clearly as a rite for mature adults. When we realize that this form of public reconciliation was the law of the official church until c. 1000, at least in practice, and until 1215 in actual written law, then our contemporary practice of children's confession is seriously questioned. Children's confession is certainly not *de iure divino.* Nor can we say that children's confession or teenage confession is pastorally obligatory, since a thousand years of the opposite pastoral practice relativizes this contemporary pastoral situation. Indeed, children's or teenage confession must be seen as a modern and even contemporary practice, not as a practice which cannot be changed.

The Council of Valence (374) forbade easy penances for lapsed virgins (can. 2); indeed, in such cases absolution ought to be postponed until the imminence of death. The Council of Elvira (306) did not even allow deathbed reconciliation for such sinners and was very severe on the issue of lapsed virgins (can. 3, 13, 14).

The Council of Elvira demanded ten years of public penance for apostates (can. 22, 59), whereas the Third Council of Carthage (397) had left it up to the bishop to determine the length of penance, based on the severity of the sin. The First Council of Toledo (400) required ten years of penance for serious sins, and also abstention from sexuality for similar cases (can. 16, 19). In this same council, penitents could not be accepted for ordination (can. 2) and subdeacons who married for a third time should be required to do penance and no longer function in their office (can. 4).

We find in these canons of various councils that the early patristic church had no single set of rules regarding post-baptismal reconciliation. Specific issues came up at these councils, because the issues were pressing and current in the geographical locales where these various councils took place. Certain things, the council bishops felt, were happening which needed some legislation. Moreover, throughout this period of regional councils, there is no mention of consulting Rome on such issues, or of asking Rome for confirmation.

The official rituals for reconciliation also varied from locale to locale; the regulations for post-baptismal reconciliation varied from locale to locale; certain sinful situations were seen in some locales to be of great significance and needing strong legislation, while the same sinful situations in other locales had minimal or lesser significance and no legislation seemed necessary. One cannot generalize on the statements of these councils, as though such conciliar legislation indicated a general trend. Regional pluralism in liturgy and pastoral practice was a normal part of church life during the first eight centuries.

4. THREE SPECIFIC PATRISTIC RITUALS

Three texts from the patristic period influenced the rite of reconciliation to some degree, namely, the *Didascalia Apostolorum,* the *Apostolic Constitutions,* and the *Sacramentary of Verona.*

A. DIDASCALIA APOSTOLORUM

In this text of Syrian provenance, written around the time of Tertullian and Hippolytus (late second and early third century, although some might place it earlier), we find in the section on post-baptismal reconciliation that there is a ritualized laying on of hands.[34] The text indicates as well that isolation from the community itself should be made if the community is seriously endangered by the presence of someone who has disregarded substantively his or her gospel commitment. Rather than a coercive rejection of the sinner by competent authority, this isolation appears to be more indirect, namely, the Christian community itself simply avoids the individual. On the other hand, as the text states, liturgical excommunication, i.e. not being able to receive the eucharist, should be for a brief time only. While community isolation is presented as a harsh penalty, liturgical or eucharistic excommunication is presented more as pedagogical in nature and as constructive of Christian life. The isolation from the Christian community, at least for those who seem repentant, is not absolute. Some Christian folk encourage the person in his or her repentance and inform the episkopos, often through the deacon, of the person's repentant state. The episkopos is the one who makes the final decision to remove the isolation and the eucharistic ban. Even before the ritual of reconciliation takes place, the episkopos is told to enjoin a few days' fast on the individual (ii, 16).

The ritual of reconciliation itself includes the laying on of hands by the episkopos (c. 7), but the role of the community is equally stressed (c. 10). Moreover, the strong relationship between baptism and reconciliation is mentioned (ibid.). We find in this text a rather mature ritual for post-baptismal penitents. Whether all sins can be forgiven is not totally clear, nor is there any mention of post-reconciliation obligations.

B. APOSTOLIC CONSTITUTIONS

In this text (c. 380) we find a lengthy exhortation, made by a deacon to the bishop, asking that the bishop, as leader of the community, reinstate the penitents to full eucharistic communion.[35] This exhortation by the deacon is part of the liturgical ritual. It represents the official attestation that the penitents, gathered at this moment, have indeed fulfilled their lengthy penitential practices (*agere poenitentiam*). The emphatic role of the deacon corresponds well with the high-profile which deacons had in the church from 300 to 600. As the role of the deacon was more and more assumed by the presbyter, the liturgical rite of reconciliation left less and less room for a diaconal ministry. Eventually, in the middle ages, the deacon had no liturgical role at all in the ritual of this sacrament.

C. THE SACRAMENTARY OF VERONA

In this text (400–500 A.D.), we find, as far as reconciliation is concerned, simply a prayer to be said when a penitent has died without imposition of hands. Of note is the fact that the prayer is connected to the ritual of reconciliation, not to the ritual of anointing the dying.[36]

This overview of the patristic texts on the ritual of reconciliation has been studied in great detail from the time of Lea to the present day. This study has been done primarily by Roman Catholic theologians. If we consider some of the major theological topics which were presented by these theologians, and often debated in a most serious way, we find: (a) the role of the church in the process of reconciliation. Is the *pax Christi* dependent on the *pax cum ecclesia,* or is the *pax cum ecclesia* declaratory of the more fundamental *pax Christi?* Poschmann, Galtier, and K. Rahner all maintained that the patristic emphasis included a role of the church. One can see, however, that if this role of the church is presented as coming first and only then can one speak of a reconciliation with God, then one raises the issue of the absolute gratuity of God's grace as well as the issue of good works and merit. (b) The discussions on the "irremissible" sins, disputed as it is by these scholars, raise the issue of the full efficacy of Jesus' salvific act. The studies, which all of these authors (not simply the three mentioned above) make on the patristic evidence of a ritual of reconciliation, focus on the rite. There is, of course, mention of the church's "power" to forgive sin or the church's continuation of the reconciling work of Christ, but none of these authors spend time relating the emerging ritual of reconciliation, with all of its elements, to the theological meaning of the life, death and resurrection of Jesus or to the theology of grace. In other words, none of these authors relate the rite of reconciliation to justification. Without such a relationship, the patristic ritual of reconciliation, with all its vagaries, makes little sense.

5. PATRISTIC THEOLOGY OF JUSTIFICATION

Early patristic writers did not express their views of salvation in terms of justification. One, of course, finds here and there the term "justification." But, McGrath notes, their interest in this term is minimal.[37] Even on the occasions when this term is used, there is generally a mere paraphrasing of Paul. In the pre-Augustinian period, the term "justification" was not a theological issue. K. Stendahl notes that during the first three hundred and fifty years of church history, "Paul is honored and quoted, but—in the theological perspective of the west—it seems that Paul's great insight into justification by faith was forgotten."[38] The fact that the term "justification" is not at all of frequent use during this patristic period, and that commentaries on Paul's letters are not abundant, is clearly correct. However, to say that "Paul's great insight into justification by faith" was a forgotten issue goes too far, for it presumes that the interpretation of "justification by faith" which we find in the reformation period clearly corresponds to Paul's intent. We shall see later that the reformation theologians read Paul with Augustinian eyes, and as a result their own interpretation cannot be judged as absolutely normative.

Moreover, given the strong fatalistic philosophy in the Hellenistic world, the early church writers felt constrained to defend the freedom of the will, and they did this, not so much by using arguments from Christian sources, but by using arguments one could find in Jewish literature generally. There is, consequently, nothing specifically Christian in the way in which Justin, for example, argues for human freedom. This need to defend the Christian teaching from philosophical fatalism influenced in a strong way the patristic emphasis on freedom (*eleutheria*) and self-determination (*autexousia*). However, the more human freedom was defended, the more restricted was God's influence on human freedom. Theophilus of Antioch, Macarius of Egypt, Gregory of Nyssa, John Chrysostom, and Nemesius of Emessa all contributed to this discussion and all strongly defended the freedom of the human will. "John Chrysostom's defence of the power of the human free will was so convincing that it was taken up by many Pelagian writers: 'good and evil do not originate from man's nature itself, but from the will and choice alone.' "[39]

In his analysis of this early patristic literature on the theology of justification, R. Eno relates such a theology to the issue of post-baptismal sin and the patristic rite of reconciliation:

> Difficulty arises with the serious sins of those already baptized. Here in many cases the patristic view of the postbaptismal Christian life seems to place the Christian back into a law situation. He must obey commandments and do good works. If he does not do these things, punishment will follow sooner or later. A closer look at the patristic data shows that most of the Fathers looked upon the old law as still in effect except for specific ceremonial, dietary, and other regulations rejected by Gentile Christians almost from the beginning.[40]

The gratuity of salvation and forgiveness of sins without our good works appears to be limited to baptism (first justification). Post-baptismal penance (second justification) in patristic thought tended to be work-oriented. Even if one were to include Augustine's development of justification, one could say that the theology of the sacrament of reconciliation, which developed in the patristic period, was not integrated into a theology of justification. In other words, the theology of justification, which means the theology of the salvific work of Christ and the theology of grace, did not influence in any large measure the way in which the sacrament of reconciliation was propounded academically and pastorally. One could almost say that the theology of the sacrament of penance on the one hand and the theology of "justification" on the other developed along parallel tracks during this early church period, but did not mutually interact in a very decisive way. This left open many questions —questions on the role of God's grace in the process of forgiveness, questions on the role of free will in this same process, questions on the theological connection between Jesus' salvific life, death and resurrection and the bestowal of the grace of salvation to a post-baptismal sinner. These open-ended and still unanswered questions were inherited by the bishops and theologians of the early and late middle ages.

All the fathers underline and agree on the mercy of God, salvation through Jesus alone, and the gratuity of grace. In his more extended study on the same period, Eno cites from the apostolic fathers, Justin, Irenaeus, Cyril of Jerusalem, Gregory of Nazianz, Origen, Cyprian, Basil, Augustine, Ambrose—all of whom evidence this agreement. Some, he notes, exaggerate the need for good works.[41] These same fathers speak about the salvation which Jesus won through his life, death, and resurrection. We have already noted that there were several approaches to the meaning of the death of Jesus in the patristic period: an emphasis on Jesus as the victor over sin, an emphasis on Jesus as a victim or atoning savior, an emphasis on the revelatory aspect of Jesus' death.

> For the first three hundred and fifty years of the history of the Church, her teaching on justification was inchoate and ill-defined. There had never been a serious controversy over the matter, such as those which had so stimulated the development of Christology over the period. The patristic inexactitude and naivete on the question merely reflects the absence of controversy which would force more precise definition of the terms used.[42]

That there was a tendency in the early western church toward a "work-righteousness" seems to be an accepted judgment by patristic scholars. McGrath cautions us to see this tendency, however, as "innocent of the overtones which would later be associated with it."[43] In the theological battles between Pelagius and Augustine, this innocence came to an end.

Augustine, as so many other Christian thinkers of his day, lauded human freedom. However, through his confrontation with the thought of Pelagius and his reflection on the New Testament, and especially Paul, Augustine made some major changes in his own thought on the matter:

1. Human election is based solely upon God's eternal decree of predestination. This is particularly clear in his writings after 410.
2. The human faith-response to God's grace is to be seen as itself a gift or grace of God. Earlier on, Augustine had taught that the human response to God depended completely upon human free will.

3. Human free will has been compromised by sin and after sin is incapable of leading one to justification. Real freedom and true justification is possible only through grace.[44]

Augustine, without any doubt, developed a theology of justification which was quite thoroughgoing: McGrath characterizes his teaching on this subject in the following way:

an astonishing comprehensiveness of its scope;

encompasses the whole of Christian life from the first moment of faith, through the increase of righteousness before God and man, to the final perfection of that righteousness in the eschatological city.

it includes the restoration of the entire universe to its original order.[45]

So vast is this theological understanding of justification in Augustine's later thought that every part of creation, and every part of one's existence, and every part of the ethical order is touched in some way or another by justification. Nonetheless, it is almost impossible to find instances in which Augustine's theology of justification significantly shaped the patristic theology and pastoral practice of the sacrament of penance. The Vandals were sweeping into the west as Augustine was wrestling with this theology, and the turmoil of the barbarian invasions can easily be seen as one of the major reasons why theology and pastoral practice might not have coincided. There is no doubt that Augustine deeply influenced the medieval world, but in the medieval world the Celtic form of penance, not the patristic form, became dominant. Thus, Augustine's teaching on justification clearly influenced the theology and pastoral practice of penance as we find it in its Celtic form. But (a) with the theology and pastoral practice of public reconciliation already quite established throughout the Mediterranean world at the time of Augustine, (b) with the patristic form of penance moving ever more rapidly in the late fifth and sixth centuries toward a sacrament of the dying, and (c) with the turmoil in the west from the migration of nations, the theological synthesis on justification, which Augustine worked out in such comprehensive detail, played almost no role in the way in which the patristic form of penance developed.[46]

Without a coherent doctrine of either the "atonement" or "justification" the legacy of the patristic form of reconciliation remained ambiva-

lent. On the one hand, the patristic writings on post-baptismal reconciliation, insofar as these were known, were respected; on the other hand, the
work-ethic which often became part of the theological and pastoral approach to post-baptismal sin in the patristic period reinforced the "satisfaction" component of the Celtic form of reconciliation along the same
lines: namely, a tendency toward a work-ethic understanding, rather than
toward a grace-ethic approach. In the fragments of patristic writings on
post-baptismal reconciliation, available to us today, we do not find a
Protocatechesis or a *Mystagogical Catechesis* for a post-baptismal penance, as we find with Cyril of Jerusalem for the ritual of baptism. The
patristic collections on this subject made by Palmer, Bourque, and Karpp
tell us about details of ritual, about laws, about pastoral problems, but
minimally about a theology of reconciliation in which grace and christology play a major role. The *De Paenitentia* of Tertullian is almost unique
among these patristic writings, inasmuch as three chapters are devoted to
post-baptismal reconciliation (cc. 4–6) (the first three chapters are on the
penance connected to baptism). Nonetheless, these three chapters are
moralistic rather than deeply spiritual and theological. In no way do they
begin to parallel the writings of Cyril of Jerusalem.

Theologians and bishops in this patristic period did not focus on the
issue of the sacrament of reconciliation in the same way that we might
today. They did not address such questions as: How does the theology
and practice of the sacrament of reconciliation reflect the full efficacy of
Jesus' salvific action? How does the theology and practice of the sacrament of reconciliation reflect the total gratuity of God's grace? In other
words, how does the theology and practice of the sacrament of reconciliation reflect justification? Such a frontal and precise interfacing of such
issues are simply not part of the patristic understanding of the sacrament
of reconciliation. That the sacrament of reconciliation was a grace of
God, a reflection of his abundant mercy, a grace of forgiveness which was
connected to the life, death and resurrection of Jesus, was certainly admitted, but these are rather generic terms. The innocence of the long
works of penance (fasting, almsgiving, etc.) which lasted years for those in
the order of penitents was never confronted by the Pelagian crisis, even
though it was this Pelagian crisis which eventually stripped this approach
to good works of its innocence. By the time that this confrontation took
place, it was the Celtic form, not the patristic form of penance which was
in the ascendancy.

In this same patristic period we note that the liturgies of baptism and
eucharist developed in a much more homogenous way than the liturgy of
reconciliation. In this patristic period, we find that the complications
caused by post-baptismal sin were often perplexing for the patristic

church leadership. Regulations regarding such sinners were not uniform. Rituals were diverse. Throughout this period, however, there was a constant belief that in the church of Jesus there was indeed a power to isolate, repel and negate sin. This was never questioned. The application of this power to individual circumstances and the ritualized celebration of this power was not always clear. Even the theological interpretation of this ecclesial power varied from writer to writer. No major theological effort was made to draw together the theology of grace, the theology of salvation and the theology of reconciliation. Pastoral needs, more often than theological positions, played a major role in the formulation of both ritual and practice. The very elasticity which we find in this early reconciliation process helps us today to open ourselves to new patterns of pastoral practice and to see how change can make this power to isolate, repel and negate sin, which we find throughout the church's life and which we find in a special way in this sacrament of reconciliation, ever more meaningful to the life and experience of contemporary Christian communities.

P. Fink in his historical analysis of reconciliation notes that two other factors played a strong role in the development of the sacrament of penance. First of all, there was change in the understanding of the sacrament of the eucharist. In early liturgies (*Didache,* and the *Anaphora* of Hippolytus) the unity of the Christian assembly was emphasized. By the fourth century personal growth and holiness became focal, and even more there was a strong emphasis on the transformation of the eucharistic bread and wine. When the eucharist gradually lost its focus as the sacrament of unity and unity-making (reconciliation), a second ritual, in a gradual way, gained importance: the ritual of penance. Secondly, Fink notes, sin, which appears to have been considered as hardness of heart and which manifested itself in all of human life, began to be centered on certain specific sins, and as time went by those substantive and serious sins which warranted eucharistic excommunication came to be seen, at least in the popular mind, as the only sins which really mattered.[47]

This interaction with the eucharist is important, since it indicates that patristic eucharistic theology shaped patristic reconciliation theology. It was not a patristic theology of justification which shaped reconciliation theology. There was a certain interrelationship among such church rituals as baptism (confirmation), eucharist, ordination, and penance. A development in the theology or practice of any one of these rituals would inevitably have repercussions on the theology of the other rituals. This means, of course, that an overemphasis on one aspect of a given ritual and its theology—an overemphasis which might not be all that correct or healthy—could possibly create incorrect and unhealthy repercussions in both the ritual and the theology of the other church rituals. With the exception of baptism, a patristic theology of salvation or justification in the west did not really affect sacramental thinking in any outstanding way. In the eucharist the main or dominating idea was real presence; sacrificial terminology remained peripheral.[48] The first theological treatise on the eucharist did not appear until that of Paschasius Radbertus, *De corpore et sanguine domini,* written about 831–833. Only with the discussions which followed did the sacrificial nature of the eucharist, i.e. the eucharist's connection with justification or salvation, come to the fore. As regards the ritual of reconciliation, there was indeed a general notion throughout the patristic period that the reconciliation of penitents corresponded to the gospel presentation of Jesus. However, the emphasis on penitential works was not integrated into this understanding of a forgiving Jesus. Cyprian had attempted to explain the necessity of these works of penance (*Ep.* 15; 16; 55; 59), but he is not always clear. He compares the works of penance to the work of a farmer who "tills his field with all his skill," but then is denied the fruit of his labor (*Ep.* 55, 27). The same theme can be found in *De Lapsis.* After reading Cyprian, one could ask: Were these truly works of grace or works of merit? Cyprian did not focus on this aspect of the question, and therefore did not consider the issue directly.

The bishops of the patristic period taught that there always had to be a full and just penance, i.e. both a time for acts of penance, and compensatory acts of penance. The various local councils tried to prevent one episkopos from countermanding what a neighboring episkopos had decreed, or to prevent on the part of the penitent what Dallen called "bishop-hopping," as one searched for a more benign penitential process. Ambrose in *De paenitentia* noted that the greater the guilt the greater the penance (1, 3, 10). Leo I stated that the "forgiveness of God cannot be obtained except by the supplications of the priests" (i.e. episkopoi) (*Ep.* 18, 3). But what is the role of the episkopos in this process of justification? What is the role of works of penance? Do such roles compromise the full efficacy of Jesus' own salvific act? Do they compromise the absolute gratuity of God's grace? In other words, do they compromise the basic aspects of what we call "justification"? Such questions were not formulated in this way by the early patristic church, nor were they really formulated in an equivalent way. As a result we do not find a clear integration of the sacramental ritual of reconciliation into a theology of "justification" in this patristic period. The ambiguity of the patristic period on this integration of the sacrament of penance, both theologically and pastorally, and a theology of justification allowed for further ambiguity in the early medieval period.

One might say, however: What about Pelagius? It had been precisely the Pelagian teaching on original sin which brought Augustine to integrate the theology of justification and baptism together. A similar situation in this patristic period cannot be found for either the eucharist or penance. There was no Pelagian assault on these two rituals. Consequently, a direct effort to integrate the process of "justification" and sacramental reconciliation came only after the Celtic form of penance had been established in the west. It was only then that the theology of justification, which Augustine had developed, began to shape both the theology and the practice of sacramental penance.

One additional item from this patristic period, which highly influenced the theology of penance in the west, deserves attention. This item was the influence of the Vulgate or Latin translation. First of all, in Matthew 3:2 and 4:17 one reads: "*Paenitentiam agite . . .*" ("Do penance"), which gradually in the early and then in the later middle ages came to be interpreted more and more as the performance of a sacramental rite of reconciliation. "Doing penance" meant receiving the sacrament. Contemporary translations tend to express the Greek in these passages from Matthew as: "Repent," which is what the original text and context means. In no way is there any reference in either the text or the context of the original Greek to a sacramental ritual. Secondly, Romans 10:10 in the Vulgate reads: "*Ore autem, inquit, confessio fit ad salutem,*" and the words "confession with the mouth" was also increasingly seen as an affirmation of the sacrament of penance or confession. Again, this interpretation is neither textually nor contextually substantiated by the Greek original. Still, these Latin approaches to the New Testament forged in the medieval theological world a strong interrelationship of forgiveness of sin and the sacrament of reconciliation. In much of the early medieval literature the very word "justification" was seen as a synonym for "forgiveness of sin" (i.e. forgiveness of sin through the sacrament of confession) and nothing more, and in the later part of the middle ages justification, forgiveness of sin, and the sacrament of penance came to be most intimately interlocked, both in theology and in practice.

SUMMARY OF CHAPTER FOUR

In this chapter we have considered the following:

1. The earliest, though very incomplete, historical evidence of a rite of reconciliation for sins committed after baptism is found in the writings of Hermas (c. 150).
2. The approach of Hermas became normative for the next nine

hundred years throughout the Christian church: namely, a rec-onciliation ritual is public and can be received only once in a lifetime.

3. Three sins caused areas of the early church considerable diffi-culty: publicly known adultery, apostasy, and murder. Not every local church handled these three sinful situations in the same way. Some churches even considered them "unfor-givable."

4. The rituals for post-baptismal reconciliation were diverse. Local and regional churches tended to develop their own patterns. Generally, a sinner remained in the "order of penitent" around three years, but this time could be shortened and for more serious crimes it could be lengthened.

5. Throughout this period there were no "confessions of devo-tion." In actual fact, only a small percentage of Christians ever received this "sacrament." Most Christians spent their entire life without ever receiving the sacrament of reconciliation.

6. During this entire period, those in the "order of penance" often did not attend Sunday "mass." Their missing mass was not considered "sinful." In fact, church legislation forbade their attendance at mass.

7. The types of sins, which required entry into the "order of peni-tent," and thereby excluded one from receiving the eucharist, do not correspond to the medieval (and later) distinction of "mortal" and "venial" sin.

8. Private confession was unknown in this patristic period. The private "confession" of one's sins to the episkopos was simply a preliminary first step in the reconciliation process, whereby the episkopos could determine the depth of sincerity of the sinner.

9. The formula "I absolve you from your sins in the name of the Father, and of the Son, and of the Holy Spirit" was unknown in this patristic period. This formula dates only from medieval times onward. Its absence during the entire patristic period indi-cates that its requirement *ad validitatem* is a requirement estab-lished by church law; it is not a requirement *e iure divino*.

10. Early councils and early church documents speak sparingly about this rite of reconciliation.

11. Nonetheless, the entire patristic period indicates that the church was aware that it shared in Christ's power to isolate, repel and negate sin, i.e. to bind and to loose.

12. "Justification" was not a term which the patristic church used to any great extent. Indeed, the development of a doctrine of

salvation through Jesus was varied and no single view dominated the patristic scene.

13. The development of a theology of salvation (justification) was
not heavily influential on the development of the ritual of reconciliation. In fact, there seems to be an emphasis on "works"
in the theological and pastoral approach to the ritual of reconciliation, an emphasis which was not well integrated into the theology of grace (absolute gratuity) or into the full efficacy of Jesus'
sacrifice.

14. Augustine's writings on salvation (justification) influenced the
Celtic form of this ritual of reconciliation, i.e. the medieval
form, far more. They had little if any influence on the patristic
form of reconciliation.

15. The Latin translation of the Bible (the Vulgate) contributed,
because of certain Latin phrases, to an integration of the New
Testament phrase "doing penance" with the sacrament of penance, and the phrase "confession of the mouth" with the same
sacrament. This gave, for the medieval theologian, an apparent
New Testament foundation for many emphases on the sacrament of penance itself.

5

Justification and the Penitential Practice of the Celtic Churches

For the next stage in the development of the sacrament of reconciliation, one must step back into the history of the church in England, but even more so into the churches of Ireland, Scotland and Wales, the so-called Celtic churches. The Celtic practice of reconciliation, developed during the fifth to the seventh centuries, became from medieval times onward the basis for the official practice of the Latin church.

In this chapter we will consider the follow topics:

1. The church structures of these early Celtic Christian communities with particular emphasis on the church structures in Ireland.
2. The Celtic missionary movement into continental Europe.
3. The clash between the Roman form of reconciliation and the Celtic form of reconciliation.
4. The theology of "justification" which developed during this period of the early middle ages.

1. THE CELTIC STRUCTURING OF THE CHURCH

The church of the British Isles, in its early period, though modeled on the Roman church structure, manifested a strong independence from Rome, and at times even an antagonism. Kathleen Hughes, in an article, "The Celtic Church and the Papacy," notes:

Celtic churchmen of the sixth and early seventh century recognized the popes as leaders of the Church and the successors of Peter, yet they did not give up their powers of independent judgement. The British refused to accept Augustine of Canter-

84

bury, appointed by Gregory the Great, and Columbanus did not hesitate to argue and rebuke the popes. . . . Though the position of Gildas and Columbanus is not unorthodox, their views and expressions could hardly have been satisfactory to papal opinion.[1]

The public form of the penitential discipline, it appears, was never practiced in England.[2] Nonetheless, it is in the Irish church particularly that one must begin to understand the new development of the sacrament of reconciliation. Palladius, but above all Patrick, converted and organized the Irish church along the Roman model, with the bishops clearly the spiritual leaders. Even a primatial see, Armagh, was established. In the church structure which Patrick built up there was little if any room for monks. John Ryan notes: "The more these documents [i.e. documents by and about Patrick] are studied, the more the conclusion imposes itself that the tradition they enshrine is strongly clerical and episcopal, as distinct from monastic. . . . Patrick entrusted the spiritual care of the country which he had evangelized to bishops, priests and inferior clergy, not to monks as such."[3]

The Roman legions had been withdrawn from Britain in 407; shortly thereafter the Picts broke through the barrier of Hadrian's wall, and the Anglo-Saxons crossed the North Sea and entered the British Isles. It was during this turmoil that Palladius was ordained by Celestine I to be the first bishop of Ireland. He survived but one year. In 432 Patrick, even with some embarrassing protests, was consecrated bishop and sent to evangelize the unbaptized people in the north of Ireland, where he had been a former slave. His knowledge of Gaelic was clearly to his advantage, and his mission was eminently successful, with thousands accepting the Christian faith.

However, things did not remain that way, and the meteoric change in church polity between the fifth century patrician church and the sixth century genuinely Celtic church is, as regards the swiftness and totality of the change, unparalleled in church annals. In the sixth century, one finds that the Irish church had become a monastic church: its center is no longer Armagh, but the monastery at Iona; its towering spiritual leader is not the bishop, but the abbot and in some instances the abbess; not a parish church provided for by a diocesan priest but a monastery becomes the spiritual center for monk, nun, and, above all, lay people. The reasons for this sudden and dramatic change are not all that clear, but certainly the fact that Ireland was almost totally rural, while episcopal churches were designed for urban populations, plays a not insignificant role. Whatever the causes, the reality was there. The Celtic church was a monastic church. By the sixth century the great abbots, generally presbyters, had completely overshadowed bishops both in authority and in prestige.

The spirituality of Celtic monasticism, however, has little rootage in Benedictine monasticism; rather, one finds its rootage in early Egyptian and Syriac monasticism. Again, the reasons for this connection are, to the historian, almost conjectural. Two issues, bearing on the sacrament of reconciliation, are of prime importance. In both early Egyptian and Syriac monasticism, and in the Celtic monasticism, the idea that a monk or nun (eventually a lay person as well) must have a spiritual director was self-understood. "A monk without a spiritual director is like a body without a head" is a truism which runs throughout the literature of this period. Secondly, it seems that early Egyptian monasticism applied to the spiritual life a dynamism taken from early Egyptian medicine and the care of the bodily life, namely, contrary cures contrary. Someone in fever is cooled by the application of cold water; someone flushed with blood is cured by leaching; etc. So, too, in the spiritual realm: someone given to overindulgence in food or drink needs to fast and abstain; someone prone to laziness ought to work more; someone tending to sleep too much should keep vigils; etc. These two factors form the context for the Celtic church's application of reconciliation.[4]

What one notices immediately in studying the Celtic form of penance is that it differs totally from the Mediterranean form:

Mediterranean Form	*Celtic Form*
Once only in a lifetime	As often as needed
Public	Private

It is not the question of a theology of redemption as such, nor a question of the need for conversion, which underlies the difference in these two approaches. Rather, it is the difference in structure which divides these two church areas. The historian needs to be alert both to the process of such structuring and to the result of such structuring. The history of the sacraments, and this sacrament of reconciliation in particular, indicates that rigidity of structure is not a part of the Christian heritage. It should also be noted that in both the early structuring of the Mediterranean form and in the Celtic form of reconciliation, the sacrament of reconciliation arose out of the spirituality of their times, and only when the structured forms at some later date became so institutionalized and routinized in themselves and thus isolated from the context of a wider and more profound spirituality was there a breakdown and consequent need for renewal.

The history of this Celtic form can be sketched as follows.[5] Once the monastic form of church polity took over, the monasteries became the virtual "parish centers" for the people and the monastic form of spiritual direction became widespread. People consulted regularly with a spiritual director, man or woman, with a private disclosure on one's un-Christian ways and tendencies. The scheme of sins which John Cassian had elaborated proved helpful: namely, gluttony, fornication, avarice, anger, dejection, languor, vainglory, and pride. The spiritual director inculcated some line of conduct opposite to such specific moral problems. It is important to realize that at first this format was simply an issue of spiritual direction, not a sacramental form for reconciliation. At this early period of Celtic history we really do not know either (a) what form of sacramental reconciliation might have been used or (b) whether there was sacramental reconciliation at all in the Celtic churches. The spiritual directors themselves were, at this early period of time, both men and women, ordained and non-ordained, although the male and the ordained person appears more often than the female or the non-ordained.

2. THE CELTIC MISSIONARY MOVEMENT IN EUROPE

Precisely when and how this form of spiritual direction regarding sin, conversion and amendment became the actual form for the sacrament of reconciliation remains shrouded in undisclosed history. The fact that it did so is clearly attested to by the **Celtic Penitentials.** These are books, providing a pastoral guideline for the care of sinful souls. They were written in either Latin or Gaelic, and through them the private form of reconciliation was transmitted first to the Roman-oriented church of England and then to that of Europe. These books list in detail various sins and indicate the appropriate penance for such sins. Because of this rather *quid pro quo* arrangement, this form eventually came to be called at times *tariff penance.* The earliest of these pentitentials are four and they stem from the church in Wales: *Gildas on Penance, Synod of North Britain, Grove of Victory* and a *Book of David.* The earliest Irish pentitential still extant was written in the mid-sixth century, supposedly by St. Finnian, abbot of Clonard (d. 549). It is a compilation of the then current penitential customs and it directly influenced the *Penitential of St. Columban,* which had enormous impact throughout Europe.

These Celtic Penitentials were the principal means whereby the Celtic system of private penance was spread.[6] In these Penitentials we do not find, oddly enough, any description of a liturgical ritual of reconciliation. We find only the listing of sins and the listing of penances. Nonetheless, these listings of sins present us with a picture of what these Celtic churches considered seriously sinful. *Gildas* and the *Synod of North Britain* treat only sins of monks and clerics. *Grove of Victory* and the *Book of David* indicate sins of both laity and clergy. An example, quite at variance with contemporary reconciliation practice can be seen in the following instruction from the *Grove of Victory*: for those who abet the Anglo-Saxon invaders there is a penance of fourteen years; if, while helping them, one sheds blood, the penance is to last one's lifetime. One notes that the very act of abetting the Anglo-Saxon invaders was a serious sin, and that the penance demanded for such a serious sin was not slight.

In the Penitential of Finnian we find sins of thought, word and deed, distinguished as far as degrees of guilt and punishment are concerned. Finnian focuses on the sins of clerics (canons 10–29) and then on the sins of the laity (canons 31–48). He appears to be preoccupied with sexual sins. Finnian, however, states that viaticum should be refused to no one, even though the person could not perform the requisite penance. The penances which Finnian advises were, for the most part, abstention from food or abstention from sex. In all of these issues, Finnian's volume had considerable influence on many other subsequent Penitentials.

Throughout these Penitentials one finds that the primary goal is to build up one's spiritual life. The model for this spiritual life remained the Celtic monk. Consequently, in the case of lay people, these Penitentials tended to make them, at least during their period of penance, "little monks," abstaining from food and drink as well as abstaining from sex.

Columban and his fellow Celtic monks, in the latter part of the sixth century and the first part of the seventh century, represent the first Celtic missionary movement into Europe. In the last part of the seventh century and the first half of the eighth century there is a second missionary movement, led by such Anglo-Saxon monks as St. Willibrord and St. Boniface. These Celtic and Anglo-Saxon monks were very successful in the conversion and reconversion of Europe, and they utilized this private and frequent form of penance wherever they went. Naturally, there was resistance on the part of the Roman-influenced churches, but the efforts by many European bishops to restore public penance failed. Some bishops railed against the use of these Penitentials, calling their very authenticity into question, but they had nothing effective to offer in their place, since the public form of penance had, by this time, become either a sacrament for those who were on the brink of death or totally unacceptable for Christians who wanted to move ahead in their human life.

Both in Celtic but especially in Germanic law, commutation and redemption was a strong element, and these legal aspects from secular life influenced the spiritual administration of the sacrament of reconciliation. Lengthy or difficult penances could be shortened to more intensive periods of penance or to the giving of alms. These money redemptions, introduced in all innocence, became one of the sources for the later practice of indulgences, with all of the tragic aspects which this entailed.

We could outline the Celtic form of the sacrament of reconciliation as follows:

1. The sacrament of penance was administered in a private way at every stage. There was no form of public penance involved.

2. Confession was to be made in secret to a qualified person, who was, most often, a presbyter. In the east confession was also made to a monk, although this was not necessarily considered the sacrament of reconciliation. This eastern practice has its counterpart in the Celtic world.

3. Even holy women, usually abbesses, acted as confessors. St. Brendan is reported to have confessed to St. Ita; St. Columban as a youth sought direction from saintly women.

4. Secrecy was enjoined. However, prior to the ninth century there is no distinctive evidence for the seal of confession, either in conciliar statements or in the Penitentials themselves. In medieval Ireland to disclose information given in confession was one of the four grave offenses which could not be atoned for by penance.

5. The acts of satisfaction according to the Penitentials were ordinarily private, though not always secret. However, Celtic sacramental penance was of its nature a private matter between confessor and penitent. The assembled church played no role.

6. The Penitentials assert again and again that this form of reconciliation may be repeated as often as necessary in the life of a Christian. The term "sacrament," applying to reconciliation, does not appear until the twelfth century, but the Penitentials leave no doubt that this frequent form of reconciliation was for their day the equivalent of the later sacrament.

7. In the spiritual life of a Christian, confession became a normal part of one's spiritual life. The Roman or public form had been, from the beginning, an extraordinary form of a Christian's normal spiritual journey. The Celtic form of reconciliation became a normal part of one's spiritual journey.

3. THE CLASH BETWEEN THE TWO FORMS

Little by little, the Celtic form of reconciliation took over, so that by the beginning of the eleventh century public penance in the west was practiced only in isolated areas. In the eastern churches a form of public penance has remained normative down to the present day. We find evidence of this medieval tension between public penance or the Roman form, on the one hand, and the private penance of the Celtic form, on the other, in some of the sacramentaries of this period. The *Gelasian Sacramentary* dates from c. 750, but it reflects here and there the ritual of the church in the late sixth century. In this sacramentary we read that public sins merit public reconciliation, while private sins should be handled in private reconciliation. Nonetheless, it should be noted that the *Gelasian Sacramentary* represents in its various parts different epochs of authorship. Parts of it stem from earlier times, parts from a later time. The section in the Sacramentary which describes the penitential ritual is part of the appendix (nn. 1726–1786), and is clearly an addition made at some later date. Consequently, the pentitential details of this appendix might very well represent a church discipline of a later period. In the various *Ordines* dependent on this sacramentary (there are three in all) we find public prayers for penitents. *Ordo* III has a public prayer of reconciliation, but it is directed to penitents who are dying. In nn. 353–354 of this *Ordo,* we find an exhortation made by the deacon to the bishop, asking the bishop to remit the sins of the penitents. This is clearly modeled after a similar section in the *Apostolic Constitution* of an earlier period. From all of this it is clear that the *Gelasian Sacramentary* by and large evidences public penance, rather than private penance, and as a book of rites and prayers it is meant to serve the public ritual of the church.

We also find in some eucharistic rituals of this same early medieval period, particularly those of the tenth and eleventh centuries, public prayers during mass which commuted lengthy and arduous penances into penances of more modest proportion. In these "apologies" we find once again indication of a public penance.

The public form of penance, in many western regions, had been relegated to the moment of death, so that the Roman form of the sacrament of reconciliation had tended to become a sacrament of the dying. The Celtic form was meant for those who were very much alive. The Roman form had the blessing of antiquity and had been encouraged by all the great patristic *episkopoi.* The Celtic form was innovative, stemming from monks who were virtually unknown to the official Roman church. When one considers the confrontation of these two forms of penance from 600 to 1000, one sees that the sacrament of reconciliation, ritually and theologically, was in a quite chaotic state. A radical change was indeed taking place, but the old official public form did not give way easily to the newer non-official private form. In many regions of the west bishops, priests and laity as well were at odds as to what procedures they might best pursue.

In 813, for instance the Synod of Chalon-sur-Saone denounced the penitential books as books of which "the errors are certain, but the authors uncertain" (can. 38). Early medieval bishops in continental Europe, however, had nothing practical to put in their place, and so these penitential books continued to exert their influence. The Council of Toledo (589) emphasized that penance was to be received only once in a lifetime; in practice, this regulation was increasingly disregarded. The Synod of Paris (829) ordered that the Penitentials be burned "that through them unskilled priests may no longer deceive men."[7]

It was not until the Fourth Lateran Council in 1215 that the western church officially endorsed the Celtic form of penance as the official form for reconciliation. The council did this more in an indirect way than in a direct way:

> Let everyone of the faithful of either sex, after reaching the age of discretion, faithfully confess in secret to his own priest all his sins, at least once a year, and diligently strive to fulfil the penance imposed on him, receiving reverently, at least during Paschal time, the sacrament of the Eucharist, unless perchance on the advice of his own priest he judges that he should abstain for a time from its reception; otherwise, while living let him be denied entrance in church and when dead let him be deprived of Christian burial.[8]

The phrase "at least once a year" and "in secret" evidences to the victory of the Celtic form of reconciliation over the public form within the official church. Later, of course, a precision had to be made, namely that this mandatory reception of the sacrament of penance on a yearly cycle was only necessary if there had been serious sin.

The missionary movement of the Celtic monks in Europe corresponded in some degree with the Carolingian reformation, and in the Carolingian reformation there was a clear clericalization of all the sacraments. In their earlier strata, the Penitentials do indicate, but not in any overwhelming degree, that "confession" at times was made to non-ordained monks. However, by the time one reaches the twelfth and thirteenth centuries the exclusive role of the priest in this sacrament dominates. This is not to say that there was not still "confession" to lay people, i.e. to the non-ordained, as even the discussions of Albert the Great, Thomas Aquinas, Bonaventure and Scotus indicate, but the sacramental administration of reconciliation was reserved exclusively to the priest.[9] This is in keeping with the entire thrust of the Carolingian reform: in the matter of post-baptismal forgiveness of sin, it is the priest alone who has jurisdiction.

Another feature should be noted: in the public Mediterranean form of penance, the severity of "doing penance" was the dominant feature, but as the Celtic form of penance took over there was in early medieval spirituality a tremendous stress on the "confession" aspect of the process. This is not to say that the penances were not somewhat severe, for they were, but what intrigued the pastoral and theological world of that time was the confession of sins.

The Celtic Penitentials reflect the society into which they were born. In them we find evidence of legal customs of both Celtic and Germanic origin. These Penitentials and the system of reconciliation which they engendered represent both a compromise with and a humanizing of these two great social groups. We find in these books a strong attempt to combat paganism. The paganism fought in these volumes is not the highly sophisticated paganism of Greece and Rome; rather it is the folk-paganism which survived in the loyalties and customs of the people.[10] This kind of paganism had withstood the pressure of both church and state. Fertility rites were still honored, and magic of all kinds was common. The celebration of the seasons was of special importance, and druids, both Celtic and continental, had great influence.

Much of this folk-paganism began to be pooled as the Germanic invasions took place: whole groups of people were uprooted and then brought into daily contact with other groups. Customs and superstitions began to blend. Imperial laws, conciliar decisions, vigorous denunciations by various bishops, all failed to extinguish this folk-paganism. The writers of the Penitentials took up this crusade, and as the Celtic penitential discipline permeated into the lives of this common people, this folk-paganism began to give way. This might be considered one of the amazing successes of this form of penance.

We should note, too, that the most effective catechesis which the early middle ages had was the sacrament of penance in this Celtic form. Through the frequent reception of this sacrament a Christian ethic was slowly developed in the consciences of people. The ministers of this sacrament used it as a forum for instruction and formation of conscience. In their private discussions with penitents there was an emphasis on the healing of sin. The minister of this sacrament might have been seen as a minister of forgiving grace, but he was also seen as a minister of spiritual growth.

Frequently the Penitentials remind the confessors that penalties are to be equated not so much with offenses but with the individual's personal stage and need. Perhaps this accounts for the fact that beneath the roughness of the times there was a humane element in the Celtic form of penance. There was personal guidance, a renewal of an individual's self-esteem, and hope for rehabilitation. The penitent, through private penance, could find his or her way back to moral values and social worth. Personal reconstruction, an inward moral change, based on the gospel life, was the intended effect of this Celtic reconciliation process.

Not all was perfect, of course. The emphasis on "confession of sin" led to agonizing scrutinies of one's past life. Even the frequent confession of venial sin became absorbingly important. In passing, one should note that whenever the confession of daily faults, venial sins, begins to dominate the penitential process, the entire process can, unfortunately, become trivialized, and the respective theology of reconciliation is skewed.

In Frankish law we find the *compositio,* i.e. the substitution of money payment for a requisite punishment. When this Frankish custom entered into the penitential process, almsgiving began to substitute for other kinds of penances, penances which might easily be more taxing and rigorous than the simple giving of money. *Compositio* even affected the theological understanding of the death of Jesus, an understanding which sees Jesus paying the price for us (vicarious substitution). When the element of *compositio* moved ever so gradually into the post-baptismal reconciliation process, the danger of abuse was never considered. Unfortunately, we know that in time, abuses on this matter, including the abuses connected with indulgences, became unbearable, and the opposition to this entire reconciliation program became increasingly strident.

In many ways the Penitentials have never died. The confessional manuals of the counter-reformation period are actually of the same genre. So, too, are the handbooks for confessors developed by certain theologians and priests just prior to the Council of Trent as also by the Jansenists in the eighteenth and nineteenth centuries. Even contemporary guidebooks for hearing confession stem from this parentage.

This Celtic form of penance, not the public form of the patristic period, was the focus of the theologizing of the scholastics. It was this praxis and its theological interpretation with which the reformation theologians took issue. It was, again, this same praxis, together with the scholastic interpretation, which focused the discussions of the Council of Trent, both as regards the bishops' efforts to provide pastorally sound guidelines, as well as regards their efforts to reform the many and glaring abuses in the administration of this sacrament.

Pastoral need in many ways engendered this Celtic form of penance. In the early middle ages the pastoral benefit of the public or Roman form of reconciliation had become almost non-existent. Clearly, a renewal was needed, and this renewal came from a grass-roots source, not from an ecclesiastically official source. The study of this period of church history indicates strongly that radical change at times is not only required but possible, that courage is needed to make sacramental forms meaningful to Christian folk generally, and that pastoral needs can indeed play a commanding role in such renewal.

4. THE THEOLOGY OF "JUSTIFICATION" WHICH DEVELOPED DURING THIS PERIOD OF THE EARLY MIDDLE AGES

It was during this same early medieval period in which the Celtic form of penance slowly penetrated the western church discipline that key and synthesizing ideas on a theology of salvation or justification began to emerge. The Latin term *justificatio* is post-classical and is almost totally used within a theological or religious context.[11] McGrath states his position on the use of this term in medieval theology as follows:

> The characteristic medieval understanding of the nature of jus-
> tification may be summarised thus: justification refers not
> merely to the beginning of the Christian life, but also to its
> continuation and ultimate perfection, in which the Christian is
> made righteous in the sight of God and the sight of men through
> a fundamental change in his nature, and not merely his status.
> In effect, the distinction between justification (understood as an
> external pronouncement of God) and sanctification (under-
> stood as the subsequent process of inner renewal), characteristic
> of the Reformation period, is excluded from the outset. This
> fundamental difference concerning the *nature* of justification
> remains one of the best *differentiae* between the doctrines
> of justification associated with the medieval and Reformation
> periods.[12]

This distinction and description of justification has its merits, but since McGrath is describing the total medieval period, some nuancing is in order. Carlson, in his analysis of all the commentaries on Pauline letters from the Ambrosiaster of the fourth century to those of Nicholas of Lyra in the early fourteenth century, shows that the Pauline term "justification" was not viewed as "a topic of major importance by the medieval exegetes." In this lengthy period called the middle ages, there are no "extended statements concerning any doctrine of justification *per se,"* until one moves into the later middle ages. Only in the latest commentaries of this period (e.g. Thomas Aquinas, Nicholas of Lyra) do we find a "developed and logically precise theological definition."[13]

> For most of the commentators, justification was a word which happened to form a part of Paul's technical vocabulary when describing the process of salvation, neither more nor less important than any one of a number of other such terms found in the Pauline epistles, and required no unusual effort of explanation different from any other aspect of Paul's teaching. In sum, justification presented no theological problem, as such, to medieval expositors.[14]

Karlfried Froehlich's article, "Justification Language in the Middle Ages," describes the view that appears to be well-founded, namely, that "the patristic and medieval tradition did not show interest" in justification as a major theme.[15] However, he goes on to say that today theologians generally agree that justification language "signals central Christian concerns which were discussed in countless ways from the beginning. Justification touches on the fundamental structure of the relationship between God and human beings; it speaks of their role in this relationship and determines the very definition of salvation."[16]

Perhaps not all the historical details have been adequately sifted and weighed, but it seems fair to say that the early medieval period was not at all overly verbose on the matter of "justification." The term was used rather sparingly and for many of the commentators it tended to be synonymous with "forgiveness of sin." The forgiveness of sin is simply one aspect in the "justification process" which only from the time of Peter of Poitiers (1205) onward began to be codifed theologically. Thus, the term "justification" as found in the very late medieval period onward, as well as in the reformation and Tridentine period, does indeed denote and connote much more than the same term as found in the writings of such authors as Rabanus Maurus, Sedulius Scotus, and Bruno of Cologne, all of whom lived in the early medieval period.

One must also state rather frankly that the medieval presentation of the Pauline letters was influenced in large measure by Augustine, and that textually the Vulgate provided the linguistic foundation, whereas in the reformation period (inchoatively) onward, the original Greek text gradually became the textual point of departure. Both this Augustinian and Latin-based grid for the medieval expositions indicate that the theological positions of Paul himself are not the focus, but rather an already to-some-degree interpreted position of Paul, that is, an Augustinian formated Paul and a Latinized Paul. One can say that with the reformation's stress on the Greek text of Paul, there was indeed a newness to the discussion on justification.

In the development of this Augustinian and Latin theology of salvation or "justification," the early middle ages of the Carolingian period were very conservative. Sedulius Scotus (c. 858), for instance, drew up a commentary on Paul, *Collectanea in omnes B. Pauli epistolas,* which presents a Pauline text and then appends a series of patristic quotations, pertaining to the Pauline text, e.g. quotations from Ambrose, Origen, Augustine, Jerome, etc.[17] Not only is the conservative element evident in this arrangement (Sedulius Scotus is "conserving" fragments of patristic thought), but such *florilegia* of patristic texts came to be considered "orthodox," and consequently these *florilegia* of patristic texts tended to control theological interpretations. Deviation from the teaching of these "sources" was viewed as unhealthy and even at times heretical. Early medieval theologians did not depart from the teaching of such quotations, and the very quoting of them "proved" or substantiated their own theological positions.

Of key importance on this issue of "justification" or a "theology of salvation" in this early medieval period is the work of Anselm of Canterbury (1109). Anselm was a major figure in the late eleventh century, and his influence has lasted down to contemporary times. In the preface to his *Monologion,* Anselm states that orthodoxy means conformity to the writings of the "catholic fathers, especially St. Augustine" ("*catholicorum patrum et maxime beati Augustini*") (I, 8, 9). In no small measure, then, Anselm can be seen as Augustinian; he carries forward the theological thinking of Augustine on such matters as justification. His major work, *Cur Deus Homo,* is an attempt to come to grips with (a) the justice of God and (b) the holiness of God. McGrath describes Anselm's overriding concern as follows:

> God is wholly and supremely just. How can he then give eternal life to one who deserves eternal death? How can he justify the sinner? This is the central question with which Anselm is concerned in *Cur Deus Homo* (1098). Earlier, Anselm had wrestled with substantially the same problem in the *Proslogion* (1079).[18]

In his struggle to come to some theological understanding of this issue, Anselm begins with the goodness of God. God is *summum bonum.* Then he points out that God's mercy is based on his justice. This is due to the fact that God is the highest good, *summum bonum: "ita iustus es non quia nobis reddas debitum, sed quia facis quod decet te, summe bonum*" ("thus you are just, not because you repay a debt, but because you do what is appropriate to you, O Highest Good").[19] Cicero and Justinian may have seen justice, as it applies to human interaction, as a rendering to each what belongs to each, but such a description of justice, Anselm argues, cannot be applied to God, who is, in his nature alone, and not in any relational way, the very basis of his justice. Rather, justice in God is an intrinsic expression of the correctness (*rectitudo*) of his own intrinsic goodness (*bonitas*); subsequently, if and when there is creation, this *rectitudo* or justice might be found in God's relationship to creation, to incarnation, to salvation. A right or just relationship to a creature is, for Anselm, not the basis of divine justice. *Summum bonum, summa iustitia,* and *summa rectitudo* (highest good, highest justice and highest rectitude)—these are the key issues in Anselm's understanding of justice, and the way in which Anselm interrelates them is the basis of his teaching on justification. This interrelationship is an *ad intra* relationship, not a relationship dependent on something *ad extra*. When one moves to the *ad extra* world, i.e. creation, this very nature of God as *summum bonum, summa iustitia* and *summa rectitudo* will, of course, be mirrored, but the relationship to creature is by no means the fundamental reason why God is just.

Creation has taken place, and sin has also occurred. Since men and women, however, have violated God's goodness by the original fall, and since original sin or original *iniustitia* is now part of human nature, a reordering of creation (*rectitudo*) is needed. This reordering cannot come from any human act. It must come from God alone, but such a redeeming act must necessarily manifest both God's holiness and God's justice. Consequently, Anselm used the now-famous dichotomy: *aut satisfactio aut poena* (either satisfaction or punishment).

It is clear that, for Anselm, things are not "just" or "unjust" simply because God wills them, in the sense that God could on one occasion decree that something is "just," while on another occasion God might name the same situation "unjust." This kind of capriciousness, as to what is just and unjust, is ruled out by the very fact that God is *summum bonum, summa iustitia,* and *summa rectitudo* (highest good, highest justice, and highest rectitude). Whatever is "just" is so because it reflects this very nature of God; whatever is "unjust" is so because it violates and thereby does not reflect the very nature of God. For this reason, God cannot capriciously declare an "unjust" man or woman "just." A justified and a justifying process has to be involved in "justification."

McGrath outlines Anselm's entire position in the following steps, which highlight Anselm's use of *iustitia*.

1. Man was created in a state of original justice for eternal felicity.
2. This felicity requires the perfect and voluntary submission of man's will to God—i.e. *iustitia.*
3. Man's present state is that of *iniustitia.*
4. Either this must result in man's being deprived of eternal felicity, or else the situation must be rectified by an appropriate satisfaction.
5. This satisfaction must exceed the act of disobedience.
6. Man cannot offer to God anything other than the demands of *iustitia,* and on account of his present *iniustitia,* he cannot even do this.
7. Therefore God's purpose in creating man has been frustrated.
8. But this is unjust (i.e. against *rectitudo*), and poses a contradiction to the divine nature.
9. Therefore a means of redemption must exist if justice is to be reestablished.
10. Man cannot redeem himself, being unable to make the necessary satisfaction for sin.
11. God could make the necessary satisfaction.
12. Since only God can, and only man ought to, make the necessary satisfaction, it must be made by a God-man.
13. Therefore the incarnation is required as an act of justice.[20]

Throughout this process of argument, *iustitia* is seen as a dominating theme, but it must be remembered that Anselm integrates *iustitia Dei* and *bonitas Dei.* By doing this Anselm strives to maintain the absolute gratutity of God's grace, and with the incarnate Jesus as the keystone, Anselm strives to maintain as well the complete adequacy of Jesus' salvific action. However, the very use of the term "satisfaction" tended to compromise the notion of gratuity. Anselm did not present his position from the standpoint of the absolute gratuity of God's grace.

B. Lonergan, in his lengthy analysis of Anselm's position, brings out many of the same issues which McGrath has highlighted.[21] After his analysis, however, Lonergan questions the adequacy of Anselm's either-or position, *aut satisfactio aut poena,* and adds a different either-or, which comes from Tertullian, *aut venia aut poena* (either pardon or punishment). Both disjunctives, in Lonergan's approach, seem to be necessary.[22] The *satisfactio* is for Anselm the preservation of God's intrinsic *rectitudo* (God's justice and sanctity); the *poena* is the negative side of this rectitude. God does not traffic in sin. On the other hand, the *venia* is for Anselm clearly part of God's goodness, which is identical with God's justice. The *poena,* once again, is the negative side of God's goodness.

How one puts justice and goodness together is the key idea throughout Anselm's many discussions on this issue.

Nonetheless, one of the major themes which Anselm brings into western theology is that of "satisfaction."[23] McGrath pointedly notes that Anselm used this term "satisfaction" rather easily, since there was an established "satisfaction-merit model of the penitential system of the contemporary church that the payment of a satisfaction by the God-man would be regarded by his readers as an acceptable means of satisfying the demands of moral rectitude without violating the moral order of creation."[24] In other words, the then-current Celtic form of the ritual of reconciliation with its emphasis on satisfaction helped shape Anselm's theory of "justification." But it is also true that Anselm's theological explanation of "justification" helped shape the theology of reconciliation, and laid the foundation for a theology of the "sacrament" of penance in the later medieval church. The two issues, the ritual of reconciliation and justification, mutually affected each other. This was not the case, as we have seen, in the patristic period, in which the two issues developed rather independently. In the early medieval world, the two issues developed with a strong theological interaction. Not only did the theological discussion of "satisfaction" allow this connection between the two issues, but a closely allied theological term, which begins to show itself with Anselm, further unites these two issues, namely, "merit."[25] The tariff-penance of the Celtic form complemented the theological discussion of merit and vice versa. Poschmann notes that the ritual of penance, in its Celtic and medieval form, had attained a certain essential format by the eleventh century: contrition, confession, imposition of a penance, and absolution.[26] Nonetheless, as we shall see, it was only with Peter of Poitiers that this fourfold listing becomes codified. At this very same time, the eleventh century, Poschmann notes that the speculative side of penance begins. Externally the ritual had become somewhat standardized; internally, or speculatively, a clear understanding of the process of "justification" was just beginning to be formulated. Anselm of Canterbury stands at the very start of this speculative process, and what he wrote provided the later scholastics with a common base for discussion. Thus the penitential ritual on the one hand and the Anselmian theology on the other form a close unit, each mutually shaping the other. In the more developed scholastic period, which we will consider in the next chapter, this interconnection of the sacrament of penance and a theology of justification remains a constant.

Moreover, it might be noted that Anselm's views not only affected the theological understanding of the ritual of reconciliation, but they also affected the theological understanding of the eucharist. Anselm's views on satisfaction contributed in no small measure to the late medieval approach to the eucharist as sacrifice.

SUMMARY OF CHAPTER FIVE

In this chapter we have seen:

1. The churches of Wales, Ireland, Scotland and England developed a form of the sacrament of penance which was private in nature and which could be repeated as often as needed. This was a total departure from the public form officially endorsed by the Roman church.
2. This form of penance originated in the monastic life of the Welsh and then the Irish churches. In this monastic life, the abbot or abbess was spiritual director of the entire community, both religious and lay. This frequent spiritual direction is at the root of the Celtic form of penance which developed at a later age.
3. The Celtic missionaries, first from Wales and Ireland, and then from Scotland, who came into continental Europe brought with them this Celtic form of penance. As a help, they had several Penitentials, books which listed sins and penances.
4. This Celtic form of penance clashed with the official Roman form of public penance and was often roundly condemned by bishops. The Roman form, however, had become more and more a sacrament of the dying; the Celtic form was seen as a pastoral help for Christians in their day-to-day life.
5. In practice, the Celtic form of the sacrament of penance eventually prevailed, but it was not until 1215 at the Fourth Lateran Council that the church officially adopted this Celtic form, thereby officially abandoning the public form of the sacrament.
6. The Celtic form of penance encouraged the "confession" of sins, which came to be seen and experienced as the more important part of this ritual. This emphasis on "confession of sins" carried on into the late middle ages.
7. The Celtic form of penance was one of the most important catechetical means the church had in this period. Through this form of the sacrament of penance, the Celtic missionaries and later the European medieval monks brought about a genuine renewal in the moral life of continental Europe.
8. A theology of "justification" began to be developed in the early medieval period, even though the term "justification" itself did

not play a major role. This theology of "justification" or salvation (redemption) relied heavily on Augustine and reached a major form of expression in Anselm.

9. Anselm's position centers on the holiness and justice of God. In his theological presentation, the absolute gratuity of grace is maintained, as is also the full efficacy of Jesus' salvific action. Nonetheless, the use of the term "satisfaction" tended to compromise the clarity of his thought on these two issues.

10. Anselm, however, highlighted "satisfaction" which he already found in the penitential ritual of his day. In spite of his efforts at integration his notion of satisfaction and the related notion of merit were not well integrated into his positions on grace and the full efficacy of Jesus' work and thereby opened the door to eventual difficulties in the process and theology of "justification."

6

The Sacrament of Penance and the Theologies of Justification from the Twelfth Century to the Reformation

In this chapter we will consider the theological reflection on the sacrament of penance and on the nature of justification in the following stages:

1. The sacrament of penance in the twelfth century
2. The major theologians of the thirteenth century
3. The medieval theologies of justification
4. An assessment of the medieval period

1. THE SACRAMENT OF PENANCE IN THE TWELFTH CENTURY

The theological source material from the twelfth century on the sacrament of penance is quite abundant, and contemporary scholars have explored it profoundly.[1] This section will provide merely an overview of this work on the subject of penance by considering the following four areas:

a. Papal, episcopal and synodal statements
b. Liturgical sources
c. Canonical literature
d. Theological literature

A. PAPAL, EPISCOPAL AND SYNODAL STATEMENTS

The major emphasis in the papal, episcopal and synodal statements is, quite expectedly, of a practical nature, namely, what should be done and what should not be done in the administration of penance. Again and again the issue of jurisdiction comes to the fore. Alexander II (1061–1073) grants to two priests the right to impose penance on those who confess to them, provided they have the authorization of their own bishop. At the Council of Rome in 1075, Gregory VII made sure that it was stated that pastors have jurisdiction over their parishioners in baptism and absolution. Innocent III (1198–1216) considers cases that ought to be reserved to Rome and forbids certain abbesses to hear confessions of their subjects, a situation which at that time was fairly common in Spain.

The Councils of Sdigenstadt (1022) and Limoge (1032) had rebuked those who took their cases in the matter of reconciliation directly to Rome. The Councils of Plaisance (1095) and of Nime (1096) had required that a priest have permission of the bishop before he could reconcile anyone. The Council of London (1102) had offered the first recorded instance of a secret sin reserved to the bishop, namely, sodomy. In the twelfth century the Council of Claremont (1130) offered the first instance of a case reserved by law, i.e. *latae sententiae,* namely when someone in violence strikes a cleric or a monk, the case was reserved to the papal court. The Council of York (1196) stated that deacons can, in cases of necessity, impose penance. Certain theologians of that time, e.g. Anselm of Lucca (1086), Lanfranc (1089), and Stephen of Autun (1130), as well as many canonists, maintained this right of a deacon to "impose penance."

A reference to the kind of ritual, namely, whether a ritual in a public form or in a private form, appears in many of the synodal documents, indicating that there was still a clash between the two forms. Papal statements still speak about public penance, and here and there also about private penance. After Lateran IV (1215) this is no longer the case. In general, however, the official magisterial literature on the sacrament of penance during the twelfth century is not extensive and provides little theological direction. The practical directives, which this literature offers, do indeed provide some small indications concerning certain aspects of actual penitential procedures.

B. LITURGICAL SOURCES

The liturgical documents of the twelfth century have, of course, histories that go back to earlier centuries. The oldest extant ritual of public penance is found in the Old Gelasian Sacramentary, transcribed at the Abbey of Chelles (near Paris) around 750. It is not well put together and seems to combine both Frankish and Roman elements; the process of amalgamating these two elements in this sacramentary is dated by scholars as beginning around the late seventh or early eighth century. In many ways it has a much different structure than the public rituals of the patristic period. One enters the penitential order on Ash Wednesday and receives reconciliation on Holy Thursday. There are prayers or rituals for reconciliation for those in the hour of death, for those near death, and for those who cannot speak. The penitential rituals of this Old Gelasian Sacramentary are also found in later rituals: the *Sacramentary of Fulda* and the *Roman Germanic Pontifical* of the tenth century. In these documents, however, one finds no single way of administering the sacrament of reconciliation. In these liturgies the word "absolve" is conspicuously rare, and the several forms of reconciliation are for the most part deprecative, e.g. "May God grant you forgiveness of sin." Already in John the Faster (596) we read the following:

> Spiritualis fili, ego confessionem tuam primario et praecipue non recipio, nec tibi absolutionem concedo, sed per me Deus (illud enim est opus eiusmodi) peccatorum tuorum confessionem suscipit, et per nostram vocem horum remissionem dispensat et largitur, sicut per propriam vocem ipse declaravit, cum secundum multam, quae exprimi non potest ejus misericordiam ita dixit: Quaecumque ligaveritis, aut solveritis super terram, erunt in coelis, illa quidem ligata, haec vero soluta.[2]

The *Roman Pontifical* of the twelfth century restates the order of reconciliation found in the *Pontificale Romano-Germanico* of the tenth century. In both, absolution is given immediately after the imposition of satisfaction. A "penitential space" between confession of sin and absolution or the public act of reconciling a sinner into the community has begun to disappear. In the patristic period this "penitential space" had been the time needed for the "satisfaction" of the works of penance.

In the twelfth century, private confession to a priest had become the more common form of this sacrament. In the *De Paenitentia* of Gratian there is even a lengthy discussion of confession made to God alone. Confession to lay people was also not unknown, particularly to those who were considered holy. As the Albigensian heresy became more extensive and intensive, stress was placed on private confession to a priest as a touchstone of loyalty to the one true church.

The *Roman Pontifical* of the thirteenth century, approved by the Roman curia, includes an *Ordo ad dandam paenitentiam,* a rite for the private form of penance. Several formulae for this are presented in this *Ordo*. There is also an *Ordo ad reconciliandum paenitentem,* a rite which focuses mostly on priestly absolution, presenting several formulae which were commonly in use at that time. There is finally an *Ordo paenitentium* which was a rite for public sinners, who came to the church to receive ashes and a hair cloth on one occasion, and some time later, often on Holy Thursday, these public sinners received absolution. Compared with the public rituals of the patristic period, this is certainly an abbreviated public form of reconciliation.

C. CANONICAL LITERATURE

The canonical literature of this early time also took up the question of penance as we find in Burchard's *Corrector,* Anselm of Lucca's *Collectio,* Yves of Chartres' *Decretum,* but above all in Gratian's *Decretals,* in which there is a complete chapter on penance. Both public and private penance are discussed in these writings, but no uniform practice is evident.

The *Corrector* is actually book nineteen of the *Decretum* by Burchard, the bishop of Worms, published between 1008 and 1012. This was a voluminous compilation of church laws which Burchard brought together for the emperor, Henry II, and the bishop of Rome, Benedict VIII. The nineteenth book was reprinted separately and thereafter came to be known as *Corrector.* This excerpt is actually a treatise on penance, and influenced many similar such treatises in the centuries which followed.[3] In this work, the bulk of the material is a sort of examination of conscience, which indicates those issues which at that time were seen as quite serious. In other words, we have here a rather detailed indicator of ethical standards for the eleventh century.

Gratian was a Camaldolese monk at Bologna who composed his famous work around 1140. It was called *Concordia discordantium canonum,* and resembles the *Sic et Non* volume of Peter Abelard. Gratian draws together sundry statements from the fathers of the church, which at times were not in harmony with one another. After this tabulation of views, he presents his own conclusions: the so-called *dicta Gratiani.* His work never became an official volume of the Roman church; nonetheless his work, often called the *Decretum Gratiani,* became a source-book for ecclesiastical legislation. After his death around 1158, other authors followed his pattern and established various collections of laws, such as the *Decretals of Gregory IX* (1234), the *Liber Sextus* of Boniface VIII (1298), the *Clementinae,* promulgated by John XXII in 1317, and much later in 1500 John Chapuis gathered all these collections of laws together with the *Extravagantes* of John XXII and the *Extravagantes communes.* These became known as the *Corpus iuris canonici,* and are the chief source of ante-Tridentine ecclesiastical law.

Gratian formulated a treatise on penance (Caus. XXXIII, q. 2 *De paenitentia*), which had significant influence throughout the middle ages. In line with the Carolingian reform, Gratian taught that public sin merited public penance, while private sin merited private penance. He hesitated on the question whether interior contrition, without priestly confession and absolution, was sufficient to obtain the forgiveness of sin, a problem which continued to tax the medieval theological mind.

D. THEOLOGICAL LITERATURE

The theologians of the twelfth century provide us with almost all the basic questions which will captivate the thinking of later scholars. The material is scattered among many theologians, some of whom add individual details. For the sake of organization, there are three major theologians who need to be mentioned and to some degree discussed, and we will also offer a brief mention of sundry theologians who contributed individual positions. The three major theologians are Peter Abelard, Peter Lombard and Peter of Poitiers.

1. Peter Abelard

It was Peter Abelard (1079–1142) who challenged the theological position of Anselm and created a major counter-position. Even though Abelard was condemned by two local councils, the Councils of Soissons (1121) and of Sens (1141), Abelard remained a powerful influence throughout the scholastic period. In contemporary times there has been considerable reevaluation of Abelard and his theological position.[4]

Abelard stressed the efficacy of contrition. At the moment when a baptized Christian is contrite of his or her sin, the sin is taken away. Penance, accordingly, is primarily internal penance; the sacrament of penance is secondary. This stress on the act of contrition, made by a sinner, raised the question of the necessity to confess such sins to a priest and to receive priestly absolution. Abelard did not deny the necessity for priestly absolution, but, given his stance on contrition, such priestly absolutions could only be necessary, in his view, because of church law. The relationship between contrition, on the one hand, which was seen as the real occasion for the forgiveness of sin, and on the other hand the absolution by the priest was not first presented by Peter Abelard. The school of Laon, especially Anselm of Laon (1117) and William of Champeaux (1121), had raised the question initially, but Peter Abelard, with his insightfulness and clarity, brought it to the forefront.[5] Does the absolution of the priest take away sin? Two theories were developed. The first theory saw in the absolution of a priest a declarative stance that God had already taken away a person's sin. Anselm of Canterbury, Peter Abelard, Peter Lombard, William of Auxerre, and in the next century Alexander of Hales and Albert the Great moved in this direction. Others, such as Hugh of St. Victor, thought that the absolution did not forgive the sin, but took away the eternal punishment due to sin, or, as Richard of St. Victor and the author of the *Praepostinus* taught, the absolution of the priest transformed a merely conditional forgiveness of sin (at the time of interior contrition) into an absolute one (at the time of priestly absolution). With William of Auvergne, Hugh of St. Cher and William of Meliton, and then more thoroughly with Thomas Aquinas, Bonaventure and Scotus, the theological position, i.e. the position in which the effect of priestly absolution consists in the forgiveness of sin by God, became the more established position in western theological thought.[6]

Peter Abelard's significance in this matter, however, lies deeper. His position on the redemption wrought in Jesus was noticeably different from that of Anselm of Canterbury. Anselm saw in Jesus' death the vicarious payment of the infinite satisfaction which sinners owed to God. Since the sinner had offended God, who was infinite, the only way to compensate for an infinite offense is by way of an infinite satisfaction. No creature, Anselm argued, could ever repay infinite satisfaction. It was the God-made-man, Jesus, who repaid this infinite debt. Abelard, however, did not focus his theology of redemption on satisfaction. Jesus, through his death, revealed the infinite and forgiving love of God for us. Rather than a payment of anything due to God, the death of Jesus was exemplary and revelatory of God's love. In the view of many contemporaries of Abelard, including Bernard of Clairvaux, this view of redemption was not acceptable. In his *Commentary on the Romans,* Abelard specifically mentions the term "justification" in this matter: "Non mediocrem movere quaestionem . . . de redemptione scilicet vel iustificatione nostra per mortem Dominis nostri Iesu Christ."[7] G. Aulén indicates that the fact that Abelard "attached no special significance to the death of Christ was sufficient of itself to make his teaching unacceptable to an age which was laying ever greater stress on the death, both in theology and in devotional practice."[8] Aulén overstates Abelard's position on the meaning of the death of Jesus. It is true that Abelard parted company with Anselm's satisfaction or atonement theory and propounded a theory in which the death of Jesus is primarily seen as a revelation of God's love, but this does not mean that it has no meaning.

In these two aspects of Peter Abelard's thought there is a clear and strong counter-thrust both on the sacrament of penance and on justification. Since Abelard stressed internal contrition, the necessity of external confession and priestly absolution was strongly challenged. More profoundly, his christological position on the redemption through Jesus raised the question of the presence of a semi-Pelagianism in the very central mystery of the Christian faith. Did Jesus have to do something so that we could be forgiven, redeemed, justified? Or is the death of Jesus not a "meritorious" act or a satisfactory act, but rather a revelatory one of God's infinite, forgiving love? At this very same time theologians were slowly developing the *de condigno* and *de congruo* understanding of merit. Most theologians reserved the term *de condigno* meriting to the salvific death of Jesus, leaving the *de congruo* understanding of merit to human good works. Still, even the *de condigno* meriting of Jesus can and at times did have a sort of crypto-Pelagianism connected with it. Jesus, in his humanity had to do something so that grace could be given. If Jesus, in his humanity, performed a "good work" to merit *de condigno* God's forgiving grace, then grace is no longer grace. The after-effects of the first issue continued throughout the remainder of the middle ages and into the debates of the reformation theologians and the Tridentine discussions. Unfortunately, the deeper issue, and therefore the very basis of the sacrament of penance, namely, the issue of Jesus himself "meriting" or "satisfying" God's justice, remained to one side. In discussing the sacrament of penance, almost all the authors of these periods clearly avoided Pelagianism of any kind. However, since there was hardly any dissent over Jesus' salvific act itself (with the exception of Abelard's position), the issue of relationship between Pelagianism and a theology of redemption did not arise. Jesus' death continued to be seen as an act which merited *de condigno,* not merely *de congruo,* the redemption or justification of the human race. If Jesus himself in his humanity had to "do" something, so that God could remit our sin or justify us, then this central mystery of Christian faith seemed to compromise the absolute gratuity of God's grace. If Jesus merited *de condigno,* then one could ask: Is grace still grace? Peter Abelard did not push his approach to its logical conclusions, but his move away from a "satisfaction" approach to Jesus' death clearly was an effort to turn theological thought on the redemption into a radically non-Pelagian approach. With the conciliar condemnations of his teachings, even though these councils were only local councils, aspects of Abelard's thought, including his reflections on redemption, did not penetrate the mainstream of medieval, reformation and Tridentine theology.

2. Peter Lombard

It would be incorrect to say that Peter Lombard's influence on scholastic theology was due primarily to his teaching on the sacrament of penance. Rather, his influence lies in the fact that his book, *Libri IV Sententiarum,* became the basis for teaching theology during the subsequent three or four centuries. In this book, his teaching on the sacraments became the standard way of presenting the theology of sacraments in general and each of the sacraments in particular.

In *Distinctio XIV* of the fourth book of the *Sentences,* Peter Lombard speaks of the sacrament of penance. He begins with a lengthy discussion on penance and its various meanings. His method, as usual, is to cite patristic statements exemplifying the various interpretations of a theological theme, and then provide some comment of his own. Penance is called an interior virtue, on the one hand, and a ritual penance, or exterior penance, on the other. Peter Lombard calls this ritualized penance a sacrament, and does so without any argumentation. Penance is, at the time of his writing, clearly accepted as one of the Christian sacraments. He speaks of solemn or single penance (*unica penitentia*), but notes that such a ritual for penance is not continued in some churches (c. III). More commonly, the sacrament of penance can be received frequently (c. IV). In *Dist. XV* Lombard teaches, rightfully, that a person who has committed several serious sins must be sorry for all such serious sin; otherwise, none of these serious sins will be forgiven. In *Dist. XVI* Peter Lombard discusses the interrelationship of contrition, confession and satisfaction, but he spends more time on the issue of satisfaction. In *Dist. XVII* he addresses the question of forgiveness of sin without priestly absolution, which includes therefore confession to lay people. In *Dist. XVIII* the issue is the remission of sin which the priest brings. As mentioned above, Peter Lombard sees only an external relationship between one's contrition, which forgives sin, and the priestly absolution. Priestly absolution is declarative. In *Dist. XIX* the author discusses the keys: particularly, when Jesus gave the power of the keys and to whom, with ramifications to this power. After this, he takes up a number of issues related to penance: how lengthy a penance is necessary; the vestiges of sin; penances unjustly given by priest; penance at the moment of death (*Dist.* XX). In the next topic (*Dist.* XXI) Peter Lombard raises sundry questions: what sins (i.e. venial sins) are forgiven after death; what is a general confession; that no one has the obligation to confess sins which he or she has not committed; that there is a confessional secrecy. In the final *Distinction* (XXII) he asks whether sins, which have been forgiven, can return, and what is the *res* and the *sacramentum* in the sacrament of penance.

In all of this Peter Lombard touches rather systematically on almost all the aspects of the sacrament of penance which were major issues at his time, and when his work became a textbook, a professor could easily expatiate on one or the other item, develop certain issues in a different way, etc. In many ways the importance of Peter Lombard, as regards the sacrament of penance, lies in this provision of a fairly systematic base for further theological discussion on the sacrament of penance. However, it is right to note that it was through Alexander of Hales that Peter Lombard's text was arranged into its present sections, and that it was because of Alexander, more than anyone else, that this work became the medieval textbook.

3. Peter of Poitiers

Peter of Poitiers (1205) should be mentioned in a special way, although not in a lengthy way, since he provided the scholastic, reformation and Tridentine periods with the accepted or standard form of the *processus iustificationis.*

> The appearance of a new doctrinal framework in which, at last a precise concept of justification was developed and applied as a major component in systematic theology is associated with several doctors of the emergent University of Paris, and approximately concurrent with the rise of its theological faculty to the pre-eminent position it was to enjoy until the close of the Middle Ages. This was the so-called *processus iustificationis,* for which priority apparently rests with Peter of Poitiers, one of the prominent late twelfth-century theologians.[9]

Peter of Poitiers, in his commentary on Peter Lombard's *Sententiarum libri quinque* establishes the fourfold components of this process: contrition, confession, absolution and satisfaction.[10] A. Landgraf has noted that Peter of Poitiers had many forerunners, some of whom used a threefold scheme, e.g. Peter Comestor (1180) and Peter Lombard. The fourfold scheme of Peter of Poitiers, however, became the ordinary way to view both the process of justification and the components in the sacrament of penance. We see this in such subsequent writers as Stephen Langton, Peter Cantor, Odo of Ourscamp, Roland of Cremona, William of Auvergne, Alexander of Hales, Albert the Great, Thomas Aquinas, Bonaventure, Scotus, and almost every other scholastic author. It was this formulation of the fourfold scheme in the process of justification which has made Peter of Poitiers eminently important for an understanding of the theology of the sacrament of penance and also the theology of justification.

4. Minor Authors

There were other medieval authors prior to the major scholastic theologians who might be mentioned. Alger of Lüttich (c. 1121) appears to be the first medieval theologian to have called the ritual of penance a "sacrament" along the lines of baptism, eucharist, orders, etc. This position came to be taken for granted at least by the time of Peter Lombard. In the school of Laon it was even called the sacrament of sacraments.

Hugh of St. Victor (c. 1096–1141) had proposed the idea that contrition removes the mortal sin, but the eternal punishment for sin is removed by priestly absolution.[11] His fellow theologians, however, roundly condemned this view. If serious sin itself is taken away, the eternal punishment due to such sin must also be remitted; the two are inseparably united to each other. In the school of Gilbert of Poitiers we have the first appearance of attrition, imperfect contrition, in contrast to perfect contrition. With Hugh of St. Cher we find for the first time the essential parts of a sacrament described not with patristic terms (the *elementum* and *verbum* of Augustine) but with Aristotelian terms, matter and form. When this Aristotelian framework was applied to the sacrament of penance, it became difficult to express theologically what the precise "matter" of this particular sacrament might be. Theologians down through the Tridentine period were not in agreement on this issue. Priestly absolution, however, was rather consistently presented as the "form" of the sacrament.

One might summarize the major points of the theologians in the twelfth century as follows:

1. It is God who remits both sin and eternal punishment.
2. The absolution of the priest is somehow involved in this process.
3. Satisfaction, especially almsgiving, prayer and fasting, is integral to this process, even though the satisfaction is performed after the forgiveness of sin.
4. Satisfaction is clearly seen as necessary, but the reason for such satisfaction is either not explored or it is not probed very deeply.
5. One is generally in the state of grace before approaching the priest for absolution, because one has already made an act of "perfect" contrition.
6. Peter Lombard and Peter of Poitiers argued that good works done in the state of sin merit nothing.
7. The confessor is required to enjoin adequate satisfaction.
8. God's grace is needed for any satisfaction to be acceptable.
9. Sorrow for sin must be universal; it cannot simply extend to some serious sins but not to others.

10. The acts of the pentitents are at first three: contrition, confession and satisfaction. With Peter of Poitiers the standard fourfold division began: contrition, confession, satisfaction and absolution. How these relate to one another remained unsettled.
11. A *processus iustificationis* was thereby set up, which provided scholastic, reformation, and Tridentine theologians with a format to discuss justification.
12. Pelagianism was considered, theologically, totally wrong; in theological discussion and in pastoral practice, however, not all Pelagian elements were eliminated.
13. Very little was done in this period to interrelate the theological elements of justification with the work of Christ. The theological understanding of redemption, i.e. the work of Christ, remained strongly under the influence of Anselm of Canterbury and the theory of satisfaction. Abelard's quite different efforts had little to no effect.

It is interesting to note that Anciaux' lengthy study on the sacrament of penance in the twelfth century revolves around the elaboration of a systematic treatise on the sacrament of penance, on the necessity of confession to a priest, and on the power of priests in the sacramental process. Anciaux touches on the theology of reconciliation, or what we might call the theology of justification, in only a cursory way. In other words, this study does not attempt to interrelate a theology of the sacrament of penance with a theology of justification, as each of these was developed in the twelfth century.

2. THE MAJOR THEOLOGIANS OF THE THIRTEENTH CENTURY

The great theologians of the thirteenth century inherited this theological discussion and attempted to work out a more coherent and richer theology of penance. It should be realized, however, that all of these major scholastic theologians considered the individual sacraments, and therefore the sacrament of penance as well, as remedial, due to the sinful state of humanity. Sacraments are remedies for a sinful human situation. Clearly each of these major scholastic theologians deserves a lengthy treatment on their approach to the sacrament of penance—a treatment far beyond the scope of this present volume—but a presentation of their key ideas on the sacrament of penance can at least be accomplished in this present volume.

The major scholastic theologians are the following:

a. Alexander of Hales (1245), an English diocesan priest who became a magister of theology at the University of Paris. At the age
   of fifty he became a Franciscan. In contemporary theology, Alexander is seen more and more as one of the most important figures
   of the thirteenth century.[12]
b. Bonaventure (1274) who entered the Franciscans at a young age
   and became a magister of theology at Paris. Later he became the
   general of the Franciscans and at the end of his life he was made a
   cardinal. He is generally associated with Alexander as one of
   major figures of the "early Franciscan school."[13]
c. Albert the Great (1280) who entered the Dominican Order when
   he was in his early twenties. He became a magister in theology
   and taught in various schools, but especially at Cologne. He was a
   professor of Thomas Aquinas. Albert's incredible scope of learn-
   ing, covering vast areas of philosophy, science, and Arabian and
   Jewish authors, as well as the newly developed Aristotelian studies, made him a major figure of the thirteenth century.[14]
d. Thomas Aquinas (1274) who was also a Dominican and a leading
   magister of theology at Paris. Author of the *Summa Theologiae.*
   Although a key professor in the thirteenth century, his popularity
   and influence from the sixteenth century onward has in so many
   ways shaped the very core of counter-reformation Roman Catholic theology.[15]
e. John Duns Scotus (1308), a Franciscan from perhaps his fifteenth
   year onward. He became a magister of theology and taught at
   Oxford, Paris and Cologne. Scotus is the major figure in the "late
   Franciscan school." He had the advantage of living slightly later
   than Thomas and Bonaventure and could, therefore, analyze and
   comment on their texts in detail.[16]

It is surely fair to say that the work which these authors did on the
theology of sacraments, and for our purposes on the sacrament of penance, remained in the Latin church the standard theological framework
from the thirteenth to the twentieth century. This is indeed a long stretch
of time, and no serious student of sacramental theology can bypass this
long-lasting and important theological contribution. Three issues, developed by these major theologians, deserve our attention.

A. THE PRIMACY OF GOD'S FORGIVING GRACE

All of these theologians stressed the action of God. In the entire
process of forgiveness God's action was primary. Probably one of the
major contributors in this matter was Thomas Aquinas, who attempted

again and again to unite the sacrament of penance itself to this process of justification. Following Anselm, Thomas also attempted to integrate the sacrament of penance into the redemptive work of Christ. In all of this, he cannot be considered Pelagian, for it is clear throughout his work that God is presented as the primary efficient cause of all grace. Still, both in the early work, the *Commentary on the Sentences,* and in his more mature work, the *Summa,* which only has an incomplete section on the sacrament of penance, absolution is in the Thomistic approach central to sacramental efficacy and is therefore causally connected to God as first cause. How the first cause (God) and an instrumental cause (priestly absolution) coincide did engender difficulties, since the interrelationship could be seen as compromising the absolute gratuity of God's grace and also rendering the salvific work of Jesus less than once-and-for-all efficacious. Priestly absolution, even though called an efficient-instrumental cause, can be seen *precisely in its causality* as compromising both the gratuity of grace and the full efficacy of Jesus' salvific action. As an instrumental cause, Thomas maintains, it must add something of its own, and it is precisely the theological interpretation of this "addition" which creates the problem.

Although the primacy of God's action must be seen very clearly in the theological appraisal of priestly absolution, Alexander, followed by both Albert and Bonaventure, did not attribute any efficient, instrumental, sacramental power to such absolution. For them, absolution is both a prayer for and a declaration of God's forgiving grace. Priestly absolution was not seen in terms of an efficient, instrumental cause. Scotus, for his part, presents a different approach to the integration of the redemptive work of Christ and the sacrament of penance. God, in the Scotistic approach, is absolute freedom. This primacy of God's freedom remains a major stress in Scotus' view. In his analysis of the sacraments *in genere,* it is not precisely the ordination of a sacrament to cause grace that Scotus takes as his starting point. Rather, it is just the opposite. In what way, Scotus asks, is God's action of giving grace compatible with the sacraments? It is God's initiative (the alpha point), not the contingent creature's initiative, which marks the real starting point for Scotus. God, as the absolutely free starting point, does not create, conserve or cooperate with the causes he creates in any necessary way. Whatever causing and whatever signing there might be in a sacrament, it is there *de potentia Dei ordinata,* i.e. because God wanted and willed that sacramental aspect to be there. God necessitates any and all salvific action of the sacrament; the sacramental action in no way necessitates God's action.

The contrasting aspects of Thomas and Scotus are important to a theology of sacraments. Poschmann notes:

It is remarkable that influential Thomists of the sixteenth century, in their efforts to find a solution to the difficulties which
beset the doctrine on penance of their master, drew close in
essential points to the conception of Duns Scotus. Therein lies
strong evidence for the important points of truth which undoubtedly it possesses.[17]

Although both the Franciscan and Dominican views stress the primacy of God's forgiving grace, the two schools go in separate ways as they
explain the interrelationship of God's action and human, sacramental
action. This becomes clear when one considers the other components of
the *processus iustificationis.*

B. THE RELATIONSHIP BETWEEN CONTRITION
AND THE SACRAMENT OF PENANCE

All of these theologians addressed the issue: What is the relationship
between contrition, which takes away sin, and the sacrament of penance?
To pursue this, these theologians analyzed more deeply a theology of sin,
with special emphasis on the gradation of sin (venial/mortal). Both
Thomas and Scotus worked out different ways to identify mortal and
venial sin.

Key to their discussions was the distinction between contrition and
attrition. William of Auvergne (1248) in *De sacramento paenitentiae* (cc.
44–48) seems to have been the first person to use the expression: *de
attritione fit contritio* (from attrition comes contrition). In subsequent
decades this phrase of William of Auvergne was recast: *ex attrito fit
contritus* (from an attrite person to a contrite person). In general one
could say that attrition was sorrow for sin, but not as profound as contrition, and the grace of sacramental absolution helped bring about the
transition from attrition to contrition. Much, however, depends on the
way one defines both attrition and contrition. Nonetheless, all the major
medieval theologians of the thirteenth century agreed that an act of "perfect contrition" by itself was the moment when serious sin was forgiven.
This position, however, raised the question: If such contrition takes away
sin, what value does the sacrament of penance have? Why is it necessary?
What does priestly absolution add?

To answer these questions, Thomas Aquinas taught that the justification of a sinner always had some intrinsic relationship to the sacrament
of penance, and more specifically to priestly absolution. Divine grace had
been given in virtue of the incarnation, and the sacraments are instrumental prolongations of this incarnation of grace.[18] The *actual* reception
of sacramental absolution, however, is not unconditionally required; in-

stead, whoever makes an act of contrition has, by the very nature of contrition itself, made at least an implicit desire to receive sacramental absolution. In this way the later absolution (at least *in voto*) was involved in the grace of contrition, and therefore in the forgiveness of sin. This *votum* was, in Thomas' view, quasi-sacramental, i.e. it had a connection with the sacrament of penance. For Thomas, then, people generally came to receive absolution, already in the state of grace. As he himself expresses it: the sacrament of penance is instrumentally effective of grace "vel in voto existens, vel in actu se exercens."[19]

Scotus, and with him the Franciscan school generally, found this theory of Thomas untenable. Scotus apparently was the first to distinguish between a sacramental way for the forgiveness of sins and a non-sacramental way. Contrition is absolutely necessary for the non-sacramental forgiveness of sin; attrition is adequate for the sacramental forgiveness of sin. Unless this were true, Scotus argues, the sacrament as gift of grace would be nothing. Contrition by itself has already brought about the forgiveness of sin. In the causality of the sacraments which Scotus developed, sacraments do not act in an instrumental efficient way (Thomas' approach), but rather are occasions in which God gives grace, not because of some causal element in the sacramental ritual itself, but because of this promise which Christ (God) has made. It is this promise alone which accounts for the sacramental bestowal of grace. Scotus' view emphasizes the absolute gratuity of God's grace and disallows any instrumentally efficient, causal activity on the part of the church or, in the case of the sacrament of penance, any instrumentally efficient, causal action of the penitent or the priest, which would compromise the absolute gratuity of God's grace. Grace is a gift, stemming solely from God's promise, not from any human action.[20]

C. CONTRITION, CONFESSION, SATISFACTION AND ABSOLUTION

A third major issue of the two schools focused on: the relationship of contrition, confession, satisfaction, and absolution, which from the time of Peter of Poitiers were considered the four elements of the sacrament of penance. For Thomas the first three acts (contrition, confession and satisfaction) were the "matter" or "quasi-matter" of the sacrament, and absolution was the "form." Thomas compares the three acts of the penitent with the water of baptism and the bread and wine of the eucharist, but admits that these three acts of the penitent can only be analogically called "matter" in a theology of the sacrament of penance. It was actually Thomas who applied in a most rigorous way the Aristotelian insight of matter and form to the theology of the sacramental sign, although he was not the first to attempt this.

For Scotus, the sacrament of penance is found almost exclusively in absolution. The acts of the penitent are only "conditions," not the "matter" of the sacrament. In moving in this direction, Scotus is highlighting that element which constitutes the sign or *sacramentum* of God's grace. It is not one's act of contrition, nor one's confession of sins, nor one's performance of a penance which sacramentalizes God's gift of grace. Absolution, however, does do this. The "I forgive . . ." of absolution is the external sign of the absolute gratuity of God's grace. In these words "I forgive . . ." there is, for Scotus, no instrumental efficient causality at work. The words "I forgive . . ." are effective, not because of anything intrinsic to the words themselves, nor because of anything intrinsic to the three acts of the penitent—contrition, confession or satisfaction—but only because of God's promise. *When* the church performs this ritual (the occasion), not *because* the church performs this ritual, God will forgive sin, for the sole reason that he has promised to do so. The three acts of the penitent, contrition, confession and satisfaction, as well as priestly absolution, are related to the forgiveness of sin *de potentia Dei ordinata,* i.e. because God has arranged it. *De potentia Dei absoluta* God could have arranged the entire matter of justification in an infinite number of other ways. Nothing intrinsic to contrition, confession, and satisfaction, on the one hand, and absolution, on the other, effects the grace of forgiveness.

It is historically evident from these major positions on various issues of sacraments generally, and of the sacrament of penance in particular, that theological discussion in the late middle ages was itself varied. There were many nuances to almost all of the sacramental questions. Official statements of the church regarding the theological value of the Dominican and Franciscan approaches are non-existent. After the work of these major scholastic theologians, we have a period highly influenced by other trends of thinking. One of these has been called "nominalist," although this particular name is called into question today, with some authors, such as McGrath, preferring the name "*via moderna.*" There were also Augustinian positions, or even schools which paralleled the Thomistic and Scotistic schools, namely, that of Giles of Rome on the one hand, and that of Gregory of Rimini and Hugolino of Orvieto on the other. These fourteenth and fifteenth century positions are themselves not uniform. What one finds regarding a certain issue on the sacrament of penance in William of Occam (1349) is not the same as what one finds in a discussion of this same issue in Gabriel Biel (1495). In another instance of non-uniform positions, William of Rubio, Peter de Palude (1342) and John Bassolis (1347) took Scotus' phrase *de potentia Dei absoluta* and taught that God could condemn a person, even if that person were in the state of grace. Nothing could be further from Scotus' own presentation.

Still another non-uniform position was that of Thomas Bradwardine (1349), an Oxford Augustinian scholar, who abandoned Augustine's position on the status of Adam and Eve. Adam and Eve, he said, required God's grace, not because of sin (Augustine's position), but *simply because they were creatures.* In this view, the human person by its very nature is incapable of doing anything good, and because of this position it appears that Thomas Bradwardine moved into a form of predestinationism.

Gregory of Rimini (1358), and Hugolin of Orvieto (1449), both members of a *schola Augustiniana moderna,* spoke hesitatingly even about meriting *de congruo* and about created grace. They emphasized *gratia increata* (the Holy Spirit). This emphasis encouraged a line of thought regarding an external acceptance of the sinner by God. These ideas, of course, applied to the contrition, confession and satisfaction of the penitent, as also to the absolution of the priest. Was the absolution merely an external declaration of God's acceptance of a sinner, with no internal change in the sinful Christian? What is merit, even *de congruo?* Does it compromise the absolute gratuity of God's grace and the full efficacy of Jesus' own salvific act? Questions such as these could not help but become central, as the issues of contrition, attrition, the value of absolution, and the necessity of satisfaction were more thoroughly studied.

The theological discussion of all these scholastic theologians focused on private sacramental penance. They mention, only in passing, and without detail, public penance. This concentration on private penance has several implications. First of all, one finds in the entire scholastic approach to the sacrament of penance a theological reflection on the *praxis* of the age, namely, private, auricular confession to a priest. In the patristic church the emphasis had been on the community and its wrestling with sin. In the patristic rituals, the assembled community played its role in the reconciling process. In the medieval period, the focus is on the individual. The community as such plays no liturgical role. This reflection on the *praxis* affected, in the second place, the liturgy of this sacrament. The assembled community has no role, although technically it is represented by the priest. The aim of the liturgical action is primarily on the health of the penitent Christian, and only indirectly on the health of the Christian community. Finally, in the third place, in the scholastic effort to pinpoint the "matter" and the "form" of this sacrament, the focus centered more and more on the words of absolution, which almost all the scholastic theologians viewed as the form. The "matter" of the sacrament was sharply contested. Since their discussions were unavoidably but narrowly pinpointed on this one historical form of reconciliation, the theologies, which they developed to strengthen this practice, can only be seen as themselves somewhat narrow. Without any doubt there are profound limitations to these various scholastic theologies of the sacrament of penance. When the reformation theologians and the bishops at Trent confronted these various theological positions, each in their different ways, they were basing their own positions not on any ideal theology of the sacrament, but on ways of theologizing, which clearly possessed inherent advantages, but also exhibited inherent disadvantages. Scholastic theologies on the sacrament of penance cannot be seen as normative theological thought. These various scholastic theologies on the sacrament of penance are, in themselves, narrow, limited, and time-conditioned. Such a criticism, however, does not mean that these theologies have no value. They certainly have great theological value, but what I am saying is this: none of them nor any one of them can be set up as the "normative" theology on the sacrament of penance against which any other theology of this sacrament must be judged.

The reformation, however, did not center on the sacrament of penance. This sacrament was simply one, and by no means the most important, example of a far deeper question: the relationship of faith and works, of God's grace and human justification. As one sees, the three issues mentioned above, which were central to the main scholastic approaches to the sacrament of penance, involved essentially that relationship of God's activity and human response. When one approaches the ritual of penance in this light, one can understand why scholastic theology on the sacrament of penance must be seen as at least one of the bases for the major disputes of the reformation period. These various scholastic theologies on the sacrament of penance were intrinsically connected to the issue of justification. To speak of the sacrament of penance was, at the same time, a speaking about justification. As we noted above, the *processus iustificationis* was at the heart of this scholastic sacramental theology, and vice versa the theology of sacramental penance was intrinsic to the scholastic theology of justification.

3. THE MEDIEVAL THEOLOGIES OF JUSTIFICATION

We have first considered the theology and practice of the sacrament of penance. Only then do we turn to a theology of justification. One might ask whether it might not be better to treat justification first and then the sacrament of penance. However, the sacrament of penance during the scholastic period was far more established, pastorally and to some degree theologically, than any theology of justification, so that the medieval views on justification were, to a large extent, based on and developed out of the theology and pastoral practice of the sacrament of penance, not vice versa. Moreover, Peter Lombard had not only left a textbook for the middle ages in his *Sentences*, but he himself had discussed the theology of justification in the very context of the sacrament of penance. McGrath notes:

> The integration of justification within the context of the sacrament of penance was greatly assisted by two developments. First, the general acceptance of Peter Lombard's *Sentences* as the basis of theological discussion during the thirteenth century led to justification being discussed with reference to the *locus* of distinction seventeen of the fourth book of the *Sentences,* i.e., within the specific context of the sacrament of penance.[21]

Rightfully, then, a study of justification in medieval theology might begin with a study of the medieval views on the sacrament of penance. The sacrament of penance, for the medieval scholar, was, generally speaking, the *locus* for their discussion on justification.

The second reason McGrath offers for this integration of justification and the sacrament of penance is this: the *processus iustificationis* indicated that remission of sin was connected to both satisfaction and absolution. Indeed, one of the major questions in high scholastic thought on the penance-issue was the relationship of absolution to the justifying process. "The justification of the sinner was therefore explicitly linked with the sacramental system of the church."[22] It was on the basis of this interrelationship that Lateran IV in 1215 established the obligation of annual confession.

When we turn to the theme of justification in the scholastic period, and particularly in the high scholastic period, we find a situation which is similar to the theology of the sacrament of penance. There was no single medieval theology of justification, just as there was no single medieval theology of the sacrament of penance. There were, rather, many theological variations on justification. Nor was there any official position of the Roman church on the matter of justification. Theologians and canonists presented a fairly wide range of views on justification. Key terms, of course, continued to appear in all the writings of these theologians and canonists: namely, remission of sin, satisfaction, justification, merit, merit *de condigno,* merit *de congruo,* free will, original sin, personal sin, etc. Many of these terms come from the New Testament and the fathers of the church, and were therefore held in highest respect. Still, theologians tended to nuance them in differing ways and to systematize them in varying patterns.

In his own historical study on justification, McGrath divides his own material under the following headings:

a. The nature of justification
b. The righteousness of God
c. The subjective appropriation of justification, i.e. the role of free will
d. Justification and the sacraments
e. The concept of grace
f. The concept of merit
g. The dialectic between the two powers of God
h. Predestination and justification

As one can readily see from the diversity of these headings, the topic of justification covers a wide range of Christian theology. We have already mentioned that the idea of "justification" in Augustine was very comprehensive; Augustine saw that justification brought about the correct ordering in the entire cosmos or in creation as such. This comprehensive and encompassing orientation of the word "justification" to a pan-cosmic situation was continued throughout medieval theology. Augustine's thought on the matter of justification dominated the medieval approach; his thought also dominated the way in which the medieval theologians and canonists interpreted the understanding of justification in the Pauline letters.

Thomas Aquinas specifically says that "justification" is the proper term to use in this context, since other terms, such as faith and love, refer to specific aspects of the process, whereas justification refers to the total process of cosmic transformation. *Iustitia* includes the notion of *rectitudo,* a correctness throughout the cosmos.[23] It should be noted here that faith is considered as a part of the process of justification, specifically, a first step in the process. Thomas is not alone in understanding faith in this limited way, but in the sixteenth century, with its hallmark of *sola fide,* this limited view of faith (based on Augustine) will be deeply challenged.

This rather global interconnection of faith, merit, grace, sin, free will, etc., under the umbrella of justification underlines the fact that the sacrament of penance, to be rightly understood and correctly implemented, must incorporate in itself the best of a theology of justification. If one were to discuss the sacrament of penance and not integrate into the theological basis for this sacrament the basic ideas from a theology of justification, there would clearly be something amiss. Although the following comments go far ahead of our discussion, they might help us understand the importance of this issue on the integration of the two theologies: namely that of the sacrament of penance and that of justification. Vatican II and the renewal of the sacrament of penance engendered by Vatican II did not address in any significant way the theology of justification. This lack has left the contemporary theology and pastoral practice of the sacrament of penance somewhat in limbo. Since the reformation theologians pointedly focused on the issue of justification and used the sacrament of penance as a clear example of an area in which there was a disintegration of a theology of justification, the renewed rite of penance from Vatican II should have evidenced in some clear way how this renewed rite and the theology of justification fit together. In the medieval period, influenced by Peter Lombard, theologians found the very *locus* to discuss justification in the theological discussion of the sacrament of penance. Today we might not make the *locus* of our discussion on justification the sacrament of penance, but we certainly need to integrate the two. This lack of integration in our own post-Vatican II church remains a serious drawback to the efforts of penitential renewal. We will take this issue up in a later chapter.

In the introduction to the *Pars Tertia* qq. 84–90 of the *Summa Theologiae* of St. Thomas Aquinas, by Blackfriars, the editors note: "The questions on Penance must be read with one finger in the *Secunda Pars* where the essential significance of sin and grace, particularly justification, is expressed."[24] Throughout these questions on the sacrament of penance, Thomas himself in the text refers again and again to *Secunda Pars,* indicating clearly that in his mind justification and the sacrament of penance are inescapably united. "This alliance of sacrament and virtue [of penance], along with one key phrase in the treatise—'Penance is concerned with sins as they are remediable by man's action co-operating with God towards justification'—lead to the core of the mystery of sin and forgiveness."[25] Thus, even though Thomas does not follow Peter Lombard and treat a theology of justification in the discussion on the sacrament of penance, he nevertheless clearly knits these two theological issues intimately together. As regards Thomas' views, one finger must be kept on the material which deals with the sacrament of penance when one is studying his material on justification, in the same way that one finger must be kept on the material regarding justification when one is studying his thought on the sacrament of reconciliation.

With this introductory material in mind, let us consider a few salient issues on the theologies of justification in this high scholastic period.

A. THE NATURE OF JUSTIFICATION

The *Summa Halensis* focused the fourfold *processus iustificationis* in the following, somewhat philosophical terms:

> In justification there are two terms: namely, [a *terminus a quo*] from evil and [a *terminus ad quem*] to good; hence on the part of God something is required on the part of the *terminus a quo,* and something on the part of the *terminus ad quem.* Similarly, from our own side ... [there is something on the part of the individual regarding the *terminus a quo* and also something on the part of the individual regarding the *terminus ad quem*]. With respect to the *terminus in quem* there is on the part of God the infusion of grace; with respect to the *terminus a quo* there is the remission of sin. With respect to the *terminus in quem* there is on our part the motion of free will [faith in God], and with respect to the *terminus a quo* there is detestation of sin.[26]

These four dimensions or aspects of the *processus iustificationis* became the framework, common to all the major scholastic theologians, to explain the nature of justification. In this there was unanimity. There was also unanimity that, in actuality (*pace* Scotus), these four dimensions or phases occur simultaneously. However, there was a wide variety of theological opinion on the logical or internal relationship of these four factors. It is precisely in this second area of interrelationship that scholastic theology developed various theologies of justification. One cannot say that there is a single "scholastic" theology of justification; rather, there are several such theologies.

Thomas Aquinas, for his part, used this same fourfold framework in the *processus iustificationis.*[27]

1. The infusion of grace
2. The movement of free will toward God through faith
3. The movement of free will directed against sin
4. The remission of sin

The same fourfold description can be found in the writings of Bonaventure,[28] and the list of subsequent scholastic theologians could go on. It is clear that for Alexander, Thomas, Bonaventure, Scotus, etc., justification does not simply mean the remission of sin, although this phrase, "remission of sin," has often been used as a code word for the fourfold process itself. In this fourfold process one begins, logically and chronologically, with the action of God, not the action of human free will. Because of this primacy of God's action, actually and logically, there is certainly no clear Pelagian overtone to the various scholastic descriptions of justification.

In the case of post-baptismal sin, Thomas connected the infusion of grace (the primordial action of God) to the desire on the part of the sinner for absolution. Thus, in the Thomistic approach contrition contained necessarily a *votum absolutionis,* in an explicit or implicit way. In a later writing, Richard of Middleton (1307) refers to five different opinions on this matter, and the first one he cites is that of Thomas, as expressed above.[29] Contrition is united to the infusion of grace *in genere causae efficientis* (in the form of efficient cause). Richard and others, however, prefer to see contrition *in genere dispositionis* (in the form of a disposition) or in some other form of interrelationship. In this discussion by Richard of Middleton we see that the issue of these various "actions," "conditions," "dispositions," even "causes," which a post-baptismal sinner needed to have, and the issue of the infusion of grace, which alone remits sin, had been argued variously by the key theologians of his day. The human aspects in this *processus iustificationis* became the arena of very divisive theological thought, and it is precisely in this area that the danger of Pelagianism becomes acute. If the human "turning to God" (called the beginning of faith by the scholastics) and the human "turning from sin" (called attrition and contrition by the scholastics) are given too powerful a role in the justification process, then the absolute gratuity of God's grace could easily be compromised, and the full adequacy of Jesus' salvific act could be nullified. It is also in this very separation of God's action and the human response that we begin to find room for the extrinsic or forensic understanding of justification which became prominent in the reformation period.

The Franciscan school, however, viewed the *processus iustificationis* in a slightly different way than Thomas had done. It too saw the goal of justification as *rectitudo,* the correct ordering of one's person and one's world, but the emphasis involved more of the psychological aspects of human nature and not merely the ontological aspects. Bonvanture, for his part, exemplified this justifying process by way of the *triplex via.* In the *Itinerarium mentis in Deum,* he used the way of purification, the way of illumination and the way of perfection, each of which has a different goal. However, in this same volume, it is clear that for Bonaventure a person stands at one and the same time in all three ways.[30] This connection to the area of lived spirituality remained a constant in the Franciscan approach to justification. Both the early and later Franciscan schools

maintained that a man or woman could merit justification *de congruo.*
Thomas in his *Commentary on the Sentences* upheld this position as well,
but in the *Summa* he apparently rejects it.

The difference between the Franciscan and Dominican approach
developed gradually and had roots prior to the rise of the mendicant
orders. Was there a preparatory disposition for the reception or infusion
of grace, for the start of the three-way journey to God? Was this preparation merely non-resistance to grace itself (apparently the view of Alexander of Hales)? Or was it some other more positive step on the part of
the sinner? Alexander of Hales appears to have been the first to formulate
a systematic view of created grace, although he is not the first to use the
term. With such a concept and term available to them, subsequent medieval authors began to express the pre-disposition to the infusion of grace
and the remission of sin in terms of created grace. Alexander had called
justifying grace, or uncreated grace, *forma transformans,* and created
grace, *forma formata,* ideas which one hears again and again, although
perhaps in some variant terminological phrasing, throughout the reformation and Tridentine period.

The issue began to focus around the following question: In what way
is the human soul open to receive grace? Is there some natural inclina-
tion? Does the openness come only from justifying grace itself? The
human creature was seen as wounded in nature, despoiled of grace
(*anima vulnerata in naturalibus, spoliata in gratuitis*). Indeed, another
phrase slowly moved into key roles: "*Facienti quod in se est, Deus non
denegat gratiam*" ("To the person who does the best he or she can, God
does not deny grace").

> With the early Thomas Aquinas it [this phrase] appeared in the
> form of a preparation in purely natural strength in which grace
> played only the role of an *auxilium,* which leads to the favorable
> opportunity, so that "grace is bestowed on him who does his
> very best" (2 *Sent.* d. 28, q. 1, a. 4).

> In Franciscan theology (*Summa Halensis,* Bonaventure) it was
> limited to a "declaration of divine goodness and generosity"
> ("*declaratio divinae bonitatis et liberalitatis*").[31]

Scotus, for his part, understands justification differently. The infusion of grace is one thing; the remission of sin is quite another. Whereas
in both Thomas and Bonaventure justification was at one and the same
time the infusion of grace and the forgiveness of sin (*via purgativa* and *via
illuminativa/unitiva*), Scotus states that at first Adam needed no remis-

sion of sin for the infusion of grace, nor did the angels. Hence, the two issues are quite distinct. Infusion of grace is truly what is meant by justification; remission of sin is secondary. The two are *de facto* united only because of God's will.[32]

With John of La Rochelle (1245) we begin to hear that the infusion of grace causes a real change: "A person is justified. If nothing takes place in the person, if no change takes place on his or her part, then the person is no closer to eternal happiness than before. If something (*aliquid*) takes place, I call it grace."[33] With this emphasis on a "real change," it is only a short step to the concept of "created grace," which one finds already in Alexander of Hales. The reification of grace had serious ramifications for the doctrine of justification, since one part, at least, in the justifying process involved the possession of some thing (created grace), which is later called sanctifying or habitual grace on the one hand, or actual grace on the other. To gain this created grace, the concept of merit, at least *de congruo* although with some authors *de condigno,* also begins to be understood in new ways.

B. THE JUSTICE OF GOD

As the idea of God's own justice began to appear in medieval theological literature, it became necessary to explain the central mystery of the Christian faith in a sharper way. God is just internally, i.e. God is *summa iustitia in se.* This means that God, simply because of divinity, will always remain true to God's nature and therefore to his covenant, to his promise, to his word. Not to do so would make God an un-God.[34] However, God is also just externally, i.e. in his dealings with creatures. This becomes theologically acute in the situation of a sinful creature.

Anselm of Canterbury in his *Cur Deus Homo,* as we saw above, presented the first major discussion of this matter. God as *summa iustitia in se* always acts for the best, the *summum bonum. This summum bonum* means that there is always an *ordo rectitudinis.* Sin, of course, has broken that correct order. From the original sin onward, human beings by themselves, individually and collectively, have been incapable of restoring the correct order, of justifying the broken or sinful situation. On the basis of Anselm's argument, McGrath writes: "If man is to be redeemed, a divine act of redemption is required *which must itself be consonant with the established order of the universe.* God, having created the moral order of the universe as an expression of his nature and will, is unable to violate it himself in the redemption of mankind."[35]

When Anselm makes this critical and central point, he is explaining to Boso why God could not simply forgive sin as a free act of mercy. Anselm throughout his writings maintains as carefully as he can (a) the goodness of God, i.e. God does not traffic in sin, belittle sin, coexist with sin, and (b) the justice of God, i.e. God must be correct to himself, to sinners, to the cosmos. An arbitrary "remission of sin" would indicate that God really did not take the sinfulness of men and women seriously and that God was capricious.[36]

It is of course important to point out that in Anselm's writings the incarnation of the Logos is key. An infinite offense has been committed which requires infinite satisfaction. No creature, not even the human nature of Jesus, can offer anything infinite. Therefore, God must become human so that the Logos in and through the humanity of Jesus is able to offer infinite satisfaction to God.[37] Not only in Anselm, but also in Thomas Aquinas, who continues this line of thought, the "infinite" satisfaction is never ascribed to a creature, not even the created humanity of Jesus. Always the "infinite" is ascribed to the *infinitum,* the Logos.

Thomas Aquinas rejects an understanding of God's *iustitia* as purely voluntary—i.e. something is just because God wills it so. Connected with *iustitia,* for Thomas, is *sapientia.* Given both this justice and this wisdom in the very nature of God, why did Jesus have to suffer death on the cross for our redemption? Thomas' answer was: it was fitting. "*Et ideo convenientius fuit quod per passionem Christi liberaremur, quam per solam Dei voluntatem.*"[38] Since God is a judge, he is not at liberty to remit our sin without some satisfaction. However, Thomas does not go as far as apparently Anselm does and require satisfaction by necessity. The aspect of satisfaction in Thomas is endorsed because it is "most appropriate to right reason and universally recognised as such by rational beings."[39]

That there is a totally capricious or voluntaristic approach to justification is neither what Scotus had in mind nor what he taught. For Scotus, the starting point is that God is first and foremost absolute freedom. Everything else flows from this. Scotus takes a very different approach to this justice of God, an approach which is generally termed "voluntaristic." His principle is clearly stated: "*Dico quod sicut omne aliud a Deo, ideo est bonum, quia a Deo volitum et non est converso; sic meritum illud tantum bonum erat, pro quanto acceptabatur.*"[40] An angel might have offered satisfaction to God for the sinfulness of men and women, if God had so chosen. "The merit of Christ's passion lies solely in the *acceptatio divina.*"[41]

Remarkably, Scotus bases his teaching on the freedom of God (the voluntaristic aspect) on Anselm. Anselm had explained that there was a common misconception about human freedom, namely that we are free because we have the capacity to sin. If this were "freedom," then God could not possibly be free, since God does not have the capacity to sin. Anselm redefines freedom as a pure perfection: "*potestas servandi recti-*

tudinem propter seipsum" ("the power of maintaining rectitude for its own sake"), and justice as "*rectitudo voluntatis propter se servata*" ("rectitude of the will served for its own sake").[42] "Under this aspect, freedom is not opposed to necessity, for 'necessary' and 'necessity' are terms with many meanings," as Wolter remarks.

God does not change, but:

> If such mutability is also lacking in God, then by the same token his will must have the pure perfection we call "firmness of purpose" or a "steadfast will." It is under this aspect that Scotus admits that, where God is concerned and with respect to his inner love-life, the freedom associated with his "unbegotten liberty" (*ingenita libertas*) must also be associated with a certain immutability or necessity.[43]

An important, recently established correction in the critical reading of the manuscript evidence of the *Quodlibet* offers us the following text from Scotus.

> Action that has to do with the ultimate end is most perfect. But firmness pertains to the perfection of such an action. Therefore, the necessity that is to be found there does not do away with, but rather demands, what is needed for perfection, namely, freedom.[44]

Justification for Scotus, then, is a most free or voluntary act, because of the very nature of God. In this way the absolute freedom of God is maintained, which implies that redemption, salvation, justification, and atonement, in his view, must be seen fully within the absolute gratuity of God's grace. Gabriel Biel, in a later century, missed this aspect of Scotus' thought and argued totally from the basis of a pact made between God and the sinful creature.

Much has been written on Scotus' teaching concerning the motive for the incarnation.[45] It is clear that for Scotus sin was not the reason for the incarnation of the Logos. It is also clear that the incarnation was accomplished freely. E. Doyle writes:

> The starting point of Scotus' Christocentric synthesis is the love of God. The supreme purpose of all God's activity *ad extra* is that he be glorified through love.[46]

In the incarnation of the Logos one sees a God who is at once *summum bonum, summa iustitia, summa libertas*. In the sense mentioned above, and only in that sense, is the incarnation of the Logos at once a free act and a necessary act. By saying this, Scotus maintains the absolute freedom of God's nature. The same must be said of the suffering and death of Jesus, considered as "redemption," "justification," "atonement." In this suffering and death of Jesus we must be able to see God who is utterly free (*summa libertas*), utterly good (*summum bonum*) and utterly just (*summa iustitia*).

C. MERIT

Of all the elements in the *processus iustificationis* which eventually came to be divisive, the element of merit stands at the head of the list. There have been a number of excellent studies, by both Protestants and Catholics, on this issue of merit.[47]

Late Judaic thought in the apocrypha and rabbinic writings developed a concept of merit, which is clearly the source of the Christian teaching on merit. There was, in this theological view, a reward for good deeds. Jesus himself did not use this reward-for-good-deeds approach in any extensive way. One can even see in the New Testament that the struggle against the Pharisees was, in part, a struggle against such a spirituality. The Pauline literature focused on grace (*charis*), not on the good works of the Torah or the wisdom of the Gentile world.

In the early church, it is really Tertullian who develops a vocabulary for a theology of merit: *Deus offensus, satisfactio, compensatio, hostia placatoria, bonum factum, meritum,* etc.[48] It is primarily in western theology that one finds a teaching on "merit." In the east there is really no corresponding and systematic approach to this theme.

Augustine, in his struggles with Pelagius, came face to face with the issue of merit and good works. It springs from the very core of Pelagius' error: the independence or neutrality of human nature. Augustine struggles with this area of merit as he discusses on numerous occasions the role of free will in the working of God's grace. Portalié notes: "The idea of merit presupposes, as a matter of fact . . . responsibility of the agent, freedom of choice and dominion over one's actions. Now he [Augustine] always asserted the merits of the just, though he maintained at the same time that these merits were due to a gratuitous gift: 'Whoever enumerates his true merits, what is he enumerating except Your gifts?' "[49] Augustine's ideas on grace, good works, free will, and merit influenced the medieval world in a most profound way. Anselm of Canterbury used merit to explain the incarnation and the death of Jesus. Gilbert de la Porrée spoke of Jesus' merits as proper: *proprie mereri*. Christians have merit only improperly: *improprie mereri*. His views were repeated by Peter Lombard. Those who disagreed with Lombard began to speak in terms of *meritum condigni* (William of Auvergne) or *meritum de con-*

digno (Odo Rigaldi), while *meritum de congruo* (Simon of Tournai, Alan of Lille) came to be used for the preparation for justification (William of Auvergne, Roland of Cremona).

These various uses of the term "merit" were applied in differing ways by the key figures in high scholasticism. There was no standard or official teaching on "merit." The key figures in high scholasticism began to integrate the various notions on merit with the newly developed term: *gratia creata.* Moreover, they also integrated merit into the phrase: *Facienti quod est in se Deus non denegat gratiam.*[50]

Two areas involving merit were of particular importance to the major theologians of the high scholastic period. The first was the area of one's preparation for grace. If one were to do good things naturally, were these meritorious for justifying grace? Generally, the answer was negative. Such "natural" good works or merits were at best "remotely dispositive." God's justifying grace (e.g. in baptism) was totally God's gift. As we saw above in both Thomas and Bonaventure, the infusion of grace is the sole reason for the remission of sin. Human effort (merit) plays no causative role.

The second area where the major scholastic theologians focused on merit was the issue of faith. From Augustine, these theologians rather consistently considered faith alone (*sola fide*) as only the initial step in the justifying process. Faith "formed by love" was seen as the perfection of the justifying process. In other words, faith by itself, in their theological approach, was incomplete. Faith needed its complete formation through love. This was stated again and again in Augustine, and repeated again and again by these medieval theologians. This "love" was charity or the infused gift of justifying love. It was the full presence of grace which one had through baptism, through the eucharist, through penance, through every sacrament, whereby one truly became a child of God, an heir to heaven, a temple of the Spirit, etc.

Luther, as we shall see, took exception to this phrase *fides caritate formata,* since in the late medieval period this love or charity was often described as "faith in action," or "faith exhibited in works of charity and love." One might speak of faith-charity as justification; one might also speak of faith alone as justification. Much depends on how one described "faith" and how one described "charity."

A person in grace, for the scholastics, should do good works. Did these good works manifest the presence of God's gift of grace, or did they "merit" further grace? Theological terminology in the middle ages spoke of some sort of meriting *de iure,* when there was question of merit *de condigno.* This is not the case when one speaks of *merit de congruo.* In both instances, however, the traditional term "merit" is retained. In discussing this issue in Scotus, for instance, Wolter remarks:

> Since merit is dependent on grace or charity, it has to do, not with the natural order, but with the supernatural state to which man has been gratuitously elevated by God. If any human act is to be rewarded with an increase of grace in this life and a face-to-face vision and love of God in the next, this is obviously a pure gift on God's part and transcends anything our human nature needs or requires.[51]

In the period after Scotus, a highly influential theologian appeared: Gabriel Biel. Biel's theology influenced Bartholomaeus Arnoldi von Usingen who in his turn was one of Luther's professors. These two men represent late medieval theological thought, and late medieval theological thought on both the sacrament of penance and on justification had, therefore, a definite role to play in unraveling the chain of events which led both to the reformation and then to the Council of Trent. In Heiko Oberman's study of Biel we find a continual interfacing of justification and the sacrament of penance.[52] Oberman comes to the conclusion that Biel presents a rather Pelagian view of justification and therefore of the sacrament of penance. He summarizes Biel's position as follows:

1. God owes it to his one immutable decision to reward those who do their best: *qui faciunt quod in se est.*
2. In this there is divine mercy and justice.
3. A sinner of his or her own power cannot move from the state of sin to the state of grace; the sinner can reach a sort of demarcation line.
4. After the fall, men and women can still detest sin and look to God.
5. Every human person has a natural knowledge of God, and knows something of what he or she should do. This is to some degree *fides acquisita.*
6. A post-baptismal sinner has only *fides informis.*
7. The "doing one's best" applies to the entire life of the baptized. The human will is responsible for one's acts; God's grace is responsible for merit.
8. Biel has a doctrine of justification which is both *sola gratia* and also *solis operibus.*[53]

In spite of this conclusion, Oberman notes that the counter-reformation cannot be seen as a reaction against nominalism. John Eck, Bartholomaeus von Usingen, and Kasper Schatzgeyer, Luther's Catholic opponents, were all indebted to nominalistic thought. Jacob Lainez, who played an articulate role at the Council of Trent, cites Biel. He goes on to remark:

> The later Middle Ages are marked by a lively, and at times bitter debate regarding the doctrine of justification, intimately connected with the interpretation of the works of Augustine on the relation of nature and grace. We have tried to show that the outer structure of the nominalistic doctrine of justification is intended to safeguard the Augustinian heritage and to neutralize the Pelagian dangers of an emphasis on the moral responsibilities of the viator. Our conclusion that nominalism has not been able to avoid a Pelagian position should not obscure the fact that nominalism was fully involved in the ongoing medieval search for the proper interpretation of Augustine.[54]

Discussion on the correct interpretation of Augustine has perdured down to the present day, and accordingly we should not fault these late medieval theologians for not arriving at "the correct view" of Augustine. Moreover, nominalistic thought on scripture and tradition appears to have been part of the basis for the Tridentine approach to this subject. Thus in many ways nominalism could be considered a "Catholic" theology, even though it was one which exemplified and in many ways intensified some of the inconsistencies found throughout scholastic thought.

4. AN ASSESSMENT

In summary, one can say that the issues involved in describing these medieval themes on the sacrament of penance and on justification are sweeping. Entire volumes can be and have been written on each of the many issues involved. There was no single medieval theology of the sacrament of penance, nor was there a single medieval theology of justification. McGrath enumerates five distinct medieval "schools" of thought regarding justification: (a) the early Dominican school; (b) the early Franciscan school; (c) the later Franciscan school; (d) the *via moderna;* (e) the medieval Augustinian tradition.[55] Each of these positions on justification had its ramification on the theology of the sacrament of penance.

One of the most penetrating and exciting (at least in my own view) aspects of this medieval discussion was the theme of God's own justice. However, it should be noted, once again, that there were in medieval thought several ways to theologize on the notion of *iustitia Dei.* The theme of God's own justice lies at the very center of every theology of justification. Justification is, at rock bottom, a statement about God and only secondarily about the human condition. This is why the many debates on justification focused so strongly on the absolute gratuity of God's grace. Without this absolute gratuity, grace is no longer grace, and God is no longer God. Once God becomes dependent, God ceases to be God. Secondly, even Jesus' role is called into question, if God's gratuitous grace is compromised. If there is another way, outside of Jesus, in which humans can find salvation, then Jesus ceases to be the Lord and savior. Even if Jesus, in his salvific action, requires help, however small, from us, he ceases to be Lord and savior. Humans, to some degree, would in this instance "merit" salvation.

Men and women, however, are not passive in this process of justification. In the Dominican school it was taught that "the formal cause of justification is defined to be the habit of created grace," and that "the necessity of a human disposition towards justification is maintained, on the basis of the Aristotelian presupposition that motion implies premotion."[56] In the early Franciscan school, it was taught that "the formal cause of justification is understood to be a created habit of grace," and that "the necessity of a human disposition towards justification is maintained upon Augustinian psychological grounds."[57] In the later Franciscan school, it was taught that "the formal cause of justification is understood to be the extrinsic denomination of the divine acceptation," and that "the necessity of a preparation for justification is upheld," but without the psychological reasons of the earlier Franciscan school.[58] The *via moderna* follows this later Franciscan school, but stresses the context of *ex pacto divino.*[59]

What is lacking in all of these attempts to integrate the human response to the divine justice is the role of the humanity of Jesus. From their analysis of the justice of God, the scholastic theologians go almost immediately to the issue of human preparation. It would have been better, so it seems, if from the presentation of the *iustitia Dei,* the next stage would have been a presentation of the way in which this *iustitia Dei* is made manifest and operative in the life, death and resurrection of Jesus. After this presentation, the next stage would have been to indicate how the *iustitia Dei* manifested in Jesus' life, death and resurrection is evident and operative in the community called church. This, of course, is hindsight. Only with Vatican II and the theology connected to Vatican II do we have Jesus presented as the primordial sacrament and the church as the basic sacrament. In the scholastic period, because of the interconnection of justification and the sacrament of penance, we have this immediate move from theological positions on justification to the particularized sacrament of reconciliation. The christological and ecclesiological element is, therefore, minimal, if indeed it exists at all. As a result both the medieval theologies of justification and the medieval theologies of the sacrament of penance are left incomplete.

The various scholastic discussions on both justification and the sacrament of penance highlighted the relationship between grace and free will. The dominance of Augustine's thought throughout this period clearly shaped the way in which the discussion was formed. Since no adequate resolution was reached on this matter, further discussion continued. This discussion went in a variety of ways, of which that of the reformation theologians constitutes only one aspect. We have, for instance:

1. Luther's approach
2. Calvin's approach
3. Baius' approach
4. Jansen's approach in the *Augustinus*
5. Quietism
6. Molina's approach
7. Banez' approach
8. The various approaches of the Tridentine bishops

All of these approaches were to some degree spawned from the same source. That some of these discussions on nature and grace were able to remain, though not without turmoil, within the Roman Catholic Church, while others of them were rejected, even through excommunication of their proponents, is not the main point. How can one explain this sixteenth and seventeenth century proliferation of divergent ideas on nature, grace, and justification, without seeing their rootage, at least to some degree, in the medieval, scholastic world. One might add that the twentieth century Roman Catholic discussion on nature, grace and justification (de Lubac, Rahner, "D," Brisbois, Malevez, Merriweather, Alfaro, etc.) is but a continuation of this same discourse.

In all of these instances, the presence of Augustine's thought is evident. A pre-Augustinian reading of scripture had to be made, but this proved to be difficult without a critical Greek text of the New Testament. Moreover, a separation of the theologizing on justification from the theologizing on the sacrament of penance had to be made. This, too, proved difficult, since for many this seemed to "empty out the baby with the bath water." Even at the Council of Trent the bishops could not address the issue of justification apart from that of the sacrament of penance.

As regards the sacrament of penance, throughout the scholastic period one certainly notes that the practice of the church was rather uncritically treated. Indeed, the *praxis* was a given; one's theology substantiated the *praxis*. This is not new in the Christian tradition. Over and over again, certain practices take shape within the church (Roman Catholic, Eastern Orthodox, Anglican, Protestant), and these practices perdure even though they are not ideal or pure. As long as these practices are not critically viewed by theology, the very theology of such practices itself cannot be seen as "ideal" or "pure." Even an appeal to "orthodoxy" or the eternal truth of the gospel, as a substantiation of such practices, can be misguided if one notes that the practice itself is not ideal and perfect. In the thirteenth to sixteenth centuries, the sacrament of penance, as a practice, was not "ideal," "perfect" or "pure." It needed reform. The theology which attempted to undergird it, as a consequence, also needed reform. An attempt at precisely such a reform, both of the practice and the theology of penance, was clearly made at the Council of Trent, but by the time the official church made such a move, the reformation churches had already been separated from the Roman church.

Nonetheless, the scholastic theologians, with their penetrating analyses on the justice of God, the key issue in this matter of justification, stand as a perduring presence to any and every theology which wishes to address the issue of justification. How one theologizes on God, the *summa iustitia, summum bonum,* and *summa caritas Dei,* will remain the key to understanding the reconciliation and justification of sinful men and women. Without this key, the door cannot be opened. In many ways, this emphasis on *iustitia Dei* is the reason why Alexander, Albert, Thomas, Bonaventure and Scotus will remain key figures in any and every struggle to understand this central mystery of our faith.

SUMMARY OF CHAPTER SIX

In this chapter we have seen:

1. Papal, episcopal and synodal statements of this period were practical; they do not provide much theological base.
2. Liturgical sources of this period indicate both public and private penance.
3. The canonical literature of this period offers us some insight into the ethical approach of the time.

4. Peter Abelard provided the middle ages with a counter-theology of contrition and justification. His views applied, to some degree, to the redemption in Jesus.
5. Peter Lombard provided the middle ages with a textbook for theology. His theological treatise on the sacrament of penance became the structure for subsequent discussion on this sacrament.
6. Peter of Poitiers formulated a fourfold process of justification which became normative in the centuries following.
7. Alexander of Hales raised the issue of sacramental causality; he was followed, in this, by the entire Franciscan school. The Dominican school maintained an instrumental efficient causality.
8. The major scholastic theologians were not at one over the relationship of contrition to absolution. Nor were they at one over the position of sacramental absolution in the process of justification. Satisfaction was variously evaluated; generally, some form of merit was involved in these theological evaluations.
9. Scholastic theologians provided a theological basis for the *praxis* of their time: namely, private auricular confession. This factor indicates a weakness and limitation to their enterprise. It also indicates the focus of their strength.
10. The sacrament of penance cannot be expressed theologically unless a theology of justification is also expressed, and vice versa. One without the other can only mean disaster.
11. In the middle ages there were several theories of justification; there was no official teaching of the church on this matter. These various theologies of justification formed the basis for the many views which appeared in the late fifteenth and throughout the sixteenth centuries.
12. The center of any and every theology of justification is the justice of God, not in the sense of God acting justly with creatures, but in the sense that God in himself is just, regardless of any creature. This justice of God is also essentially related to God's freedom and God's goodness.
13. Merit remains the issue which creates problems for any and every discussion on justification.

7

Justification, the Sacrament of Reconciliation, and the Reformation Theologians

Both the scholastic theology and the actual practice of sacramental penance provided a major base for the critique of the reformation theologians. In both areas, reform was indeed needed. Moreover, the various theologies of justification provided an even deeper base for their critique. Furthermore, it is fairly well-known that the reformation theologians rejected the view that the ritual of penance was a "sacrament." They rejected this ritual since the New Testament did not clearly indicate an institution by Jesus together with a promise of grace. Baptism and the eucharist alone can be found clearly in the New Testament as sacraments instituted by Jesus with a clear promise of grace. Nonetheless, both the theology and practice of penance in the church on the eve of the reformation provided the reformation theologians with, in their view, a clear example of an unacceptable doctrine of justification.

In this chapter I will consider both issues together and organize the material around the following:

1. The Teaching of Martin Luther
2. The Teaching of John Calvin
3. The Teaching of the English Church

1. THE TEACHING OF MARTIN LUTHER

In the first of Luther's *Ninety-Five Theses,* he wrote: "When our Lord and Master Jesus Christ said: 'Repent,' he willed the entire life of believers to be one of repentance."[1] Reconciliation is at the heart of the

Christian life, not simply one moment of sacramental activity. In *Theses* two and three Luther went on to explain that this repentance was not merely an internal repentance, nor did it mean simply the sacrament of penance administered by the clergy. Reconciliation is much more extensive and intensive than this. Luther, at first, did not object to private confession, but after some wavering on the matter, he concluded that it could not be called a "sacrament" on a par with baptism and the eucharist. Still, in Luther's view the ritual of private confession had its place in the Christian life. In the *Large Catechism* Luther wrote: "When I urge you to go to confession, I am simply urging you to be a Christian."[2] Contrition, of itself, forgives sin. When one confesses to a priest and receives absolution, the person must believe that the Lord truly has overcome sin and has bestowed on us the grace of reconciliation. Without this realization of sin and this faith in Jesus' salvific action, the sacrament of penance, or any sacrament for that matter, is meaningless.

Article twelve of the *Augsburg Confession* indicates that "true repentance is nothing else than to have contrition and sorrow, or terror, on account of sin, and yet at the same time to believe the Gospel and absolution (namely, that sin has been forgiven and grace has been obtained through Christ), and this faith will comfort the heart and again set it at rest."[3]

P. Meinhold begins his discussion on the ritual of confession in the Lutheran Church with the statement: "The reformation of the sixteenth century, which was shaped by Luther, had its beginning in a break from the then current teaching on penance and in a break with the then current practice of confession."[4] In a limited sense this judgment is correct; however, the reason for the break is much more focused on "justification." The sacrament of penance in Luther's view provided a clear incidence in which a correct theology of justification was being compromised. In the *Babylonian Captivity of the Church,* we find how deep Luther's concern on this matter truly was. Luther takes exception to the patristic phrase, popularized in particular by Jerome, that penance is a "second plank of salvation." This means, he argues, that some sort of shipwreck has already taken place, which can only mean that one's baptism has fallen apart. For Luther, faith in baptism can never end in shipwreck; otherwise, what God has promised in baptism is denied. Baptism lasts forever and ever, and we must be able to have a sure confidence in God's baptismal word to us.[5] Consequently, if our baptism can never be shipwrecked (the first plank), there cannot even be a second plank (penance). Even in this criticism of a patristic phrase, however, Luther points up the essential connection of a ritual of penance to the ritual of baptism. Without this relationship, both in pastoral practice and in theological reflection, neither the practice of penance nor its theological explanation is meaningful. A sacrament of reconciliation must be theologically explained in a baptismal way.

In all of this, the starting point was, for Luther, his christology. Already in his early writings, such as the *Dictata super Psalterium* and the *Commentary on the Letter to the Romans,* Jesus is presented as the "sacrament and example" of justification. He writes: "The death of Christ is the death of sin, and his resurrection is the life of justice, for through his death he satisfied for sin and through his resurrection he has given us his justice. Accordingly his death not only signified, but also brings about remission of sin as the most sufficient satisfaction. Moreover, his resurrection is not only a sacrament of our justice, but it also effects it in us and is its cause, if we believe in the resurrection."[6] This christological starting point remains a constant throughout Luther's life. Jesus has saved us in a complete way. Jesus has justified us totally. No explanation of the church or of any of its sacraments and rituals can compromise this foundation.

G. Tavard in his analysis of Luther's position on justification compares the writing of an early Luther, the *Commentary on Galatians* of 1519, with the writing of a more mature Luther, the *Commentary on Galatians* of 1535. One sees through this methodology the growth and clarity of expression in Luther's position on justification, even though the latter commentary has a harsher and more strident tone, as Luther inveighs against both the *Schwärmer* and the pope. Nonetheless, in both commentaries we find the typical language of Luther on this matter of justification: sin and freedom, law and gospel, twofold justification, one from works and one from God, faith and above all *sola fide.* In all of this we see Jesus as the sole reason for human justification.[7]

When one turns to the later *Commentary on Galatians,* lectures which were delivered in 1531 and thereafter revised and published by Luther in 1535, one sees his foundational thoughts. The central issue remains justification by faith. Still, Luther, more carefully in 1535 than was the case in 1519, delimits the role of intellect, of reason, and of philosophy. Theology must take place totally within the framework of faith: "In theology, faith is perpetually the divinity of works and is so present in the works as the Divinity in the humanity of Christ."[8] In the same text, Luther makes the following summary:

> Christian justice should be properly and accurately defined as trust (*fiducia*) in the Son of God, or trust of the heart in God through Christ. Here one should add this specific note: this faith is imputed as justice for the sake of Christ. These two elements,

as I have said, make Christian justice perfect: one, faith (*fides*) itself in the heart, which is a gift divinely given and formally believes in God; the other, that God considers this imperfect faith to be perfect faith for the sake of Christ, his Son, who suffered for the sins of the world, in whom I have begun to believe.[9]

Tavard calls this passage in Luther: eloquent, christocentric, unimpeachable. If the above ideas, summary though they are, express an unimpeachable Christian stance, then merit *de congruo* must rightfully be repudiated. Such was Luther's logic.

McGrath, in his analysis of Luther's teaching on justification, also stresses the fact that Luther developed his understanding of justification over many years. From 1509 to 1514 Luther made his own the teaching on justification which one finds in the *via moderna,* with its emphasis on the pact-theory as also on the phrase *facienti quod in se est Deus non denegat gratiam.* It was only in the period 1514–1519 that Luther made a radical break with this line of thinking, which one begins to see in the *Commentary* of 1519. The 1545 autobiographical fragment indicates that Luther's struggle had been with the theology of the *via moderna,* i.e. the *via moderna* view of justification.[10]

In the *Lectures on Romans* of 1515–1516 Luther taught that the human person is passive vis-à-vis God, and that the human will without grace cannot attain righteousness. Therefore, McGrath notes, Luther characterizes the justice of God (as it applies to sinners) as:

1. A righteousness which is a gift of God.
2. A righteousness which is revealed through the Cross.
3. A righteousness which contradicts human ideas.[11]

G. Yule begins his study with these words:

When one studies Luther's works chronologically, it becomes apparent that more and more he discussed justification by grace alone in terms of the traditional Christology of the Church. The originality of Luther's theology is the way he interwove its anti-Pelagian slant with the central affirmation of the Christian faith, that Jesus, though of one nature with God the Father, became our brother man.[12]

At the end of his study he states the same material, but more point-edly on the issue of justification:

> An essential element of Christology has now been underlined —the cost of redemption—so that if one says *sola gratia* one points to the incarnation, and if one says Jesus Christ, truly God and truly man, one can only say *sola gratia.* Adoration and theology are again knit together.[13]

Christology lies at the base of Luther's theology of justification, and it is with Christology that one must begin either to affirm or to criticize his stance. Once this foundation is made, then one can move into other areas of Luther's theology, and in many ways ecclesiology is the logical next area of Luther's thought which deserves investigation.

When one asks about Luther's understanding of the mediation of the church, this christological sufficiency must be kept in mind. For Luther, of course, the church has been divinely established, and therefore only in and through the church can one discover both the will of God and the revelation of Christ. At times, arguments are made that Luther is indi-vidualistic and over-personal to the detriment of his theology of church. Without any doubt his ecclesiology differed from the ecclesiology of many Roman theologians of his time, but what Luther attempted to defend, as he developed his ecclesiology, was his christology. The church, he maintained, cannot be put into Jesus' place. As a consequence, the church becomes more and more "revelatory" and "declaratory" of Jesus. If one uses the theological term "cause," one finds its meaning in Jesus, not in the church. God/Jesus is the cause of grace, the cause of justifica-tion, the cause of remission of sin, etc. The action of the church is revelatory and declaratory. If an ecclesiology attempts to see the church itself as causing justification, then, in Luther's view, there is an unaccept-able union of christology and ecclesiology. For Luther, absolution is not a cause of forgiveness, but a declaration that God has forgiven sin.[14]

Besides the christological base and its ramifications in ecclesiology, there is also an anthropological base for Luther's view of justification. In some key ways, McGrath argues, Luther parted company from Augus-tine, particularly from Augustine's anthropology. For Augustine "the righteousness bestowed upon man by God in his justification was recog-nisable as such by man—in other words, the justified sinner was *iustus coram Deo et coram hominibus.*"[15] For Luther, with his theological un-derstanding of the human person as a *caro* and *spiritus,* a person might be righteous *coram Deo,* but not *coram hominibus;* or a person might be righteous *coram hominibus,* but not *coram Deo.* The human person remains *caro* and therefore *simul iustus et peccator.* The righteous human person remains an enigma to other humans, who judge only on the basis of *caro.* The righteousness which a human person has, therefore, is not his or her own, but *iustitia Christi aliena.* This move eventually provides the basis for forensic justification or external justification.[16]

Moreover, Luther noted that the three acts of the penitent—contrition, confession, and satisfaction—are nowhere found in the New Testament. These are, rather, theological contrivances, and their explanations, in his view, often did not square with God's merciful grace. The stress from the scholastic period on perfect contrition was particularly questionable to Luther, since, if someone could make an act of perfect contrition, then where is God's freely given grace? How can the absolute gratuity of God's forgiving grace co-exist with an explanation of perfect contrition? One notes that Luther found a Pelagian interpretation in some of the then-current theological presentations of perfect contrition and of absolution. Even some forms of theological discussion on the church were, in his view, Pelagian. This theological tendency toward Pelagianism was also reflected in the pastoral practice of the church at his time. Pastors and preachers were advocating the "doing" of some "good work" in order to merit grace. Such works could have a valid theological meaning, but they could also be used in a Pelagian way. God's word alone, not some human act, Luther argued, is the basis for all forgiveness.

The same critique was raised against the issue of satisfaction. For Luther, satisfaction can only be seen as an effect of God's forgiveness, not a cause nor a condition to such forgiveness. No one through works of satisfaction merits grace; otherwise, grace is no longer grace. In Luther's reflections on satisfaction, we see the very core of the reformation controversy: namely, the call for a Christian theology and practice which takes seriously the full sufficiency of Jesus' salvific action and the complete gratuity of God's forgiving grace. Any dimunition of the full sufficiency of the work of Jesus or any dimunition of the absolute gratuity of God's grace can only be seen as a distortion of Christian theology and practice.

In his *Small Catechism,* Luther presents a form of priestly absolution for private confession: "Be it done for you as you have believed. According to the command of our Lord Jesus Christ, I forgive you your sins in the name of the Father and of the Son and of the Holy Spirit. Amen. Go in peace." This absolution of the priest is good, Luther tells us, because it is from God; it also provides spiritual instruction to the penitent.[17] Absolution for Luther, as we have mentioned above, is declaratory of what God has done and is doing: namely, forgiving our sins.

No wonder then that B. Lohse notes: "The private confession is a point of crystallization for several theological and ecclesial problems. Of importance for private confession is not only the teaching on sin and grace, but also ecclesiology, in which the interpretation of the ordained ministry and the power of the keys is particularly meaningful."[18]

In the history of the Lutheran churches, we find diverse rituals for confession of sin. In many of these rituals private confession to a priest was included and even urged. In many ways this retention of private confession marked the difference between the Lutheran and the Reformed churches. When pietism became strong within the Lutheran communities, private confession to a priest began to be minimized. To compensate for this reduction, Lutheran communities, particularly in southern Germany, began to celebrate *Busstagen* and *Bettagen*, which included hymns, prayers, scriptural readings, sermons, general confession and even absolution. There were many forms for such liturgical celebrations of reconciliation.[19]

From all of this, one sees that private confession to a priest remained, and even today remains, a part of the Lutheran tradition. Lutherans may not call this ritual a sacrament in the same sense as the sacraments of baptism and the eucharist, but the ritual of private confession has remained a hallowed one with long historical roots.[20] In this profession of ritualized reconciliation, the Lutheran Church bears Christian witness to Christ's power within the church to isolate, repel and negate sin. However it is also true to say:

> Despite the high reverence for confession as a means of grace in its own right in Luther and in the dogmatic and liturgical tradition of Lutheranism, there is, in fact, the broadly shared consciousness that: "In the Evangelical [German Lutheran] view of things, Christians who are conscious of their sin before the face of God experience justifying grace through faith in the Gospel of Jesus Christ. Justification through faith which holds fast to Christ is not tied to a priestly administered sacrament of penance" (Reinhard Schwarz, in *Luther,* 1986).[21]

The above few paragraphs indicate a Lutheran position on the issue of a ritual of reconciliation (confession to an ordained minister). The focus, however, throughout Luther's discussion of reconciliation is much more on justification. J. Heinz has indicated that it was precisely in the rejection of the theological concept of "merit" which allowed Luther to present his theology of justification.[22] The rejection of "merit," however, is not the heart of Luther's critique; rather, the heart of his critique is his rejection of any theology or pastoral practice which denies the absolute freedom of God's grace and compromises the full adequacy of Jesus' salvific act, both of which are, of course, related to the concept of "merit." The theology and pastoral practice regarding merit caused Luther serious pause precisely because these two foundational issues were, in many instances, being compromised. Faith, in Luther's approach, was the acceptance of these two issues: namely that (a) we have been saved solely by God through Jesus, and that (b) we have been saved by the absolutely free gift of God's grace.

Heinz summarizes Luther's position as follows:

1. The human will does nothing toward conversion and justification.
2. A person acts in the process of conversion as Paul acted before the Damascus experience; he struggles against God.
3. The Holy Spirit draws the sinner through the Word to God and changes the will of the struggling one.
4. This will, changed by God, is now so constituted that it agrees with God and gladly wills what God requires of it.
5. The recognition of the sole agency of God should not terrify us, but call us to prayer, whereby we rely wholly on God.[23]

One can say that the main lines of justification were expressed in the various writings of Luther. He arrived at his position only gradually, but in the development of his thought he came to see more clearly that justification is from God alone, *sola gratia,* and that our only response is one of faith, *sola fide.* But this "faith" must be clearly understood.

Many Protestants assume that when Luther said justification by faith alone he meant that we are saved not by our works but by our existential decision of faith. But this, as Cranmer crisply remarked, makes faith into a work, and it would have been for Luther just another type of Pelagianism. "Faith," he [Luther] wrote, "is something done to us rather than by us (*magis passio . . . quam actio*) for it changes our hearts and minds."[24]

This is why Luther preferred the term *fiducia* for faith rather than *assensus,* since *fiducia* pointed away from us, while *assensus* pointed toward us. Faith, for Luther, was a far deeper and more comprehensive aspect of Christian life than the definition of "faith" in the scholastic theologians. The scholastic theologians followed Augustine, for whom faith needed to be formed by charity. In this view, faith was seen as only an initial stage in justification, and completed solely when charity (sanctifying grace) began to "inform" this initial faith. For Luther, faith must be the full turning to God of a person's heart and life, a complete entrustment of one's being to God; otherwise, it is really not "faith." Unfortunately, the bishops at Trent did not really come to grips with this definition of faith; they clung closely to the Augustinian and scholastic approach to "faith" and "informed faith," in which faith is seen as merely the beginning of justification. For Luther faith was the beginning, middle and end of justification. As a result, Luther's position and Trent's position often become two discussions about two different theological and spiritual realities.

Luther's doctrine of *servum arbitrium* stems from this same concern. A thorough study of this aspect of Luther's thought has been made by H.J. McSorley, *Luther—Right or Wrong? An Ecumenical-Theological Study of Luther's Major Work, "The Bondage of the Will."* [25] For Luther the human will remains captured no longer by sin, but by God's forgiving grace. The role of God remains absolute.

Even during Luther's lifetime, but especially after his death, the Lutheran theologians were not at one in their explanation of justification: Philip Melanchton, Andreas Osiander, Francesco Stancari, Johann Agricola, Georg Major, and Martin Chemnitz all had varying and at times opposing views on this matter of justification.

> It will therefore be clear that the *Formula of Concord* marked not only the ending of an important series of controversies in the Lutheran church immediately after Luther's death; it also marked the victory and consolidation of the critique of Luther from within Lutheranism itself. Luther's concept of justification, his concept of the presence of Christ within the believer, his doctrine of double predestination, his doctrine of *servum arbitrium*—all were rejected or radically modified by those who followed him. It would be improper to inquire as to whether this critique and modification was justified; it is, however, right and proper to note that it took place. [26]

Even though there was some reshuffling of the issues involved in the doctrine of justification, the very reshuffling indicates that "final" statements on this central teaching of the church are not easy to establish. Still, the majority of Lutheran theologians were clearly in agreement in their stress of the gratuity of God's grace and the full efficacy of Jesus' salvific action.

2. THE TEACHING OF JOHN CALVIN

John Calvin, at first, agreed with Zwingli as regards the sacrament of penance. Some of his strongest statements of such agreement can be found in *The Necessity of Reforming the Church.* However, in the *Institutes of the Christian Religion*[27] (which Calvin revised on several occasions) he tended to follow Luther's views. In these *Institutes,* Calvin, like almost all other scholars of his day, indicated only the fairly thin knowledge of the history on public penance which was available at that time (IV, 19, 14). This knowledge however was enough to call into question some of the apodictic statements which scholastic theologians were attempting to maintain. When Calvin took up the issue of the "sacrament" of penance (IV, 19, 15) he noted that various theologians held different views as to the "matter" of this sacrament. Calvin, moreover, found no scriptural basis to maintain that the rite of confession should even be called a sacrament, much less that there be a discussion of a "sacramental matter and form." Rather, in Calvin's view, this ritual appears to have been developed during the course of church history (IV, 19, 17). With Luther, Calvin sees baptism, not confession, as the sacrament of repentance, and he too argues strongly against the phrase "second plank of salvation."

> They have adorned this feigned sacrament with an appropriate title, "the second plank after shipwreck," for if anyone has stained, by sinning, the garment of innocence received in baptism, he can restore it by penance. But it is, they assert, Jerome's saying. No matter whose it may be, it cannot be excused of manifest impiety (IV, 19, 17).

Calvin, in an earlier section of the *Institutes,* had considered the scholastic discussion on attrition and contrition (III, 4, 1). Calvin insisted that the real issue is the mercy of God, not the human effort, to make an act of perfect or full contrition (III, 4, 3). Nor is confession of sins clearly enjoined by scriptures, in the way the medieval theologians and the canonists maintained. Indeed, Calvin notes, these theologians and canonists are not in agreement themselves on this issue of confession of sin (III, 4, 5–6). Auricular confession is a later establishment in the church (III, 4, 7–8), and therefore goes back neither to Jesus nor to the New Testament.

When Calvin discusses the issue of private confession two items stand out: first of all, the impossibility of confessing all sins, and, secondly, the question of the power of the keys. That a person must confess all one's sins is according to Calvin virtually impossible. Even after one has confessed one's sins, one is still sinful. This inability to enumerate all one's sins can only augment the torment of one's conscience. Rather than focusing on a full rendition of each and every sin, one should focus on the infinite mercy of God, who forgives us our sins. God's merciful and infinite forgiveness, not the human endeavor of enumerating sins, is the basis for our faith. As far as the power of the keys is concerned, Calvin interprets scripture more in keeping with contemporary biblical scholarship, namely, that there is in the church a power to isolate, repel and negate sin. That this power is given to priests alone is a misreading of scripture and, as Calvin says, a tyranny over God's forgiving love (III, 4, 16–23).

The issue of satisfaction is likewise criticized (III, 4, 25) since it makes good works more important than God's grace of forgiveness. It is God's grace, manifested in Jesus, that provides full satisfaction (III, 4, 26–27). Once again, we see that the issue is christological. How does one view the death and resurrection of Jesus? If the church requires some human action, either on the part of the Christian himself or herself, or on the part of the church minister (whether pope, bishop, or priest) as a pre-condition or pre-cause for God's forgiveness, then is there not a Pelagian approach to grace, and, in this present instance, the grace of forgiveness of sin? In Calvin's view, the scholastic approach to the matter was clearly Pelagian, and the endorsement by Roman authority of the power of the keys appeared to be an endorsement of this Pelagian approach.

For Calvin there were three forms for the confession of sin: the first is between the person and God; the second is a confession of faults and sins to one's neighbor; the third is private confession made to the ministers of the gospel. Calvin saw that sin was indeed an offense against God, but that it was also an offense against the church. Serious offenses against the church, which were also serious offenses against God, demanded some form of church reconciliation. In all of this Calvin states that this was the teaching of the patristic church, not some formulation of the scholastic or Roman church (III, 4, 11–12).

These are some of Calvin's basic views on the ritual of reconciliation, and once again it is evident that the main argument is not on the "sacrament" as such, but on the theology of justification which underlies this ritual. When Calvin takes up his explanation of faith (III, 2, 1) he focuses on Jesus. After stating that we are to live in conformity with God's law

(*rectitudo* or *ordo,* as Augustine would have said), and after indicating
that sin separates us from God in such a way that it is "above our
strength" and "beyond all our abilities" to free us from sin, Calvin concludes:

> There is but one means of liberation that can rescue us from
> such miserable calamity: the appearance of Christ the Re-
> deemer, through whose hand the Heavenly Father, pitying us
> out of his infinite goodness and mercy, willed to help us; if,
> indeed, with firm faith we embrace this mercy and rest in it with
> steadfast hope. (III, 2, 1)

He then takes to task the scholastic view of "implicit faith," a view
which is found in Peter Lombard, Thomas Aquinas and Bonaventure.
Implicit faith, for Calvin, is a fiction which destroys true faith. An implicit faith is a faith in a church or someone wiser, but this is a faith based
on ignorance, not on Jesus. "We do not obtain salvation either because
we are prepared to embrace as true whatever the church has prescribed,
or because we turn over to it the task of inquiring and knowing" (III, 2,
2). We obtain salvation only by believing in Christ.

In the Introduction to the *Institutes,* the editors summarize Calvin's
position:

> In his treatment of faith, repentance and justification he [Cal-
> vin] deals with these doctrines so much discussed in the Refor-
> mation. Faith is more than an assurance of God's veracity in the
> Scripture; it is also a full persuasion of God's mercy and of his
> favor toward us. It stands clear of works and of the law, since it
> has for its primary object Christ and is imparted to us by the
> Holy Spirit. Calvin denounces certain Scholastic treatments of
> faith in which it is severed from piety and love. Although with
> Luther he uses the phrase "justified by faith alone," he is careful
> to say too that faith does not of itself effect justification, but
> embraces Christ by whose grace we are justified.[28]

Calvin spends considerable time on *Poenitentia.* In Latin this word
refers both to repentance and to penance. Basing himself on the Greek
original, *metanoia,* Calvin stresses the fact that we change: we depart
from ourselves and turn to God; repentance is "the true turning of our
life to God, a turning that arises from a pure and earnest fear of him; and
it consists in the mortification of our flesh and of the old man, and in the

vivification of the Spirit" (III, 3, 5). Calvin, in this definition, describes in his own way the *processus iustificationis* and there is a fourfold aspect to this:

a turning to God (III, 3, 6)
an earnest fear of God (III, 3, 7)
mortification of the flesh (III, 3, 8)
vivification of the spirit (III, 3, 8)

The turning to God is a transformation, a circumcision of the heart. That this transformation and turning comes from God's initiative had already been stressed (III, 2, 1). This action of God leads us to a fear of God. This involves a hatred of sin, a turning from sin, a mortification of the flesh. And all of this leads to the presence of the Spirit: "This comes to pass when the Spirit of God so imbues our souls, steeped in his holiness, with both new thoughts and feelings, that they [the inclinations to righteousness, judgment and mercy] can be rightly considered new" (III, 3, 8). But the mortification and vivification happen to us only in and through Jesus, and thus repentance is a regeneration, "whose sole end is to restore in us the image of God that had been disfigured and all but obliterated through Adam's transgression" (III, 3, 9). This takes place because "no one ever hates sin unless he has previously been seized with a love of righteousness (*nisi prius iustitiae amore captus*)" (III, 3, 20). Repentance, however, of itself is not, properly speaking, the cause of salvation. Salvation comes to us because repentance is inseparable from faith and from God's mercy (III, 3, 21).

With this lengthy description of the *processus iustificationis,* Calvin then takes up the issue of sacrament of penance (III, 4, 1–39), and presents the basic issues mentioned above. It is more than evident that Calvin's presentation further exemplifies the union between a theology of justification on the one hand, and a theology of the "sacrament of penance" on the other. There can be no theology of such a sacrament unless there is a genuine theology of justification. The difficulties which one might experience in a theology of the sacrament of penance very often are difficulties inherent in a more basic area, namely, the theology of justification. The two issues are intimately bound together.

Calvin's discussion on justification, in the 1559 edition of the *Institutes,* is found, as we have seen, in Book III. Many Lutheran scholars find this rather late discussion of the issue of justification embarrassing, since one might question how focal justification is to Calvin's thought if it only appears in Book III.

Calvin's concern is with the manner in which the individual is incorporated into Christ, and the personal and corporate consequences of this insertion *in Christum*—of which justification is but one way. Calvin thus expresses systematically what Luther grasped intuitively—the recognition that the question of justification was essentially an aspect of the greater question of man's relation to God in Christ, which need not be discussed exclusively in terms of the category of justification.[29]

There is, indeed, some truth to this Lutheran criticism of Calvin. Justification, as a doctrine, might not be the word which best summarizes Calvin's foundational thought. Nonetheless, one can certainly see that the twin issues of (a) the full efficacy of Jesus' salvific act and (b) the absolute gratutity of God's grace, even without being formally called "justification," do lie at the base of Calvin's entire approach to the Christian kerygma.

3. THE TEACHING OF THE ENGLISH CHURCH

The reformation in England reflects the continental reformation to some degree, but it is clearly quite different as well. Rosemary O'Day describes the situation quite well:

Process or event? If we have to define historical phenomena in such terms, then the English Reformation is more properly described as process than as an event. So much so that it is difficult to decide precisely who was and who was not a contemporary of the English Reformation. John Foxe? Of course. Thomas Cranmer? Yes. But what about John Whitgift, Richard Bancroft, William Laud, even John Strype? Just where do we draw the line? . . . The idea of a continuing reformation—the completion of a half-finished job—remained with the English well into the nineteenth century.[30]

There were, indeed, major theological figures in the English reformation, such as Tyndale, Cranmer, Lattimer, etc., but none of them individually were quite as influential and powerful as Luther and Calvin. Moreover, the Church of England remained in many ways quite similar to its pre-reformation character. Of course, there was the break with the Roman papacy, the dissolution of the monasteries, but bishops in many ways kept on being bishops, priests kept on being priests, and lay people kept on being lay people in much the same way as before the Henrician or Elizabethan acts of supremacy.

Tavard makes a similar judgment:

> In Anglicanism, Luther's theology of justification has never been much at home. For one thing, Thomas Cranmer (1489–1555) was more Calvinist than Lutheran. For another, Richard Hooker (1554–1600), the great theologian of the Elizabethan period, struck out on his own. He could "speak of that grand question which hangeth in controversy between us and the Church of Rome, about the matter of justifying righteousness." But he also judged the "opinion of the Lutherans" to be "damnable."[31]

When one reads the English theologians of this reformation period, however, one hears many of the same positions on justification that one heard from Luther and Calvin.

> We are accounted righteous before God, only for the merit of our Lord and Saviour Jesus Christ by faith, and not for our own works or deservings; wherefore that we are justified by faith only is a most wholesome doctrine.[32]

> Note now the order: first God giveth me light to see the goodness and righteousness of the law, and mine own sin and unrighteousness; out of which knowledge springeth repentance. Now repentance teaches me not that the law is good, and I evil, but a light that the Spirit of God hath given me out of which light repentance springeth.[33]

> Justification is not the office of man, but of God: for man cannot justify himself by his own works, neither in part, nor in the whole; for that were the greatest arrogance and presumption of man that antichrist could erect against God, to affirm that a man might by his own works take away and purge his own sins, and so justify himself.[34]

Philip Edgcumbe Hughes weaves together citation after citation of such comments by key English reformation theologians in his book, *Theology of the English Reformers,* and as one peruses these passages, one hears again and again: justification comes from the Lord through

Jesus alone, and we sinners are saved by faith alone. Hugh Latimer might be cited, but he is one with the other authors to indicate that all of this talk on justification, merit, and grace is fundamentally christological:

> "Forgive us our trespasses, as we forgive them that trespass against us." Do I now, in forgiving my neighbor his sins which he hath done against me, do I, I say, deserve or merit at God's hand forgiveness of my own sins? No; no; God forbid! for if this should be so, then farewell Christ; it taketh him clean away, it diminisheth His honour, and it is very treason wrought against Christ.[35]

The full efficacy of Jesus' salvific act and the absolute gratuity of God's grace are the key elements in this discussion of justification, just as these elements were the key elements in Luther's or Calvin's discussion on justification. Tyndale echoes this same thought: "Now to have heaven for mine own deserving is mine own praise and not Christ's. For I cannot have it by favour and grace in Christ and by mine own merits also; for free giving and deserving cannot stand together."[36]

When we consider the English reformation and the sacrament of penance we see that the Church of England retained the ritual of reconciliation, though not calling it a sacrament. Henry VIII wanted no change on this issue. Cranmer, for his part, said that such confession was voluntary. The *Prayer Books* of 1549 and 1552 included private confession to a priest. J. Jewell in his *An Apology* of the Church of England and in his *Defense of the Apology* in many ways summarized the position of the Church of England on confession to a priest. It was not enjoined by Christ nor is it necessary for salvation, but when used rightly it is beneficial to Christian life.[37]

The Church of England, more than any other church of the reformation, maintained the tradition of a ritualized penance. Again we see in the tradition of this church the acknowledgement that Christ's power to isolate, repel and negate sin is operative within the church at many levels.

A discussion of the theology of justification or the theology of the ritual of reconciliation is but one part of the English reformation. In the past century, historians have reconsidered this reformation process and they have moved in several ways.[38] A. Pollard stands as a watershed historian in this endeavor, for he attempted to present a picture of Henry VIII as objectively as possible. He wanted to present the reasons for the English reformation, without making a moral judgment on the matter. Pollard was concerned with the question: What are the factors which allowed the reformation in England to succeed? After the long civil strife of Lancaster and York, the people of England wanted peace, and for Pollard this desire of the public made room for the Tudor kings to be supreme. "The Reformation was an act of Henry VIII's will . . . it could not have happened, had his people not allowed it."[39] Pollard himself says the English reformation was "not in essence doctrinal," but "an episode in the eternal dispute between Church and State."[40] Henry VIII was the sole creator of the English reformation, in this view, a view which went unchallenged until mid-century.

Geoffrey Elton became the leader of the change, arguing that Thomas Cromwell, not Henry VIII, was the real creator of the reformation. The break with Rome, for Cromwell, was a political act, not a religious one. Joel Hurtsfield challenged both Pollard's and Elton's position by focusing on parliament. J.J. Scarisbrick then attempted to reconstruct Pollard's view. The reformation was imposed on the people of England by Henry VIII, with the help of Cromwell. A.G. Dickens moves differently. Protestant thinking, in his view, was already making headway in England by 1530, and the Catholic England was too enfeebled to withstand this new movement.

Who is correct? Has the historical study of this period reached a momentary deadlock? It would seem so. However, interest has been raised in studying not merely the main figures in the drama, but to consider the English people as such. This has been done by A.G. Dickens, in *The English Reformation,* which is a study in the devotion or lack of it among the English people of the late fifteenth or early sixteenth centuries. C.S.L. Davies expressed the situation this way:

> Protestantism was to triumph in England, initially at least because it was given a lead from above by the king. . . . Without that lead it is impossible to know what would have happened in sixteenth-century England. Almost certainly, there would have been a powerful Protestant party; very probably powerful enough to exploit particular political situations and bring about civil war. But there is no guarantee that a Protestant rebellion would have succeeded any more than it succeeded in France.[41]

The Church of England, however, did not remain unreformed. It was not simply a "Catholic" Church without a Roman pope. But it was also not a totally "Protestant" Church. The fact that the theology of justification as expressed by the English theologians parallels the continental reformation theologians speaks strongly; the deep spirituality in hierarchy and ritual and ceremony also speaks strongly. For centuries English people have argued "convincingly on all sides that the Church of

England was Catholic, Protestant or, indeed neither. Historians are still rehearsing the pros and cons of the case."[42]

Tavard notes that the Puritan wing of the Church of England, which later on came to be a strong element in English Presbyterianism, endorsed the views of the Dutch Calvinists, established at the Synod of Dort (1617–1618). These formulas, however, were certainly quite right of Calvin's own theology.[43] Still another approach to these issues came from John Wesley (1703–1790), whose writings are strongly anti-Protestant. "To tie Wesley to any one line of thought and call him, for instance, Lutheran, Calvinist (Reformed), or Catholic will always be a distortion; he is so much of an eclectic that he belongs to all—and still has a theology uniquely his own."[44]

McGrath's treatment of justification in the English Church extends from Tyndale to Newman. He traces the many vicissitudes in the theological discussion on justification made by Anglican scholars. The grand question of justification, as Hooker called it, became itself a question among the Caroline divines of the seventeenth century. McGrath rightfully points out that the influence of the Calvinist tradition, rather than that of the Lutheran tradition, played a more significant role among the English theologians, but in the end there remained an open-question quality about the issue of justification within the Anglican Church.[45]

Whether one considers the reflections of Luther or Calvin or scholars of the English Church, one sees that the real issue in all of the above is not the "sacrament of penance." Nor can one say that the real issue is whether or not penance is a "sacrament." The real issue is not even ecclesiology, i.e. what is the "power" of the church over the forgiveness of sin? Or what does the "power of the keys" in the gospels really mean? This ecclesiological element is vital, of course, but in reality it is the twin issues of (a) the full efficacy of Jesus' salvific action and (b) the absolute gratuity of God's grace which are the main focus of the dispute. In the life, death and resurrection of Jesus do we ourselves have the complete "expiation" of sin or does the church or the individual Christian have to add some additional component to this "work of Christ"? If the latter, then Jesus is no longer the true "savior of the world," for in this instance we would, to some slight degree, be saving ourselves. Connected to this christological issue is the second issue: Is God's grace truly a gift, or do Christians in some form or another have to "do" something first in order to obtain God's grace? This latter is Pelagian, and has to be rejected. By the time that the Council of Trent addressed these issues, as far as justification, on the one hand, and the sacrament of penance, on the other, was concerned, a divided church had already and unfortunately been formed. The reformation churches had taken root, and the documents of Trent on justification and on the sacrament of penance were unable to rekindle a dialogue. These statements from Trent, as we shall see, remained just that: statements of the Roman church. Only in the twentieth century has the dialogue on these issues finally been established through the efforts of the current ecumenical discussion.

From the twelfth through the sixteenth centuries all these varying issues on justification had recurred again and again. Various answers had been proposed throughout this long stretch of time. Some of these answers emphasized one aspect, while other answers stressed different facets. However, there was an ongoing questioning, in a rather circular way, around justification. For the first time in Christian history, it should be noted, basic issues were beginning to be clearly presented, and even more importantly the interrelationships and implications were also being more clearly expressed. In this period of time, the interrelationships of justification and the sacrament of penance were sharply and probingly discussed. The implications of justification for a ritual of penance were beginning to be spelled out. Nonetheless, the practice of this sacramental ritual continued on, in many ways, undisturbed by this theological discussion. The reformation movements of the sixteenth century are, in many ways, a culmination of these discussions. Trent, too, must be seen as another culminating point of these same discussions. In the fifteenth and sixteenth century church, reform was clearly needed, both theologically and pastorally. It is, however, unfortunate that the reform movements, Protestant, Anglican and Tridentine, ended up in a divided church, which itself called for reform: a reform to bring back unity.

SUMMARY OF CHAPTER SEVEN

In this chapter we have seen:

1. The sacrament of penance, either theologically or pastorally, was not the central issue of the reformation critique. The central issue was the theology of justification. The theology of justification found expression in the sacrament of penance, and consequently the sacrament of penance became an issue of focus.

2. The main problem which the reformers brought against the sacrament of penance was not the question of its sacramentality. In many ways the Catholic response focused on the denial of sacramentality, rather than on the interrelationship of the theology of justification with the theology of penance.

3. For Luther the theological beginning of his critique lies in christology. The full efficacy of Jesus' salvific act must be uncondi-

tionally stated and maintained throughout any discussion on penance.

4. The second step for Luther is ecclesiology. The church, however, cannot be seen as adding anything to the work of Christ. Rather, the church is declaratory and revelatory of God's grace to us in and through Jesus.

5. Lutherans have maintained in many ways some form of ritualized penance, even though the ritual is not counted as one of the sacraments. This retention of the ritual, and the discussion of it in Lutheran literature, attests to the esteem which the Lutheran Church has for such a ritualized celebration of penance.

6. Faith, in Luther's works, is often called *fiducia,* since this word looks toward God. The Roman term for faith, *assensus,* is not used often, since it is human-centered. Indeed, the bishops at Trent did not face the Lutheran use of faith in a direct way; the bishops argued only on the basis of the Augustinian-scholastic view of *fides caritate formata.*

7. Calvin considered the pastoral practice of penance a development by the later church, and therefore not a sacrament. This practice of penance included in it many issues which compromised the full efficacy of Jesus' salvific act and the gratuity of God's grace.

8. Calvin did emphasize the ecclesial nature of penance and reconciliation, not however at the expense of the christological base. This ecclesial nature can be seen in Calvin's description of the process of reconciliation.

9. Doctrinally, Calvin takes up the issue of justification only in Book III of the *Institutes,* a lateness which some Lutherans criticized as depreciation of justification. In their view Calvin did not appear to make justification central enough to Christian faith.

10. The reformation in the English Church is quite different from the many reformations on the continent. Justification plays a role in this reformation, but the theology of the English reformation on this issue tends to be more Calvinist than Lutheran.

11. There is no doubt that the two issues—the full efficacy of Jesus' salvific act and the absolute gratuity of God's grace—played a major role in the theologies of the English reformers.

12. The reformation and the response from Trent gave rise to the need for a new reform: a reform of a divided Christianity. This new reform can take place only by a dialogue on the issue of justification.

8

Reconciliation and Justification at the Council of Trent

For the Roman Catholic Church the decisions made at the Council of Trent on the issues of justification and of the sacrament of penance have been and still are the official teaching of the church on this sacrament. In order to grasp both the intent of the statements themselves as also the implications these statements involve, this chapter will be organized around the following points:

1. The sacrament of penance in the ordinary life of a Christian in the late fifteenth and early sixteenth centuries.
2. Trent's discussion of the sacrament of penance.
3. The canons of Trent on the sacrament of penance.
4. General conclusion on the Tridentine doctrine.
5. The teaching of the Council of Trent on the theology of justification.

1. ORDINARY CHRISTIAN LIFE AND THE SACRAMENT OF PENANCE

In order to appreciate the pastoral situation regarding the sacrament of penance in the latter part of the fifteenth and the early part of the sixteenth century, let us consider some of the more salient aspects of confessional practice.

A. *Frequency of Confession.* In church documents of this period and in the ordinary preaching of clerics, the church's official teaching about annual confession (Lateran IV) was mentioned again and again. Nevertheless, numerous Christians did not receive the sacrament even yearly.

Particularly in the villages confession was severely neglected. In monasteries, however, the custom of confessing several times in a week continued to flourish. Except for this statement of Lateran IV there had been no clear guidelines issued by the official church on this matter of confession. As a result, both the over-use and the under-use of the sacrament co-existed.[1]

B. *Penitential Formalism.* There were the so-called "Holy Saturday" penitents in that era, just as there are today. One Franciscan preacher of that period castigated these "once-a-year" penitents as follows:

> How can you confess, you who have not confessed for a year? Now you come in Holy Week to a priest, praying that he dispatches you as quickly as possible! . . . And so the priest, who wants only quick action (for the confession itself) and money, takes care of you immediately. He gives you absolution and says to you: "Friend, go!" But where does one go with such an absolution? To all the devils and the man prepares a place for his confessor (with them).[2]

Moreover, many priests (and at the time of Trent there were too many priests) were professionally untrained to hear confessions, and as a result they simply "gave absolution." Untrained for the task of confessor, they had no ability to check circumstances, frequency, etc. In 1547 a document was given to the bishops assembled at Trent, describing the "worst plague among all the abuses of the church: namely, the fact that priests, without any consideration of their competence or moral life, heard confessions." This was seen as the source of many other abuses in the church and a source of grave scandal. These incompetent priests abused confessional secrecy, imposed penances of almsgiving which actually profited the priests themselves, rather than the poor, and engaged in immoral intimacies with women who came to be absolved.[3]

C. *Penitential Handbooks.* Throughout this period, many manuals for confessors had been developed. There was a mixed reaction to such manuals. They focused almost exclusively on the confessor, not on the penitent; they were often used by priests with a certain moral imperialism, which meant that the penitent had to follow the priest's instructions, no matter what he might have said. At Trent some of the bishops wanted the manuals of the Dominican, Antoninus, or that of Albert Castellan, to be officially adopted. Other bishops openly criticized all such manuals.[4]

D. *The Power of the Keys.* In case of reserved sins, there was much discussion on "who had the power" to forgive. The mendicant orders had received many confessional privileges, touching on reserved sins. At times, they exploited these privileges. One Gallic bishop at Trent mentioned that Franciscans in his area claimed that only they could truly hear confessions. Sins reserved to bishops or to the Holy See had become a complicated situation with, unfortunately, an involvement of money on occasion.

In practice, the sacrament of confession at the time of the reformation and the Council of Trent was pastorally in need of a radical reformation. Theological discussion on the sacrament of penance, with all of its diversity, stayed rather consistently within the academic world and did not affect the ordinary pastoral practice. On the other hand, liturgy, preaching and pamphlets, written in the vernacular and for the less educated, had tremendous influence. The Protestant reformation succeeded in great part because of these popular writings and preachings; the academic and the theological arguments continued on, long after Luther's and Calvin's deaths, often with little resolution other than an anathema. One can certainly show that liturgy, preaching, pamphlets for the common folk became a major channel of change.

2. TRENT'S DISCUSSION OF THE SACRAMENT OF PENANCE

In the sixth session, 1547, the Council of Trent took up, for the first time, the issue of the sacrament of penance. This was done during the bishops' discussion of the decree on justification. The fourteenth chapter of that decree dealt with those who sin after baptism and the means for their reconciliation to the church and to God. It was not, however, until 1551 that the bishops focused clearly on the sacrament of penance itself. From October 15 to November 25, 1551, the document on the sacrament of penance was deliberated, refined and promulgated.[5] The usual pattern for the bishops for such documentation had by then become standardized: (1) first, prepare a doctrinal statement, usually called today the "chapter"; (2) then prepare propositions or "canons," based on the doctrinal chapter. With the sacrament of penance the bishops spent almost the entire time on the propositions or canons; the chapter on the sacrament of penance, drawn up by a special commission, was first presented to the bishops on November 22, discussed on November 23, and voted in on November 25, a matter of only four days in all.[6] This indicates to us that the canons served as the major focus for the Tridentine bishops as regards their discussions on the sacrament of penance.

It is important to understand this historical background of these Tridentine texts, but it is equally important to consider the criteria for judging the value of these Tridentine texts. In contemporary theology, there has been considerable discussion on the theological value, technically called the *valor theologicus,* of the chapter but above all of the canons, not only those connected with the sacrament of penance, but all of the chapters and canons of Trent. The canons begin with the words: "If anyone shall say . . ." and conclude with the words of anathema: "anathema sit—let that person be anathema." Does this mean that if someone maintains the teaching expressed in the canon, he or she is *ipso facto* a heretic? Is the teaching there stated against God's own law (*de iure divino*) or merely against a church law (*de iure ecclesiastico*)? One realizes, of course, that whatever is from God's law, *de iure divino,* brooks no rebuttal, while whatever is only from the church's law, *de iure ecclesiastico,* has of itself no divine sanction. With this distinction of divine and ecclesiastical law, one can ask: With the anathemas do we have revealed truth or merely a disciplinary regulation of the church?

In 1929 J. Umberg, who was one of the editors of the *Enchiridion Symbolorum, Definitionum Declarationum* (commonly called *Denzinger*), compared the censures of Pius VI against the propositions of the Synod of Pistoia with the canons found in the decrees of Trent. Did the Synod of Pistoia, he asked, dissent from Trent, and, if so, were these instances of their dissent heretical? Umberg found two instances in which the Synod of Pistoia had clearly contradicted Trent, and in which Pius VI had concluded that such contradictions were heretical. However, he argued, what about the other one hundred and eighteen canons of Trent? Umberg pointed out that there were, indeed, other instances in which the Synod of Pistoia had contradicted Trent, but which Pius VI had not judged heretical.[7] Did this not mean the following, namely, that the mere fact that there was something contradictory to the canons of Trent in itself could not be considered an adequate basis for heresy?

Following this work of Umberg, H. Lennerz examined the canons of Trent and came to the conclusion that many of the canons must be interpreted as penalties, *latae sententiae.*[8] Lennerz states, however, that if one is going to deny a tradition of the church, one must first know what that tradition is, and if one has such knowledge and still denies the tradition, then there is an anathema because of the contempt (*pro eius contemptu*) not specifically because of the denial of the tradition. R. Favre continued this line of research on a number of the Tridentine canons. He found that *anathema sit* had several meanings even during the council. To prove his point he lists one canon after another.[9]

In turn, A. Lang reviewed the teaching of Melchior Cano, a major figure at the time of Trent, and concluded that *anathema sit,* by itself, cannot be taken to mean heresy. Lang argues that other factors, from other sources, must be present and operative before a condemnation of heresy is warranted.[10] H. Jedin, through his historical research on the Council of Trent, arrived at the same conclusion.[11] P. Fransen also researched the material and came to a similar conclusion. Faith and heresy have, in the documents of Trent, a meaning which is far more comprehensive than merely a divinely revealed truth (faith) or its denial (heresy).[12] Under "faith" Trent refers not only to items found in scripture, but also to items proposed for the universal church, including ecclesiastical laws. On this topic, Karl Peter states: "An anathema meant a major excommunication, as canonists have remembered better than theologians. Heresy, by the same token, involved disobedience to the religious leaders Christ left to guide us to salvation."[13]

On many occasions during the Council of Trent, the issue under consideration focused more on the rejection of church authority by the reformation theologians, rather than on an issue of heresy. At times it was this contempt for authority which was anathematized, rather than a specific theological position. In the following discussion, the mere recital of the canon, then, cannot be understood, of itself, as a statement of divinely revealed truth, on the one hand, and its denial, on the other hand, as an heretical position. In the analysis of each canon, an attempt will be made to state carefully the central issue or issues involved and to indicate which of these central issues are doctrinal and which are disciplinary.

If such a nuanced interpretation affects the Tridentine canons, an even wider berth must be accorded to the chapters. In the chapter on the sacrament of penance, which as we noted was not discussed at great length, the bishops intended to present only key points for the teaching and above all for the preaching on the sacrament of penance of their day. No effort was made by the bishops during the development of this chapter to sort out in an academic way theological opinion and defined doctrine. Rather, the bishops simply presented a general overview of the sacrament of penance, as it was to be practiced and preached for that particular period of time.

3. THE TRIDENTINE CANONS ON PENANCE

Both the doctrinal chapter and the canons regarding the sacrament of penance, promulgated at Trent, follow the same outline:

1. The necessity and the institution of the sacrament of penance.
2. The sacrament of penance differs from the sacrament of baptism.
3. The constitutive parts and effects of this sacrament.
4. Contrition.

5. Confession of sins.
6. The minister of the sacrament and absolution.
7. Reserved cases of sin.
8. The necessity of satisfaction.
9. Works of satisfaction.

Let us consider these issues by studying the canons or propositions, using the material in the chapter itself as additional background.

CANON 1: If anyone shall say that in the Catholic Church penance is not truly and properly a sacrament, instituted by Christ our Lord for reconciling the faithful to God as often as they fall into sin after baptism, a.s.

It is clear that the main focus of this canon was to reaffirm the sacramentality of penance. Luther and Calvin, as well as other reformation theologians, had limited the term "sacrament" to baptism and eucharist alone. The other five rituals, helpful though they might be to Christian life, were not, according to the reformation theologians, sacraments, since there was no clear scriptural proof that they had been instituted by Jesus himself. Rather, the reformation theologians maintained that the church itself in the course of history had instituted these additional five rituals, penance included. In this canon the Roman church officially affirms the sacramentality of penance, distinct from that of baptism.[14]

Certain issues are implied in this canon: if Jesus, not the church, instituted this sacrament of reconciliation, the sacrament is of divine right (*de iure divino*) and not merely of human origin (*de iure humano*). Our contemporary knowledge of the history of this sacrament indicates that Jesus nowhere specifically established such a rite, and that the various rituals of penance have come about through historical development. Calvin had stated in the *Institutes:* "I deny that it [penance] is rightly reckoned as a sacrament. First, because no special promise of God to this effect—the only basis of a sacrament—exists. Secondly, because every ceremony displayed here is a mere invention of men" (IV, 19, 17). Melanchthon had proposed something quite similar.[15]

When Luther and Calvin explained how such rituals arose in the church, both men engaged in a polemical and strongly-worded rejection of church authority. More than anything else, this ridiculing of church authority riled the bishops at Trent.

The scholastic theologians had maintained that penance was instituted as a sacrament in the classical gospel passages discussed in chapter one: Matthew 16:16; 18:18; John 20:22–23. This interpretation was not questioned by the Tridentine bishops. For all intensive and extensive purposes, then, the bishops felt (a) that Jesus had instituted this sacrament, and (b) that it was a genuine sacrament of the church, distinct from baptism.

Today, we would want to nuance and qualify both of these statements. The relationship of the gospel accounts to reconciliation in general, and to a ritual of reconciliation, has been explained in chapter two of this volume. That there is a power in the church to isolate, repel and negate sin is unquestioned. The development of a ritual of reconciliation, which in the twelfth century was technically called a sacrament, is but one expression of this power. The contemporary understanding of Jesus as the primordial sacrament and the church as a basic sacrament helps us to relate this ritual of reconciliation to Jesus, but even this contemporary approach does not allow us to claim that at a given historical time Jesus himself instituted a ritual of penance or reconciliation.

That the sacraments of both baptism and eucharist have a superior position in both the church's theology and practice of sacraments is also unquestioned. That the two rituals of baptism and eucharist should be called "sacrament" has remained, for the most part, unquestioned throughout the Christian tradition. That the other five rituals might be seen as "secondary sacraments" or "rituals of a second order" is a real possibility which contemporary theologians are presently considering.[16]

> **CANON 2: If anyone, confounding the sacraments, shall say that baptism is itself the sacrament of penance, as though these two sacraments were not distinct, and that penance is therefore not rightly called a second plank after shipwreck, a.s.**

In this canon the bishops focused on those particular statements of reformation theologians which claimed that at best the sacrament of reconciliation was simply a renewal of the sacrament of baptism. In the second section in the "chapter" of this document on penance a number of reasons are stated why these two sacraments are distinct: namely, (a) there are ritual differences; (b) baptism is administered once in a lifetime but penance is received many times; (c) priestly absolution has a juridical character, while baptism is not presented in this juridical way.

F. Cavallerra, in his analysis of these canons, notes that the three following issues, excerpted from the writings of Luther, Melanchthon and Calvin, had been specifically presented to the bishops:

a. Penance is not really a sacrament.
b. It is not called a second plank of salvation.
c. Baptism is the real sacrament of penance.[17]

Time and time again, the theologians and the bishops spoke against these three statements, calling them blasphemous, impious, and heretical. The proof for the sacramentality of penance was based on:

a. Scripture, particularly John 20:22–24; some, such as Lainez, Tapper and Gropper, also cited Matthew 16:16 and 18:18.[18]
b. Patristic sources, with citations from Tertullian, Hilary, Ambrose, Jerome, Augustine, Cyril of Alexandria, Leo I, Gregory the Great, and an account of the famous case of Nectarius of Constantinople.[19]
c. The Councils of Vienna, Constance and Florence, all of which had mentioned the sacrament of penance as distinct from the sacrament of baptism.[20]

The bishops at Trent with this array of tradition on the sacramentality of penance, considered any denial of such sacramentality to fly in the face of the church's long-standing position. The bishops were quite aware of Luther's and Calvin's position that the sacramentality of penance could not be found clearly in scripture; still, the patristic and conciliar material warranted, in their eyes, the *de iure divino* approach to the sacrament of penance.

It was precisely this authority from tradition which had been challenged by the reformers. The central point of these two initial canons, then, focuses much more on a matter of church authority than on a defined interpretation of some scriptural passages (Mt 16:16; 18:18; Jn 20:22–23). Moreover, the criticism of the reform theologians had been that there were Pelagian overtones both in the theological understanding of this sacrament of penance and in its practice. In the course of time, the practice of the church regarding the sacrament of penance, with its demand for contrition, confession, absolution and satisfaction, seemed to disparage the full efficacy of Jesus' salvific activity, and also seemed to present a Pelagian approach to the grace of Christ which alone offers forgiveness of sin. These precise issues were not addressed in either of these initial canons, since in the mind of the Tridentine bishops the decree on justification had already been promulgated and had treated these points. Rather, the bishops, realizing that the post-baptismal ritual of penance was rooted in the early patristic church and had perdured throughout the centuries, felt that such a traditional ritual could not in essence, therefore, be Pelagian. Heretical elements, they argued, never lasted long in church history. The protest of the reformation theologians was, as a result, interpreted as a protest against the very meaning of the church's sacred tradition, as well as against the authority of traditional church leadership to regulate such a ritual. To deny the sacramentality of penance did not mean, then, that one must find in scripture a clear institution of penance by Jesus himself. Rather, the denial of the sacramentality of penance meant, according to the Tridentine bishops, a denial of a long-standing and therefore orthodox tradition of the true church.

That there is a relationship between the sacrament of baptism, on the one hand, and the sacrament of penance, on the other, cannot be denied. Indeed, the Tridentine bishops openly admit this.[21] This indicates to us today that the sacrament of penance makes no sense if it is theologically and liturgically interpreted in a non-baptismal way. The patristic church, with its public penance, clearly related penance to baptism. Indeed, many fathers of the church throughout the first three centuries had used Matthew 16:16 and 18:18 or John 20:22–23 in connection with baptism. This relationship to baptism is the very reason why some of the patristic writers had referred to reconciliation as the "second plank" of salvation. There could hardly be a "second" plank if there had not been a "first" plank. Only when one's baptismal life has become seriously distorted did the *ordo paenitentiae* of the patristic church make any sense. Both the Tridentine bishops and the reformation theologians concur on this point: there is, both theologically and pastorally, a necessary connection between baptism and penance. The *way* in which these two elements of the Christian life are connected was indeed disputed.[22]

What, then, is at stake in this canon? What fundamental truth of the Christian faith undergirds these words? At stake, it seems to me, is a christological focus, namely the extent of Christ's forgiving grace. To deny that Christ's forgiveness extends even to those who, after baptism, have fallen in a most serious way from their life in Jesus, which, they have pledged, would indeed be contrary to the very message of Jesus. The power to isolate, repel and negate sin extends even to post-baptismal sin. God's forgiveness, and therefore the church's forgiveness which is the sacrament of God's own forgiveness, must be seen as seventy-times-seventy-times-seventy-times seven. Even a post-baptismal serious sin does not outrun the mercy of God's love. The metaphor of a shipwreck with its image of a second plank is purely secondary. Luther indeed has a valid point: if one ever says that one's baptism has become shipwreck, then what kind of faith can we have in baptism itself? To describe baptism in such a way that baptism might be something which falls apart is poor theology. The bishops at Trent were not defending the phrase "second plank" as though it were *de iure divino*. Nonetheless, the rejection of this hallowed phrase, in their view, seemed to be a rejection of church tradition and church authority.

Summary of Canons 1 and 2: Given all the nuancing that needs to be made, because of biblical and historical data, we could say that the solemn teaching of these two canons can be summed up as follows:

a. Jesus is the source of all reconciliation of sin. The sacrament of penance has its meaning for reconciliation only in virtue of its relationship to Jesus, the single source of all reconciliation (i.e. institution by Jesus).

b. Penance is a sacrament of the Christian church, but it is not a sacrament of the same rank as that of baptism and eucharist. How this ranking is to be understood is still a matter of theological discussion.

c. There is an essential relationship between baptism and penance. The two should not be identified, but neither should they be so separated that theologically and pastorally they become independent of each other. Theologians are still clarifying this interrelationship.

CANON 3: If anyone shall say that those words of the Lord Saviour, "Receive ye the Holy Ghost, whose sins you shall forgive, they are forgiven, and whose sins you shall retain, they are retained" (Jn. 20:22–23), are not to be understood as applying to the power of forgiving and retaining sin in the sacrament of penance, as the Catholic Church has always understood them from the beginning, but distorts them, contrary to the institution of this sacrament, as applying to the authority of preaching the gospel, a.s.

In this canon, with its corresponding chapter, the bishops focus once more on a statement made on many occasions by the reformation theologians, namely, that the power to forgive sins resides in the power of preaching. In itself, this is incontrovertible. In preaching, God's own word comes into the heart of the faithful, and this word is a word of reconciliation and forgiveness. The power to forgive and retain sin, the power, therefore, to isolate, repel and negate sin, is exercised in every aspect of Christian life, and in a most special way this power is active in the preaching of God's word, not because of the preaching itself, but because of the presence of God's word in and through the preaching.

The difficulty arose when this preaching of God's word seemed to be presented as the *primary locus* in which such power to forgive and retain sin was to be found, coupled with the denial that such power was to be found in the ritual of reconciliation. It was precisely the denial of any gospel effectiveness in the sacrament of reconciliation which occasioned this solemn statement. The bishops were reaffirming officially that in the sacrament of reconciliation there is indeed forgiveness of sin.

It is evident, however, that the Tridentine bishops' scriptural interpretation needs to be reinterpreted. As we saw in chapter two, with these words of the New Testament there is no "proof" of an immediate and direct institution of the sacrament of penance by Jesus himself. John 20:22–24, neither textually nor contextually, allows such an interpretation. The focus of this canon, therefore, cannot be centered on some "historical fact" regarding the institution of the sacrament of penance. Rather, the focus is both a negative one: the power to forgive sins, which Jesus exercises through the church, cannot be restricted to preaching; and a positive one: this power of Jesus is operative, though not exclusively, in the sacrament of reconciliation, a ritual which enjoys a long tradition in the church.

> **CANON 4: If anyone shall deny that for the full and perfect remission of sins, three acts are required of the penitent, constituting as it were the matter of the sacrament of penance, namely, contrition, confession, and satisfaction, which are called the three parts of penance, or shall say that there are only two parts of penance, namely the terrors of a smitten conscience, convinced of sin, and the faith received from the gospel or from absolution by which one believes that one's sins are forgiven through Christ, a.s.**

In this canon, the bishops take up the theological presentation of the so-called "acts of the penitent." This systematic way of theologically presenting the sacrament of penance had only begun in the twelfth century, but over the subsequent decades it had become rather standard in all the theological and canonical schools of thought. Since the terms contrition, confession and satisfaction are not biblical terms, their validity had been contested by the reformation theologians.

The discussion on these "acts of the penitent" once again raises some of the fundamental issues, which go far beyond the sacrament of penance. The sacrament of penance itself, however, is only one instance among many in which such issues emerge. The basic issues raised here are those which were fundamental to the entire reformation critique: namely, the full efficacy of Jesus' salvific activity and the absolute gratuity of God's grace. At the time of the reformation and of Trent, there were indeed preachers who explained the three acts of contrition, confession and satisfaction as "good works" which contributed to the forgiveness of sin. In the *Institutes* (III, 4, 2–3) Calvin had argued that no matter how deep one's contrition, how precise one's confession of sins, how intense one's satisfaction, these all remain human actions, and as such cannot establish with any certainty the forgiveness of sin. One can always ask: Was my contrition adequate? Was my confession of sins all inclusive? Was my satisfaction enough? None of these, Calvin argued, is the basis for real forgiveness; rather, the basis is the merciful grace of God which alone causes forgiveness of sin and is, therefore, the surety of our good standing before God. Not what we do, but what God does, is paramount. Because of this, both Luther and Calvin argued that the human person must first realize that he or she is indeed a sinner, and second, believe in God's merciful grace which has been revealed to us in Christ. It is evident that the argument of the reformers was against any Pelagian approach to the "acts of the penitent": contrition, confession, and satisfaction.

Moreover, at the time of the reformation and of Trent, there were a number of theological positions regarding contrition, confession and satisfaction. There was no official church teaching on these matters. The Franciscans and the Dominicans, in particular, presented two differing interpretations. The *via moderna* school had also contributed a variety of views. Likewise, the question of the role of faith in the conversion process was an essential part of the theological discussion of that time, if not the essential issue. Cajetan, in his debate with Luther on this point of faith, went far beyond the thought of his mentor, Thomas Aquinas, for in this debate Cajetan had presented many of his own personal stances on the issue of faith and sacraments. During the Council of Trent there were even theologians and bishops who agreed basically with Luther's own stance on the role of faith in the sacraments.[23]

The addition of the phrase, "constituting as it were the matter of the sacrament of penance," is evidence of the argument between the Franciscan and the Dominican schools. Since the acts of the council clearly show that the bishops in no way wished to settle the issues separating these two schools of theological thought, the insertion of "as it were" allows both a Thomistic and a Scotistic approach, that is, these words leave open the question whether the three acts are in some way the "matter" or merely "conditions" in the sacrament of penance.[24] Both opinions are still viable within solid Catholic teaching; no solution has as yet been reached.

The Tridentine bishops in no way wanted to teach that contrition, confession and satisfaction could be theologically described in terms which detract from the once-and-for-all sacrifice of Jesus nor in terms which detract from the absolute gratuity of God's grace. This canon, therefore, must be interpreted in the light of the Tridentine statements on justification and the eucharist, which had already been promulgated and had clearly maintained both of these theological points. In the decree on justification, God is presented as the sole efficient cause of justification, thereby officially excluding all Pelagianism or semi-Pelagianism. It would have been very helpful, however, if the bishops had in this present canon pointedly addressed these two basic issues with reference to the decree on justification. Since the matter had been addressed previously, however, they did not wish to reopen the question. As a result the focus of the canon appears to be narrowly centered on those who denied validity to the acts of contrition, confession and satisfaction, but the canon does not focus on the reasons for such a denial.

Given the decree on justification, one must say that this canon inculcates the following:

> Only those theological ways which explain contrition, confession and satisfaction, and which simultaneously maintain the full efficacy of Jesus' salvific action and the full gratuity of God's grace, are acceptable within the Christian church.

The bishops in this canon maintain that there clearly does exist a way of theologically presenting contrition, confession and satisfaction which in no way contradicts either of those two fundamental issues. Therefore the point of the canon seems to include as well:

> To deny that there is or can be such a valid explanation of contrition, confession and satisfaction would be against the long-standing teaching of the Christian church.

The reformation theologians had rightfully pointed out that these three terms, contrition, confession, and satisfaction, were not biblical terms. A conscience, keenly aware of sin and faith, was, however, quite scriptural. For instance, Psalm 41:4: "Lord, have mercy on me, help my soul, for I have sinned against you." Or Psalm 51:2: "Oh wash me more and more from my guilt and cleanse me from my sin." Or John 8:11: "Go and sin no more; your faith has healed you." These, and many others like them, are scriptural terms, and as such have a canonical status. The more technical terms, contrition, confession and satisfaction, derive only from academic and theological discussion. Because of this, the reformation theologians considered them suspect, but the bishops at Trent indicated that if the terms "contrition, confession and satisfaction" were theologically interpreted in a way that accords with scripture, then the use of such terms is valid. In this sense, and only in this sense, to deny the validity of contrition, confession and satisfaction would be tantamount to denying the validity of scriptural passages as well.

> **CANON 5: If anyone shall say that contrition which is evoked by examination, recollection and hatred of sins, whereby a person recounts his years in the bitterness of his soul, by reflecting on the grievousness, the multitude and the baseness of his sins, the loss of eternal happiness and the incurring of eternal damnation, with a purpose of amendment, is not a true and beneficial sorrow, does not prepare for grace, but makes a man a hypocrite and a greater sinner or finally that this sorrow is forced and not free and voluntary, a.s.**

Canon five addresses in a more detailed way the issue of contrition, and in doing so makes even more specific the two fundamental issues which underlie the whole discussion on the sacrament of penance. From the time of Peter Abelard, the issue of contrition had been highly controversial among theologians. The connection of contrition and the sacrament of penance had been debated throughout the late medieval period, and not always in a satisfactory way. Through contrition, one clearly reflects on the evil of sin, both in its offensiveness against God and in its implications for human life. In sin, then, there is both offense and guilt. If one believes, however, that one must "do" something on one's own power in order to gain forgiveness, one is indeed Pelagian. Chapter one of the *Decree on Justification* states clearly that all men and women are unable to be freed from sin by their own will. Chapters two and three of that same decree state that it is through Christ alone that the grace of forgiveness has been given to all men and women. Chapter five declares that "the beginning of that justification must proceed from the predisposing grace of God through Jesus Christ, that is, from His vocation, whereby, without any merits on their part, they are called." In this decree on justification, then, the bishops clearly state that only God's grace is the cause for the forgiveness of sin. Of itself, contrition does nothing; even the turning to God in sorrow for sin must be understood theologically as an effect of God's grace.

Contrition, then, is part of the process of justification. The very act of contrition is possible only by a predisposing grace, which comes to us without any merits of our own. Chapter four of the *Decree on Justification* notes that adults are "disposed to that justice when, aroused and aided by divine grace, receiving faith by hearing, they are moved freely toward God, believing to be true what has been divinely revealed and promised, especially that the sinner is justified by God by his grace, through the redemption that is in Christ Jesus."

In these passages from the *Decree on Justification* we see that the contrition, mentioned in canon five in the *Decree on the Sacrament of Penance,* can come only from God's prevenient grace and that justification is effected not by human contrition but by God himself. Contrition must be explained in a way which preserves this absolute gratuity of God's grace. Moreover, the *Decree on Justification* clearly states that it is through faith by hearing that one attains such justification (c. 6). The church, therefore, cannot demand a contrition contrary to this; if the church were to make such a demand, then clearly the sorrow for sin would neither be free nor voluntary, and the church would be making a hypocrite out of the sinner.

The meaning of this canon as well as its corresponding chapter (c. 4), then, can only be understood against the declarations of the *Decree on Justification.* By itself, the interpretation of this canon, therefore, is not self-evident. Moreover, the discussion in the chapter itself on contrition and attrition, as also on the relationship of both contrition and attrition to sacramental absolution, can only be seen as a presentation on contrition, drawn up in very general terms. One must also keep in mind that the bishops had no intention of settling the theological discussions between the Thomists and the Scotists. This means, as a consequence, that the chapter and canon (a) by not reiterating or even deliberately referring to the material from the *Decree on Justification* and (b) by not taking sides as regards the legitimate disputes in the various schools, retains a certain ambiguity about it. It is not a self-evident canon.

> **CANON 6: If anyone shall deny that sacramental confession was instituted by divine law or is necessary for salvation; or shall say that the manner of confessing secretly to a priest alone, which the Catholic Church has always observed from the beginning and still observes, is at variance with the institution and command of Christ and is a human contrivance, a.s.**

The second "act" of the penitent is treated in this canon: confession of sins. The key to this canon's interpretation are the final two words: "human contrivance." These two words refer back to the first part of the canon which says: "instituted by divine law." Whatever is of divine law is not merely a human arrangement. God's action and God's power stand behind those issues which are *de iure divino.* Some reformation theologians had indeed said that the sacramental confession of sins was a contrivance of church people, and a Pelagian one at that. Because of this, their argument went on, the power of Jesus had been removed from such a ritual of confessing sins.

The bishops wanted to stress that the sacrament of penance, and particularly the confession of sins, was not some human arrangement. However, given the history of this sacrament of penance, it is clear that over the centuries there have indeed been arrangements for confessing sins, which are not *de iure divino* but merely *de iure ecclesiastico.* Secret confession to a priest alone is not a form of this sacrament which goes back to the very beginning of the church. In the early patristic church, we realize, presbyters (priests) were not the leaders of the ritual of reconciliation; the episkopoi were. Moreover, the penance ritual was a public ritual, not a secret one.

It is clear that the intent of this canon cannot be understood as defining some "historical situation." The bishops and theologians at Trent, as well as the reformation theologians, had only vague ideas about the history of this ritual in patristic times. What the bishops at Trent did know well was the decree from Lateran IV on private confession to a priest at least once a year, if there were serious sin involved. In this canon, then, the bishops are simply reaffirming Lateran IV as the discipline of the church. Consequently, one cannot read into this canon that the secret confession of sins to a priest is the only way in which reconciliation can be celebrated. Secret confession of sin is simply one way to celebrate the sacrament. Whether it is pastorally the better way remains an open question. Adnès in his volume on the sacrament of penance indicates that confessing one's sinfulness is of divine mandate; the modality of such a confession has been established by church authority and practice.[25] Unless someone admits that he or she is truly a sinner, forgiveness of sin remains meaningless.

One must also take into account the various formulae used by the eastern churches as regards the ritual of reconciliation. In some of them, there is a formal admittance to the commandments or to sins generally, without any detail. A study of penance rituals in the Syriac, Alexandrian, Byzantine, and Russian liturgies evidences a wide variety in this matter of confession of sin, and most of these ways of confessing sin are not auricular or detailed confession to a priest.[26] This very practice and theology of the eastern churches, which is firmly rooted in the patristic period, also militates against the divine institution of secret confession of sin to a priest.

CANON 7: If anyone shall say that in the sacrament of penance it is not required by divine law for the remission of sins to confess each and all mortal sins which are recalled after a due and

diligent examination, also secret ones and those that are a violation of the last two commandments of the Decalogue, as also circumstances that change the nature of a sin, but that this confession is useful only to instruct and console the penitent and in olden times was observed only in order to impose a canonical satisfaction, or shall say that they who strive to confess all sins want to leave nothing to the divine mercy to pardon; or finally that it is not permitted to confess venial sins, a.s.

This canon continues the presentation on "confession of sins" and includes a wide variety of items: (a) confession of serious sin in detail as regards species, number and circumstance; (b) confession merely as a canonical satisfaction; (c) the confession of venial sins.

Confession of sins in detail was challenged by the reformation theologians on two counts: the first was pastoral, since it is nearly impossible for some to recall each and every "mortal" sin. One should remember that yearly confession was enjoined but by no means the actual practice. Intervals of time longer than a year were more frequent than even an annual confession. Painstaking searches of conscience to recall each and every mortal sin could end in anxious consciences.

Secondly there were theoretical questions: not without good reason did Luther, for instance, emphasize that every person is both justified and sinful, *simul iustus et peccator.* There is an acceptable Roman Catholic approach to this phrase, as Karl Rahner has pointed out.[27] If the forgiveness of sin depended on an accurate confession of each and every sin, then where, Luther asked, is the mercy of God? Where is God's grace? Once more the spectre of Pelagianism raises its head. If the confession of sin is so explained, either as part of the quasi-matter or as the condition for the sacrament of penance, so that without it God cannot forgive sin, then grace ceases to be grace. It is no longer a gift but something earned. No matter how hard one tries to recall and confess all sins, a Christian is truly unable to account for each and every sin. Each Christian remains a sinner. Therefore, it is not the ability to recount all sins which causes the forgiveness of sin, but rather the grace of God which one, in faith, sees as the only source of forgiveness.

Moreover, nowhere in the New Testament is there a command of Jesus to "confess each and every mortal sin." The canon, however, seems to state that this is required by divine law. If such a required confession cannot be found in the New Testament, then on what basis can the law be called "divine"? The answer to this question is complex. One must even begin with the meaning of "mortal" and "venial" sin, which in contemporary Roman Catholic theology has become a matter of some dispute.[28]

It is clear from the scriptures that a sinner must acknowledge his or her sinfulness. For instance, God does not allow Adam, in the Genesis account (3:8–13), to make some sort of excuse: "I was afraid because I was naked, so I hid" and "It was the woman . . . she gave me the fruit." In the case of Cain, God would not allow the rationalization: "Am I my brother's keeper?" The intrigues of David to hide over his sin with Bathsheba are disallowed by God through his prophet Nathan (2 Sam 11:12). The fraud of Ananias and Sapphira (Acts 5:1ff) must be acknowledged for what it truly is. Again and again throughout the Old and New Testaments there are instances in which the sinful person is held accountable. Denial of one's wrongdoing is disallowed. In this sense, one can say that "confession of sin" is *de iure divino.* The same holds true in the matter of reconciliation. Each and every Christian must act like the tax collector who goes to the temple to pray, and not like the Pharisee. The former confessed his sinfulness: "God, be merciful to me a sinner." The latter confessed no sins, but only the "good things" that he had done. The scriptures clearly tell us (*de iure divino*) that we cannot disclaim our sinfulness; we must confess ourselves to be sinners and unworthy of God's mercy and love. Divine law obliges us to be truthful in our appraisal of ourselves. We are not to gloss over times that we knowingly committed some sin. We are not to cover up the type of sins we commit. We are not to rationalize our way out of our own wrongdoing. This honesty and truthfulness before God, ourselves and our neighbor is clearly *de iure divino.*

Likewise, the confession of venial sins is certainly not central to the sacrament of penance. Such sins are forgiven through many other ways; the most important of these other ways is, of course, the eucharist. There is also prayer, fasting, almsgiving, and almost all works of the spiritual life. Any undue focusing of the sacrament of penance on the forgiveness of venial sins can only trivialize the very meaning of this ritual of reconciliation.

Perhaps we might say that this canon teaches:

a. Confession of venial sin is not a reprehensible practice, but neither theologically nor liturgically can it be seen as central to the sacrament of penance.
b. The sacrament of penance is meant to be more than a privileged moment of spiritual guidance.
c. The sacrament of penance is not simply an occasion to impose a canonical penance. This can be done outside the sacramental rite.
d. The core of this canon then is this: the theological and liturgical center for an understanding of the sacrament of penance can only

be found in (1) the sinful situation of a Christian who has seriously and substantively broken with his or her baptismal-eucharistic life, a break both with God and with the church; and (2) the
gratuitous mercy of God to all sinners which heals that break; and
(3) the willingness on the part of the Christian community to
make evident the seventy-times-seven forgiveness of Jesus within
its own attempt to follow the gospel.

e. Such sinful Christians must acknowledge: (1) their serious and
substantive break from the gospel life which they had promised;
(2) their faith in the limitless mercy of God's forgiving love.

Reconciliation is a two-way street. After baptism a Christian, who
has substantively broken with the Christian life, but again wants to rejoin
the Christian community and strive once more to lead a full gospel life,
cannot accomplish this reunion by a simple "return." The church or the
Christian community plays a role in this return of the sinner. The community must itself acknowledge that the sinner is repentant enough to
resume Christian life, or, more accurately stated, the Christian community must say something about itself, namely, that the community itself
wants to reflect the forgiving love of Jesus in the way it deals with this
sinful member. Confession of sin within an ecclesial setting is not merely
a case of an individual penitent Christian confessing his or her sins, but it
is also a case of a penitent, forgiving, Christian community trying to live
up to God's own command to forgive seventy times seven times. In this
approach, the canon from Trent makes solid theological sense. When
there is indeed a breakdown between an individual Christian and the
community, then (1) a full acknowledgement of one's anti-gospel behavior is requisite, and (2) the forgiveness of the community in some official
way is equally requisite so as to make manifest the community's own
reflection of the forgiving Jesus.[29]

> **CANON 8: If anyone shall say that the confession of all sins as it is
> observed in the Church is impossible and is a human tradition to be
> abolished by pious people; or that each and all of the faithful of
> Christ of either sex are not bound thereto once a year in accordance
> with the constitution of the great Lateran Council, and for this reason
> the faithful of Christ are to be persuaded not to confess during
> Lent, a.s.**

In this canon, which continues the presentation on confession of
sins, we see that the main issue is respect for church authority. There had
been a belittling of this authority, particularly as it affected the sacrament

of penance, and the bishops were quick to reaffirm the authority of the hierarchy, particularly its manifestation at the Lateran Council. This canon, then, does not focus so much on the sacrament of penance per se but rather on the issue of the magisterium. The discipline, mandated by Lateran IV, is to be respected and maintained.

In the analysis of the Tridentine canons on penance, which Ramos-Regidor presents, he spends considerably more time on the three canons concerning the confession of sins (canons 6, 7 and 8) than he does on any of the other canons. Evidently these canons have engendered more discussion on their precise interpretation than the others. Ramos-Regidor appends a series of hermeneutical observations on the issues involved.[30] The first of these hermeneutical observations deals with the concept of mortal and venial sin at the time of Trent and the various ways in which scholars have been interpreting this (Gründel, Alszeghy, Meier). The second observation deals with the question of the juridical aspect of confession, and he cites K. Rahner and P. Charles on the matter. Lastly, he takes up the issue of an "integral confession," with a long list of authors: Alszeghy, Corrigan, Eppacher, Heggen, McCormick, Peter, Vorgrimler, Curran, K. Rahner, Neumann. It is evident that there is not an accord among theologians and moralists on this issue. It is equally evident that the position taken by Trent on this matter is not clear-cut either.

We are indebted to Braeckmans and Arendt for detailed studies on the issue of individual confession as understood at the Council of Trent. Both authors provide us with important background and analysis. On many occasions, during the Tridentine sessions, reference was made to the *Omnis utriusque* decree of Lateran IV (1215). The promulgation of this decree was the first time in which the church expressed such a universal law. The bishops, abbots and lay people who were the "council fathers" at Lateran IV offered no theological justification for this law of annual confession and annual communion. Nor is it clear if there is any intrinsic connection between the law regarding annual confession and the law regarding annual communion. When the Tridentine bishops refer to *Omnis utriusque,* they, too, do not offer theological reasons for such legislation. The appeal is simply an appeal to church authority. The question naturally arises: On what basis does the church hierarchy legislate an annual confession and in a private manner, as also an annual communion? The basis can be, of course, church authority, but if this is the case, then we are dealing with situations which are *iure ecclesiastico.* Such situations can be changed by later church authorities. Is there, on the other hand, something which touches on *iure divino?* Is there, in this legislation, anything which cannot be changed? Recent theological discussion, as evidenced in the two authors mentioned above, indicate that there is to some degree room for change.

CANON 9: If anyone shall say that the priest's sacramental absolution is not a judicial act, but the mere ministry of pronouncing and declaring that sins are forgiven the one who confesses, so long as he believes that he has been absolved and this even though the priest does not absolve seriously but in jest; or shall say that confession is not required of the penitent that the priest may absolve him: a.s.

This canon takes up the minister of the sacrament of penance and the issue of absolution. Reference to the corresponding chapter (n. six) should be made in interpreting this canon. In the chapter, but not in the canon, the meaning of Matthew 18:18 and John 20:23 is referred to. Both Luther's discussion of this matter in the *Babylonian Captivity*[31] and Calvin's discussion in the *Institutes*[32] serve as specific background for this particular canon. The bishops at Trent wished to state two things: (a) absolution is not simply a declaratory act; (b) a priest who absolves only in jest effects nothing.

To say that absolution is merely a declaratory act of sins already forgiven would make absolution a rather unnecessary part of the penitential ritual. The Dominican and the Franciscan schools, however, differed on the matter of the way in which absolution was effective in the sacrament of penance, and this dispute was not resolved by Trent. The positions of both these schools remain acceptable even today. Neither school, however, maintained that the absolution of the priest was merely declaratory, for such a view seemed to emasculate the very sacramentality of penance. By maintaining a more integral role for absolution in the process of reconciliation, without, however, advocating either the Dominican or Franciscan approach, the Tridentine bishops wanted to uphold the full sacramentality of this ritual. This appears to be the main thrust of this canon: a defense of the full sacramentality of the sacrament of penance in all its parts, including the absolution by a priest.

Secondly, the matter of "jest" is brought forward. This is but a corollary of the above. If absolution is central, in some way, to the penitential process, then if it were done simply in jest, the entire sacramentality of the ritual would be rendered void. The wording we find in the respective chapter is very circumspect in the way in which it describes this issue: "While it is true that the priest's absolution confers a benefit that is not his own, yet it does not consist solely in the ministry of announcing the Gospel or of declaring that sins have been forgiven." The Latin of the first section is: "Quamvis autem absolutio sacerdotis alieni beneficii sit dispensatio ..." This phrasing deftly avoids the term "cause" or even "confer," which is precisely the focal point of the Dominican-Franciscan difference. The second part says that absolution does actually announce the gospel, but "non solum," i.e. it does announce the gospel, but this is not its only signification. Absolution does declare the remission of sin, but again "non solum." The wording indicates that both Luther and Calvin are correct in stating that absolution does announce the gospel and declare forgiveness. However, the bishops state that besides this there is something more. This "something more" has, in the period after Trent, played a major role in the Catholic interpretation of penance. To understand this, the Latin is helpful: "Sed ad instar actus iudicialis, quo ab ipso velut a iudice sententia pronuntiatur." ("Rather, the absolution is like a judicial act in which the priest himself passes sentence as a judge.") Absolution, in this context, is not said to be a judicial act, but rather "like" a judicial act: *ad instar* and *velut a iudice sententia pronuntiatur.* The bishops, in this chapter, make a comparison and use metaphorical language. On the other hand, in the corresponding canon, the metaphorical language has disappeared: "If someone shall say that the sacramental absolution of a priest is not a judicial act . . ." The chapter and the canon, linguistically, differ. Since Trent there has been an intense argument among theologians and canonists on this matter: Is absolution only analogous to a judicial act or is it actually a judicial act? Is it comparable to a judge's decision or is it more an act of one who dispenses privileges? Catholic authors to date have not and do not agree on the correct interpretation.[33]

F. Gil de las Heras states that the issue was not presented at Trent in the same way theologians and canonists present it today. At the time of Trent, the Protestants, he writes, "had come to deny the judicial character [of absolution] understood in a broad sense, equivalent to our administrative act."[34] The bishops at Trent, he argues, affirm that absolution is an administrative act of the church. Ramos-Regidor notes that the *ad instar* and *velut* were added rather late to the definitive text precisely to emphasize the analogical meaning of the juridical terms. Consequently, he maintains that there is only an analogical interpretation of absolution on the one hand and the juridical language on the other. He cites three reasons for this stance. (a) First of all, the church itself can only be analogically called juridical, so that any and all jurisdiction in the church must be considered only analogically juridical in comparison with human law. (b) Second, the power to forgive sin comes to a priest through ordination, and the ordaining prelate in no way delegates sacramental power. Sacramental power is given *vi sacramenti,* not *vi delegationis.* (c)

Third, one must take into account the difference between a juridical act in the social order and any action in the sacramental order.[35]

All of this means that one today could maintain that absolution is a clear judicial act, but such a position would be merely a theological opinion, not an official church interpretation. One could also maintain that absolution is not a judicial act but only analogously called a judicial act, and this too would be correct, but again merely as a theological opinion. There are still other authors, such as Morsdorf and Ternus, who have advocated a biblical interpretation of this "juridical" aspect of absolution. None of these opinions has been officially rejected nor officially adopted by the church. Whenever, then, one finds a heavy emphasis by some author or preacher on the juridical aspect of absolution, one should be cautious. The precise Tridentine meaning of "judicial" when applied to absolution remains open to several acceptable interpretations.

> **CANON 10: If anyone shall say that priests who are in mortal sin have not the power of binding and of loosing; or that priests are not the sole ministers of absolution, but that to each and everyone of Christ's faithful it was said: "Whatever you shall bind on earth, shall be bound also in heaven, whatever you shall loose on earth, shall be loosed also in heaven" (Mt. 18, 18); and "Whose sins you shall forgive, they are forgiven them, and whose sins you shall retain, they are retained" (Jn. 20, 23); and that in virtue of these words anyone can absolve from sins, from public sins by correction alone, if the one corrected shall submit, but from secret sins by voluntary confession, a.s.**

Several items are gathered together in this canon, which continues the discussion on absolution:

(a) Sinful priests still celebrate the sacrament of penance validly. This discussion on the spiritual integrity of the minister goes back to the early patristic times, particularly in the question of rebaptism and reordination. The bishops had no intention of reopening these questions; these questions had already been decided, in their judgment, by church authority. Neither baptism nor ordination, for its efficacy, depended on the spiritual integrity of the minister. So, too, penance did not depend, for its efficacy, on the spiritual integrity of the minister. From an ecumenical standpoint this is an important point: absolution is not seen as a "good work" performed by a minister which effects God's grace. The efficacy of absolution—however this might be described theologically—does not depend on the minister's spiritual integrity, but solely upon God's grace, which acts independently from the minister.

(b) Enough has been said about the classical New Testament passages to indicate that there is no official interpretation given to them. That these passages do refer to all Christians is the common teaching of contemporary biblical scholars as we have seen above. That all Christians can be seen as active in the ritual of reconciliation, which developed after New Testament times, is equally valid. Exclusivity, that is, a reference only to hierarchical figures, cuts against a valid interpretation of these classical New Testament passages.

(c) That priests (the Latin reads: *sacerdotes*) alone are the ministers of this sacrament also needs nuancing, because of the history of the sacrament of orders. In the early patristic church it was the episkopos, not the presbyter nor the deacon, who presided over the ritual of reconciliation. Only after 400 do we find more generally presbyters presiding over the ritual of reconciliation. In the Carolingian reformation (751–1000) the theological position came about that only priests can forgive sins, whether in this sacrament of reconciliation, or in the sacrament of anointing of the sick. However, even during this same period, deacons occasionally heard confessions at times, as also did lay people. The reformation theologians had downplayed the role of the priest in the process of reconciliation. The bishops at Trent took a strong stance against the involvement of deacons, and lay people in the process of reconciliation; and opposed the virtual negation of priestly (and therefore church) authority in the process of reconciliation.

CANON 11: If anyone shall say that bishops have no right to reserve cases to themselves, unless they pertain to the external government, and that as a result the fact that cases are reserved does not prevent a priest from truly absolving from reserved sins, a.s.

The challenge from the reformation theologians, as regards reserved sins, had been this: On what New Testament authority do bishops claim the right to reserve certain sins to themselves for absolution? Is such reservation simply a matter of church discipline affecting external factors (the external forum) and not the forgiveness of sin itself? If priests (*sacerdotes*) can forgive sin in virtue of their ordination, how can a bishop deny such a power or restrict such a power, which does not come from them by way of delegation but comes from the Lord himself by way of ordination?

At the beginning of this chapter we saw that reservation of certain sins, juridically speaking, was something which began to occur in the early middle ages. We also saw that there had been abuses on this matter by bishops themselves and by priests, in particular the mendicant order priests, since at times the removal of reserved sins involved the payment of money. Without any doubt, then, a reform of the entire issue of "reserved sins" was needed at the time of Trent. The reformation theologians had also considered the abuses of that time, and in their judgment they advocated a complete rejection of episcopal and papal power to reserve sins. Bishops and popes could reserve cases involving the external forum, but not the internal forum. Such reservations of sin was, in the judgment of Luther, simply another case of the "Babylonian captivity" of the gospel.

The focus of the canon is clearly a defense of church authority, rather than a defense of some particular heretical position.

> **CANON 12: If anyone shall say that God always remits the entire punishment along with the guilt of sin, and that the penitent's satisfaction is nothing, that faith whereby they come to realize that Christ has satisfied for them, a.s.**

> **CANON 13: If anyone shall say that satisfaction for the temporal punishment due to sin is in no way made to God through the merits of Christ, by punishments which God inflicts, or by those enjoined by the priest, or those voluntarily undertaken, such as fastings, prayers, almsgiving or other works of piety, and that as a result the best penance is simply a new life, a.s.**

> **CANON 14: If anyone shall say that the penitent's works of satisfaction, whereby they redeem their sins through Christ Jesus are not expressions of divine worship but human traditions which obscure the doctrine of grace, the true worship of God and the very benefit of Christ's death, a.s.**

> **CANON 15: If anyone shall say that the keys of the Church have been granted for the sole purpose of loosing and not also of binding, and that as a result, when priests impose penances on those who confess, they act contrary to the purpose of the keys and contrary to Christ's institution; and that it is sheer fiction that, after eternal punishment has been taken away in virtue of the keys, the debt of temporal punishment normally remains to be paid, a.s.**

These four canons deal with the theologically difficult question of satisfaction. Catholic theologians of the fifteenth and sixteenth centuries were not in agreement on the issue of satisfaction. The reformation theologians had brought to the fore new and sharp questions on this matter.

We are brought once more to issues which go far beyond the sacrament of penance but which were at the very core of the reformation, namely:

    a. The full efficacy of Jesus' salvific action;
    b. The absolute gratuity of God's grace.

The Tridentine bishops, in these canons and in the corresponding chapters, did not resolve all the theological questions in these intricate issues, but in these canons certain guidelines were established for an understanding of the question on penitential satisfaction. These guidelines reflect the theological positions commonly held by the Roman theologians of that time.

1. Sin, eternal punishment and temporal punishment are three somewhat separate issues. God forgives each and every sin; God also remits all eternal punishment due to sin. Even with the forgiveness of sin and the remission of eternal punishment, temporal punishment might still remain. The entire issue of "satisfaction" in connection with the sacrament of penance becomes intelligible only in this area of temporal punishment.

2. The forgiveness of temporal punishment stems from the merits of Jesus' salvific action. If one loses sight of this Christocentric efficacy in the matter of the remission of temporal punishment, the entire theological question of temporal punishment becomes unintelligible. Satisfactory acts, such as fasting, prayer, and almsgiving, either enjoined by a priest or privately adopted by a Christian, have validity only in their relationship to Jesus' salvific action. Separated from Jesus, such actions have no validity in the Christian life.

3. The goal of such acts of satisfaction is indeed a renewed Christian life. Fasting, prayer, almsgiving, etc. therefore must be seen as an integral part of one's renewed Christian life. The Tridentine bishops indicate that any derogation of such acts is a derogation of the very meaning of a renewed Christian life.

4. The satisfactory acts are true acts of worship. Canon fourteen says specifically that Christians do such acts for the redemption of sins "through Jesus Christ." This connection with Jesus is crucial. In the discussions and promulgations of Trent the full efficacy of Jesus' life, death and resurrection was unequivocally maintained.[36] Satisfactory acts, therefore, cannot be seen as adding to or completing Jesus' salvific action. Consequently, a theological explanation of "satisfaction" must be explained so the doctrine of

the full efficacy of Jesus' work is preserved intact, the full gratuity of grace is maintained, and in this sense be understood as true acts of worship. In many ways, canon fourteen is one of the most important, since it clearly confronts the two central issues of the reformation complaint and answers them in a way which is ecumenically acceptable.

5. Imposing penance is to be seen as part of the power of the keys. This power is both a binding and a loosing power. In the church disciplines which follow the theological presentations of Luther, Calvin, Zwingli and the Anabaptist tradition, separation from the community of a sinful Christian and eventual reconciliation is a constitutive part of the church. The reformation theologians insisted much more on the community's involvement in this process of binding (excommunication) and loosing (readmission), while the Roman church exercised this power almost exclusively through popes and bishops. To some extent, priests (*sacerdotes*) are also involved in this binding/loosing inasmuch as they impose penances, in the sense that the remission of temporal punishment due to sin was considered "bound" until the satisfactory acts were performed. All of these actions of binding and loosing, however, so the bishops at Trent imply, are to be seen as part of the power of Jesus in the church to isolate, repel, and negate sin.

Even with these five points, theological questions to this complex issue of "satisfaction" remain.[37] Pelagianism, which in many ways had crept into the church, remained stubbornly entrenched. This Pelagian quality compromised, at times, the very direction which the bishops at Trent attempted to emphasize. Both the theology and practice of "satisfaction," at times, continued to compromise the absolute gratuity of God's grace and the complete efficacy of Jesus' salvific work.

4. GENERAL CONCLUSION ON THE TRIDENTINE DOCTRINE

H. Vorgrimler, at the end of his presentation of Trent's teaching on the sacrament of penance, notes:

As regards the theologically central question of Luther—the question of faith—Trent, as far as the sacrament of penance is concerned, did not address it. The core of Luther's teaching is: No one receives God's grace mechanically, simply because he has been absolved. One receives God's grace, *because* one believes that *through* absolution one receives grace. Insufficient is a general belief, that God *can* forgive sinners. A firm and certain faith is unconditionally required, that the sins *are* forgiven. One can be sure of forgiveness only through the words of the priest and through faith in the promise of Christ. It is Luther's point that one who wishes to receive sacramental absolution, must necessarily believe that he or she will receive God's grace. Luther was not of the opinion that priestly absolution was unnecessary for the forgiveness of sins.[38]

Neither canon six nor canon nine even touches on this issue of faith as Luther had been proposing it. Canon four, which speaks of the acts of the penitent, makes no mention of faith, but at the same time canon four makes no rejection of Luther's main point. For the bishops at Trent, faith was acknowledged as the basis and presupposition for sacramental activity. Actually, the bishops addressed Luther's central issue, not in this discussion of the sacrament of penance (1551) but in the discussion on sacraments generally (1547). Nonetheless, by not bringing this question of faith and its answer directly into the discussion on the sacrament of penance, the Tridentine presentation on the sacrament of penance is left, in many instances, quite unclear. What Vorgrimler called Luther's central question—the question of faith—I have called, throughout this chapter, the twofold issue of the absolute gratuity of God's grace on the one hand and the full efficacy of Jesus' salvific action on the other.

Poschmann, at the end of his presentation on the Tridentine teaching of the sacrament of penance, notes:

This [the emphasis on the role of absolution] does not mean that a complete solution had as yet been found of the chief problem at which theology had been labouring since the early scholastic period, that of the relation of the subjective and personal factor to the objective and ecclesiastical one in the production of the forgiveness of sin.[39]

Poschmann, as well as Vorgrimler, indicates certain inadequacies to the Tridentine presentation on penance, inadequacies at the very core questions surrounding both the theology and the practice of this sacrament. These inadequate confrontations with core issues of this sacrament have perdured down to the present day. Even the renewal of the sacrament of penance, therefore, which came about in the aftermath of Vatican II, inherited the limitations of Trent. To bypass these limitations in a discussion of Trent and to mention only the positive aspects of the Tridentine doctrine can only do harm to both the theology and practice of this sacrament of penance.

In each of the canons listed above, I have attempted to enumerate the positive gains which the bishops at Trent worked out. That these gains were valuable is clearly proven by the enormous impact Trent had on subsequent church theology and practice of the sacrament of penance. From the sixteenth century to the time of Vatican II, all Roman Catholic theology and practice regarding the sacrament of reconciliation has been shaped by the Tridentine approach to this sacrament. Four hundred years of such strong influence certainly indicates and validates the positive aspects of the Tridentine synthesis. Nonetheless, the *lacunae* in Trent's doctrine present the Catholic community with as yet unresolved problems.

5. THE TEACHING OF THE COUNCIL OF TRENT ON THE THEOLOGY OF JUSTIFICATION

Since the focus of this book is on the sacrament of reconciliation, it seemed better to present the Tridentine understanding of the sacrament first and only then take up the Tridentine decree on justification. Historically, however, the bishops at Trent had formulated the decree on justification *before* writing the decree on the sacrament of penance. One of the major themes of this present book has been the need to interrelate, pastorally and theologically, both penance and justification. One without the other is impossible. Nonetheless, at Trent this interrelationship was not totally successful, as we shall see.

There was no doubt in the minds of the bishops and theologians at Trent that the major issue between the Roman Catholic and Protestant positions lay with a theology of justification. The issue itself had been, as we have seen, a matter of discussion since late Carolingian times, but more especially in the scholastic period of the twelfth, thirteenth and fourteenth centuries. Neither the reformation theologians nor the bishops and theologians at Trent began with a *tabula rasa*. Both groups were conditioned by the very history of this theological and pastoral discussion, and both groups made their theological response within an historically conditioned framework.

On September 23, 1546 a draft of a decree on justification was given to the assembly of bishops at Trent. Work on this so-called "September draft" had been going on privately, under the direction of Cervini, since the previous July. This draft represented a break with the usual conciliar manner of formulating doctrine, since it presented a very lengthy statement on justification, followed by a series of canons. Ordinarily, councils, e.g. Nicaea, Chalcedon, Lateran IV, Vienne, etc., had issued merely a series of canons. Since the issue of justification was so important, this novel way of formulating conciliar thought was broached. We have, then, not merely a series of somewhat disjunctive canons on a given topic, but a fairly coherent and carefully formulated presentation of a theology of justification. In no way was this lengthy "chapter," of and by itself, presented or promulgated as infallible doctrine. It is certainly a solemn and official statement by the Roman church, but it is the canons, which are attached to this chapter, that might include teachings *de fide definita*. It is in the canons that the bishops at the Council of Trent wished to express church doctrine, at times even *de fide definita*. The chapters, then, must be considered as official explanations of the doctrine expressed in the canons.

This "September draft" went through a number of revisions before it reached its final formulation. Throughout these revisions, specifically scholastic vocabulary was deliberately avoided, and the wording of the statement kept close to biblical terms and to the teaching of Augustine. The statement itself is focused almost exclusively on the teachings of Luther and the *Confessio Augustana*. Teachings on justification by Zwingli and Calvin are only tangentially treated. Moreover, throughout the deliberations a concerted effort was made to avoid a judgment on the so-called internal disputes, i.e. the differences between the Thomists and the Scotists. Since on several occasions official mention was made that the bishops were not gathered to settle these internal arguments, it is clear that the decree on justification cannot be read in a way which opts for either a Thomistic or Scotistic approach. These differences remain, even today, matters of open discussion.

From the "September draft" to the final formulation, the following issues were those which absorbed the major efforts and time of both Tridentine bishop and theologian:

1. The contribution of the human factor in the preparation stage of the *processus iustificationis*.
2. The issue of a dual-justification, i.e. inherent justice (*iusitia inhaerens*) and the justice of Christ himself (*iustitia Christi*). This dual-justice was argued most forcibly by Seripando.
3. The certitude which one could have on the matter of justification. This was an argument between the Thomists and the Scotists, but it also was based on the Lutheran position of certain faith: *fides certa*.

The history of the debate on justification at Trent has been treated elsewhere in careful fashion.[40] In these pages we will consider only those aspects of this decree which bear strongly on the interrelationship with the sacrament of penance. The three issues mentioned above tended to focus the discussion both of the theologians and of the bishops during the months of discussion on justification.

The first issue, the contribution of the human factor in the preparations stage of justification, was central to the entire debate, since it clearly raised two questions. The first concerned a Pelagian stance, in which human nature is neutral before God and in which, therefore, human nature of its own efforts does something to gain grace or merit damnation. What does a person do, if anything, prior to justification? Is this preparatory phase under the influence of grace or not, and to what degree? (b) The second question was the question of merit. Does a person merit the grace of justification in any way at all? Does one merit at least the preparation for justification, or is this preparation a work of human nature? Throughout the medieval period, lengthy discussions had taken place on this preparatory stage. Already in Augustine's dispute with Pelagius the question of God's grace and human will came to the fore again and again. The "merit question" certainly lies at the heart of the reformation critique of several medieval theologies of justification, and merit was also part of the reformation critique of such pastoral practices as that of the sacrament of penance, of indulgences, of good works, etc.

The second issue, the dual-justification, was especially dear to Seripando, the superior general of the Augustinians. Seripando, however, was not alone in this view; other authors of note held the same view: namely, Aurelio of Rocca Contracta, Mariano of Feltre, Stephen of Sestino, Gregory of Padua, Antonio Solis, Pedro Sarra, and Lorenzo Mazochi. The Tridentine opponents of this dual justification view were quite vocal and cogent: Vincenzo de Leone, a Carmelite; Vicenzo Lunello, the superior general of the Conventual Franciscans; Richard of Le Mans and John du Conseil, also Franciscans; and Diego Lainez, a Jesuit. The thrust of Seripando's argument in favor of this dual-justification was this: no matter how holy a person might be, at the time of final judgment each person must still look to the merits and justification of Christ for salvation. This distinction between the "justification" which a person has (merits?) in this life, and the "justification" which only comes from the superabundance of Jesus' salvific work, was, however, rejected by the Council of Trent. There is but a single justification, a *iustitia Christi*.

The third issue, the certitude of faith, was primarily directed against the position of Luther. However, it involved a difference of opinion between the

Thomists and Scotists as well, and at times during the discussions it seems that the latter dominated over the former. In the end, the intra-school dispute remained unresolved; the Lutheran view became the only focus. As we shall see below the certitude of faith cannot be fully resolved unless one addresses the very meaning of "faith." The Lutheran position on faith and the Roman Catholic position on faith, at this period in history, were quite far apart. If faith is only preparatory or dispositive, then faith brings no certitude. If faith is the very center of justification, then how can one believe and at the same time call such belief into question? The issue is extremely complex.

Such were the three major topics of discussion which controlled much of the discussion on justification during this period of the Council of Trent. This does not mean that other issues were not debated, for they were. It does mean, however, that these three issues took the lion's share as regards time and effort. Because of this dominance by the three issues, other aspects of justification did not receive due attention, as we shall see.

In this present book, the heart of the justification-dispute has been presented as centering around two fundamental issues: (a) the absolute gratuity of God's grace, and (b) the complete adequacy of Jesus' redemptive act. Let us consider the Tridentine decree on justification and these two fundamental issues.

A. THE ABSOLUTE GRATUITY OF GOD'S GRACE

The decree states on many occasions that without God's grace no good work is possible. There is a clear renunciation of a "human-merit" doctrine. We read, for instance:

> The impotency of both nature and law to justify a human person (Title, c. I).

> Not only Gentiles . . . but also Jews . . . were unable to be freed or rise [from sinfulness] even though there was in them a free will . . . (c. I).

> If men and women were not born again in Jesus Christ, they would never be justified (c. III).

> The beginning of justification in adults must be based on the prevenient grace of God through Jesus Christ, by which they are called through no existing merits of their own (c. V).

> We are therefore called justified because none of those things which precede justification, be it faith or good work, merits the grace of justification (c. VIII).

There are other passages as well which might be cited, but these indicate clearly that the decree proposes as a matter of Christian belief the absolute gratuity of God's grace. The decree also states that the human will is free, and therefore the question might still remain: how to put into some sort of cogent unity this complete gratuity of God's grace, on the one hand, and human freedom on the other. Nonetheless, that God's grace is absolutely gratuitous is clearly a teaching of this decree.

B. THE COMPLETE ADEQUACY OF JESUS' REDEMPTIVE ACT

H. Latimer's description, mentioned above, expresses this idea so well. He was commenting on the Our Father and then rhetorically asks: "Do I now, in forgiving my neighbor his sins which he hath done against me, do I, I say, deserve or merit at God's hand forgiveness of my own sins? No, no; God forbid! for if this should be so, then farewell Christ; it taketh him clean away." In this Tridentine decree on justification the full adequacy of Jesus' salvific work is, indeed, not stressed. The notion of "farewell Christ" remained apart from the discussion. Unfortunately, this precise christological theme was not one of the topics which focused the discussion of the various drafts of this decree.

In 1562, some fifteen years after this decree on justification was promulgated, the Tridentine bishops took up the issue of the "sacrifice of the mass." Alphonso Salmeron was the opening speaker, and although the question he was addressing was the issue of the "sacrifice of the mass" and the "sacrifice at the last supper," his lengthy presentation centered around the mass on the one hand and the cross of Jesus on the other. Through the subsequent discussion, it was this interrelationship: mass/cross of Christ, not the interrelationship: mass/last supper, which came up again and again. The background for this eucharistic discussion was clearly the full adequacy of the redemptive work of Christ. Did the mass in any way "complete," "add to," or "fill up" the redemptive work of Jesus? If so, "then farewell Christ!" as Latimer remarked.

The very fact that this issue had to be debated *per longum et latum* in 1562 indicates quite strongly that it had not been adequately debated prior to this. It had not been debated in the discussions on justification. The Tridentine policy was: Whenever there were issues which had already been dispatched by the Council of Trent, they were not reopened. I think one can fairly state that in the decree of justification there is no statement which denies the full adequacy of Jesus' redemption, but there was no satisfactory confrontation of this issue either in its preliminary discussions or in its final formulation. In other words, this is one area which not only Luther, but also Zwingli, Calvin, and the English reformation theologians had raised in a very focused way regarding the question of justification. However, this precise area was not answered by this Tridentine decree in any adequate way. Indeed, it was not even discussed! Only with the debates in 1562 do we find a response to this fundamental issue. In a sense, then, the Tridentine decree on justification, as a deliberate answer to Luther's critique, is, as regards this central theme, quite insufficient. Even the lengthy debates on dual-justification never addressed the issue of the full adequacy of Jesus' salvific work in a satisfactory way.

C. THE ISSUE OF FAITH

Undoubtedly, one of the major controversial issues which the Tridentine decree mentions is that of faith, particularly the *sola fides.* Faith for the theologians and bishops at Trent was consistently understood as part of the preparation for justification. Jedin states that the bishops and theologians "all conceived it [justification] as an entitative, supernatural elevation, through sanctifying grace and the meritoriousness of good works performed in a state of grace."[41] Prior to this elevation by sanctifying grace, faith, in the bishops' view, performed only a preparatory function. In the November draft of the decree, the text stated: "We are said to be justified by faith because the preparation for justification begins with faith" ("*quia in ea, quae ad iustificationem est dispositio, prima est fides*").[42] On this draft, Seripando wrote in the margin: "What do I hear? All that we read in the Scriptures about justification by faith is to be understood of the disposition?" In this marginal remark, Seripando summed up the reformation critique of the scholastic approach to faith. Does Paul, does Mark, does the entire New Testament speak of "faith" merely in a preparatory or dispositive way? Rather, is not "faith" in the New Testament far more than a mere disposition? Are such words as "Go and sin no more; your faith has healed you?" merely a statement about a preparation, a disposition? There was a major discrepancy between a biblical understanding of the term "faith" and the Augustinian-scholastic understanding of the same term "faith." From the New Testament approach, faith is a saving faith: faith alone is presented as salvific. From an Augustinian-scholastic approach, faith is a *fides informata;* only when formed by charity (grace) can one speak of *fides formata,* a faith which saves. Subtle though the difference might be, faith, in this latter view, is inadequate, preparatory, dispositive. But, the reformers objected and with vehemence: Is such a view of faith biblical? Does it have endorsement and validity on the basis of God's own word as the church finds it in the holy scriptures?

The final formulation of this Tridentine document speaks this way about "faith":

"For God designed him [Jesus] to be the means of expiating sin by his sacrificial death, effective through faith" (c. II, citing Romans 3:25).

Now they [adults] are disposed (*disponuntur*) to that justice when, aroused and aided by divine grace, receiving faith by hearing, they are moved freely towards God (c. VI).

This disposition or preparation (*hanc dispositionem seu praeparationem*) is followed by justification (*iustificatio ipsa consequitur*) (c. VII).

But when the Apostle says that one is justified by faith alone, these words are to be understood in the sense in which the uninterrupted unanimity of the Catholic Church has held and expressed them, namely, that we are therefore said to be justified by faith because faith is the beginning of human salvation, the foundation and root of all justification (c. VIII).

The scholastic view of a *fides formata* dominated the thinking of the bishops and theologians at Trent. Faith needed to be perfected or formed by love. The *habitus* of faith could exist in a human person without sanctifying grace; therefore, faith by itself (*sola fides*) is inadequate for justification. Faith by itself is dispositive and preparatory, not adequate to justify the sinner. Although the decree avoided the use of almost any scholastic terms on this matter of justification, still the decree embodies the thought-patterns of the scholastics, and it is on the basis of these thought patterns that the decree speaks of faith.

In Luther, however, faith is not dispositive or preparatory. Calvin, as we saw above, had found such notions as *fides formata* or *fides inchoata* contradictory to the New Testament. On the issue of "faith" this scriptural base for one's interpretation of faith is precisely where the problem between the Roman Catholic side and the reformation side stood. On the basis of revelation, the New Testament in particular, can one truly say that faith is merely dispositive, merely preparatory for justification, or can one truly say that faith is at the very core of justification itself, not merely its disposition or preparation? This issue was neither argued nor answered by Trent. This is precisely why Vorgrimler can say, as we mentioned above: "As regards the theologically central question of Luther—the question of faith—Trent . . . did not address it."

One almost gets the impression that on this issue of faith, as the saying goes, two ships were passing each other in the night. These two views of faith needed to be discussed *per longum et latum.* The bishops at Trent simply did not enter into this kind of discussion. Undoubtedly, this is the reason why even today there remains a great need to discuss the issue of justification once again. This discussion has at least begun in the contemporary Lutheran-Roman Catholic dialogues, but it is nowhere near completed.

D. THE *PROCESSUS IUSTIFICATIONIS*

In c. VII the decree on justification describes the causes of justification in the *processus iustificationis.* The bishops used the Aristotelian categories of cause, which had been modified by the scholastic theologians: final, efficient, meritorious, instrumental, and formal causes.

Final cause:	the glory of God and of Christ
	eternal life
Efficient cause:	the merciful God who gratuitously
	washes and sanctifies
Meritorious cause:	Jesus Christ
Instrumental cause:	the sacrament of baptism
Formal cause:	the justice of God by which he
	justifies us

In this analysis of the process of justification, God, in his mercy alone, is seen as the efficient cause: *justification comes from God only.* Human merits are no part of the efficient cause of justification. Baptism (and one could add any of the other sacraments, or even good works of any kind) are seen as instrumental causes. This phrase "instrumental cause" is not further explained, and there were and remain within the Roman Catholic tradition a variety of theologies on this matter, all of which are tenable.[43] Certain of these explanations raise, in a pointed way, major questions on the core issues of "good works," "merit," and "the adequacy of Jesus' own redemptive action."

The meritorious cause is Jesus. Again and again throughout the decree, the bishops and theologians at Trent understood this meriting of Jesus in terms of his passion and death. In their comments and their written conclusions, neither the life of Jesus itself nor the resurrection is brought into their understanding of the redemptive act of Jesus. The exclusive emphasis on the passion and death of Jesus, which one finds throughout the documents of Trent, is, from a christological standpoint, defective. The salvific act of Jesus involves not simply his passion and death, but his life and his resurrection as well.

Calvin, in his discussion of merit, retained the idea that Jesus "merited," but that he did not merit for himself, but only for us (III, 17, 1–6). For Calvin, the use of the term "merit" was not totally rejected. There was a clear theological place for this term "merit," namely, in christology. Jesus, in Calvin's view, clearly "merited." Nor was Calvin the only reformation theologian who spoke in this way. These reformation theologians agreed that Jesus merited, though not for himself but for us. This was a manner of speaking about Jesus and merit which was common in scholastic theology, and therefore this manner of speaking about Jesus and merit could be considered acceptable, at the time of the reformation, by both reform and Catholic scholar alike. Today, both Protestant and Catholic theologians might want to reconsider this interrelationship of merit and Jesus. Although the threat of Pelagianism hovers on every page of a book which deals with grace, one seldom hears the term "Pelagian" when one reads a theological analysis of Jesus' own salvific work. Nonetheless, that there might be some "crypto-Pelagianism" in a given theologizing on the redemptive act of Jesus is often quite clear. This kind of questioning was not, however, part of the medieval and reformation discussions.

The formal cause was the *iustitia Christi* which was at the same time *iustitia inhaerens;* it was not the very justice of God. The bishops and theologians saw this *iustitia Christi* or *iustitia inhaerens* as an entitative, supernatural elevation of the soul, through sanctifying grace, which was both *gratia increata* (the very being and presence of God) and *gratia creata* (God's created gift). *Iustitia Christi,* however, was not the same as faith, for faith was only dispositive and preparatory. It was, nonetheless, the same as *fides formata,* since *fides* in this instance had been formed by *gratia creata* or charity. From this analysis of the decree's approach to faith, one sees again that the bishops at Trent did not confront the core issue of Luther: his understanding of faith as the very core of justification.

E. GOOD WORKS

The decree explicitly states that there are no good works which merit anything prior to first justification (c. V). The human person, however, is not passive: the human person does not absolutely do nothing (*homo ipse nihil omnino agat*). Still, by one's free will, we do not of our own accord move to justification. The interrelationship of these two aspects, grace and free will, is not developed further.

In cc. X and XI the decree addresses the issue of good works on the part of those who are justified, i.e. in the state of grace (*fides formata*); c. X is a florilegium of scriptural texts on good works. The phrase "faith cooperating with good works" (*cooperante fide bonis operibus*) is specifically stated, again indicating the council's view of faith. On the basis of this scriptural evidence, c. XI more pointedly addresses the good work issue or the merit issue. Again, the decree picks up on the term: faith alone. Faith alone, it says, is inadequate; good works are needed. Canon 24, however, raises some major issues:

> If anyone shall say that the justice received is not preserved and also increased before God through good works, but that those works are merely the fruits and signs of justification obtained, but not the cause of its increase, a.s.

How does one understand "cause" against the background of the absolute gratuity of God's grace which the decree clearly states? How does one understand "cause" against the complete adequacy of Jesus' own salvific act, which the decree at least implies? One cannot take this canon by itself, without taking into consideration much more fundamental positions of the Tridentine decrees. On the other hand, one must admit that the meshing of God's gratuitous grace and human "merit" was not completely resolved by the Council of Trent. That the very term "merit" was retained is due to the long tradition it has had in the Christian world. As mentioned above, even some of the reformation theologians, like Calvin, continued to use this term. One of the bases for this canon is the theological statement, to some degree found in Augustine: *facienti quod est in se Deus non denegat gratiam.* For the one who does what he or she can, God will not deny grace. The reason why God does not refuse grace was explained differently by the Thomists and the Scotists. With Gabriel Biel the pact theory was in the forefront: God gives grace to those who do good works because he has promised through a pact that he would do so. Biel's approach, however, was a long way from that of Scotus, and rightly criticized by Luther. Nonetheless, the fact that both Thomistic and Scotistic theologians disagreed on this relationship, and still do, is another indication that a "final word" on the matter was not attained by Trent. Even today, particularly in ecumenical dialogue, the issue remains an open one.

McGrath in his summation of the Tridentine decree on justification makes this observation:

> The degree of latitude of interpretation incorporated into the Tridentine decree on justification at points of importance makes it impossible to speak of "the Tridentine doctrine of justification" as if there were *one such doctrine.* In fact, Trent

legitimated a range of theologies as catholic, and any one of them may lay claim to be a "Tridentine doctrine of justification."[44]

McGrath's judgment that there are several Tridentine doctrines of justification is valid. Clearly, the Thomists and Scotists had legitimate approaches. The *via moderna* theologians also formulated the doctrine of justification in a slightly different format. The Augustinian school presented still another approach to justification. In many ways, the decree on justification affirmed many of the issues which reformation theologians had made.

Any decree which tries to be broad enough to encompass so many schools of thought, a sort of umbrella decree, cannot help but be seen as "vague," "ambivalent," "unclear," at least in a variety of areas. If the decree were not vague, ambivalent and unclear, it could hardly "legitimate a range of theologies as catholic." To some degree, however, this "umbrella" aspect of the decree on justification is its strongpoint, but to some degree it is also its Achilles' heel. A decree can only allow a number of varying views, if it does not address itself forcefully and clearly to certain issues. Some of these issues which were not addressed clearly enough by Trent need, in our present age, a better confrontation: faith, merit, the meaning of Jesus' saving action. We will see in the final chapters how the non-addressing in a clear way of these fundamental issues continues to harass theological thought on the issue of the sacrament of reconciliation.

Finally, let us consider the two decrees together: that of justification and that of the sacrament of penance. Even when the discussion on the sacrament of penance was under discussion by Trent (1547), the full adequacy of Jesus' redemptive act had not yet become a matter of full-scale debate at Trent. This only took place in the discussion on the mass. Since this particular issue was not debated or discussed in the formulation of the decree on justification, it was therefore not fully operative in the discussion on the sacrament of penance and not fully integrated into the discussion on penance. Secondly, the understanding of faith throughout the discussion and final formulation on justification did not come to terms with the Lutheran approach to faith, and as a result the Lutheran critique of the sacrament of penance, theologically and pastorally, was not fully met, since faith and the forgiveness of one's sins are essentially bound up together, given our present sinful condition. The decree on justification from Trent certainly moved the theological discussion forward. Even Harnack could write: "The decree on justification, though an artificial product, is in many ways an excellent piece of work;

in fact one may doubt whether the Reformation would have developed if this decree had been issued by the Lateran Council."[45] This is indeed high praise, and although the decree did not cover all the problems adequately, it moved Catholic thought into definite areas. The movement, however, was not always successful; other issues in Roman Catholicism arose which stymied and even contradicted the theological orientation of this document. These contradictory areas were particularly pronounced in the area of the sacrament of penance, both theologically and pastorally. In the third quarter of the sixteenth century, there was still not a totally satisfactory wedding between the theology of justification on the one hand and the theology and practice of the sacrament of penance on the other. But this is the topic of the next chapter.

SUMMARY OF CHAPTER EIGHT

In this chapter we have seen:

1. The sacrament of penance was not received frequently at the time of the Council of Trent, except in monasteries and religious houses. Many priests were misusing the sacrament, so that there were a number of abuses connected to the pastoral ministry of confession.
2. The first time that the sacrament of penance was discussed at the Council of Trent was in the discussion on justification. This indicates that there is an essential connection between the two issues.
3. The anathemas in the canons of Trent cannot be interpreted per se as a censure of "heresy." Heretical aspects must be established through other means than a mere citation of anathema sit.
4. Each of the canons must be considered against the background of the decree on justification. Unfortunately, the bishops at Trent did not make any effort to interrelate the material on the sacrament of penance with the already formulated decree on justification.
5. In the body of the chapter each canon is considered individually, and a summary of this material does not seem to be necessary at this point. However, in the canons we see that the bishops often felt that a criticism of long-standing traditions was a criticism of church authority itself. This kind of criticism is often the focus of the anathema.
6. The canons cannot be read as though they "define" the scrip-

tural passages of Matthew 16:16 and 18:18 and John 20:22–23. Nor can the canons or the doctrinal chapters be read as though they officially interpreted the history of this sacrament. Scriptural exegesis and historical data have, since the time of Trent, necessitated a rethinking of some of the Tridentine statements.

7. The canons on confession, contrition and satisfaction claim the lion's share of the bishops' attention. This fact alone indicates that it was in these three areas that the bishops found the most serious difficulties for the theology of the sacrament of penance. Since the bishops did not wish to settle issues between the various schools of that time, there is a certain ambiguity inherent in these very canons.

8. It is not clear from the statements of Trent that priestly absolution is in itself a judicial act. Even today Catholic scholars are not in agreement on this issue.

9. The central question of Luther, namely that of the meaning of faith, was not even addressed by the bishops at Trent, as far as the sacrament of penance is concerned.

10. The decree on justification maintains the absolute gratuity of God's grace in the process of reconciliation. It does not address the question of the full efficacy of Jesus' salvific work. This issue was faced by the bishops at Trent in the decree on the eucharist as sacrifice, in which the bishops expressly maintained the full efficacy of Jesus' once-and-for-all sacrifice.

11. Still, there is not one theology of justification which emerges from the Tridentine decree on justification. The decree actually allows for several variant theologies of justification, any of which could be considered Tridentine.

12. The presentation of the bishops at Trent on the sacrament of penance became the dominant approach to this sacrament within the Roman Catholic Church for the next four hundred years. This perdurance alone indicates the worth of this presentation. Still, today one must face up to the limitations of the Tridentine presentation and modify those areas which certainly demand it.

9

The Sacrament of Reconciliation, Justification and Vatican II

From the decree of Lateran IV (1215) to the decree promulgating the new rite of penance (1973), there were no official changes by the Roman church regarding the sacrament of reconciliation. Even the Council of Trent, as we just saw, made no substantive innovation in the theology and practice of this sacrament. However, it may seem strange that we are moving from a study of the Council of Trent to a study of the Second Vatican Council without mentioning much on the intervening centuries. Surely, important issues occurred in that period which affected both the Christian understanding of justification and the Roman Catholic theology and practice of the sacrament of penance. None of these issues, on the other hand, changed the Roman Catholic theology of penance in any fundamental way. In Roman Catholicism the theology of the counter-reformation period continued the main theological positions of the Council of Trent, attempting to clarify more precisely the relationship between contrition, confession, absolution and satisfaction. In general, one could say that counter-reformation Roman Catholic theology made no radical innovations, regarding this sacrament of penance.

However, several situations occurred which altered to some degree the way that both the theology and the practice of this sacrament was understood.

(I) The first was a shift from a dogmatic understanding of sin to a moral one. During the counter-reformation period a gradual separation took place between dogmatic and moral theology. This had its advantages, but also its disadvantages. The major disadvantage, as far as the sacrament of penance was concerned, lay in the fact that sin was explained more and more from its moral base, not from its theological base. The development of various "schools" of moral theology within Catholicism, such as the tutiorist school, the probabilist school and the equiprobabilist school, and even a so-called laxist school, further ingrained the moral interpretation of sin over the theological interpretation. As a result, a juridical aspect of the sacrament of penance was emphasized. Naturally, pastoral practice softened, on many occasions, the rather juridical approach to penance, but in the long run the sacrament of penance was practically and on many occasions theologically explained through juridical and moral categories, rather than through biblical and theological categories.

(II) The second situation had a much more deleterious influence on this sacrament, namely the influence of Jansenism. The two sacraments which were most affected by Jansenistic spirituality were the eucharist and penance. As far as the eucharist was concerned, Jansenism stood in the way of frequent reception of the eucharist. As far as penance was concerned, absolution was often refused, making the sacrament of penance even more distasteful in the eyes of the faithful.[1] Under the Jansenistic influence, confession of sins abounded, but the granting of absolution did not.

(III) Third, the antagonistic positions between Catholics and Protestants in the main disallowed any dialogue on the issue of justification. In his historical survey on justification during this post-Trent period, Tavard mentions: (a) the intra-Catholic squabble between the followers of Molina (1536–1600) and those of Banez (1528–1604); (b) the controversy over quietism which went on between Bossuet (1627–1704) and Fenelon (1651–1715); (c) a lengthy analysis of a book on grace by Jean-Martin Moye (1730–1793), *Le Dogme de la Grace,* which was a volume written not by a professional theologian but by a pastoral individual. In this volume Tavard indicates that Roman Catholicism really focused on the question of grace, not that of justification per se. (d) On the Protestant side, Tavard presents the thinking of Wesley. This section of his overview ends with a few pages on John Henry Newman, for whom the major issue was the way in which one could determine the formal cause of justification.[2]

Dallen, in his review of the same period, mentions that Trent had really paved the way for a more frequent reception of the sacrament of penance, but that Jansenism nipped this movement in the bud. He also mentions the many efforts at liturgical reform in Germany and how such reforms were labeled, by various contemporary Catholics, as either Protestant or Jansenistic. Some of these liturgical reforms focused on a ritual of public and communal penance. Dallen ends this section citing *Mirari vos* of Gregory XVI, written in 1832, which denied that the Roman Catholic Church ever needed reform.[3]

(IV) Finally, there is the historical change. At the end of the nineteenth century and throughout the first half of the twentieth century a new interest in the history of this sacrament gradually emerged. It was precisely this historical material which prompted, in many ways, the call for renewal by Vatican II. That no major change occurred from the Council of Trent to Vatican II is indicative of the power and solidity of the Tridentine approach. Such a conclusion cannot be denied. It cannot be maintained today that the Tridentine reform of this sacrament was adequate. The reform of the sacrament of penance, stemming from Vatican II, has its obvious roots in the heritage from Trent. However, Vatican II went far beyond Trent.

All of the above topics deserve full attention, of course, but for our present purposes we can merely enumerate these themes and move from the Tridentine study to the renewal of the sacrament of penance, called for by the bishops at Vatican II and promulgated in 1973 by Paul VI. To understand the renewal of this sacrament, we will consider the following:

1. The renewal of the rite of reconciliation mandated by Vatican II.
2. The contemporary theological understanding of Jesus as the primordial sacrament of reconciliation and the church as a basic sacrament of reconciliation.
3. The issue of justification in the theological thought of Vatican II.

1. THE NEW RITUAL FOR RECONCILIATION

The promulgation of the *Ordo paenitentiae* on December 2, 1973 is a milestone in the renewal of the sacrament of penance, and the final draft represents the work of two different Vatican committees. The first study group for this renewal of the sacrament of penance was constituted by the *Consilium ad exsequendam constitutionem de sacra liturgia* in December 1966, with P. J. Lecuyer as chairman and F. Heggen as secretary (succeeded by F. Nikolasch in 1967). Members of the groups were: Z. Alszeghy, K. Rahner, P. Anciaux, C. Florestan, L. Ligier, A. Kirchgassner, and C. Vogel. This group prepared the first draft of the new ritual, submitted to the Concilium in April 1968. With their draft they submitted a list of the criteria which they had followed in composing the text, and a summarized history of the sacrament of penance in the eastern and western churches. In this draft, three rites for reconciliation were proposed: (1) one for individual and private confession and absolution; (2) another for a communal penance with individual and private confession and absolution; (3) another for a communal celebration with general absolution without a previous private confession. The committee also expressed the view that in the foreseeable future a new formula of absolution might be used which would express more clearly the effects of grace proper to the sacrament of penance. The draft also included four formulae for absolution, which had strong historical rootage.[4]

In October 1968 the *Consilium* examined and with some changes approved the *Praenotanda* of this draft, but asked that the committee rework the issue of absolution. In 1969 the *Consilium* studied the draft again, with a view to incorporating several formulae for absolution. However, on May 8, 1969 the Consilium itself was terminated, and the former Congregation of Rites was officially divided into a Congregation for Divine Worship and a Congregation for the Beatification and Canonization of Saints.

The new Congregation for Divine Worship took up the issue, but with great reserve, asking the committee to rework areas on communal penance and absolution. The committee did this and resubmitted its work. There then occurred a lengthy period of silence. What, if anything, happened remains classified. Only in 1971, after two years of no public information, a report on the proposed new ritual was issued, but shortly afterward, on June 16, 1972, the Congregation for the Doctrine of the Faith issued *Pastoral Norms on the Administration of General Absolution,* and consequently, in the same month, a new study group was formed to reword the draft in keeping with these newly promulgated norms. No member of the previous committee was placed on this new committee. P. Jounel was appointed chairman; F. Sottocornola was the secretary; A. Gracia, P. Visentin, H. Meyer, K. Donovan and G. Pasqualetti were the appointed members. Their task was to review the proposed new rite and adapt it to the norms on general absolution which had just been published. They were also instructed to provide only one formula of absolution. The revised text was again examined by the consultors of the Congregation for Divine Worship in November 1972, and then in its newly revised form it was sent to the total congregation on November 22, 1972. Further changes were asked for, which were made, and this draft was then approved by the Congregation and circulated to the Congregation for the Doctrine of the Faith, the Congregation for the Sacraments, the Congregation of the Clergy, and the Congregation for the Evangelization of Peoples. It was also sent to the Apostolic Penitentiary. Numerous changes were suggested, suggestions which indicated the bias and preference of various groups and individuals. Jurisdictional elements between the various congregations also entered into the picture, with the competencies of these various congregations being defended. Further meetings took place, but finally the document was approved, with the Congregation for the Doctrine of the Faith playing a fairly definitive role. The new ritual was then approved by Paul VI on November 29, 1973, and promulgated by the Congregation for Divine Worship on December 2, 1973.

Such in broad outline is the history of the writing of this document. It is obvious that some of the best Roman Catholic theologians and liturgical scholars of that period of time worked on this document at some stage of its conception and refinement. It is also obvious that some political, inner-church activities played a role in the construction of this document.

A. CRITERIA

First of all, the documents of Vatican II, particularly the *Constitution on the Liturgy,* provided the authors of this document with some general, but pointed criteria:

1. "The rite and formulae of penance are to be revised so that they more clearly express both the nature and effect of the sacrament."[5]

2. "The role of the church in penitential practices is not to be passed over, and the need to pray for sinners should be emphasized."[6]

3. "In sacred celebrations a more ample, more varied, and more suitable reading from sacred scripture should be restored."[7]

4. "Liturgical services are not private functions, but are celebrations of the church which is 'the sacrament of unity'; namely, 'the holy people united and arranged under their bishops'."[8]

5. "The rites should be distinguished by a noble simplicity. They should be short, clear, and free from useless repetitions. They should be within the people's power of comprehension, and normally should not require much explanation."[9]

Other Vatican II documents than the *Constitution on the Liturgy* were also helpful as criteria:

1. "Those who approach the sacrament of penance obtain pardon from God's mercy for the offense committed against him, and are, at the same time, reconciled with the church, which they have wounded by their sins and which by charity, by example and by prayer labors for their conversion."[10]

2. "By the sacrament of penance they (priests) reconcile sinners with God and the church."[11]

From these and other passages found in the documents of Vatican II, the committees were guided by three essential elements:

1. First of all, a realization that sin, besides being an offense against God, is a wound in the body of the Church as well.
2. Secondly, the penitential process is a reconciliation of the sinner both with God and with the Church.
3. Thirdly, the entire people of God collaborates in the conversion and reconciliation of the sinner.[12]

Other elements were likewise employed as criteria for composing this renewed formula of reconciliation.

1. The importance of the spoken word, especially that of scripture, in the sacramental liturgy.
2. The importance of a communal liturgical celebration, based on, but not imitating, that communal liturgical penance of the first centuries.
3. The preference for a simple and sober rite, which would at the same time be both noble and clear in its expression.
4. The importance to take seriously contemporary historical and theological studies on the sacrament of penance, which have emphasized the central role of the paschal mystery in the reconciliation process, and their love and mercy of God as the source of the forgiveness and salvation of our world.

These various criteria played a role in shaping the document, but they also provide us with the keys to interpret the ritual of reconciliation.

The listing of these criteria is of basic importance, since they indicate to us the major theological *foci,* which shaped the final document.

An awareness of these criteria helps us to see why there was a need for a revised ritual of penance. It is not enough simply to tell our Christian communities that the rite of the sacrament has been renewed and to explain the various parts of the new ritual. One must also indicate the reasons for these changes. The *National Bulletin on Liturgy,* drawn up by the Canadian Catholic Conference, answers this fundamental question as follows:

Why was it revised?
To show its relationship with Jesus' paschal mystery.
To point out its ecclesial dimensions.
To give proper place to God's word.
To make the rite more expressive, understandable,
  and to increase participation.
To be a celebration of faith.
To leave room for adaptation to various cultures
  and situations.
To bring out the nature and effects of this
  sacrament more clearly.[13]

B. STRUCTURE OF THE DOCUMENT
The document, containing the new rite, can be outlined as follows:

1. The *Praenotanda* [1–40] or prefatory remarks, explaining the new ritual.
2. A rite for the reconciliation of an individual penitent [41–47].
3. A rite for the reconciliation of many penitents with individual confession and individual absolution [48–59].
4. A rite for the reconciliation of many penitents with a general confession and a general absolution [60–63].
5. A rite in case of necessity or imminent danger of death [64–66].
6. Various biblical readings and prayers which can be used in any of the three major rites, mentioned above [67–214].
7. Appendix I: Absolution from censures, and dispensation from irregularity.
8. Appendix II: Sample penitential services, for the liturgical seasons of Lent and Advent; for various groups of people, such as children, young people, and the sick.
9. Appendix III: Form of examination of conscience, which can be adapted for times, places and persons.

Appendixes I and II indicate that the framers of this new rite wanted and expected variety and creativity; they did not present us with a monolithic or mechanistic ritual. The *Praenotanda* and Appendix III help us understand the theological meaning of sin and reconciliation which is embodied in the rituals.

C. KEY THEOLOGICAL IDEAS

From all of this material we can select key theological ideas which surface again and again.

1. The Name: Reconciliation

Rather than "confession" or "penance" the preferred name for this rite is "reconciliation." It is true that the entire document is entitled *Ordo paenitentiae,* and that the people who worked on the document were reluctant to abandon summarily the term "penance," which had served the Christian community for centuries and which had received official sanction in the documents of such councils as Florence, Trent and Vatican II. Moreover, the total document, *Ordo paenitentiae,* addresses itself not only to the liturgical celebrations of the sacrament of penance, but also touches on non-sacramental penitential services [37–37]. By and large, however, the sacrament itself, throughout the document, is seen and called "reconciliation." The decree of promulgation begins with the words: "*Reconciliationem inter Deum et homines*"; and each of the three rites are called: "*Ordo ad reconciliandum . . .*" In the title of the first three chapters of the *Praenotanda* the word "reconciliation" appears as well. Sottocornola remarks that this word "reconciliation" seems to "make more evident the essential content of the sacrament."[14] From an historical standpoint, the *Gelasian Sacramentary* of the seventh century spoke of the *reconciliatio paenitentis* and provided some prayers: *ad reconciliandum paenitentem.*[15] Rather than penance, a word which stresses, at least in the contemporary mind, some work to be done, or confession, which highlights only one aspect of the process, the term "reconciliation" seemed to represent the entire process by its focus on the culminating moment.[16]

When the revised Code of Canon Law appeared in 1983, it was clear that the framers of the new code had no liking for the term "reconciliation." Almost invariably the code uses the term "penance." Only twice in all thirty-nine canons devoted to this sacrament is the term "reconciliation" used. We see here one official document of the Vatican, the new Rite of Penance, going in one direction, and another official document of the Vatican going in another.

2. The Sacrament of Penance and Salvation History

Even more important theologically, however, is the fact that the penitential process throughout is more clearly inserted into salvation history. The *Praenotanda* begins with the role of Christ as reconciler, and his life-work and his very existence is presented as reconciliation [1–2]. Secondly, the *Praenotanda* speaks of the church as a *locus* of reconciliation [3–5]. This methodological concern, proceeding from Christ to church and only then to the sacrament itself, provides the horizon within which the sacrament of reconciliation becomes more lucid, and with which, too, the liturgical celebration can be better expressed.

This salvation history theme also affects the life of each Christian, since each Christian has a personal history of salvation and reconciliation. Reconciliation is indeed a process; it is not instantaneous. The lengthy penitential process of the patristic church was a witness to this in its own time, whereas the highly abbreviated form of more modern times tended to obscure this process, this penitential space, this personal salvation history. The church itself is historical and has a history. We read in the *Praenotanda:* "The Church, which embraces sinners to her own bosom, and which is holy but at the same time always in need of purification, continually seeks out penitence and renewal" [3]. Again, "In many and various ways the people of God perform and perfect this continuous penance" [4]. There is a self-conversion whereby the church itself from day to day becomes more and more conformed to the likeness of Christ [4]. Even the progression: contrition, confession, satisfaction and absolution [6] indicates the processive historicity of reconciliation. The non-sacramental celebrations of penance [36–37] have as some of their goals: helping the faithful prepare for a sacramental celebration at some later date; the education of younger people, so that they gradually develop a formed conscience; and a means to aid interested, non-baptized people toward a final step of conversion [37]. In all of these statements, we see that the document clearly describes reconciliation as a progression, a process, an historical part of the very history of salvation.

It must be stated, however, that the final document in no way altered the pre-Vatican II understanding of absolution. Even with the introductory prayer expressing the trinitarian dimension of reconciliation and the role of the church, the stark phrase: "and I absolve you from your sins in the name of the Father, and of the Son, and of the Holy Spirit," retains a judicial and instantaneous character about it. On the one hand, the document throughout envisions reconciliation as part of the life-process of a Christian; on the other hand the document does not clearly involve the meaning of these words of absolution [I absolve you, etc.] in this life-process. The ecclesial moment of absolution is not presented as a celebration but, in keeping with pre-Vatican II theology, a judicial act. We will consider the absolution prayer shortly, but its rather instantaneous quality seems to militate against the clear thrust of the whole document to include reconciliation in the total process of salvation history.

3. The Relationship to Baptism and Eucharist

The term "reconciliation" helps to indicate the affinity which the sacrament of penance has to both baptism and the eucharist. Baptism is, of course, a major reconciliation-event, and the connection of baptism to penance is alluded to in the document: "In obedience to this command, on the day of Pentecost Peter preached the forgiveness of sins by baptism: 'Repent and let every one of you be baptized in the name of Jesus Christ for the forgiveness of your sins' (Acts 2:38)" [1]. A more lengthy passage on this same theme follows:

> This victory is first brought to light in baptism where our fallen nature is crucified with Christ so that the body of sin may be destroyed and we may no longer be slaves to sin, but rise with Christ and live for God. For this reason the Church proclaims its faith in "the one baptism for the forgiveness of sins" [2].

Naturally, a thorough theological explanation of the baptism-reconciliation relationship should not be expected from this document, but it is clear that a non-baptismal theology of the sacrament of penance is essentially unacceptable. The insistence of such reformation theologians as Luther and Calvin on this link between baptism and penance has never been fully elucidated in any official Catholic document, and therefore this present official document, with its mention of the link between baptism and penance, is a strong impetus to contemporary Catholics to study and explain more deeply this interrelationship of the two sacraments.

The eucharist is likewise mentioned in the *Praenotanda* as an essential part of reconciliation:

> In the sacrifice of the Mass the passion of Christ is made present; his body given for us and his blood shed for the forgiveness of sins are offered to God again by the Church for the salvation of the world. In the eucharist Christ is present and is offered as "the sacrifice which has made our peace" (Euch. prayer III) with God and in order that "we may be brought together in unity" (Euch. prayer II) by his Holy Spirit [2].

In this passage, the deliberate reference of the new eucharistic prayers is an effort to unite the post-Vatican II renewal of the eucharist with the post-Vatican II renewal of penance. The language of the paragraph is theologically traditional in Roman Catholic eucharistic discussion. Of itself it is quite acceptable; if explained in a Pelagian way (e.g. the interpretation given to such phrases as "offered again" and "offered as sacrifice"), then the foundational complaints of the reformation theologians reenter the scene: Is the mass a good work? Is Jesus' expiation complete or must the church add to it?

Nonetheless, the document highlights the truth that a non-eucharistic theology of the sacrament of penance is likewise faulty. Precisely what this interrelationship involves is not stated in any detail, but that there is such an interrelationship is stated.[17]

4. The Social Nature of Sin and Reconciliation

On the subject of sin, the document presents us with some very clear guidelines: (a) sin must be seen as both an offense against God and as an offense against others; in other words, there is a social dimension to every sin; (b) the document nowhere uses the standard phrase: mortal and venial sin.

(a) The Social Nature of Sin

No sin is a strictly private matter, affecting only the sinner himself or herself. Nor is sin simply a matter between an individual and God. This does not mean that the very basis of sin is not an offense against God. It clearly is.

> Since every sin is an offense against God which disrupts our friendship with him, "the ultimate purpose of penance is that we should love God deeply and commit ourselves completely to him" [5] (citation is from Paul VI).

This offense against God, however, has adverse effects on the individual sinner and on the society in which he or she lives. This is stated clearly in the document on reconciliation.

> "By a hidden and loving mystery of God's design men are joined together in the bonds of supernatural solidarity, so much so that the sin of one harms the others, just as the holiness of one benefits the others" [Paul VI, *Indulgentiarum doctrina*, 1967]. Penance always entails reconciliation with our brothers and sisters who are always harmed by our sins.

In fact, men frequently join together to commit injustice. It is thus only fitting that they should help each other in doing penance so that freed from sin by the grace of Christ they may work with all men of good will for justice and peace in the world [5].

The Canadian Catholic Conference, commenting on this social nature of sin, remarks: "Sin is also a community act. We cannot ignore the sins of government, large corporations, or of the Churches. We cannot divorce ourselves from our share in these, at least by our silence or by turning a blind eye to such crimes."[18]

The Congregation for the Doctrine of the Faith, in its *Instruction on Christian Freedom and Liberation,* reinforces this social dimension of sin. In this document sin is seen fundamentally as a separation from God: "Man's sin, that is to say, his breaking away from God, is the radical reason for the tragedies which mark the history of freedom."[19] However, the document goes on to say:

By sinning, man lies to himself and separates himself from his own truth. But seeking total autonomy and self-sufficiency, he denies God and he denies himself. Alienation from the truth of his being as a creature loved by God is the root of all other forms of alienation. By denying or trying to deny God, who is his Beginning and End, man profoundly disturbs his own order and interior balance and also those of society and even of visible creation.[20]

The document reaffirms the basic principles of human freedom. First, it mentions the supreme commandment of love which "leads to the full recognition of the dignity of each individual, created in God's image" [73]. This "essential prerogative" of human freedom is manifested in all the dimensions of human life. Human persons then are the "active and responsible subjects of social life" [73]. The principle of solidarity and the principle of subsidiarity are "intimately linked to this foundation" [73].

Reconciliation, then, is also not a matter of a relationship between an individual and God. Reconciliation is reconciliation both with God and with one's neighbor. Sottocornola comments:

Recent studies and polls have brought to light that one of the more frequent criticisms of confession was its excessive ritual and psychological-moral individualism. It was requested that the following be brought into greater evidence: the relationship between good and evil, the understanding of sin not only individually but also collectively, and the ecclesial nature of the sacrament of reconciliation. All this should be done not only in the catechesis, but also and above all in the rite of penance itself, which must appear as an action of the Church to which each individual penitent associates himself.[21]

The revised ritual of reconciliation stresses the reconciliation not only with God but also with the church. The church as a basic sacrament is given a place of prestige in this new ritual. The assembled community is not merely present in an observing way, but the assembled community is present in a participative way. The assembled community shares sacramentally in the reconciliation of sinners. The assembled community is an agent of reconciliation, and thus the ecclesial dimension should be evident throughout the ritualized celebration of this sacrament. We will return to this theme below, since it is so key to an understanding of the theology of reconciliation and therefore the ritual of such celebration.

(b) Mortal and Venial

The new rite of reconciliation, *Ordo paenitentiae,* nowhere uses the terms "mortal" and "venial." Clearly the framers of this document could have used such terms. Clearly the final arbiters, whether in the sacred congregation or other Vatican agencies, could have used these terms. Their absence seems to indicate that such terms as mortal and venial are inadequate. All sin is serious.

The revised Code of Canon Law uses the term *gravis* (960, 962, 963, 988); in can. 988, § 2, it uses the term "venial." The 1972 norms for general absolution use the term "lethal" (*lethalis*). One could say that there is, at present, no set terminology. From official statements from the Vatican, we have a variety of terms. From moral theologians we have, as well, a renewed discussion on the issue of sin itself.

Still, from the new rite of reconciliation, there is a clear step, especially through terminology, toward a clearer realization that all sin is serious. Such notions as "only a venial sin," "light sin," etc. do not mesh well with the theology behind this new ritual of reconciliation.

5. The Communal Nature of Sacramental Celebration

There is no doubt that the communal character of sacramental life is a major part of this new ritual. Sacraments are not to be considered private matters. They are, rather, celebrations of the assembled community. The documents of Vatican II had already stated that *preference was to be given to communal celebrations over more individual or private celebrations (SC, 27).* In the new ritual there are both sacramental and non-sacramental communal celebrations, i.e. forms II and III and the penitential services spoken of in numbers 36 and 37. Form I remains quite private and individual in structure, and as such does not measure up to the preference for communal sacramental services which Vatican II requested.

In the new Code of Canon Law, we read: "Liturgical actions, to the extent that by their proper nature they involve a common celebration, are to be celebrated where possible with the presence and active participation of the Christian faithful" (837 § 2). However, in the section on the sacrament of penance, 959–997, communal celebration is referred to only when the code speaks about the restrictions on general absolution. The tenor of this section of the code is, in many ways, antithetical to the new ritual itself, so that once again we have divergent voices from varying, official Vatican documents on this matter of reconciliation.

Even the very stilted definition of the sacrament of reconciliation, which the revised Code of Canon Law offers us, in no way measures up either to the theology of the Vatican II documents on sacraments, or to the theology of reconciliation which one finds in this new ritual of reconciliation. In can. 959 we read:

> In the sacrament of penance the faithful, confessing their sins to a legitimate minister, being sorry for them, and at the same time proposing to reform, obtain from God forgiveness of sins committed after baptism through the absolution imparted by the same minister; and they likewise are reconciled with the Church which they have wounded by sinning.

When one compares this to the definition of sacrament in general given in can. 840, we see severe differences. Can. 840 reads:

> The sacraments of the New Testament, instituted by Christ the Lord and entrusted to the Church, as they are the actions of Christ and the Church, stand out as the signs and means by which the faith is expressed and strengthened, worship is rendered to God and the sanctification of humankind is effected, and they thus contribute in the highest degree to the establishment, strengthening and manifestation of ecclesial communion.

In canon 959 on the sacrament of penance, where is the action of Jesus, the primordial sacrament? Where is the action of the church, the fundamental sacrament? Where is the ecclesial community? Where is the sign of faith and the moment of worship? The entire tenor of the section on reconciliation, presented by the revised Code of Canon Law, seems almost oblivious to the rich teachings of Vatican II; instead, this section clearly harks back to an understanding of the sacrament of reconciliation which dominated the code of 1915.

6. The Presence of the Word in the Sacrament

Even in form I, which seems so particularized and individualistic, the word of God plays a key role. It is unfortunate, however, that this aspect of the rite in form I can be omitted (n. 17), which can easily give the impression that the word of God is not so key to the sacramental act, that it is only tangential to the sacrament. Rather, the word of God should be seen as integral to each and every sacramental celebration. Although one might say that a major step forward in this meshing of word and sacrament has been taken by the Roman church in the new ritual of reconciliation, still the full integration of the word has as yet not occurred.

With the presence of this word of God in the sacrament the emphasis is seen as God's action—even more sharply stated, God's merciful and forgiving action. The new rite does stress conversion or metanoia, just as the RCIA does. But it is the grace of God which is placed in the foreground, not human action. God's grace which comes to us first is center-stage. God first loves us, and therefore we can love God. God first loves us, and therefore a conversion or metanoia becomes possible and desirable. As many a German theologian points out, there is first of all the word, *das Wort,* and only then the response, *die Antwort.* This aspect of the new ritual will be focused on in the section concerning justification and Vatican II below.

With these ideas on the key theological issues of the new ritual, let us widen our approach by looking at the theology of reconciliation itself, as we find it developed in and through the currents which gave rise to, were expressed by, and emerged after Vatican II.

2. JESUS, THE PRIMORDIAL SACRAMENT OF RECONCILIATION; THE CHURCH AS A BASIC SACRAMENT OF RECONCILIATION

In so many ways, chapters two and three of this present volume are the key to both a theological understanding and a pastoral practice of the sacrament of reconciliation. Jesus, in those two chapters, was presented as the primordial sacrament of reconciliation. The new rite of penance, in its *Praenotanda,* situates the renewed sacrament of reconciliation precisely in the Christ-event as a reconciling-event. It also situates the renewed rite of reconciliation within the church-event as a reconciling-event. This could be diagrammed as follows.

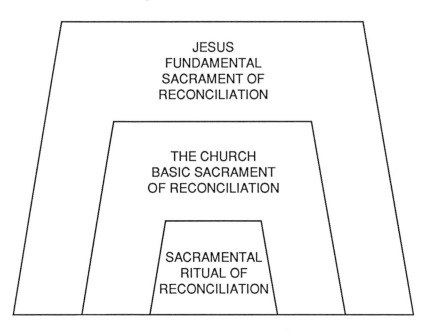

JESUS
FUNDAMENTAL
SACRAMENT OF
RECONCILIATION

THE CHURCH
BASIC SACRAMENT
OF RECONCILIATION

SACRAMENTAL
RITUAL OF
RECONCILIATION

The value of this diagram is twofold:

(I) It indicates the milieu in which, or the sounding board against which, the celebration of reconciliation becomes significant. Without the christological aspect and without the ecclesiological aspect, the celebration of the sacrament of reconciliation would be meaningless.

(II) The second value to the diagram is its indication that the church-event as a reconciling-event is larger, more extensive, and more intensive than any single celebration of a sacrament of penance, for ecclesial reconciliation is not limited simply to the moments of the sacrament of penance, nor to any sacramental celebration. Moreover, the Christ-event as a reconciling-event is likewise seen as even larger, more extensive and more intensive than the ecclesiological sphere. Jesus is not limited to the church to bring the kingdom of reconciliation to men and women. The church and the kingdom are not co-extensive, and since the kingdom is God's own kingdom of the reconciled, reconciliation occurs quite beyond ecclesiological boundaries. This is a major element in the theological statement: Jesus in his humanity is the primordial sacrament of reconciliation.

Nonetheless, the diagram is limited, since it does not clearly express the full primordiality of the sacrament of the humanness of Jesus, nor the way in which the sacramentality of Jesus is constitutive for the sacramentality either of the church as a reconciling-event or of the sacrament of penance as a reconciling-event. The sacrament of penance is constituted a sacrament, not by matter and form, not by some "fiat" of institution which Jesus once made, but rather and only because Jesus himself, in his humanity, is the primordial sacrament of God. The church itself is a sacrament not by some "fiat" of Jesus, nor by any "matter/form" argument, but because Jesus in his humanity is the constitutive and primordial sacrament. Jesus, as the primordial sacrament, totally redefines what Christian theology has meant by "sacrament."

When the framers of the new rite of penance came to the prayer of absolution, they attempted to express the christological and ecclesiological framework of revelation. The prayer reads as follows:

The Father	God, the Father of mercies
Jesus	through the death and resurrection of his Son has reconciled the world to himself
Holy Spirit	and sent the Holy Spirit among us for the forgiveness of sins;
Church	through the ministry of the Church may God give you pardon and peace,
	and [because of all this] I absolve you in the name of the Father and of the Son and of the Holy Spirit. Amen.

The "absolution" is presented against a trinitarian and salvation history background: what the Father has done in and through his Son and in and through the Spirit within the holy church now comes to the individual. Reconciliation has meaning only on the basis of God's initiative: the prayer itself starts with this divine initiative, indicating that reconciliation is a gift of God, a grace, absolutely gratuitous. But this is not directly given to an individual; reconciliation comes to all of us only in and through the [life, which unfortunately is not mentioned in the document,] death and resurrection of Jesus. Jesus has reconciled *the world* to the Father, not just Christians. Outside of Jesus there is no salvation. This is the negative side. The positive side is: Jesus is the primordial sacrament of God's reconciliation of all men and women. The presence of God's Holy Spirit, the very Spirit of Jesus, is among us as reconciliation. Once more this expression of the Spirit's role indicates the full gratuity of the divine initiative.

The church is presented in a ministerial role, a servant role. The church is the sacrament of Jesus. When the church reflects Jesus, the primordial sacrament of reconciliation, then the church, too, is part of the reconciliation process; the church, too, is a "minister" of God's reconciliation.

The framers of the new rite had submitted their draft with words which the bracketed phrase expressed, namely, "because of all this." The words of the priest: "I absolve you, etc." were not seen in a vacuum; they have meaning only against the background of Father, Son, and Spirit, and of the church. Unfortunately, when the rite was promulgated, someone had removed those bracketed words, leaving the priestly words: "I absolve you, etc." as an almost totally unconnected phrase. The omission of the bracketed words or their equivalent clouds the very meaning of the last sentence. Theologians, like Sottocornola and Jounel, who had originally worked on the draft, in subsequent writings complained of this omission, and rightfully.

In spite of this omission, the point is clear: we are celebrating a concrete moment of God's forgiveness, a moment of grace and gift, which has come to us in and through Jesus, the primordial sacrament of reconciliation. In this prayer Jesus is seen as the primordial sacrament who makes present God's forgiving love. In the sacrament of penance one can and must truly, not analogously, speak of the "real presence" of Jesus. Without this real presence of the foundational sacrament, Jesus, the ritual of penance has nothing to offer.

Although we today are living almost two decades after this new ritual has been promulgated for the Roman Catholic Church, few Catholics, even theologians, priests and bishops, think of Jesus when they hear the words: sacrament of reconciliation. Yet, if Jesus is truly the primordial sacrament of reconciliation, then the very phrase "sacrament of reconciliation" should make us think first of Jesus, secondly of the church, and, only in a very relativized and tertiary way, of this ritual of penance. The fact that few Catholics think in this form indicates how thin the true renewal of the sacrament of penance still is within the Roman Catholic Church.

In the Dogmatic Constitution on the Church, *Lumen Gentium*, Jesus alone is presented as the *light of the nations*. The church is never called the light of the nations. Vis-à-vis Jesus, the church is relativized. In this image of light, the bishops at Vatican II deliberately indicated that the mystery and nature of the church lies in its reflection of Jesus. Since the church has no light of its own, it becomes light and light-giving only insofar as it reflects Jesus, the true and only light. In all of this the mystery of the church is portrayed as a sacramental mystery. The church, then, is only a mystery and thus true to its nature when it reflects the one, true mystery of Jesus, who is the primordial sacrament of the divine mystery itself, God.

When this sacramental process is applied to reconciliation, we see that the church, in order even to be church, must reflect the forgiving love of God, which one sees in Jesus, the light of the nations. Whenever the church, at any and all of its levels, reflects the prodigal forgiveness of God as revealed to us in Jesus, then the church is truly fulfilling its nature. Whenever, on the other hand, the church, at any and all of its levels, does not reflect God's prodigal forgiveness, it is distorting the gospel and camouflaging what should be the very revelation of God.

If there is going to be a true renewal of the sacrament of reconciliation, then the place to start is not with the ritual of penance. Rather, the place to start is with a catechesis on Jesus, the light of the world, the sacrament of God's prodigal, forgiving grace. Once this beginning is made, then one must experience and understand the church as a locus of reconciliation. One must find forgiveness at every level of church life. This means that prior to a renewal-effort regarding the individualized sacrament of reconciliation, the local church community needs to be renewed, to be made into an even more reconciling community than it is. Only then should one begin to discuss the sacrament of reconciliation as an individual rite within the church.[22]

3. JUSTIFICATION AND VATICAN II

The bishops at Vatican II nowhere addressed the issue of justification. Nor did the theologians who constructed the new ritual on the sacrament of reconciliation address the issue of justification. This is a regrettable situation. At the time of Luther and Calvin, and ever since then, most Protestants have considered the issue of justification as the principal teaching of Christianity. By it the church stands and falls, or as Luther himself said: "*quia isto articulo stante stat Ecclesia, ruente ruit Ecclesia*" (if this article stands, the Church stands; if this article comes to naught, the Church comes to naught).[23] The bishops at Vatican II had as their main agenda a theological and pastoral statement on the church, its nature, its mystery, its function. How the issue of justification could not have been a major theme of their discussions remains unclear.

J. Heinz, at the conclusion of his book *Justification and Merit,* spends fourteen pages on justification and Vatican II, but many of these pages are indicative of the lack of material on justification from Vatican II, rather than on an even modest amount of material. With the announcement of the council, there was an expectation by many that the council would speak to the issue of justification, and thereby speak in dialogue to the Protestant churches. This expectation was totally deflated. G. Marron, who attended the council as an observer, stated: "The texts from Vatican II contain 'expressis verbis' as good as nothing on justification."[24]

Otto Pesch, in his essay "*Gottes Gnadenhandeln als Rechtfertigung des Menschen*," says that the Protestant thinker was looking for a comprehensive ecclesiology from Vatican II, but "as regards the justification of a sinner as the measure for the church there is not one word!"[25] Schillebeeckx notes that Vatican II in many ways complemented Vatican I, but not Trent.[26]

The official *Constitutiones, Decreta, Declarationes* of Vatican II, published by the office of the secretary general of the Second Vatican Council, contains an analytical-alphabetical index. The entry "justification" is listed with only two references: one to paragraph three of the *Decree on Ecumenism,* and the other to paragraph nine of *Lumen Gentium.*[27] Actually the word *iustificatio* is used twice, and the verb *iustificare* is used three times. Twice they refer to something quite secular (*Gaudium et Spes,* 2, 3, 67 and 2, 4, 74). In *Lumen Gentium,* 2, 9, the passage from Romans (4:22) is cited, but without any additional comment. We end up, then, with two instances in which these texts use the term "justification" or "to justify." The first is in the *Decree on Ecumenism* mentioned above:

> The ecumenical movement is striving to overcome these obstacles. But even in spite of them, it remains true that all who have been justified by faith in baptism are incorporated into Christ (n. 3).

The second is in the chapter on holiness found in *Lumen Gentium:*

> The followers of Christ, called by God not in virtue of their works, but by his design and grace, and justified in the Lord Jesus, have been made sons of God in the baptism of faith and partakers of the divine nature, and so are truly sanctified (n. 5, 40).

The mystery of salvation is central to the church, since Jesus is central to the church. There was no overt christology at Vatican II nor any expression of this central mystery of our faith. One can only say that the ecclesiology of Vatican II is good as far as it goes, but without a major consideration of salvation (justification, deification), the ecclesiology remains incomplete and thereby inadequate. This is not to say that the documents of Vatican II do not offer us major aspects of ecclesiology: the discussion on the people of God, on holiness in the church, on religious freedom, on ecumenism, etc., are in many ways a true renewal, an *aggiornamento*. Still, the steps taken at this council did come up short on this central issue of justification.

When one turns to the renewal of the sacrament of penance which the bishops of Vatican II mandated, it should have been clearly evident to anyone who has studied the history of the sacrament of reconciliation that such a renewal of the sacramental ritual could not be done except within the framework of the issue of justification. We have seen that already from the twelfth century onward, these two issues, justification and the sacrament of penance, have been theologically intertwined. Peter Lombard used the section on the sacrament of penance as the very locus of his treatment of justification. This was followed by all the major scholastic theologians, including Thomas Aquinas, who treated justification in another section, but with clear textual cross-references between the section on justification and the section on the sacrament of penance. Moreover, the Council of Trent clearly discussed the two themes in an interrelated way. How, then, given this lengthy "tradition" in the Roman Catholic Church, could a renewal of the sacrament of penance be made without a corresponding renewal of the theology of justification? The shortcomings of this new ritual are due in no small measure to this lack of a theological foundation regarding justification. In the following chapter we will consider some of this unfinished agenda, but it should be noted that the shortcomings might not reside in the ritual itself, but rather in the as yet unsettled issues regarding justification.

SUMMARY OF CHAPTER NINE

In this chapter we have seen:

1. The new rite for the sacrament of penance was promulgated on December 2, 1973, but only after many modifications and after the work of two committees. One of the main reasons for the lengthy time of preparation was the issue of general absolution, which various congregations discussed and even argued over.
2. The general criteria for the renewal were taken from the docu-

ments of Vatican II, particularly *Lumen Gentium* and *Sacrosanctum Concilium*. From these criteria sin is presented as an offense against God and an offense against the church; reconciliation therefore is reconciliation with God and reconciliation with the church. All sin is social by its very nature, and all reconciliation is communal by its very nature.

3. The celebration of reconciliation must be a communal, not a private celebration. It must also be expressed in a simple and non-repetitive way.

4. The use of scripture is highly important in the liturgical celebration of the sacrament of penance. The term "reconciliation" brings out this relationship to the word of God and to salvation history.

5. The theology of the sacrament of reconciliation must be both baptismal and eucharistic. Without such relationships to these sacraments of initiation, the theology of the sacrament of reconciliation is essentially misleading.

6. The terms "mortal" and "venial" are not found in the new ritual. Even the new code speaks of grave and lethal sin, rather than mortal sin.

7. Jesus, in his humanness, is the basic or fundamental sacrament of reconciliation. This understanding of Jesus relativizes the sacrament of penance. Moreover, the church is a basic sacrament of reconciliation; this further relativizes the sacrament of penance.

8. Jesus as the fundamental sacrament of reconciliation indicates the theological point of departure for a theology of the ritual of reconciliation. The ritual must express the very meaning of Jesus, the reconciler.

9. The local church community must itself be a sacrament of reconciliation. Without a reconciling community, a ritual of reconciliation will be meaningless.

10. The prayer of absolution was meant to indicate the trinitarian and ecclesial presence in this moment of liturgy. Unfortunately, the official prayer of absolution, by leaving out a connective phrase, makes the words "and I absolve you from your sins in the name, etc." somewhat decontextualized.

11. Vatican II did not address in any way the issue of justification, a deficiency which to some degree calls into question the adequacy of its ecclesiology. The committees which worked on the

new ritual of reconciliation did not address the issue of justification nor attempt to bring the theology of justification into the renewal effort. This lack, to some degree, calls into question the adequacy of the renewed sacramental rite and its underlying theology.

10

Post-Vatican II Theology and Unresolved Issues on Justification and the Sacrament of Reconciliation

The new rite of reconciliation for the Roman church has not resolved all the issues regarding the sacrament of penance. Indeed it has raised anew many issues regarding the theology of justification. In some ways the new ritual has not only not resolved such matters but it has heightened these issues. In this chapter we will consider five such unresolved issues, not because these five are the only ones, but rather because these five issues in a very pressing way affect the theoretical and pastoral approach to the sacrament of reconciliation. The chapter, then, is divided as follows:

1. The issue of general absolution
2. The issue of private confession to a priest
3. The issue of the age for first reconciliation
4. The issue of frequent confession
5. The issue of justification

No intention is made in this chapter to provide an over-arching resolution to any of these issues. The goal is simply to present the situations as they are. Some comments, of course, will be made, but merely as suggestions for possible resolution.

1. THE ISSUE OF GENERAL ABSOLUTION

When the new ritual for the sacrament of reconciliation was promulgated in 1973, a use of general absolution in the Roman church, to some degree wider than church law had allowed in previous decades, was established. In the *Praenotanda* to the new rite, for instance, we read:

> It is for the diocesan bishop to determine, after consultation
> with other members of the episcopal conference, when general
> absolution may be permitted under the conditions laid down by
> the Holy See (n. 39).

The conditions laid down by the Holy See are those norms, *Sacramentum paenitentiae,* which had been issued in June 1972.[1] On the basis of these general guidelines, national conferences of bishops are now authorized to determine the times, within their jurisdictions, when general absolution might be allowed. If such regulations are not made by a national conference of bishops, then regional conferences of bishops can determine such occasions. If neither the national nor the regional conferences have made any such regulations, then the local ordinary is competent to allow general absolution, as long as he remains within the guidelines of *Sacramentum paenitentiae.* As a result, there is throughout the Roman church at this present time a lack of uniformity on this issue. Certain dioceses allow instances of general absolution which other dioceses do not. Certain national conferences of bishops allow for instances of general absolution which other national conferences do not. This lack of uniformity is not at all regrettable, but it underlines the flexibility bishops have in determining such instances, and it sends a message to the Christian people generally that a given diocesan restriction is merely local and by no means necessarily founded on any immutable teaching of the church.

In principle, then, general sacramental absolution has been officially given a much wider berth in the Roman church than it had been awarded in the past. This openness to general absolution in the current pastoral practice of the church is the starting point for any discussion on the discipline of general absolution.

Secondly, the *Praenotanda* of the new ritual went on to say:

> It is for priests, and especially parish priests, to decide to give
> general sacramental absolution, preceded by only a generic
> confession, when a grave necessity not foreseen by the diocesan
> bishop arises and when recourse to him is not possible (n. 40).

As is evident, this regulation from the ritual opened the door further. Even priests, but especially those in the parish ministry, might judge a situation serious enough to warrant general sacramental absolution.

Priests in such situations are told to use their own judgment on the matter and only afterward inform the bishop of their decision. This entire prescription, however, is no longer applicable.

The new Code of Canon Law, promulgated after the new ritual of reconciliation, has dropped this paragraph regarding priests making a judgment on the use of general absolution.[2] What the new ritual had allowed, the new code has taken away. The code has to be seen, therefore, as more restrictive in this matter than the original ritual itself. Today, then, only bishops, either nationally, regionally or individually, are by law allowed to determine the instances, in accordance with the 1972 norms, for the celebration of general sacramental absolution. This reluctance by the framers of the code should not surprise us. Throughout the lengthy history of the two committees which drew up this new rite of reconciliation, the question of general sacramental absolution was one of the major factors which prevented either agreement between the committees and the congregations and/or the ability of the congregations themselves to come more quickly to an adoption of the revised rite.

In both of these instances, the one involving the decision of the bishop(s), the other involving the decision of a priest, the central factor is stated as follows: there must be a "case of necessity." The question naturally arises: What is this "case of necessity"?

To answer this, let us consider the new rite. The new rite has not only the three forms which are customarily enumerated, but there is also a fourth form (form IV), namely, the form to be used when death is imminent (nn. 64–65). The general absolution, referred to in the norms of 1972 and also in form III of the new ritual, does not refer to a case of imminent death. When one speaks of a "case of necessity," imminent death is certainly such an instance. But this situation has its own form (form IV). When the ritual presents us with form III, it is not focusing on an instance of imminent death. Therefore, to interpret the phrase "cases of necessity," when applied to form III, as a case only of imminent death would be a total misreading of the ritual and of the Vatican regulations of 1972. "Case of necessity" has, evidently, a wider meaning than "imminent death."

The 1972 regulations (*Sacramentum paenitentiae*) tell us that general sacramental absolution should be used only in "cases of necessity." This is certainly true, but such a statement cannot allow us to say that *only* a general absolution situation involves a case of necessity. In no way can we read the new ritual as if either form I or form II is to be used *when there are no cases of necessity.* Actually it is theologically more correct to say that all the forms of the new ritual apply to cases of necessity. Indeed, if there were no "case of necessity," we would have none of the forms of this new ritual. We would have no sacrament of reconciliation at all. Accordingly, every time the rite of reconciliation is celebrated, there is operative in one way or another a "case of necessity."

One sees immediately that the very phrase "case of necessity," as used in the documents under discussion, is unhealthily ambiguous, and, in reality, this phrase "case of necessity" when applied only to form III (general absolution) is theologically incorrect. The choice of this phrase is not felicitous, and its continual appearance in discussions on general absolution—and often only then—contributes in a quite substantial way to the difficulty involved in more comprehensive discussions on general absolution. Rather, whenever there is a celebration of the sacrament of reconciliation, under whatever form, I, II, III or IV, there is a case of necessity. To say otherwise would make certain celebrations of reconciliation trivial and insignificant.

Moreover, in n. 64 of the new ritual, which deals with general absolution, we read: "In case of necessity, the rite for reconciling several penitents with general confession and absolution may be shortened." The phrasing of this paragraph is interesting: there is an authorized shortening of form III (general absolution) "in case of necessity." The longer and standard ritual of form III should be seen, then, as the "normal" way of celebration, when there is no case of necessity. This is undoubtedly not what is intended, but one can see that the phrase "in case of necessity" even in church documents is vague and ambiguous.

In n. 65 of the ritual we read: "In imminent danger of death, it is enough for the priest to use the form of absolution itself. In this case it may be shortened to the following: "I absolve you from your sins, etc." Clearly this is an exceptional circumstance: the imminence of death. This is a clear "case of necessity."

However, the point to be stressed is this: in the new ritual, form I, form II and form III are neither presented as nor called extraordinary. Rather, they are presented in the ritual as the three *ordinary* forms in the Roman church today for the celebration of the sacrament of reconciliation. Nn. 64 and 65 (dealing with imminent death) present us with an extraordinary situation. In the new ritual no one of these forms (I, II, III) is called "normal" or "ordinary." Nor are they called "extraordinary" or "exceptional." Thus, it is totally beyond this new ritual, which has the highest church authorization, to say, for instance, that form I, i.e. the individual form of reconciliation, is the normal and normative form, while forms II and III are meant for special or extraordinary times. Such a view cannot be substantiated by the new rite of reconciliation. Rather, all three forms are, according to the new ritual, normal and normative. All three forms are ordinary and acceptable forms of reconciliation. Consequently, in any discussion on general absolution, it is totally beyond the authorized ritual of the church to imply that general absolution is to be used only as a "last resort."

It is undeniable, of course, that certain people within the Roman church are trying to restrain as far as they can even the legitimate use of general absolution. On the other hand, it is undeniable that there are certain people in the Roman church who are trying to extend the use of general absolution even beyond the limits presently acceptable. In the introductory paragraphs of *Sacramentum paenitentiae*, it is mentioned that some bishops had asked the Holy See for a clarification on general sacramental absolution, and that they had asked for this clarification because (a) the lack of priests in some areas had become alarmingly acute and general sacramental absolution seemed the only practical pastoral solution under such circumstances; and (b) some erroneous teachings on the sacrament of penance had apparently been encouraging general sacramental absolution beyond acceptable limits. *Sacramentum paenitentiae* does not state in any way precisely what these erroneous teachings might be.

Since these regulations from the Vatican have been cited again and again in discussions on general absolution, it would help us to consider them carefully. They can be summarized as follows:[3]

1. The norms first restate the official Tridentine doctrine on integral confession. An integral confession is called the "only ordinary way" (outside of moral or physical impossibility) by which those separated from God and from the church through lethal (*lethalis*) sin can be reconciled after baptism both to God and to the church.
2. Having stated this official doctrine, the pastoral norms go on to indicate that a general sacramental absolution without an integral confession of sin can be licit and even necessary in case of imminent death. No ritual is indicated in this second norm for such a circumstance.
3. The pastoral norms, having treated the "case of necessity" of imminent death, go on to treat other instances when general sacramental absolution is both licit and possibly even necessary. These instances are:
   a. When there are too many penitents and an insufficient number of priests who can hear confessions "*rite*," i.e., following the correct ritual of the church. Besides this first condition, a

second is also necessary, namely, when the faithful would be deprived of the eucharist for a long time (*diu*). No further specification of this long time (*diu*) is provided.

    b. Missionary countries are particularly singled out, but other areas, such as gatherings of large groups, are also mentioned as presenting situations in which n. a (above) might apply.

    c. If there is an adequate number of priests available in these instances, then the use of general sacramental absolution, as described in n. a (above), is not licit.

4. In this fourth regulation, priests are to be encouraged by their bishops to schedule their time, so that they will be free to hear confessions. Significantly, it is added that tasks which deacons and lay people can perform should be entrusted to them so that priests have adequate time for this sacrament.

5. The local bishops, in conjunction with the national conferences of bishops, have the task of deciding on whether or not general absolution can be given within their jurisdictions. A priest who experiences a "case of necessity" should, if possible, consult his bishop first; if this is not possible, he should inform the bishop later, if he has given general absolution.

6. Those who have received general absolution must be willing to confess their serious sins privately to a priest when this becomes possible. This willingness (*dispositio*) is described as necessary for a valid reception of the sacrament. Priests are mandated to explain this requirement.

7. Those who have received general sacramental absolution, unless justifiably impeded, are not to receive this form of the sacrament a second time unless they have first made a private confession. This should be done within a year unless some moral impossibility arises. This regulation, the norms state, is in keeping with the decree of Lateran IV on annual confession of all serious sins.

8. Priests, particularly, are not to instruct the faithful to avoid private confession, either deliberately or negligently, so as to avail themselves of general confession. This seems to be one of the abuses mentioned in the opening paragraph of the decree.

9. Priests are advised once again to provide time for confession, particularly at those times and locations which fit best into the schedules of the faithful. In remote places, where priests come only irregularly, special care should be taken so that the faithful have the opportunity to confess privately at least once a year.

10. Penitential services, which are not the sacrament of penance,

are encouraged, but they are not to be explained in a way which confuses them with the sacrament. This seems to be another abuse which occasioned the decree. In these penitential services individual confession might also be available; and, if permitted by these norms, even general absolution might be given. One should, however, use the correct formula. Such a celebration should be kept separate from the mass.

11. Someone whose life has been a serious scandal to the community may receive general absolution, but before receiving the eucharist he or she should remove the scandal. Reserved cases must comply with these regulations.

12. Frequent confession, or confession of devotion, is to be encouraged. Disparagement of such confessions of devotion and of frequent confession seems to be yet another abuse which occasioned this document.

13. General absolution, given beyond the above norms, must be considered an abuse.

In these pastoral norms we find that there is indeed a licit and necessary use of general absolution far beyond the case of imminent death. This openness to general sacramental absolution is the basic premise of these norms. If there were no openness, there would have been no norms. Instead there would have been merely a castigation for anyone who presumed to give general sacramental absolution. Even if one takes into account the complaints against certain abuses which appear to be alluded to in the document, there is still a basic openness, though cautious, to a more extensive use of general sacramental absolution. The door may not be open in too wide a fashion, but it is open to a greater extent than in previous decades, even centuries.

After the publication of these norms, as well as after the promulgation of the new ritual on reconciliation, both Paul VI and John Paul II have referred to the issue of general absolution. In an allocution to some American bishops, Paul VI in 1978 referred to these 1972 norms regarding general absolution. However, he then went on to state:

In the life of the church, general absolution is not to be used as a normal pastoral option or as a means of confronting any difficult pastoral situation. It is permitted only for the extraordinary situations of grave necessity as indicated in norm 3. Just last year we drew attention publicly to the altogether exceptional character of general absolution. . . . We ask for a faithful observance of these norms.[4]

These are strange words, indeed. Nowhere in the new ritual of reconciliation is form III (general sacramental absolution) called "extraordinary" or "exceptional." Nowhere is general absolution said to be not "normal." Norm III of *Sacramentum paenitentiae,* to which Paul VI refers specifically, does not use these terms "extraordinary" and "exceptional" either. In norm I, *Sacramentum paenitentiae* does state: "Individual, complete confession and the receiving of absolution remain the only ordinary way for the faithful to obtain reconciliation with God and the church, unless physical or moral impossibility excuses them from this manner of confessing." The term "ordinary" seems to imply that all other forms are not-ordinary or extraordinary. However, *Sacramentum paenitentiae* was drawn up so that there would be orderly regulations for the orderly use of general sacramental absolution, within orderly limits, of course. Moreover, *Sacramentum paenitentiae,* in norm II, says: "By reason of special conditions occasionally arising . . ." It is the condition or circumstance which is "special," but it must also be stated that any and every time one celebrates the sacrament of reconciliation, even using forms I and II, there are special circumstances or conditions. The use of this term "special," just as the use of the phrase "in case of necessity," is ambiguous, and if applied solely to form III and denied to forms I and II, there is clearly a theological problem, not just a linguistic one.

Three situations are presented by the norms *Sacramentum paenitentiae* for a licit use of general absolution: (1) a large number of Christians who wish to receive reconciliation; (2) an inadequate number of priests who can celebrate the sacrament of reconciliation *rite* (according to the approved rite) individually with all of these Christians; (3) these Christians would as a result have to wait *diu* (a long time) before the sacrament of reconciliation would be available to them. At best the norms call this circumstance "special" (n. II). One is well aware that in current church life it is not "extraordinary" or "exceptional" to have a large group of Christians gathered together who would want to receive the sacrament of reconciliation. In current church life, it is not "extraordinary" or "exceptional" to have a lack of priest-confessors. It would be "extraordinary" and "exceptional" to make these Christians wait a long time before another opportunity for reconciliation would arise. In other words, *Sacramentum paenitentiae* can be seen as a document which provides *ordinary* norms for the above situation of large numbers/few priests. To describe the situation as extraordinary does not necessarily make the norms for them extraordinary. Moreover, even calling the described situation extraordinary is quite often incorrect, since such situations can indeed be the ordinary situations in a local church. There appears to be an arbitrariness in the way one uses "extraordinary" and "ordinary." What might be ordinary in one locale could easily be extraordinary in another locale and vice versa.

According to a letter from the Sacred Congregation for the Doctrine of the Faith to the bishops of the United States, January 14, 1977, the norms in *Sacramentum paenitentiae* were drawn up to assist pastors in situations which were attended by extraordinary circumstances. Once again, it is the circumstances which are designated "extraordinary," not the ritual of general absolution. The implication, however, is again the same, namely, that circumstances in which forms I and II might be used are "ordinary." Is this the kind of theological thinking the church authorities wish to foster? When a Christian in mortal or lethal sin, for instance, asks for form I, is this circumstance to be designated, from a theological standpoint, "ordinary"? Are not these very terms "ordinary/extraordinary" theologically imprecise?

In a reply from the Sacred Congregation for the Doctrine of Faith to a query from the United States, January 20, 1978, a case was presented in which it was briefly presented and the question asked whether it was in conformity with the 1972 norms for general absolution. In the reply proper, we hear that the particular case does not conform: "because the conditions listed for the use of the extraordinary practice of general absolution are not necessarily verified."[5] Again, we are confronted with new terminology, namely, "the extraordinary practice." *Sacramentum paenitentiae,* however, does not describe general absolution as "the extraordinary practice of general absolution." Nor does one find in norm III, in which the conditions for general absolution are listed, this specific way of speaking, namely, "the extraordinary practice of general absolution." It is clear that in this statement from the Sacred Congregation for the Doctrine of the Faith there is an extension or even a new interpretation to the meaning of general absolution, beyond the interpretation found in *Sacramentum paenitentiae.*

One year later, 1979, John Paul II, in an allocution to some Canadian bishops, made reference to this allocution of Paul VI.[6] John Paul II reiterates the phrase of Paul VI: the "exceptional character" of general absolution, but without any further comment. In March of that same year, John Paul II issued his first encyclical, *Redemptor hominis.* In this encyclical he mentions general sacramental absolution, but emphasizes that true conversion is essentially a personal conversion. The communal aspect of reconciliation, he notes, cannot exclude the individual aspect of conversion. In *Redemptor hominis* the footnotes for this reference to general absolution include the 1972 norms, his own allocution to the Canadian bishops and Paul VI's allocution to the American bishops.[7]

In an address to priests, dedicated to the confessional ministry, John

Paul II encouraged them to be generous with their time and energy in administering this sacrament.[8] In 1986, in an address to some priests from India, John Paul II again urged generosity in their pastoral service to this sacrament.[9] On October 4, 1986, in an allocution to some Spanish bishops, the same pope spoke about abuses in the practice of general absolution. He referred to the 1972 norms and to the Code of Canon Law, nn. 961–963. He urged these bishops, and, through them, their priests, to provide ample time for individual confessions.[10]

From all these papal statements it is clear that the 1972 regulations, namely *Sacramentum paenitentiae,* served as the framework for their sections on general absolution. With the exception of the encyclical *Redemptor hominis,* these papal statements are not officially addressed to the universal Roman church. Paul VI's adjectives "exceptional," "extraordinary" and "normal" are repeated only once by John Paul II and on two occasions by the Sacred Congregation for the Doctrine of the Faith in responses. In the Code of Canon Law, the section dealing with general absolution is likewise based on the 1972 regulations, but the code itself does not use the terms "extraordinary" or "exceptional" to delimit the occasions when general sacramental absolution might be licitly given.

Quite apart from such terms as "case of necessity," "exceptional character," "extraordinary," etc., it is patent that the 1972 regulations suffer a major deficiency. These regulations are not placed within a sacramental or theological context. These 1972 regulations give no evidence of the sacramental theology found in the documents of Vatican II. Without such a context, the norms are theologically, juridically and pastorally isolated and in themselves subject to distortion. Even though papal statements on general absolution, brief as they are, and even though the Code of Canon Law on this same subject of general absolution, are based on these 1972 regulations, the 1972 regulations in no way can be seen as the "starting point" or the "major criteria" for a discussion on general sacramental absolution. Rather, based on the documents of Vatican II and the entire theological discussion on sacraments which gave rise to and developed from Vatican II, the starting point must be the primordial sacrament, the humanness of Jesus.

A. THE STARTING POINT IS JESUS

Jesus in his humanity is the primordial sacrament of reconciliation. In himself alone, he offers us the essential meaning of sacramental reconciliation. In Jesus alone, not in some sacramental form, do we find the real key to Christian reconciliation. Catechesis on the sacrament of penance which begins simply with the ritual itself or with regulations is bound to become self-defeating. One asks, when perusing the 1972 regulations summarized above: Where is Jesus in all of this? The absence of any reference to Jesus as the primordial sacrament of reconciliation is a glaring absence, an absence which decontextualizes the entire document.

Both in sacramental theology and in sacramental pastoral work, beginning with a ritual or with a set of norms will remain inevitably sterile. The new ritual of reconciliation itself serves as a model for us, for the ritual itself does not begin immediately with the rite or with norms. Rather, the ritual begins with Jesus, as we saw in the *Praenotanda*. Jesus, the primordial event of reconciliation, provides the essential context for any and every ritualization or legislation. Without Jesus, such rites and regulations cannot find their substance.

Nonetheless, what we see in this issue of Jesus as the starting point is, once again, the importance of the issue of justification. The Jesus-event as the primordial reconciliation-event could also be named: the Jesus-event as the primordial justification-event. The name might also be: the Jesus-event as the primordial deification-event, or the primordial salvation-event. One of the key reasons why there is such a dispute over the issue of general sacramental absolution, a dispute which centers around the ambit of its licit use, lies in unclarified presuppositions over justification. Unless this key issue of justification is made center-stage and discussed openly, the haggling over the use or ambit of use for general sacramental absolution will go on *ad infinitum* and be, therefore, infinitely worthless. The issue of justification, however, is intrinsically connected to Jesus as the primordial sacrament of reconciliation. Jesus the reconciler is precisely Jesus the justifier.

B. THE ECCLESIAL DIMENSION

Although Jesus as reconciler is the primordial starting point, one cannot immediately move to rituals and regulations. The church itself must be formed into a reconciling community. Long before one urges priests to provide more time for confession, bishops and priests should be urged to form communities of reconciliation at the local level. The ritual of reconciliation might be magnificently structured and liturgical laws might be duly observed, but if these rituals are not themselves contextualized within a broader ecclesial context of reconciliation, they will have little lasting value. The church, to be a genuine event of reconciliation, must have a leadership, both cleric and lay, which takes the initiative for reconciliation. The church leadership, however, cannot wait for the people themselves to come to them to be reconciled. The leadership must go out to those who need reconciliation. Like Jesus, these leaders must go the extra mile. They must leave the ninety-nine, in order to search for the one who is lost. They must put aside their money and sweep until the mislaid coin is found. The leaders must go out to sinners and eat with them. They must wander through the Palestine of their own milieu, giving sight to the blind, hearing to the deaf, firmness to the lame, and life to the dead. The leaders must go out to the highways and hedgeways and invite those whom they find to the banquet. Our generation will truly experience a reconciling church if today's church, particularly in and through its leadership, moves out to the alienated and to the sinners. To stay comfortably at home, in the churches and in the sacristies and in the rectories and in the church offices, "waiting" for the sinners to return is without any doubt a characteristic of an unreconciling church community.[11]

Again, it is clear that the issue of justification lies at the heart of this church issue. Is God's grace absolutely gratuitous? Or is the church leadership, as the "mediators" and "dispensers" of this grace, also co-causes of God's grace? Even more, is God's grace operative only if church leadership "deems" the giving of grace appropriate? In other words, does God's grace depend on the leadership's judgment or action? If so, one can ask: Is grace still grace? Do sinners, in turn, have to "do" something, i.e. come to the church, so that Jesus will save them? Or is the salvific work of Jesus totally efficacious in itself? Did the salvific action of Jesus' life, death and resurrection depend on the sinner's "doing something"? If so, then Jesus is clearly not the savior of the world, as the scriptures portray him to be. He is savior of the world, but only insofar as we assist him.

How church leadership acts, how church leadership portrays itself, the very self-identity which church leadership has of itself, is shaped by the way a theology of justification is formulated. In this issue of general sacramental absolution, ecclesiology is clearly at stake, but it should be an ecclesiology which is based on *Lumen gentium:* that is, an ecclesiology which understands the church as the mirror of the true light, Jesus. Whenever the church reflects Jesus, who is the *lumen gentium,* it is church. Whenever it reflects itself and not Jesus, it is un-church. In the issue of general sacramental absolution, then, a question clearly is presented: Does the use or restriction of such general sacramental absolution reflect Jesus, the only light of the world? Or does the use or restriction of general absolution reflect the viewpoint of church people and not necessarily that of Jesus? If it reflects Jesus, then it is reflecting the issues of justification mentioned so often in this volume: grace that is absolutely gratuitous and Jesus' salvific work that is totally efficacious.

Protestants and Catholics may differ on ecclesiology, and when faced with such questions as: How are sins forgiven? Is the sacrament of reconciliation necessary, and if so, why and how? Is general absolution adequate, and if so, or if not, why? Leadership people in both Protestant and Catholic groups will almost instinctively begin to defend their positions and their practices whenever these issues are presented. This defense of position and practice, however, should not be the immediate response. Rather, the immediate response should first of all be: What does Jesus as the reconciling and justifying one mean? And secondly: Is this the heart of our own ecclesiology?

C. RITUALS AND REGULATIONS

On the basis of Jesus as the primordial and basic sacrament of reconciliation, and on the basis of the church as a foundational sacrament, rituals and regulations can become true channels of Christ's power to isolate, repel and negate sin. In the case of general sacramental absolution, parish communities and diocesan structures need to establish a catechesis which aids people to see Jesus as their reconciling Lord and savior. There is a need to build up local communities, remarkable in their efforts to go out to those who are hungry for reconciliation. In this way, even with a shortage of priests, general sacramental absolution is not singled out as *the means of confronting difficult pastoral situations.* Making the gospel alive, evangelization, really becomes the key and indeed the major means of confronting difficult pastoral situations. However, in the context of a reconciling church community, general sacramental absolution can and does play a role, for it can be a significant and important moment in the lifelong process of reconciliation, in a way which forms I and II cannot ever attain.

That general absolution plays such a major role can be seen, for example, in the comments made by the bishops of Switzerland. In 1975 the *Newsletter,* published by the Bishops' Committee on the Liturgy, cited the bishops of Switzerland on this issue of general sacramental absolution:

> The [Swiss] bishops recognize that the penitential services are among the best attended church services. . . . The bishops rely upon the responsible consciousness and prudence of their priests. Occasional abuse does not justify limiting what is permitted by the new Rite of Penance.[12]

These comments by the Swiss bishops have a healthy ring about them. The bishops indicate their trust in their priests. They indicate that an occasional abuse should not defraud the people of God from such a healthy experience of reconciliation.

From all of the above, it can be stated that general sacramental absolution cannot be seen as the panacea for all the difficulties we find in the sacrament of penance today. General sacramental absolution has its rightful place in the Christian life, and pastorally it is an enormous boon. It must equally be stated that pastoral regulations, such as those of *Sacramentum paenitentiae* of 1972, are also not the panacea for all the issues surrounding general sacramental absolution. Neither form III itself nor the regulations of 1972 can serve as the focus of attention. Without a deep experience of Jesus as reconciler and of the church as a reconciling community, rituals and norms have no theological vigor. The evangelization of both church leadership and church membership regarding Jesus, the primordial sacrament of reconciliation, is primary. The building of a true reconciling ecclesial community locally is equally prerequisite for any and all penitential forms and rituals, norms and regulations.

A second issue, however, arises. In n. 66 of the new ritual we read:

> A person who receives general absolution from grave sins is bound to confess each grave sin at his/her next individual confession.

Whenever general sacramental absolution is offered, those who avail themselves of this form truly make a "good confession." Their sins are truly forgiven. They are able to receive the eucharist and any other sacrament, e.g. ordination, matrimony, etc., worthily. This is common theological teaching throughout the Roman church, but it can only be theologically maintained if one simultaneously acknowledges that those who have received general absolution have made a "good confession." Without a good confession, no form of reconciliation is valid or licit. Evidently this term "good confession" must apply as validly to form III as it does to forms I and II. Without a "good confession," there is no sacrament of reconciliation. However, in the administration of general sacramental absolution, there exists, in the best of Roman Catholic theology, a true sacrament of reconciliation, and consequently the sorrow one has for sin and the confession one makes of sin, even in this form of general reconciliation, can only be called "good." If this is so, then what is the difference between a "good confession" and an "integral confession"? Why must a penitent "reconfess" his or her sins in a private way after general sacramental confession if all grave sins and all eternal punishment for such grave sins have been removed? General sacramental absolution is not given "conditionally." Even if a penitent were to receive general absolution and still not make a "private" confession within a year, as the regulations state, none of the person's sins return. There would be no condemnation to hell because of the grave sins which were taken away through general sacramental absolution.

It is true that in *Sacramentum paenitentiae* we read in n. VI: "With respect to the faithful, it is absolutely required for the reception of general sacramental absolution that they have the proper dispositions. This means [among other basic items] that they intend to make an individual confession in due time of those serious sins they cannot at the present time confess." Priests are told to instruct the faithful about these "dispositions and conditions." In the letter from the Sacred Congregation for the Doctrine of the Faith, January 14, 1977, it is stated: "Norm VI explicitly requires the diligent reminder that the penitent's sincere intention to bring his serious sins to individual confession within a reasonable time is a condition necessary for validity."[13] This letter is, of course, more strongly worded than one finds in *Sacramentum paenitentiae*. By raising the issue of validity one raises the whole issue of the validity of the sacraments. Even if it is the intention of the penitent to confess his or her grave sins individually at a future date, how does this intention, theologically, enter into the issue of a valid sacrament? These issues lead us to the next unresolved issue.

2. PRIVATE CONFESSION TO A PRIEST

In the historical sections of this book, we have seen that confession privately to a priest was not part of the public ritual of the patristic period. This practice stems more from the Celtic form of reconciliation. We have also seen that this Celtic form of reconciliation was officially opposed by bishops and by local councils in the early medieval church. Private confession to a priest does not, therefore, enjoy an unbroken history in the church's official practice. In 1943 Pius XII noted: "Not without inspiration of the Holy Spirit was this practice [auricular confession] introduced into the church."[14] In saying this, Pius XII clearly indicates that private confession of sins to a priest cannot be understood as a *de iure divino* situation, in the usual way that *de iure divino* is theologically understood. Confessing individual sins privately to a priest, even though brought into the church by the inspiration of the Holy Spirit, remains more a church law than a divine law.[15]

We have also seen that the relationship between contrition, which of itself takes away sin, and private confession of serious sin to a priest, together with priestly absolution, has never been satisfactorily presented in theology. The names of Peter Abelard, Hugh of St. Victor, Peter Lombard, Thomas Aquinas and John Duns Scotus come readily to mind in this theological debate. The Council of Trent, for its part, made no theological decision on this issue. If, then, one's sins through contrition have been taken away, why is it necessary to confess already-forgiven-sins to a priest in a private and detailed manner?

We have, consequently, the following separate but related issues:

a. That an act of contrition of itself removes sin and all eternal punishment due to sin is an official teaching of the Roman church (*D. 1676, 1647, 1743*).
b. That priestly absolution given generally (form III) is a valid and licit form for the sacrament of reconciliation. Through such absolution all serious sins and the eternal punishment due to such sins are removed. This, too, is an official teaching of the Roman church (*New Ritual*).
c. That an integral confession of all serious sins is necessary for absolution of sin is also an official teaching of the Roman church (*IV Lateran, D. 812*).

How does one bring these three teachings of the Roman church into some sort of theological and pastoral unity? This is no mean task. Certain factors have further complicated the issue.

A. MORTAL AND VENIAL SIN

Contemporary moral theology has called into question the very names of "mortal" and "venial" sin, at least in the way these categories had been explained in the counter-reformation period. Even the new ritual for reconciliation avoids using these terms: mortal and venial. All sin is serious, but the degree of seriousness which would cause eucharistic excommunication or even ecclesial excommunication has not been constant throughout church history, nor is it clearly presented today in moral theology. If contemporary moral theology is nuancing sin in a slightly different way than previous Catholic moral theology had done, then there must be a corresponding nuancing of the minister's role in reconciliation.

In the 1984 post-synodal apostolic exhortation, *Reconciliatio et paenitentiae,* John Paul II spends a great deal of time on the issue of mortal and venial sin.[16] John Paul traces the examples of serious sin from the Old Testament through the New Testament. Of course, he reminds us, the terms "mortal" and "venial" are not biblical terms, but he goes on to stress those sins which "lead to death" and those sins which do "not lead to death," citing the passage in 1 John 5:17.[17] However, even though John Paul is careful in his interpretation of this passage by using such words as "seems"—"seems to say . . ." "seems to be . . ."—neither the text nor the context of 1 John 5:17 is clearly adaptable to a mortal/venial context. R. Brown gathers together centuries of biblical scholarship on this particular passage from 1 John and presents the four different views on the Johannine distinction of sin, which historically come down to us from patristic times to the present. The interpretation that attempts to see in this Johannine passage a connection to mortal and venial sin is neither exegetically nor historically the more solid interpretation.[18]

John Paul also places an emphasis on Augustine with his terms of *lethalia* and *mortifera crimina,* as also *venialia, levia,* and *quotidiana.* That Augustine influenced the medieval theologians is clear, but it is less than clear that "After him, it was Saint Thomas who was to formulate in the clearest possible terms the doctrine which became constant in the church."[19] It is well known that Scotus had a quite different approach to mortal and venial sin than that of Thomas, and it is equally well known that the Council of Trent had no intention of settling disputed issues between the various schools of theology which were extant in the sixteenth century. As a consequence, both the views of Scotus and of Thomas on this matter, as also other options such as those of the Augustinian school, remained quite acceptable, and remain so down to the present. Actually, Thomas' doctrine on this matter of mortal and venial sin has never become the "constant teaching of the church."

In the references which this apostolic exhortation makes at this juncture, the Tridentine decree on justification is mentioned. In this decree on justification, we find that chapter XII mentions venial sin (*levis, quotidianum, veniale*), and that in the appended canons, namely, nn. 23, and 25, there is also mention of venial sin. However, in these three passages no definition is given of venial sin, nor is there presented in any of the documents of Trent a teaching by which venial sin might be distinguished from mortal sin, the precise issue which Thomas and Scotus argued. In chapter XV and in canon 27 of this decree, one finds the term "mortal sin," but again without any clarification or theological definition.[20] In citing chapter XV of the Tridentine decree on Justification, the apostolic exhortation indicates that the Council of Trent taught that some sins "are intrinsically grave and mortal by reason of their matter. That is, there exist acts which, per se and in themselves, independently of circumstances, are always seriously wrong by reason of their object."[21] This position seems to go a tad beyond the actual wording of the chapter in the Tridentine document, for the position stated above specifies far more pointedly than the Tridentine document that there are acts which are per se evil in themselves, and that there are acts which are always serious precisely by reason of their object. Ch. XV is entitled: *Grace, But Not Faith Is Lost by Every Mortal Sin.* The text goes on to say that only by a sin of unbelief is faith lost; the grace of justification is lost by any other mortal sin, sins which separate men and women from the grace of Christ but which can be avoided with the help of divine grace. The scholastic terminology "per se," "independently of circumstances," "by reason of their objects," are words and phrases which this chapter from Trent does not contain.

The apostolic exhortation makes mention that in the synod on reconciliation, held shortly before the publication of this apostolic exhortation, some bishops had proposed a threefold classification of sin. If the teaching of the church on mortal and venial sin, a twofold classification, however, were crystal-clear, few if any bishops would have dared make such a proposal openly. The very fact that some bishops, in a public way, voiced a different approach to the twofold classification of all sins is a sign that there is even today no constant determination of the church on this matter. The apostolic exhortation makes a brief mention of the "fundamental option" approach, current in today's theology, but John Paul raises a rather cautious voice to this approach.[22]

As careful a theologian as Karl Rahner once wrote on this matter:

As long as the integration of the world, which must come from God, is delayed, man continues to yield (though freely), in one fashion or another, to the pressures of the unintegrated world. This he does in two essentially different ways: either by a pseudo-integrist absolutizing of a moment of the world, radically engaging his liberty ("mortal sin"), or by freely slackening the dynamic which tends towards authentic integration . . . ("venial sin"). These two ways of yielding to the pressure of the unintegrated world cannot be clearly distinguished from one another in the concrete.[23]

In many ways Rahner reflects the current reconsideration of the very meaning of mortal and venial sin. He is not alone in this reflection. Such reflection on the distinction between mortal/venial could not be undertaken if the Roman Catholic position on the issue were air-tight.

For all of these reasons, one must admit that there is actually no theological view, with precise distinctions between mortal and venial sin, which can claim "official status." That there needs to be a distinction in the gravity of sinfulness is essential to any solid moral theology. This is not the issue. Rather, the issue focuses on the way in which one theologically presents such a distinction, and in current Roman Catholic moral theology these ideas are being reevaluated in a very comprehensive way.

Since the question regarding a *necessary* private confession to a priest is applicable only with "mortal" sins, not "venial" sins, the way in which current moral theologians might reclassify sin will surely have an effect on the question of the necessity for such private confessions of "serious" sin. The very renewal of moral theological thinking on the matter of mortal and venial sin cannot help but complicate further the issue of the necessity to confess one's sins privately to a priest.

B. THE SOCIAL NATURE OF SIN

The new ritual of reconciliation instructs us that all sin is an offense against God and an offense against the community. There is no such thing as a completely private or personal sin. So, too, we are instructed that reconciliation at all levels is both reconciliation with God and reconciliation with the community. There is no such thing as a private or merely personal reconciliation.[24]

This social dimension of sin and reconciliation may not be new to Christian theology, but it is clearly a new stress in contemporary Roman Catholic theology. Contrition, of itself, involves forgiveness of sin, and therefore in the way one expresses contrition, this social nature of both sin and reconciliation needs to find expression. Consider the formula suggested for an act of contrition, which was so prevalent in Catholic life for generations:

> O my God, I am heartily sorry for having offended Thee, and I detest my sins above every other evil because they displease Thee, my God, Who for Thine infinite goodness art so deserving of all my love; and I firmly resolve by Thy holy grace, never more to offend Thee, and to amend my life. Amen.

Nowhere in this prayer do we find a trace that sin has offended the community. Nowhere do we find a trace that reconciliation is a reconciliation with the community. It is all personally oriented to God alone. This act of contrition is, indeed, a little prayer, but it is one which generations of Catholics have said over and over again. It is a prayer which has clearly shaped the thinking of many Catholics on the matter of sin and reconciliation. If the prayer is focused on sin as a personal offense against God and reconciliation as a personal reconciliation with God, then Catholics will think that this is precisely what sin and reconciliation are all about. They will not think of a social dimension, either to sin or to reconciliation. It is one thing for the new ritual to stress the social aspect of both sin and reconciliation, but it is quite another to bring this new approach into the prayer-life of individual Christians, which has been so deeply affected and in such a personal way by the sentiments expressed in the act of contrition cited above.

Moreover, the confession of sin privately to a priest tends to rein-

force the private character of reconciliation, rather than its social reconciliation. How is the private confession of one's sins to a priest an acknowledgement of the social dimension of sin? How is the private
reception of priestly absolution an acknowledgement of the social dimension of reconciliation? The priest may represent the community, but
the format of the sacrament was so privately structured that this repre-
sentational and social aspect of the church came to be almost unnoticed.
In the new ritual, the rite for individual reconciliation (form I) does not
clearly do justice to the basic thrust of the documents of Vatican II, which
stated that a communal nature of sacramental celebration is to be preferred over a more private celebration. Nor does the ritual of individual
private confession do justice to the *Praenotanda* of the new ritual itself,
which inculcates, as we have seen above, this strong emphasis on the
social dimension of both sin and reconciliation.

Sin which separates one from the eucharistic community and perhaps even from the ecclesial community itself must clearly be a post-
baptismal sin which in a serious and substantive way has offended both
God and the community. Any theological grounding for the requirement
to confess one's grave sins privately to a priest must indicate that the
situation in question is clearly a serious and substantive offense against
both God and the community.

Canon law, to some degree, collaborates this basic principle. Canon
959 states that "individual and integral confession and absolution constitute the only ordinary way by which the faithful person who is aware of
serious sin is reconciled with God and with the Church." Canon law has
included this notion of reconciliation both with God and with the church.
However, it might be noted, as we have already seen, that (a) the three
forms in the new ritual are presented to us as "ordinary" ways for celebrating the sacrament of reconciliation; (b) individual confession to a
priest is only one of these "ordinary" ways; (c) reception of general
absolution forgives all serious sin and all eternal punishment due to such
sin, and therefore one must say that a person makes an "integral" or good
confession in the case of form III. It is evidently not the individual and
private confession of sins to a priest which makes a sacramental celebration good or "integral." The term "integral" can only refer to a person's
sorrow for all one's serious sins: that is, a person is not sorry simply for
one or the other sin in his or her life, but a person is sorry for all (integral)
grave sins. In this way, the general confession of sin found in form III can
be called "integral."

This same canon goes on to state that "only physical or moral impossibility excuses the person from confession of this type." The canon
implies that form III is permissible only if there is some physical or moral

impossibility. Nowhere in the new ritual is this approach validated, nor is this stated in the 1972 norms.

If one takes into consideration (a) the statements in canon law, (b) the norms of 1972, (c) the new ritual itself, and (d) statements made by the popes themselves or by one of the Vatican congregations, one is not always hearing the exact same message. The nuancing, and even some outright statements, tend to differ. Different messages are being given to the church at large on this matter. The church at large is receiving mixed signals. No wonder it is difficult to find theological and pastoral agreement on the issue of reconciliation.

The principle that the sacrament of reconciliation is required only when there has been a serious and substantive offense against God and the community has the following three components:

1. Acknowledgement of one's sin
2. An official minister of the church community
3. Serious and substantive offense

1. Acknowledgement of One's Sin

In one way or another, that is, either privately or publicly, the sinful Christian must acknowledge his or her sinfulness whenever there is a question of sin. Unless a sinner admits his or her sins, and admits them "integrally," that is, admitting all sins, and not admitting only some sins but refusing to admit others, no reconciliation is possible. The Tridentine insistence on an "integral confession," that is, a confession of sin which specifies both the nature and frequency of sins, might be considered as overly intrusive. On the other hand, one could also see this regulation, both psychologically and morally, as quite sound. If a husband, for instance, were to batter his wife in a very serious way and then simply say that he struck someone, not indicating that the person was his wife or that he left her impaired, does not do full justice to his claim to acknowledge his evil-doing. Similarly, as we hear so frequently today, an alcoholic or drug addict must admit the addiction and reject the denial before any health promotion can begin. If an alcoholic or drug addict simply acknowledged that he or she drank too much on some occasions, or used drugs heavily here and there, the denial factor remains very evident. In both instances they are denying the addiction. So, too, with sin. The denial factor disallows us from admitting our sinfulness. "Integral" confession or acknowledgement means, therefore, that one does not deny any of the sinfulness of one's life. One makes a full admission or avowal of the extent and the gravity of one's sinfulness.

2. An Official Minister

Since reconciliation is reconciliation not only with God but with the community as well, someone representing the community must accept a sinner's repentance. Reconciliation is never a one-way street. One does not leave the church and reenter the church at will. The church community, which accepted the person originally into the assembly, must reaccept such a person when there has been serious and substantive rejection of both the Lord and the church itself.

3. Serious and Substantive Offense

One is not ejected from the community for any and every failure, but only for those failures which in a serious and substantive way make the sinner's behavior totally unacceptable to the church community. It is evident that in the patristic church the rite of reconciliation was used almost exclusively for such instances. The sinner had in his or her behavior so broken with the basic and fundamental ideals of the church that union with the church was considered impossible. Only when repentance of such sinful behavior was evident did the church, in those patristic times, readmit or reconcile the sinner.

In these cases of extremely serious and substantive sinful behavior, it becomes clear that there must be a recognized acceptance by the church of the penitent sinner. This recognized acceptance takes place in what the Catholic Church more recently has called "private confession to a priest." It seems that all three elements—the acknowledgment of one's sins, the role of the official church minister, and a situation of clearly serious and substantive offense—must be operative. In such situations, then, the "confession to a priest" makes theological sense.

However, if there is not such a clearly serious and substantive sin which breaks the union of sinner and community, the need to confess one's sins privately to a priest becomes unintelligible. This indicates that the key to the problem is to be found in the third issue: What is a serious and substantive break with the Christian community?

3. THE AGE OF FIRST CONFESSION

In the twentieth century there have been four major documents from the Vatican on the issue of the age for first confession.

A. The decree *Quam singulari* of Pius X (August 8, 1910), which allowed both penance and eucharist to children.[25]
B. *The General Catechetical Directory,* promulgated by the Sacred Congregation for Clerics (April 11, 1971), in which the custom

and prescription of children receiving first confession and eucharist as established by Pius X was reiterated (n. 5), but permission was also given to continuation of experiments of the celebration of first eucharist with no prior first penance, provided such experiments are in accordance with the Holy See.[26]

C. The joint declaration, *Sanctus Pontifex,* from the Sacred Congregations for the Discipline of the Sacraments and also for the Clergy, in which, after citing both of the above documents, it was determined that the time of such experimentation was to end with the conclusion of the school year, 1972–1973. This was issued on May 24, 1973.[27]

D. The clarification, *In quibusdam Ecclesiae partibus,* made to the conferences of bishops by the Sacred Congregation for the Discipline of the Sacraments and the Sacred Congregation for the Clergy, March 31, 1977.[28]

In these documents, *Omnis utriusque* of Lateran IV is mentioned again and again, a constitution which prescribed annual confession and communion. The Latin term used to designate this constitution is *praescriptio.* Pius X in *Quam singulari* is said to have determined (*statuit*) that children could receive both penance and eucharist. This regulation of Pius X is also called a *praeceptum.* The *General Catechetical Directory* speaks of the common practice (*praxis communis et generalis*) and a custom (*consuetudo*). Having children receive communion without first confession is called a "new practice" and an "experiment." The joint declaration of the two congregations (n. c above) "declares" the time of such an experiment closed.

This language has been carefully chosen: *praeceptum, statuit, praescriptio, consuetudo, praxis communis.* These words usually indicate more a matter of ecclesiastical law than of a *de iure divino* ordinance.

In the Latin church communicating infants after baptism was the usual practice from the time when infant baptism became common down to the tenth century. When the chalice was no longer given to the lay people at communion, but only the consecrated bread, then the custom of infants making their first eucharist, generally with a spoonful of consecrated wine, gradually disappeared. In the eastern churches, the custom of communicating children has remained down to the present century. L. Gaupin has sketched the Roman church's history of this relationship between first eucharist and first penance from the post-reformation period to the present age.[29] In the latter part of the seventeenth century, because of the virtual breakdown in the initiation-sacraments, and because of the decline in faith on the part of many Catholics, the reform of the sacramental pastoral practice began to focus on the early age, particularly children. Catechisms were developed precisely for children. Baptism continued to be administered in infancy. First confession was introduced to children around the age of five or six, together with confirmation at some time close to this age. First eucharist was celebrated around the age of twelve to fourteen. Following these stages of catechesis was an ongoing religious formation on adult perseverance in the faith. In this framework, the catechesis of first penance was clearly separated from the catechesis of first eucharist. Different catechetical objectives were envisioned for the preparation of first penance and the preparation for first eucharist. The two were not, because of the separation of age, joined together. First penance preceded first eucharist not because of any theological position regarding the flow of sacraments. It was much more the catechetical needs for faith-development which prompted this structuring of the various sacraments. This structuring of the sacramental process remained until Pius X's *Quam singulari.* Pius X wanted to correct some abuses which had entered this process, primarily from Jansenistic spirituality. These abuses were an exaggerated demand for moral perfection and for a Christian intellectual expertise as far as the eucharist was concerned, together with an effort to keep advancing the age of first eucharist.

Quam singulari, with its openness to children's eucharist, created havoc with the then current catechetical processes. This is not to say that the action of Pius X did not have advantages. Still, one must today candidly admit that *Quam singulari* created a number of difficulties at the same time that it attempted to remove abuses. The first and perhaps most immediate of these disadvantages was catechetical. Catechists had to revise their entire formation structures and processes. Instead of a catechesis for first confession separate from that of first eucharist, they had to condense them into a single unit. The issue of the age for confirmation was, at this time, equally placed into an uncertain situation. Gaupin notes:

> The situation regarding sacramental order was never resolved.
> In most cases, the pattern set out by the seventeenth-century
> catechetical reform, whereby penance preceded first eucharist,
> was maintained as the given order without any critical examination of the ramifications of this for the catechesis of young
> people.[30]

The catechesis of first penance and even of the sacrament of penance which had taken place over a period of four or five years (i.e. from first penance to first eucharist) was suddenly collapsed into a process of only a few months at best. This structuring of first penance and first eucharist in close proximity of age was at first uncritically followed, but several factors began to change this. Gaupin lists the following five factors as particularly significant: (a) the development of the liturgical movement in the United States, particularly through the efforts of the Benedictines at St. John's Abbey, Collegeville, Minnesota; (b) the general advances in sacramental theology made throughout the Roman church prior to Vatican II; (c) the documents and reforms of Vatican II; (d) the developments in child psychology; (e) the writings of J. Jungmann.[31]

Out of all of this came the unrest in the American Catholic Church over this issue of first penance and first eucharist. The structuring of these sacraments in the catechesis of children was seriously questioned and a change was increasingly demanded. In many ways, this call for change was the first well-researched and critical response to *Quam singulari.* The fact that *Quam singulari* had not been so profoundly critiqued is very significant, for it indicates that the foundational ideas behind *Quam singulari* had until then not been theologically and pastorally reviewed.

Both the *Addendum* to the *General Catechetical Directory* and the declaration *Sanctus pontifex* were setbacks to this critical and serious reflection. The response given to the conferences of bishops from the two congregations only added to the confusion, since the response was itself ambiguous. The *National Catechetical Directory, Sharing the Light of Faith,* reflects both the controversy and the ambiguity which has come from this current analysis and from the ambiguity created by Vatican statements.

From all of this historical material it is clear that first confession prior to first eucharist is not of apostolic, patristic or even early medieval origin. Indeed, for almost ten centuries in the west the opposite custom was to communicate the infant immediately after baptism, a tradition which the east has retained down to the present. The sacrament of reconciliation was seen throughout this period of time more as a sacrament of an adult Christian than as a sacrament of children.

The custom of first penance prior to first eucharist, which began to develop in the post-reformation period, has to be seen, then, as no more than a custom or a church prescription at a given time in history. In sacramental theology, there is absolutely no essential relationship between the eucharist on the one hand, and on the other a *necessary prior reception* of the sacrament of penance, with the one exception, namely, when there has been a serious and substantive separation by a Christian both from God and from the community.

If this is the principle for a solid eucharistic theology, namely, that one must first receive reconciliation *only when* there has been a substantive and serious break with the church, and if this is the way Roman Catholic Christians have understood the issue of sin and eucharist for adults, one cannot devise different rules or regulations for children. In other words, there cannot be one eucharistic and reconciliation theology for children and another eucharistic and reconciliation theology for adults. Whatever sinful situation might prevent an adult from receiving the eucharist must be the same when children, not adults, are involved.

None of the regulations, prescriptions, customs, etc. which the Roman Church leadership has adopted from time to time can be said to *require* first confession before first eucharist in an absolute way. The four directives cited above can only be interpreted as endorsing and encouraging a pastoral practice, which may or may not be the most theologically correct pastoral practice. If these documents were to be interpreted in a way other than a mere recommendation or a pastoral prescription, we could easily be faced with a situation of erroneous theological doctrine. Both in the case of a child and in the case of an adult, prior confession is *only necessary* when there has been a serious substantive sin. No regulation from whatever church source can be in opposition to that foundational stance.

Without any doubt, both children and adults *may* receive the sacrament of reconciliation prior to eucharist, and the above documents encourage such a practice in the case of children. However, this can only be seen as an "encouraged practice." Neither parents nor the children themselves nor those in pastoral care can be forced into an unbending regulation which apodictically demands first confession before first eucharist.[32]

Whatever solution might be developed on this matter of first penance, it will not be developed outside the context of baptismal theology and its questions as to age; outside the context of eucharistic theology and its questions as to age; outside the context of a theology of sin; and above all outside the context of a theology of justification. Indeed, unless one enters more fully into the theology of justification with its two major issues, the absolute gratuity of God's grace and the full efficacy of Jesus' salvific work, neither the issue of the age for first penance nor any of the key issues regarding the sacrament of reconciliation will ever be on target.

The issue of first penance for children generally focuses on the material we have just put together: the documents which have come from the Vatican, catechetical problems, the issue of serious and substantive sin. These are, of course, important matters, but in many ways they are the wrong starting points for discussion. One needs to move to a far more fundamental issue: namely, that of justification. Does justification in Christ mean that grace is absolutely gratuitous? Does justification mean that the salvific work of Jesus is in itself fully efficacious? The Council of Trent eventually said "yes" to both of these issues, but, one can rightfully ask, are these issues apparent in the way in which the official Roman church speaks about the first penance for children? In the 1973 declaration from the Sacred Congregation for the Discipline of the Sacraments in which the "experiment" was declared ended, Jesus is not mentioned once throughout the document. The April 30, 1976 rather long letter from the Sacred Congregation for the Sacraments and Divine Worship and the Sacred Congregation for the Clergy, which was sent to the national conferences of bishops, focused entirely on the matter of first penance for children. Again, in this entire document Jesus is not mentioned once. A year later, March 31, 1977, the same two congregations issued another letter, *In quibusdam Ecclesiae partibus,* to the conferences of bishops, and in this fairly lengthy letter Jesus is mentioned only once: namely, the reception of penance prior to eucharist "arouses in them [the children] the awareness of moral good and evil and aids them to bring a more mature disposition to their happy meeting with Christ in the eucharist."[33] Even the Addendum of the *General Catechetical Directory* mentions Jesus three times, twice in the section on the formation and growth of the moral conscience of children (n. 2), but only in the briefest way. The third and final time is in the next paragraph (n. 3) when the text speaks of advancing in a more intimate love of the Lord Jesus. Once the focus of the Addendum turns to "certain new experiments" (nn. 4 and 5), Jesus is not even mentioned. Rather, the stress is on obedience to the regulations set up by the Vatican. One can legitimately ask: Are we talking about obedience to church authority and church regulations, or are we talking about the celebration of a justifying Jesus in our midst? What is more central in this issue: Jesus or church authority? In this document, the very lack of centralizing one's position in Christ raises serious questions as regards its theological value.

One wonders whether the teaching from Vatican II of the church as a basic sacrament, whether the teaching of theologians who developed this sacramental approach to the church and who based it on Jesus as the primordial sacrament, will ever penetrate into Roman Catholic sacramental thought. In many ways the argumentation on the time for a child's first reception of the sacrament of reconciliation is based on and nourished by the church as the foundational sacrament and Jesus, especially, as the most basic sacrament of all. The reception of penance by children will only be theologically and pastorally meaningful if and when such a reception evidences both the church and above all Jesus as the basic sacraments. To present a case in which the only argument seems to be that the church authority has established this prescription cannot help but falter. Unless one sees in children's reception of penance as in every reception of penance an image of the justifying Jesus, there will be no solution. But what do we mean when we say that Jesus is justifying? The christological base on this matter of reconciliation must be faced forthrightly. The fact that church authority, even at Vatican II, did not address this issue of justification and ecclesiology, nor that the renewal of the sacraments after Vatican II did not address the relationship between justification and the sacrament of reconciliation, nor that any of the statements which have come from the Vatican since Vatican II have addressed the issue of justification, lies at the root of almost every problem of sacramental theology today. The question of first penance is no exception.

4. FREQUENT CONFESSION

In many ways, different factors are involved in the issue of frequent confession, although many similar issues remain operative. There is little doubt that the frequency of confession in the Roman church, worldwide, has declined in the last twenty-five years. The renewed rite of reconciliation, helpful as it is, in many ways militates against frequent confession. Form I, i.e., private confession to a priest, if done *rite,* according to the prescriptions of the ritual, takes more time now than the pre-Vatican II ritual of private confession to a priest had required. Of course, many of the prayers and readings are optional in this new ritual, but if these optional parts are systematically and ordinarily omitted, then the efforts at a renewal of this sacrament will be sharply curtailed. In its full structure, form I militates against frequent confession. Neither the penitent nor the priest has the time for this full-structured ritual on an ongoing basis. The penitent will not wait for the priest if there are three or four penitents ahead of him or her. Three or four penitents could mean a wait of forty-five minutes to an hour. Again this is presupposing that the ritual is being performed in its full structure, which is precisely what *rite* means. The priest also does not have the time to spend in such lengthy periods of reconciliation.

Still, church officials, from the pope down, have continued to encourage frequent confession. The ritual, however, militates against this. In many ways there is a "catch-22" situation. The ritual signals priests to spend more time with each penitent; the church officials signal priests to confess large numbers of penitents. The two signals do not fit well together.

There is an added problem. The theology of the priesthood which the documents of Vatican II have inculcated envisions the priest from the standpoint of the threefold mission and ministry of Jesus: prophet, priest and king (teacher, sanctifier, and leader). More often than not, the documents of Vatican II place the prophetic ministry in first place, that is, the preaching of the word. This primacy of the prophetic ministry over the sacramental ministry signals priests to spend more time in that area of their work. These documents of Vatican II have clearly moved away from a sacrament-centered approach to the priesthood, an approach which the scholastic theology of priesthood had fostered. Frequent confession, with its demands on priestly time, places the priest back into the scholastic view of priesthood which the teaching of Vatican II did not accept as an adequate theology of ordained ministry for our times. Again mixed signals are being given by church authorities. Admonitions to priests to spend more time hearing confession seem to run counter to the doctrinal and rather solemn statements on priestly ministry which Vatican II promulgated for the entire church.[34]

The issue of frequent confession, tied as it is to an understanding of the role of the ordained minister on the one hand, and to the theology of reconciliation on the other, cannot be adequately dealt with unless a theology of justification is presented as the foundation for one's theology. Why should a Christian "frequently" receive the sacrament of reconciliation? Does this frequent reception of reconciliation foster a doubt that one's sins are forgiven? Does it imply that the penitent must "do" something, perhaps again and again, so that one's sins can be forgiven? Does not frequent reception of the eucharist forgive sin? There are too many questions which frequent confession, as a studied practice, raises, and the questions all have to do with the full and absolute gratuity of God's grace and the full efficacy of the salvific work of Jesus. Perhaps an urging for frequent confession might be theologically and pastorally more meaningful if those who urged such a practice would make it clear how such frequent reception of reconciliation reflects the justifying Jesus. If such a reflection is not made clear, then the very practice of frequent reconciliation is rendered questionable. The very lack of an integrated presentation of frequent confession and a theology of justification continues to give rise both to unhealthy pastoral positions and to ambiguous theological positions.

There are many ways in which one's everyday sinfulness is uprooted from our hearts, and the church has always held these many avenues for reconciliation in highest esteem: prayer, fasting, and almsgiving have been the ones most often mentioned. The sacrament of the eucharist is in current theology more and more described as a sacrament of reconciliation. Over-stress on confession of venial sins, i.e. over-stress on the sacrament of reconciliation as *the* means for uprooting such sin, does not take

into account all these other ways and means which Christians have and
have had at their disposal for the process of reconciliation.

5. THE ISSUE OF JUSTIFICATION

It is certainly clear, from this entire volume, that the issue of justification lies at the heart of a theology on the sacrament of reconciliation.
Without a clear understanding of justification, as regards both its theology and its practice, this sacrament of reconciliation cannot help but
become ambiguous and, at times, unintelligible. The Council of Trent,
some four centuries ago, did indeed present the Roman church with a
statement on justification. This statement, as we have seen, has both
strengths and weaknesses. Nonetheless, from 1547 to the present day, the
leadership of the Roman church has not officially addressed the question
of justification. When one studies, for instance, the analytical index of
Denzinger, the compilation of official and important church statements,
under the rubric of justification, there are only passing references to
justification beyond this Tridentine decree. The expectations of many
Protestants and Catholics just prior to the Second Vatican Council that
this council would say something on the issue of justification were pain-
fully disappointed. From a theological position, a discussion about the
very nature and mystery of the church, which the documents of Vatican
II clearly attempt to express, must include something substantial on the
issue of justification. That the ecclesiology of Vatican II did not take this
issue into account raises questions on the adequacy of the ecclesiology
which the council presented.

One of the first issues regarding justification which remains unresolved is that of faith. The theology of faith which the reformation theologians maintained was not directly considered in the 1547 document of
Trent. Rather, the Tridentine bishops remained with the Augustinian
view of faith: namely, *fides caritate formata,* a faith formed by charity.
Faith alone, *sola fides,* was considered by the Tridentine bishops as only
an initial disposition to the justification process. Seripando's marginal
note on one of the drafts of this document, namely whether faith in the
New Testament is merely an initial disposition, needs to be better analyzed by Catholic authority, both theological and hierarchical. It is clear
from the many current studies of New Testament exegesis that the New
Testament writings do not use the term "faith" in the Augustinian sense.
In fact, the New Testament writings tend to use the term "faith" much
more in the reformation theologians' approach and interpretation. Since
the issue of faith is so fundamental, the very issue of the theological
meaning of faith, based on solid biblical foundations, remains part of the

unfinished agenda which Trent did not resolve and which subsequent Roman Catholic official teaching has not faced.

Second, the issue of justification includes the faith-position that God's grace is absolutely gratuitous. The "Judaizers" mentioned in the letters of Paul; the critique Paul makes of both Jew and Gentile in the early section of his letter to the Romans; the struggles between the *hebraioi* and *hellenistai* of the apostolic church; the issues raised by Pelagius in the fourth century, and by the semi-Pelagians in subsequent centuries; the criticism of the semi-Pelagian aspects of Roman Catholic practice and theology which the reformers continually expressed in their writings; the teaching of *homo in puris naturalibus* of Baius; the teaching of Jansenius in the *Augustinus;* the issues surrounding the question of the "natural desire for the supernatural" in the *Nouvelle Théologie* of the mid-twentieth century—all of these positions were challenged, precisely because they compromised the absolute gratuity of God's grace. Nonetheless, the far-reaching influence of Jansenism in the post-reformation period and the intense theological discussion which clustered about the *Nouvelle Théologie* in the twentieth century makes a reexamination of this issue imperative for our day.

The new rite of penance was not developed within the context of this aspect of justification, and as such the new rite remains in many areas ambiguous. Besides the rite, we have as well various theologies of the sacrament of penance. With all the emphasis which some theologies of the sacrament of penance place on the "works of the penitent" and on the "efficacy of the priestly absolution," and with all the emphasis which the pastoral practice of the sacrament of reconciliation brings to the "dispositions" of the penitent and the "intentions" of the priest, the absolute gratuity of God's grace has at times appeared to be compromised. As we have just seen above, the "need" to confess privately already-forgiven-sins, the "need" to put first penance prior to first eucharist, and the "emphasis" on frequent confession can easily be presented in a way which compromises the absolute gratuity of God's grace. In all of these instances (and many others as well) it appears that we, as creatures, must *do something first;* then, and then only, does or can God give us grace. Merely to call such penitential activities "dispositions" does not avoid the issue of God's gratuitous grace. In each of the instances mentioned in this chapter, the integration of the issue (general absolution, first penance, etc.) must take place within a theology of God's gratuitous grace. The very fact that so much of the written discussion on these issues does not even mention this aspect of God's grace indicates that these issues are being handled outside the very question of justification.

Third, in some christological writing, particularly in the discussion on the death of Jesus, the "work" of Jesus itself in many ways becomes a "good work." Jesus himself *must do something first,* so that God can or does give us forgiveness. In such explanations, there appears to be a sort of crypto-Pelagianism. Even in the middle ages and in the reformation period, the term merit *de condigno,* although most often used only in the case of Jesus, can imply that Jesus performs some good work first, i.e. he offers himself as "victim," or he "atones" for sin, so that God can offer us forgiveness. This line of thinking almost compromises the faith-stance that our salvation through Jesus is the supreme instance of God's absolute gratuitous gift of grace.

Moreover, in ecclesiology, Roman Catholic practice and at times Roman Catholic teaching, though not with a solemn, official status, seem to indicate that the church itself offers something along with the offering of Jesus. This appearance of co-offering has often been central to eucharistic theological debate. The view that the salvific and propitiatory work of Jesus was efficacious by itself was indeed taught by Trent, as we saw. But the post-Tridentine explanation of the term "sacrifice of the Mass" often did not reflect the Tridentine approach. Even though the eucharist is by far the lightning rod for this debate, the sacrament of penance shares in this line of questioning as well. Today, especially, Roman Catholic theologians have discussed the role of the church in the reconciliation process. The new ritual of reconciliation itself teaches that there is both a reconciliation with God and a reconciliation with the church. Some theologians indicate that the reconciliation with God depends on the reconciliation with the church, and this interpretation raises the issue of the adequacy of Jesus' salvific action. Other Catholic theologians indicate that the reconciliation with the church is the sacramental reflection of one's reconciliation with God. In this latter case, the argument goes, absolution is merely declaratory.

Latimer's rhetorical phrase: "If this [that we ourselves merit salvation] be so, then farewell Christ!" remains as valid today as it did in Latimer's own time. There is but one savior, Jesus. Neither the church itself, nor any member of the church, can be considered a second savior or even (though in miniscule fashion) a co-savior. An official statement of the Roman church on this matter of Jesus' full efficacy is needed today as Christians move together more and more. The Lutheran/Roman-Catholic dialogue on justification presents both traditions, down to post-Vatican II times. At the end of its joint statement, it lines up the issues which still need clarification: (1) forensic justification; (2) sinfulness of the justified; (3) sufficiency of faith; (4) merit; (5) satisfaction; (6) criteria of authenticity.[35] McGrath's study on the history of justification ends with open questions as well.[36] Tavard indicates that "the entire edifice of

Catholic thought since the sixteenth century stands in need of recon-struction," precisely because of this issue of justification.[37] J. Heinz, in his *Justification and Merit,* studies the contemporary material on these two issues and notes that there really is not a consensus.[38]

The continued study on justification is foundational. Nonetheless, it remains a separate factor from the factor which lies at the heart of current Roman Catholic uncertainty in the theology and practice of the sacra-ment of reconciliation. This factor can be stated as follows: In what way does the sacrament of reconciliation, in its currently revised form, cele-brate the central mystery of justification? The way in which this question is answered, both theologically and pastorally, will be the measure by which the revised rite of reconciliation succeeds or fails.

The revised sacrament of penance, in some of its theological de-scription and in some of its pastoral practice, has given rise to the view that what one has lost through sin is now regained. Nothing could be further from New Testament thought. The offense, we read, is not like the gift. Sinners through the sacrament of reconciliation do not simply "regain" a lost innocence. Reconciliation is not a personal paradise re-gained. Rather, sinners are inundated with a superabundance of God's forgiving and gracing love, far beyond anything which sinners lost and which sinners might strive to regain. It is this super-abundance of God's grace which the sacrament of reconciliation is meant to celebrate. The sacrament of reconciliation cannot be presented as a "means" to regain what was lost. It cannot be presented in the words of the *Baltimore Catechism:* "the sacrament by which sins committed after Baptism are forgiven through the absolution of a priest" (q. 379). Such a description is far too narrow, and because of its narrowness it actually distorts the very meaning of the sacrament of reconciliation. The sacrament of penance is a celebration of justification: a justification, a salvation, a deification, in which God not only forgives seventy-times-seventy-times-seventy-times-seventy-times seven times, but also gives to us, sinners, what eye has never seen, ear has never heard, nor has it ever entered into our hearts. The height, the breadth, the depth and the length of this mystery of God's forgiving grace is what the sacrament of reconciliation is meant to cele-brate. To celebrate anything less caricatures the very meaning of this sacrament.

But on what basis can one say such things, and say them so critically? To answer this we must return to the very place where this volume began in the opening chapters: there one read that the real sacrament of recon-ciliation is Jesus in his humanity. If Jesus is the basic, primordial, foun-dational, root-meaning sacrament of reconciliation, then the ritual of reconciliation must be a sacrament of this same Jesus. Only when and if this ritual of penance is indeed a sacrament of Jesus, then is it clearly a sacrament of the very meaning of justification: a justification which includes the absolute gratuity of God's grace and the full efficacy of Jesus himself; a sacrament of the superabundant love and mercy of a reconciling, justifying, divinizing God.

Notes

1. Reconciliation and Justification: Their Interrelationship

1. *Lehrverurteilungen-kirchentrennend? Rechtfertigung, Sakramente und Amt im Zeitalter der Reformation und heute,* ed. K. Lehmann and W. Pannenberg (Freiburg i. B.: Herder, 1986) pp. 45–46. This volume is one of a series, arising from the ecumenical dialogues between Protestant and Catholic theologians in Germany.

2. E.W. Gritsch, "The Origins of the Lutheran Teaching on Justification," *Justification by Faith,* ed. H.G. Anderson, T.A. Murphy, J. Burgess (Minneapolis: Augsburg, 1985) pp. 163–164.

3. F. Sottocornola, "Commentarium: il nuovo 'Ordo Paenitentiae'," *Notitiae* 90 (1974) pp. 63–79; P. Jounel, "La Liturgie de la réconciliation," *La Maison-Dieu* 117 (1974) pp. 7–37; A. Tegels, "The New Order or Rite of Penance," *Worship* 48 (1974) pp. 242–246; R. Ling, *Worship Resources* 3 (1974); Z. Alszeghy and M. Flick. *Il sacramento della riconciliazione* (Turin: Marietti, 1976); *Sacramento della Penitenza* (Zurich: Pas, 1974) G. Pianazzi and A. Triacca, eds.

4. M.-J. Le Guillou, "La Sacramentalité de l'Église," *La Maison-Dieu* 93 (1968) p. 15. In this article the author summarizes the teaching of Vatican II and the sacramentality of the church and connects this sacramentality to the mystery of salvation or justification.

5. C.P. Osborne, K., *Sacramental Theology* (N.Y.: Paulist, 1988).

6. K. Rahner, "Salvation," *Sacramentum Mundi* (N.Y.: Herder & Herder, 1970) v. V p. 428.

7. A.E. McGrath, *Justitia Dei: A History of the Christian Doctrine of Justification* (London: Cambridge University Press, 1986) v. I, p. 2.

8. Ibid., p. 3.

9. Ibid., p. 3.

10. R.W. Bertram, " 'Faith alone justifies'; Luther on *Iustitia fidei,*" *Justification by Faith,* p. 174.

11. Ibid., p. 177.

12. H. Jedin, *A History of the Council of Trent* (St. Louis, Mo.: Herder Book Co., 1958), trans. by E. Graf, v. II, p. 170.

13. Ibid., pp. 170–171.

14. Historical studies on the redemption have been numerous. Some of the older works are: F. Chr. Baur, *Die christliche Lehre von der Versöhnung* (Tübingen: C.F. Osiander, 1838); R.S. Franks, *A History of the Doctrine of the Work of Christ* (London: Hodder and Stoughton, 1918); L.W. Grensted, *A Short History of the Doctrine of the Atonement* (Manchester: Longmans, Green and Co., 1920); H. Rashdall *The Idea of Atonement in Christian Theology* (London: Macmillan and Co., 1919); J. Rivière, *Le dogme de la Rédemption, Essai d'étude historique* (Paris: Lecoffre, 1905); ibid. *Le dogme de la Rédemption. Études critiques et documents* (Louvain: Bureau de la revue, 1931); ibid. *Le dogme de la Rédemption chez saint Augustine,* 3e éd. (Paris: Gabalda, 1933); ibid. *Le dogme de la Redémption après saint Augustine* (Paris: Gabalda, 1930); J.N.D. Kelly, *Early Christian Doctrines* (London: Adam & Charles Black, 1965); G. Aulén, *Christus Victor* (New York: Macmillan, 1969) trans. A.G. Herbert.

15. For a general history of the sacrament of reconciliation, cf. B. Poschmann, *Penance and the Anointing of the Sick* (N.Y.: Herder and Herder, 1963) trans. F. Courtney; H. Vorgimler, "Der Kampf des Christen mit der Sünde," *Mysterium Salutis* (Einsiedeln: Benziger, 1976) v. V, pp. 363–440; Paul Palmer, *Sacraments and Forgiveness* (Westminster, Md.: Newman Press, 1959); E. Bourque, *Histoire de la Pénitence-Sacrement* (Quebec: Laval Univ., 1947); P. Galtier, *L'Église et la rémission des péches aux premiers siècles* (Paris: Beauchesne, 1931); ibid. *De Paenitentia: Tractatus Dogmatico-historicus* (Rome: Gregorian Univ., 1956); K. Rahner, "Vergessene Wahrheiten über das Busssakrament," *Schriften zur Theologie* (Einsiedeln: Benziger, 1964) pp. 143–183; P. Anciaux, *La théologie de pénitence au Xiie siècle* (Louvain: E. Nauwelaerts, 1949); ibid. *Histoire de la discipline pénitentielle* (Paris, 1963); O.D. Watkins, *A History of Penance* (N.Y.: Burt Franklin, 1961); H. Karpp, *La Pénitence* (Neuchâtel: Delachaux et Niestlé, 1970) trans. A. Schneider, W. Rordorf, P. Barthel; J. Ramos-Regidor, *Il sacramento della penitenza* (Turin: Elle de Ci, 1974); J. Dallen, *The Reconciling Community* (N.Y.: Pueblo, 1986). J.A. Favazza, *The Order of Penitents* (Collegeville, Minn.: The Liturgical Press, 1988). Cf. also the detailed bibliography in *The Renewal*

of the Sacrament of Penance, published by The Catholic Theological Society of America (1975) pp. 49–95.

16. A. McGrath, *Iustitia Dei: A History of the Christian Doctrine of Justification,* v. I cf. above; v. II, from 1500 to the present day (Cambridge: Cambridge University Press, 1986); G. Tavard, *Justification an Ecumenical Study* (N.Y.: Paulist, 1983). Authors could also be cited as regards an historical account of justification for a particular individual theologian or for a particular period of history. Mention will be made of such writings in the course of this volume.

2. Jesus: The Primordial Sacrament
of Reconciliation

1. R. Brown, *The Gospel According to John* (Garden City, N.Y.: Doubleday and Co., 1970) v. 2, p. 1044.

2. John the Deacon, "Letter to Senarius," *PL,* v. 59, 171.

3. Cf. on the issue of these Johannine passages and baptism, T. Worden, "The Remission of Sins," *Scripture* 9 (1957), pp. 65–79, 115–127. Worden notes that in the first three centuries, the fathers of the church interpreted this Johannine passage in reference to baptism, but Brown indicates both the textual and contextual reasons why such an interpretation cannot be maintained with any assurance.

4. Brown, op. cit., p. 1044.

5. Ibid., p. 1045.

6. B. Rigaux, " 'Lier et délier' Les ministères de réconciliation dans l'Église des temps apostoliques," *La Maison-Dieu,* 117 (1974) pp. 86–135.

7. Ibid., p. 134. J. Dallen, op. cit., pp. 5–28, presents the same view.

8. A. Nocent, "Il sacramento della penitenza e della riconciliazione," *I Sacramenti: teologia e storia della celebrazione* (Genoa: Marietti, 1986) pp. 133–203.

9. Ibid., pp. 144–147.

10. Ibid., p. 144.

11. Ibid., p. 145.

12. Ibid., pp. 146–147.

13. On this subject, cf. E. Martinez, "The Interpretation of *oi mathetai* in Mt. XVIII," *Catholic Biblical Quarterly,* 23 (1961) pp. 281–292; J. Murphy-O'Connor, "Péché et communauté," *Révue Biblique,* 74 (1967) 161–193, esp. 186–187. P. Adnès, *La Penitencia* (Madrid: BAC, 1981) pp. 36–37 interprets Matthew 18:18 in close relationship to rabbinical loosing/binding. He sees this as "the more common" opinion, citing

Strack-Billerbeck, Buchsel, Jeremias, Vögtle, Schmitt, Giesen, Cothenet, and Derousseaux. Adnès raises the issue whether this binding/loosing affects merely the external forum or applies to the internal forum as well. He opts for the latter, pp. 38–40, an indication that this issue is still undecided by biblical scholars and theologians. However, he does add: "Hay que reconocer, sin embargo, que, si bien los textos de Mateo hablan de un poder confiado a la Iglesia para perdonar los pecados cometidos después del bautismo, lo hacen unicamente de una manera velada, implícita. Podríamos dudar de la realidad de este poder si no tuviéramos un testimonio escriturario mas claro, mas formal. El evangelio de Juan va a proporcionárselo" (p. 39). Adnès openly indicates that there is no clear indication in Matthew alone on a power conferred to the church to forgive sins committed after baptism. Only with the gospel of John does this aspect, so he states, become clear. However, when he focuses on John 20:22–23, he says: "Pero la Iglesia no se engañara cuando, cada vez mas, vaya discerniendo en este texto de Juan el fundamento escriturístico mas importante del sacramento de la penitencia" (p. 47). Two items should be mentioned: for a Catholic theologian, specializing in sacramental theology and writing in 1981, Adnès totally overlooks contemporary Vatican II theology on Jesus and the church as the fundamental sacraments, and therefore Jesus and the church must be seen as "el fundamento escriturístico" for the sacrament of penance. Not John 20:22–23 but Jesus himself and the church itself are the fundamental sacraments. Secondly, the fact that he totally disregards contemporary Catholic and Protestant scholarship, summarized as we have seen by Brown, Rigaux, and Nocent, indicates again that he has not advanced beyond pre-Vatican II theological positions.

14. Ben F. Meyer, *The Early Christians* (Wilmington, Del.: M. Glazier, 1986) p. 57.

15. Ibid., p. 65.

16. Ibid., p. 82.

17. Ibid., p. 68.

18. Ibid., pp. 76–77.

19. Ibid., p. 80.

20. Poschmann, op. cit., p. 18.

21. Favazza, op. cit., p. 81.

22. Ibid., p. 81.

23. J. Jeremias, *New Testament Theology* (N.Y.: Charles Scribners, 1971) pp. 76–121.

24. J.H. Charlesworth, *Jesus Within Judaism* (N.Y.: Doubleday, 1988).

25. Ibid., p. 7, n. 22.
26. Ibid., p. 71.
27. Ibid., pp. 45–53 for an overview of current considerations on the issue of sin and forgiveness during first century Palestinian Judaism.
28. Ibid., esp. pp. 48–51.
29. Ibid., pp. 68–71, in which Charlesworth cites passages from various Dead Sea scrolls which focus the term "poor" on the Essenes, who used these terms, the "poor," or the "poor in spirit," as technical terms to describe themselves. The origin of this technical derivation seems to be based on the Righteous Teacher who had been exiled from the temple priesthood. Once again, there is an exclusion from those in the religio-social world who had power. The Righteous Teacher now had only God's power to rely on. That the Essenes lived simply in the Qumran monastery cannot be denied, but that they were beggar-poor is quite a different question.
30. Ibid., pp. 206–207; the work of E.P. Sanders to which Charlesworth refers is: "The Search for Bedrock in the Jesus Material," *Proceedings of the Irish Biblical Association,* 7 (1983) pp. 74–86.
31. Meyer, op. cit., p. 42.

3. The Life, Death, and Resurrection of Jesus

1. "Praenotanda," *Rite of Penance,* n. 1.
2. "Common Statement," *Justification by Faith,* p. 16.
3. E. Schillebeeckx, *Jesus, An Experiment in Christology* (N.Y.: The Seabury Press, 1979) trans. H. Hoskins, p. 37.
4. *The Baltimore Catechism* (N.Y.: Sadlier, 1941) p. 34.
5. N. Flanagan, *Friend Paul* (Wilmington, Del.: M. Glazier, 1986) pp. 153–157.
6. Ibid., p. 156.
7. J. Fitzmyer, "Pauline Theology," *The Jerome Biblical Commentary* (Englewood Cliffs, N.J.: Prentice-Hall, 1968) pp. 807–808.
8. D. Stanley, *Christ's Resurrection in Pauline Soteriology* (Rome: Pontificio Instituto Biblico, 1961) pp. 69–80, 277–279.
9. E. Käsemann, "Die Heilsbedeutung des Todes Jesu nach Paulus," *Zur Bedeutung des Todes Jesu* (Gütersloh: Gert Mohn, 1967) p. 34. Cf. also B. Meyer, op. cit., pp. 114–158.
10. E. Schillebeeckx, op. cit., p. 294.
11. Ibid., pp. 274–282.
12. Ibid., p. 282.

13. Ibid., pp. 283–291.

14. D. Senior, *The Passion of Jesus in the Gospel of Matthew* (Wilmington, Del.: Michael Glazier, 1985), p. 164.

15. Ibid., p. 166.

16. Schillebeeckx, op. cit., pp. 286–287.

17. Senior, op. cit., p. 166.

18. Schillebeeckx, op. cit., pp. 291–294; this is the least developed of Schillebeeckx' threefold interpretations. Perhaps the brevity is due to the fact that this interpretation has been so dominantly used in Christian tradition, particularly in this present century.

19. Ibid., p. 293.

20. W. Kasper, *Jesus the Christ* (N.Y.: Paulist, 1976) pp. 113–123, esp. p. 115.

21. Ibid., p. 114.

22. J. Sobrino, *Christology at the Crossroads* (N.Y.: Orbis, 1982) trans. J. Drury, pp. 179–235. Cf. also, Sobrino, *Jesús en América Latina* (San Salvador: UCA/Editores, 1982) pp. 173–183.

23. Sobrino, *Christology at the Crossroads,* pp. 184–187.

24. Ibid., p. 190.

25. Ibid., p. 202.

26. Ibid., p. 224.

27. G. Aulén, *Christus Victor,* p. 1.

28. J.N.D. Kelly, *Early Christian Doctrines,* p. 163.

29. J. Riviére, *Le dogme de la Rédemtion, Essai d'étude historique.*

30. J. Pelikan, *The Emergence of the Catholic Tradition* (Chicago: University of Chicago Press, 1971) pp. 141–155.

31. G. Ghiberti, *Resurrexit: Actes du symposium international sur la Résurrection de Jésus* (Rome: Libreria Editrice Vaticana, 1974) ed. E. Dhanis, pp. 643–745.

32. W. Künneth, *The Theology of the Resurrection* (London: SCM, 1965) trans. J.W. Leitch, p. 16.

33. F. Schleiermacher, *Der Christliche Glaube* (Berlin: Walter De Gruyer & Co., 1960) ed. M. Redeker, 2:82.

34. J.A. O'Brien, *The Faith of Millions* (Huntington, Ind.: Our Sunday Visitor, 1938) 11th ed. p. 118.

35. A. Tanquerey, *Manual of Dogmatic Theology* (N.Y.: Desclée, 1959) trans. John J. Burns, v. 1, p. 76.

36. F.X. Durwell, *La Résurrection de Jésus, Mystère de Salut* (Paris: Xavier Mappus, 1950) trans. Rosemary Sheed, *The Resurrection* (N.Y.: Sheed and Ward, 1966).

37. Ibid., Durwell, Eng. trans. op. cit., pp. 149–150.

4. Justification and Reconciliation in the
Patristic Period, 150 to 700 A.D.

1. H.C. Lea, *A History of Auricular Confession and Indulgences in the Latin Church* (Philadelphia: Lea Bros. & Co., 1896), three volumes.

2. E. Bourque, *Histoire de la Pénitence-Sacrement,* pp. 63–65. J. Dallen, op. cit., cautions us not to overstress this idea of early encratism, since the documents are not that conclusive; cf. pp. 2–3, 15–22; but it is safe to say that in some patristic churches encratism was clearly evident. Favazza, op. cit., pp. 96–99, notes that some Catholic authors stress the rigorism of this early period, while others tend to modify the rigorism. Favazza seems to agree with R. Joly, "La doctrine pénitentielle du Pasteur d'Hermas et l'exégèse récente," *Revue de l'histoire des religions,* 147 (1955) pp. 32–49, by maintaining that there was both a rigorist element in the church alongside a more lenient tradition (p. 99). M.-F. Berrouard, "La pénitence publique durant les six premiers siècles: Histoire et sociologie," *La Maison-Dieu,* 118 (1974) 92–130, indicates that a rigorism set in during the third century, but there seems to have been some rigorism already in the latter part of the first and beginning of the second century as well, a rigorism which might have been localized rather than general, but one, nonetheless, which affected the way some churches dealt with the post-baptismal sinner.

3. For an outline of the theory that Hermas began something quite new, cf. Poschmann, op. cit., pp. 26 ff.; Adnès, op. cit., pp. 85–87. Defenders of Hermas' innovation were Petau, Sirmond, Funk, Battifol, Harnack, Loofs, Seeberg, Windisch, Preuschen, Schwartz, Koch, Dibelius, Weinel, Puech, and Bihlmeyer. Those who maintain that Hermas was simply advocating a practice which was already a part of church practice, at least in Rome, were: d'Alés, Bardenhewer, Hünermann, Galtier, Tixeront, Altaner, Poschmann, and Adnès. On both sides of this argument, dogmatic stances at times seem to predetermine the interpretation of historical data.

4. Cf. Hermas, *Commandment,* 4, 3, in which the author clearly states the once-only quality of post-baptismal reconciliation; cf. also ibid. 4, 1, 8. An ecclesial or ritual dimension is not stated in Hermas. However, if the issues revolved simply around a personal prayer for God's forgiveness, then this once-in-a-lifetime reconciliation makes little sense. Hermas' influence on church discipline in the centuries which immediately followed his writings indicates that church leaders understood Hermas in the sense of an ecclesially sponsored ritual. Cf. Karpp, op. cit., pp. 56–57 for the text.

5. Cf. Poschmann, op. cit., pp. 26–34; a similar judgment is found in Quasten, *Patrology* (Westminster, Md.: Newman Press, 1951) v. I, pp. 98–99.

6. Tertullian, *De Baptismo,* 7.

7. This is the thesis of Watkins, Mortimer, Harnack, Funk and Battifol.

8. This is the thesis of d'Alés, Galtier, Poschmann, Palmer and Adnès.

9. For the texts of Tertullian on this matter, cf. Palmer, op. cit., pp. 27–32; these are all taken from *De Pudicitia,* written when Tertullian had become a Montanist. For the historical interpretation of these texts, cf. Poschmann, ibid., pp. 39–44; Bourque, op. cit., pp. 83–89; Watkins, op. cit., pp. 118–125; Adnès, op. cit., pp. 93–105. For the controversy involving Hippolytus, we have only his writings. Nothing written by Callistus has come down to us. It may be, but this is not sure, that Hippolytus was not against the total exclusion of an adulterer in the process of reconciliation, but only the relaxation of the time required, which Callistus seemed to allow. Cf. Poschmann, op. cit., pp. 49–52; Watkins, op. cit., pp. 109–113; Bourque, op. cit., pp. 89–92; Favazza, op. cit., pp. 174–178. Gy, *La Maison Dieu* (1974) pp. 92–130, presents a lengthy description of the rigorism in this early church period and various moves for the relaxation of the rigorist position.

10. Cf. Bourque, op. cit., pp. 95–114; Poschmann, op. cit., pp. 52–62; Watkins, op. cit., pp. 176–222.

11. For the pertinent passages, cf. Palmer, op. cit., pp. 41–42.

12. On the various stages of lapsi, cf. John T. McNeill and Helena M. Gamer, *Medieval Handbooks of Penance* (N.Y.: Columbia University Press, 1938), pp. 7–9.

13. On murder, cf. Bourque, op. cit., p. 87, n. 1.

14. Cf. Tertullian, *De Paenitentia,* 9. Text in Karpp, op. cit., pp. 176–178.

15. Cf. Cyprian, *De Lapsis,* 16, and passim.

16. On Origen, cf. A. Nocent, "Il Sacramento della Penitenze e della Riconciliazione," *I Sacramenti,* p. 160; Poschmann, op. cit., pp. 62–75; Bourque, op. cit., pp. 75, 267–271; Palmer, op. cit., pp. 33–40. Dallen speaks of a *ius communicationis*—cf. pp. 38–39, 72–73. This is an entire controversy by itself, namely, whether this sacramental ritual means first reconciliation with God (*pax cum Deo*) and only then reconciliation with the church (*pax ecclesiae*), or vice versa. In the passages noted above, Dallen seems to say that Cyprian opted for the second. The second opinion theologically appears to be the weaker position, and is clearly open to the criticism of the reformation churches.

17. On Innocent, I, cf. *Epistula Innocentii Papae I ad Decentium*

Episcopum Eugubinum (Turin: Tiposervizio) ed. A. Ferrua, undated, c. 6, n. 9; c. 7, n. 10.

18. On Ambrose, cf. F. Homes Dudden, *The Life and Times of St. Ambrose* (Oxford: Clarendon Press, 1935) two vols. esp. v. II, pp. 555–679 for a lengthy study of Ambrose as a theologian; pp. 624–634 for Ambrose's approach to grace and sin; and pp. 634–636 for Dudden's comments on Ambrose's approach to the ritual of reconciliation; Ambrose, *De Paenitentia;* Nocent, op. cit., p. 164.

19. On Augustine, cf. Poschmann, op. cit., pp. 96–109; Nocent, op. cit., p. 164; Bourque, op. cit., pp. 129–132; E. Portalié, *A Guide to the Thought of Saint Augustine* (Chicago: Henry Regnery Co., 1960) trans. R.J. Bastian, pp. 260–267.

20. On Leo I, cf. Bourque, op. cit., pp. 127–128; Nocent, op. cit., p. 165; Palmer, op. cit., pp. 115–120.

21. Dionysius of Alexandria, *Fragment of the Letter to Connon;* the fragments of his writings have been gathered together by C.L. Feltoe, *The Letters and Other Remains of Dionysius of Alexandria* (Cambridge: Cambridge University Press, 1904).

22. Gregory the Wonderworker, *Canonical Epistle,* Eng. text in Palmer, op. cit., pp. 63–65.

23. Basil, *Ep.* 199, c. 22, *PG,* 32, 727.

24. Sozomen, *Ecclesiastical History,* 7, 16; Eng. trans. from Palmer, op. cit., pp. 122–123. Cf. Dallen, op. cit., p. 68.

25. *Acts of the Council of Nicaea,* Eng. text in Palmer, op. cit., p. 70.

26. Poschmann, op. cit., pp. 105–106; cf. also the letter of Pope Siricius (384–398) to Bishop Himerius of Tarragona, Spain, *PL,* 12, 1137.

27. Cf. Watkins, op. cit., p. 465.

28. Cf. Cyprian, *Ep.* 9, 10–11; *Ep.* 12 in which a deacon is explicitly mentioned. One needs to remember that by the time of Innocent I the term "sacerdos" which previously had referred almost exclusively to the episkopos, was gradually being applied to the presbyters as well.

29. On the issue of private penance, cf. Galtier, *De Paenitentia,* pp. 218–260; Bourque, op. cit., pp. 37–45. Older authors defended private penance in the early church; cf. A. Lagarde, "La pénitence dans les églises d'Italie au cours des IVᵉ et Vᵉ siècles," *Révue de l'histoire des religions,* 42 (1925) pp. 108–147; Poschmann, *Kirchenbusse und correptio secreta bei Augustinus* (Braunsberg: Bender, 1923); Galtier, "Comment on écarte la pénitence privée," *Gregorianum* 31 (1940) pp. 183–202; K. Adams, "Die abendländische Kirchenbusse im Ausgang des christlichen Altertums, Kritische Bemerkungen," *Theologische Quartalschrift,* 100 (1929) pp. 1–66. More contemporary authors find no private penance in the patristic church; cf. Adnès, op. cit., pp. 130–136; Nocent, op. cit., p. 166.

Dallen, op. cit., p. 81, notes that in the descriptions of death rituals which involved the Roman form of penance and which date from the early part of the seventh century one finds "the only clear instance in the ancient period of something approaching private sacramental penance."

30. For Caesarius of Arles, cf. G. Millenkamp, *Penance in Transition and Caesarius of Arles* (Rome: Gregorian University Press, 1973).

31. On the question of mortal and venial sin, cf. D. Mongillo, "Natura del Peccato," *Dizionario Enciclopedico di Teologia Morale* (Milan: Edizioni Paoline, 1987) pp. 737–741; P. Schoonenberg, "Der Mensch in der Sünde," *Mysterium Salutis* (Zürich: Benziger, 1967), v. 2, pp. 845–941, esp. 854–861; Dallen, op. cit., pp. 59–60.

32. Cf. H. Vorgrimler, "Der Kampf des Christen mit der Sünde," *Mysterium Salutis* (Zürich: Benziger, 1976) v. 5, p. 414.

33. On these early councils of the church, cf. Nocent, op. cit., pp. 165–166; also Dallen, op. cit., pp. 58–62; Poschmann, op. cit., pp. 82–84.

34. On the *Didascalia apostolorum,* cf. R. Hugh Connolly, *Didascalia Apostolorum* (Oxford: Clarendon Press, 1929), pp. liv–lvi for general introductory remarks; Chapter VI, pp. 40–55 for text. Favazza, op. cit., pp. 122–129 has a brief but well-organized summary of the material on a ritual of penance in this text.

35. On the *Apostolic Constitutions,* particularly the lengthy attestation by the deacon, cf. English text in Palmer, op. cit., pp. 72–74.

36. On the *Sacramentary of Verona* cf. the brief analysis of its importance for reconciliation in Nocent, op. cit., p. 159.

37. A. McGrath, op. cit., p. 19; cf. also a general survey in C.P. Carlson, Jr., *Justification in Earlier Medieval Theology* (The Hague: Martinus Nijhoff, 1975) pp. 1–17.

38. K. Stendahl, "Paul among Jews and Gentiles," in *Paul Among Jews and Gentiles and Other Essays* (Philadelphia: Fortress, 1983) p. 83.

39. McGrath, op. cit., p. 21.

40. R. Eno, "Some Patristic Views on the Relationship of Faith and Works in Justification," *Justification by Faith,* p. 130. Eno's longer article on the same subject and with the same title, *Recherches Augustiniennes* (Paris: Études Augustiniennes, 1984), pp. 3–27, leads to the identical conclusion. In this latter form, Eno treats specifically of the interrelationship between the patristic theology of justification and the theology of the sacrament of reconciliation, pp. 23–25.

41. Ibid., pp. 112–125, 4–19.

42. McGrath, op. cit., p. 23.

43. McGrath, ibid.; cf. Carlson, op. cit., pp. 17–20 for the *Commentaria in xiii epistolas Paulinas* by Ambrosiaster, written about this same time.

44. Ibid., p. 25.

45. Ibid., p. 36.

46. Eno, op. cit., pp. 122–125, 15–19 shows that Augustine's thought on grace and justification was applied to baptism. Augustine's treatment of original sin almost forced him to move in this direction. H. Pope, *Saint Augustine of Hippo* (Westminster, Md.: Newman Press, 1949), makes no mention of the sacrament of penance in Augustine's thought. E. Portalié, *A Guide to the Thought of St. Augustine,* gathers together almost every item on the penitential ritual which can be found in Augustine's writings (pp. 260–267). In this material, however, one does not find a wrestling with the gratuity of grace, the freedom of human will, and the ritual of reconciliation. Portalié spends considerable time on the way in which Augustine appears to have divided sin: those requiring public penance, and those which are taken away by other spiritual means. For those who have sinned and are required to submit to public penance Augustine speaks of *poenitentia laboriosa,* of due satisfaction, of painful and grievous penance (pp. 263–265). In all of this we find a fairly standard patristic approach, but nothing which indicates a meshing of his teaching on the gratuity of God's grace and the ritual of penance.

47. P. Fink, "History of the Sacrament of Reconciliation," *Alternative Futures for Worship: Reconciliation* (Collegeville, Minn.: Liturgical Press, 1987) pp. 73–75.

48. Cf. G. Macy, *The Theologies of the Eucharist in the Early Scholastic Period* (Oxford: Clarendon Press, 1984), pp. 18–21. This is a fine reconsideration of these eucharistic controversies.

5. Justification and the Penitential Practice of the Celtic Churches

1. Kathleen Hughes, "The Celtic Church and the Papacy," *The English Church and the Papacy in the Middle Ages* (N.Y.: Univ. Press, 1965) ed. C.H. Lawrence, pp. 16–17; cf. also J. Ryan, "The Early Irish Church and the See of Peter," *Medieval Studies Presented to Aubrey Gwynn* (Dublin: Colm O. Lochlainn, 1961).

2. J.T. McNeill and Helena M. Gamer, op. cit., p. 26.

3. John Ryan, *Irish Monasticism* (Dublin: Talbot Press, 1931) pp. 92–93.

4. Cf. McNeill and Gamer, op. cit., pp. 44–46.

5. Cf. L. Bieler, *The Life and Legend of St. Patrick: Problems of Modern Scholarship* (Dublin: Clonmore and Reynolds, 1949); idem, *The Works of St. Patrick,* Ancient Christian Writers v. XVII (Westminster: Newman Press, 1953); idem, *The Irish Penitentials* (Dublin: The Dublin

Institute for Advanced Studies, 1963); Eleanor S. Duckett, *Gateway to the Middle Ages: Monasticism* (Ann Arbor, Mich.: Univ. of Michigan Press, 1938) v. 3; Hans von Campenhausen, "The Ascetic Idea of Exile and Medieval Monasticism," *Tradition and Life in the Church* (Philadelphia: Fortress, 1968) trans. A.V. Littledale.

6. Cf. an unedited manuscript by W. Storey, "The Tradition of Christian Penance: Celtic Monastic Penance and Its Influence in the West." Cf. also P. Galtier, "Les origines de la pénitence irlandaise," *Recherches de science religieuse,* 42 (1954) 58–85, 204–225; C. Vogel, "La discipline pénitentielle en Gaule des origines au IXe siècle: le dossier hagiographique," *Recherches de science religieuse,* 30 (1956) 1–26, 157–186.

7. Mansi, XIV, 102, 559; cf. also C. Carlson, *Justification in Earlier Medieval Theology,* pp. 82–87.

8. *Conciliorum oecumenicorum decreta,* p. 221; Eng. trans. from Palmer, op. cit., pp. 197–198.

9. Cf. A. Teetaert, *La Confession aux laïques dans l'Église latine* (Paris: J. Gabalda, 1926). The major scholastics, however, were not at one on the question of the sacramentality or non-sacramentality of confession to lay people. John Duns Scotus, more than any other scholastic theologian, appears to have made the strongest and most influential argument against the sacramentality of a confession to a lay person. However, the custom of confessing to lay people outlasted the entire scholastic period, at least in some areas of the western church.

10. Cf. McNeill and Gamer, op. cit., pp. 38–44. In this section of the chapter I am highly indebted to this work for its summation of the importance and influence of these penitentials.

11. Cf. McGrath, *Iustitia Dei,* p. 40. G. Tavard, *Justification, an Ecumenical Study,* pp. 23–30 outlines the influence of Augustine on the deliberations of the late patristic and above all the early medieval western church.

12. McGrath, ibid., p. 41.

13. C. Carlson, op. cit., pp. 65–66.

14. Ibid., p. 66.

15. Cf. K. Froehlich, "Justification Language in the Middle Ages," *Justification by Faith,* p. 143.

16. Ibid., p. 143.

17. Carlson, op. cit., pp. 29–33. The author presents the text based on A. Souter, and indicates in the margin the various authors cited. This text by Sedulius Scotus is typical of Carolinigian biblical scholarship.

18. McGrath, op. cit., p. 55.

19. Anselm, *Proslogion,* 10.

20. McGrath, op. cit., p. 59.

21. B. Lonergan, *De Verbo Incarnato* (Rome: Gregorian University, 1964) [Thesis decima quinta ad decimam septimam] pp. 497–520.

22. Ibid., pp. 516–520.

23. McGrath, op. cit., p. 60; he cites F. Hammer, *Genügtuung und Heil: Absicht, Sinn und Grenzen der Erlösungslehre Anselms von Canterbury* (Vienna: 1966).

24. Ibid., p. 60.

25. Cf. J. Heinz, *Justification and Merit: Luther vs. Catholicism* (Berrien Springs, Mich.: Andrews University Press, 1981) pp. 136 ff. Heinz is heavily indebted to J. Riviére, "Mérite," *Dictionnaire de Théologie Catholique;* M. Landgraf, *Dogmengeschichte der Frühscholastik* (Regensburg: Pustet, 1952–1956); J. Auer, *Die Entwicklung der Gnadenlehre in der Hochscholastik* (Freiburg i. Br: Herder, 1951).

26. Poschmann, *Penance and the Anointing of the Sick,* p. 156.

6. The Sacrament of Penance and the Theologies of Justification from the Twelfth Century to the Reformation

1. Cf. P.J. Anciaux, *La théologie du sacrement de pénitence au XIIième siècle;* E. Amann, "Pénitence," *Dictionnaire de théologie catholique,* v. 12, cc. 722–1138 (Paris: Letouzey, 1933); L. Braeckmans, *Confession et communion au moyen âge et au concile de Trent* (Paris: Gembloux, J. Duculot, 1971); C. Vogel, *Le pécheur et la pénitence au Moyen Age* (Paris: Ed. du Cerf, 1969).

2. *Enchiridion Euchologicum Fontium Liturgicorum* (Rome: Edizioni liturgiche, 1979) ed. E. Lodi, pp. 570–571. Cf. also Palmer, op. cit., p. 175, who notes that it is difficult to say when absolution formulae were first introduced into the penance liturgies or even when they came to be seen as the sacramental form. Both deprecative (more common) and indicative forms are used throughout the twelfth century. Cf. also J. Jungmann, *Die lateinischen Bussriten in ihrer geschichtlichen Entwicklung* (Innsbruck: Rauch, 1932).

3. Cf. Bourque, op. cit., pp. 325 ff. Bourque includes the Latin text of the *Corrector* taken from *PL* 140, 949–978.

4. In the introduction to *Libri IV Sententiarum* of Peter Lombard (Quarrachi: College of S. Bonaventure Press, 1916) the editors note: "Quisquis Magistri libros 'Sententiarum' attente examinaverit, facile animadvertet quam multa ex illis, tacito autoris nomine, afferat, et praesertim quam constanter simul et prudenter methodo Abaelardi inhaereat"

(pp. xii–xiii). Since Lombard's work became the basic text throughout the scholastic period, Abelard's influence, though unnamed, remained equally present. Cf. also R.R. Bolgar, *The Classical Heritage* (N.Y.: Harper and Row, 1964) pp. 158–162; H. Wolter, "The New Theology: Abelard, Peter Lombard, Gratian," *Handbook of Church History,* ed. H. Jedin, J. Dolan, v. IV (N.Y.: Herder and Herder, pp. 47–49). Cf. also E.F. Rogers, *Peter Lombard and the Sacramental System* (Merrick, N.Y.: Richwood Publishing Co., 1976) pp. 47–50. Also, Anciaux, op. cit., 64–70, who along with M. de Wulf, J. de Ghellinck and others (p. 65) affirm the ranking position of Abelard.

5. Peter Abelard, *Ethics, PL* 178, 664 ff; *Sic et Non,* c. 151. Anciaux, op. cit., pp. 177–186, presents this aspect of Peter Abelard's thought very clearly.

6. H. Vorgrimler, "Der Kampf des Christen mit der Sünde," *Mysterium Salutis,* pp. 414–419.

7. P. Abelard, *In Rom.* II, 835–836. Cf. also J. Riviére, *Le Dogme de la Rédemtion au debut du moyen-âge* (Paris: J. Vrin, 1934) pp. 96–129.

8. G. Aulén, *Christus Victor,* pp. 96–97.

9. C. Carlson, *Justification in Earlier Medieval Theology,* p. 108. Anciaux, op. cit., pp. 126 ff.

10. *Sententiarum libri quinque, PL,* 211, 1044a; cf. also *Compilatio praesens,* ed. J. Longère, *CCSL,* 51 (Turnholt: Brepols, 1980).

11. Hugh of St. Victor, *De Sacramentis fidei, PL* 176, 565; cf. also Anciaux, op. cit., pp. 164–174.

12. Cf. A. Vanneste, "La Théologie de la pénitence chez quelques Maitres Parisiens de la première moitié du XIIIe siècle," *Ephemerides theologicae lovanienses,* 28 (1952) pp. 24–28; K. Lynch, "The Doctrine of Alexander of Hales on the Nature of Sacramental Grace," *Franciscan Studies,* 19 (1959) 334–383. In 1946 Alexander's lectures on the *Sentences* were discovered and then published: *Glossa in Quattuor Libros Sententiarum Petri Lombardi* by the Quarrachi editors. The *Summa Halensis* is, today, considered the work of several authors, basing themselves to a strong degree on Alexander; cf. J. Auer, "Textkritische Studien zur Gnadenlehre des Alexander von Hales," *Scholastik,* 15 (1940) pp. 63–75.

13. Bonaventure, *Opera Omnia* (Quarrachi: Ad Claras Aquas, 1889) v. 4, pp. 314–586; J. Guy Bougerol, *Introduction to the Works of Bonaventure* (Paterson, N.J.: St. Anthony's Guild Press, 1964) trans. by J. de Vinck; B. Marthaler, *Original Justice and Sanctifying Grace in the Writings of St. Bonaventure* (Rome: Miscellanea Francescana, 1965); V. Heynck, "Zur Busslehre des hl. Bonaventura" *Franziskanische Studien,*

36 (1954) 1–82; R. Ohlmann, "St. Bonaventure and the Power of the Keys," *Franciscan Studies,* 6 (1946) 293–315.

14. Albert the Great, *Opera Omnia: Commentarium in IV Sententiarum* (Paris: Vives, 1884) v. 29, 1. IV, d. XIV to XXII, pp. 400–901; M. Entrich, *Albertus Magnus: Sein Leben und seine Bedeutung* (Graz: Styria, 1982).

15. Thomas Aquinas, *Summa theologiae* (N.Y.: McGraw-Hill, 1963) ed. and trans. by Blackfriars; J. Gottler, *Der h. Thomas von Aquin und die vortridentinischen Thomisten über die Wirkungen des Busssakraments* (1904).

16. John Duns Scotus, *Quaestiones in Librum Quartum Sententiarum;* N. Krautwig, *Die Grundlagen der Busslehre des J. Duns Skotus* (Freiburg i. Br: 1938); V. Heynck, "Attritio sufficiens," *Franziskanische Studien,* 31 (1949) 76–134; J.P. Benabarre, "La penitencia sacramental según J. Duns Escoto," *Verdad y Vida,* 31 (1973) 317–380.

17. Poschmann, op. cit., p. 184.

18. Cf. Adnès, op. cit., p. 149.

19. Thomas Aquinas, *Suppl.* q. 18, a. 1; *Summa Theologiae,* III, q. 84, a. 1 ad 3; q. 86 a. 6 ad 1. This interpretation of Thomas' thought is presented by Poschmann, op. cit., pp. 171–172, as also J. Ramos-Regidor, *Il Sacramento della Penitenza,* p. 196.

20. Adnès, op. cit., p. 152, considers the issue between the Franciscan and Dominican theological schools as one which centers on the subjective/objective aspects in the sacrament of penance. Adnès completely misses the issue which Scotus is treating. Scotus is focusing primarily on the absolute gratuity of God's grace, on the one hand, and the actions of men and women, on the other, whether or not these actions are those of the penitent ("subjective" in Adnès' view) or of the church ("objective" in Adnès' view). Adnès writes: "El mérito de Santo Tomas es haber intentado resolver el problema sin sacrificar la eficacia de la absolución ni la necessidad de la contrición." By this Adnès implies that only the Thomistic efficient instrumental causality preserves the efficacy of absolution. Such a position is simply his own personal theory. Scotus' position clearly maintains both the efficacy of absolution and the necessity of contrition, but also, as regards both contrition and absolution, Scotus maintains the complete gratuity of God's grace. It is the issue, therefore, of sacramental causality, not the subjective and objective issue, which divides these two schools of thought on this matter. Even more fundamental is the different emphases each school places on the relationship of God's freedom on the one hand, and human action on the other.

21. McGrath, op. cit., p. 94.

22. Ibid.

23. Thomas Aquinas, *Summa Theologiae,* Ia IIae, q. 83, a. 4.

24. Thomas Aquinas, *Summa Theologiae,* v. 60, ed. and trans. by R. Masterson and T.C. O'Brien (N.Y.: McGraw-Hill, 1966) p. xx.

25. Ibid.

26. Alexander of Hales, *Summa,* p. IV q. 17, m. 4, a. 6, §4.

27. Thomas Aquinas, op. cit., Ia IIae, q. 113, a. 8.

28. Bonaventure, *Commentaria in IV Libros Sententiarum,* 1. IV, d. XVII, p. i, a. 2, q. 1.

29. Richard of Middleton, *Supra quattuor libros sententiarum* (Brescia: 1591).

30. Bonaventure, *Itinerarium mentis in Deum,* c. 4, n. 4; *De Triplici Via* (Prol.). Cf. J.G. Bougerol, *Introduction to the Works of Bonaventure,* pp. 156–160.

31. Cf. J. Heinz, *Justification and Merit: Luther vs. Catholicism,* p. 139.

32. Scotus, *Opus Oxoniense,* IV d. xvi. q. 2.

33. John of La Rochelle, *Quaestiones disputatae de gratia,* q. 2; ed. Doucet, 45–49.

34. McGrath, op. cit., p. 54, cites a clear passage from Julian of Eclanum on this very point: "Est igitur procul dubio iustitia, sine qua deitas non est; quae si non esset, deus non esset; est autem Deus, est itaque sine ambiguitate iustitia."

35. Ibid., p. 57; cf. also a lengthy discussion on the positions of J. Ratzinger and H. Kessler concerning Anselm's satisfaction-theory in R. Haubst, "Anselms Satisfactionslehre einst und heute," *Analecta Anselmiana* (Frankfurt am Main: Minerva, 1975) pp. 141–157.

36. Cf. W.J. Courtenay, "Necessity and Freedom in Anselm's Conception of God," *Analecta Anselmiana,* pp. 39–64; throughout Anselm's life he struggled with the concept of necessity in God, and his writings indicate a development, even change in his thought on this matter. In *Cur Deus Homo* he reaches his final position on the issue.

37. Cf. Haubst, op. cit., pp. 146–148. Anselm uses the term "infinite" only twice and Haubst believes that authors, such as Ratzinger, have overstressed this aspect of Anselm's argument. Sometimes this has been done to play down the Scotistic approach of God's acceptance.

38. Thomas Aquinas, op. cit., IIIa q. 46, a. 3.

39. McGrath, op. cit., p. 64.

40. Scotus, *Opus Oxoniense* III dist. xix q. 1, n. 7.

41. McGrath, op. cit., p. 64.

42. Cf. A. Wolter, *Duns Scotus on the Will and Morality* (Washington, D.C.: The Catholic University of America Press, 1986) p. 12; text from

Scotus, *Ordinatio* IV, dist. 46 ix, ibid., pp. 241ff. Courtney, op. cit., in his analysis of Anselm reaches the identical conclusion.

43. Ibid., p. 14.

44. Ibid., p. 15.

45. Scotus, *Reportata Parisiensia* III, d. 7, q. 4, n. 5. This is the key passage in Scotus himself. Cf. *Franciscan Christology* (N.Y.: St. Bonaventure University, 1980) ed. Damian McElrath; O. Schaefer, *Bibliographia de vita, operibus et doctrina Ioannis Duns Scoti* (Rome: Herder, 1955); ibid., "Conspectus brevis bibliographiae scotisticae recentioris," *Acta Ordinis Fratrum Minorum*, 85 (1966) pp. 531–550.

46. E. Doyle, "John Duns Scotus and the Place of Christ," *Clergy Review*, v. 57 (1972) p. 777.

47. Cf. J. Heinz, op. cit.; J. Riviére, "Mérite," *Dictionnaire de théologie catholique;* A. Landgraf, *Dogmengeschichte der Frühscholastik;* J. Auer, *Die Entwicklung der Gnadenlehre in der Hochscholastik* (Freiburg i. Br.: Herder, 1951); W. Detloff, *Die Entwicklung der Akzeptations- und Verdienstlehre von Duns Skotus bis Luther* (Münster: Aschendorff, 1963); J. Kunze, "Verdienst," *Realencyklopadie für protestantische Theologie und Kirche;* B. Hamm, *Promissio, pactum, ordinatio* (Tübingen: J.C.B. Mohr, 1977); R. Schinzer *Die doppelte Verdienstlehre des Spätmittelalters und Luthers reformatorische Entdeckung* (Munich: Chr. Kaiser, 1971).

48. Cf. Heinz, op. cit., pp. 114–116; this is based on O. Pesch, "Die Lehre vom 'Verdienst' als Problem für Theologie und Verkündigung," in *Wahrheit und Verkündigung* (Munich: F. Schoningh, 1967) ed. L. Scheffczyk, W. Dettloff, R. Heinzmann, v. II.

49. Portalié, op. cit., p. 275.

50. Augustine in *Enarratio in Ps. 145* says: "Non enim deseret opus suum, si ab opere suo non deseratur." Auer and Ratzinger, *Kleine katholische Dogmatik* (Regensburg: Pustet, 1972), 5:87, state that the phrase itself in its usual Latin form comes from the school of Peter Abelard.

51. Wolter, op. cit., p. 17; cf. also pp. 48–51.

52. H. Oberman, *The Harvest of Medieval Theology* (Cambridge, Mass.: Harvard University Press, 1963).

53. Ibid., pp. 175–176.

54. Ibid., p. 427.

55. McGrath, op. cit., pp. 155–179; this is a key section of McGrath's work.

56. Ibid., p. 160.

57. Ibid., p. 161.

58. Ibid., p. 166.

59. Ibid., p. 172.

7. Justification, the Sacrament of Reconciliation, and the Reformation Theologians

1. Luther, "Ninety-Five Theses or Disputation on the Power and Efficacy of Indulgences." *Luther's Works*, v. 31 (Philadelphia: Fortress, 1957) p. 25.

2. Luther, "Large Catechism," *Book of Concord* (Philadelphia: Fortress, 1959) ed. T.G. Tappert et al., pp. 460–461.

3. Luther, "Augsburg Confession," *Luther's Works*, v. 35, p. 11.

4. P. Meinhold, "Entwicklung des Busswesens und Handhabung der Beichte im Lutherischen Protestantismus," *Busse und Beichte* (Regensburg: Friedrich Pustet, 1972) p. 81.

5. Luther, "The Babylonian Captivity of the Church," *Luther's Works*, v. 36, pp. 58–61.

6. Luther, "Commentary on the Romans," 4, 25, *WA*, 56, 296, 15–22.

7. Tavard, op. cit., pp. 49–58 for discussion on the *Commentary* of 1519.

8. Ibid., p. 60, citing Luther's 1535 *Commentary on Galatians* 3:19.

9. Ibid., p. 66, citing Luther, op. cit., 3, 6.

10. McGrath, *Iustitia Dei*, v. II, p. 4.

11. Ibid., p. 7.

12. G. Yule, "Luther's Understanding of Justification by Grace Alone in Terms of Catholic Christology," *Luther, Theologian for Catholics and Protestants* (Edinburgh: T. & T. Clark, 1985) p. 87.

13. Ibid., p. 107.

14. Cf. M. Gesteira Garza, "El Sacramento de la Penitencia en Lutero hasta el año 1521," *El Sacramento de la Penitencia* (Madrid: Aldecoa, 1972) pp. 272–276; Luther himself states: "Verisimilius est quod sacerdos novae legis declarat dumtaxit et approbat solutionem Dei (id est ostendit) et hac ostensione et iudicio suo quietat conscientiam peccatoris, qui eius iudicio tenetur credere et pacem habere" (*WA* 1, 542, 14).

15. McGrath, op. cit., p. 12.

16. Ibid., pp. 11–14.

17. Luther, "Liturgy and Hymns," *Luther's Works*, 53, p. 121.

18. B. Lohse, "Die Privatbeichte bei Luther," *Arbeitstagung und Sitzung der Kommission für Gottesdienst und geistliches Leben des lutherischen Weltbundes* (Hannover: 1967) p. 1 (privately printed). A study which focuses more on the liturgy of reconciliation in the Lutheran Church is that of O. Jordahn, "The Practice of Penance in the Lutheran Church," *Studia Liturgica*, 18 (1988) 1, pp. 103–107.

19. Cf. H. Nyman, "Die Beichte im Luthertum des 17. und 18. Jahr-

hunderts, Orthodoxie und Pietismus," Anlage B, *Arbeitstagung und Sitzung* (privately printed) (Hannover: 1967).

20. Ibid.

21. O. Jordahn, op. cit., p. 107.

22. J. Heinz, op. cit., pp. 158–174.

23. Ibid., p. 205.

24. G. Yule, "Luther: Theologian for Catholics and Protestants," *Luther,* p. 15.

25. H.J. McSorley, *Luther—Right or Wrong? An Ecumenical-Theological Study of Luther's Major Work, "The Bondage of the Will"* (N.Y.: Newman, 1969).

26. McGrath, op. cit., p. 32.

27. J. Calvin, *Institutes of the Christian Religion* (Philadelphia: Westminster, 1960) ed. by J.T. McNeill, trans. by F.L. Battles. References in the text are to this translation. Cf. also A.R. George, "The Ministry of Reconciliation in the Evangelical Tradition," *Studia Liturgica* 18 (1988) 1, pp. 112–116.

28. Ibid., p. LX.

29. McGrath, op. cit., p. 38.

30. R. O'Day, *The Debate on the English Reformation* (London: Methuen, 1986) p. 1.

31. Tavard, op. cit., p. 68.

32. Article 11 of the *Thirty Nine Articles.*

33. W. Tyndale, "Answer to Sir Thomas More's Dialogue," *The Works of William Tyndale* (Appleford, Eng.: The Sutton Courtenay Press, 1964) v. I, pp. 369–370.

34. T. Cranmer, "Homily on Salvation," in P.E. Hughes, *Theology of the English Reformers* (London: Hodder and Stoughton, 1965) p. 50.

35. H. Latimer, *Works,* v. I, p. 419; cited in Hughes, op. cit., p. 54.

36. Tyndale, cited in Hughes, op. cit., p. 60.

37. J. Jewell, *The Works of John Jewell, Bishop of Salisbury* (Cambridge: University Press for the Parker Society, 1948), ed. J. Ayre. Cf. also D.R. Holeton, "Penance in the Churches of the Anglican Communion," *Studia Liturgica,* 18 (1988) 1, pp. 96–102. Holeton offers only a brief overview, and concentrates on contemporary practice. His footnotes cite in full a number of relevant texts.

38. Cf. O'Day, op. cit., pp. 102–132.

39. Ibid., p. 105.

40. A.F. Pollard, *Henry VIII* (N.Y.: Harper, 1966), p. 187.

41. C.S.L. Davies, *Peace, Print and Protestantism* (London: Paladin, 1976) p. 155.

42. O'Day, op. cit., p. 1.

43. Tavard, op. cit., p. 69. Cf. also McGrath, op. cit., pp. 111–121;

McGrath notes that a central idea of Puritan thought on justification is its federal foundation. This federal or covenanted foundation is found in the *via moderna,* the young Luther, and Reformed Orthodoxy, and it is associated with H. Bullinger, Z. Ursinus, K. Olevianus and G. Zanchius.

44. Ole E. Borgen, *John Wesley on the Sacraments* (Zurich: Gotthelf, 1972) p. 48; cf. also pp. 131–136, 197–202.

45. McGrath, op. cit., pp. 98–134.

8. Reconciliation and Justification at the Council of Trent

1. Cf. A. Duval, *Les Sacrements au concile de Trente* (Paris: Les Éditions du Cerf, 1985) pp. 153–154. Cf. also J. Ramos-Regidor, *Il Sacramento della Penitenza* (Turin: Elle di Ci, 1974), pp. 187–189 for a description of the frequency of penance in the late middle ages. Cf. Braeckmans, op. cit., pp. 20–36.

2. Duval, op. cit., pp. 154–155. The citation is taken from *Sermons choisis de Michel Menot,* ed. J. Neve (Paris: 1924).

3. *Concilium Tridentinum* (hereafter *CT*), ed. Görresgesellschaft (Freiburg: Herder, 1919ff.) VI, 403.

4. *CT,* VI 404, 581, 585, 586, 587, 588.

5. *CT,* VII, 234–359. The English translation of the canons used in this current chapter is taken from that of Palmer, op. cit.

6. *CT,* VII, 334.

7. J.B. Umberg, "Die Bewertung der Trienter Lehren durch Pius VI," *Scholastik,* 4 (1929) pp. 402–409. Cf. also H.-P Arendt, *Bußsakrament und Einzelbeichte* (Freiburg: Herder, 1981) pp. 174–193 for a detailed examination of the theological valency of the Tridentine canons.

8. H. Lennerz, "Das Konzil von Trient und theologische Schulmeinungen," *Scholastik,* 4 (1929) pp. 38–53; idem, "Notulae Tridentinae, Primum Anathema in Concilio Tridentino," *Gregorianum* 27 (1946) pp. 136–142.

9. R. Favre, "Les condamnations avec anathème," *Bulletin de Litterature Écclésiastique,* 17 (1946) pp. 226–241; 18 (1947) pp. 31–48.

10. A. Lang, "Die Bedeutungswandel der Begriffe 'fides' und 'haeresis' und die dogmatische Wertung der Konzilsentscheidungen von Vienne und Trent," *Münchener Theologische Zeitschrift,* 4 (1953) pp. 133–156.

11. H. Jedin, *A History of the Council of Trent* (St. Louis, Mo.: B. Herder Book Co., 1961) trans. E. Graf, v. II, p. 381.

12. P. Fransen, "Réflexions sur l'anathème au Concile de Trente," *Ephemerides théologiques lovanienses,* 29 (1953) pp. 657–672.

13. K. Peter, "Auricular Confession and the Council of Trent," *The Jurist*, 28 (1968) p. 287. Peter cites other theologians who are in agreements with this position, cf. p. 287; cf. also Duval, op. cit., pp. 170–171. The same conclusion is expressed by J. Lecler, H. Holstein, P. Adnès, and C. Lefebvre in *Trente* (Paris: Editions de l'Orante, 1981) pp. 550–551: "On voit dès lors avec quelle prudence il faut traiter les canons avec anathème dans les décrets dogmatiques du concile de Trente. La contradictoire de chacun des canons n'est pas nécessairement de 'foi divine' au sens précis des terms. Chaque cas est à étudier pour lui-même. Les propositions de 'foi divine', irrévocables, parce que l'Église y a engagé toute son autorité, sont à distinguer des conclusions théologiques, des propositions dites de 'foi ecclésiastique', des décisions touchant la discipline générale, que l'Église pourrait un jour soumettre à révision."

14. Cf. *CT,* VII, 233; the Tridentine text refers pointedly to Calvin's *Institutes of the Christian Religion,* IV, 19, 1–3; 14–17, and to Melanchthon in the chapter on penance of the *Loci Communes.*

15. Melanchthon, *Corp. Ref.* XXI, 215, in *CT,* VII, 233.

16. Cf. Osborne, *Sacramental Theology* (N.Y.: Paulist, 1988) pp. 20–31, 106–109; idem, *The Christian Sacraments of Initiation* (N.Y.: Paulist, 1987) pp. 11–14, 80–96.

17. F. Cavallera, "Le décret du concile de Trente sur la pénitence et l'extrême onction," *Bulletin de Littérature ecclésiastique,* 25 (1924) 56–63.

18. For Lainez, *CT,* VII, 241; for Tapper, *CT,* VII, 248; for Gropper, *CT,* VII, 266.

19. Nectarius was the patriarch of Constantinople (397), just prior to John Chrysostom. He suppressed the ministry of presbyters in the *ordo paenitentiae* at Constantinople. This was considered by many bishops of his time as heretical. The reformation theologians challenged the historicity of this entire situation, and other theologians saw it as an indication of traditional discontinuity. Cf. Duval, op. cit., pp. 188–191.

20. Cf. for example Paul Gregorianz, bishop of Zagabrien, *CT,* VII, 295; Georg Flach, auxiliary bishop of Herbipolen, *CT,* VII, 310.

21. *CT,* VII, 296–297, 304–305, 337, 344–345.

22. Adnès, op. cit., p. 177, in his comments on this canon, stresses that baptism "confiere gratuitamente el perdón pleno y totál de todos los pecados; el sacramento de la penitencia no se hace sin esfurezos y lágrimas, exigidas por la divina justicia, de manera que los Santos Padres pudieron llamarlo 'bautismo laborioso.'" When a theologian emphasizes that baptism is gratuitous, but penance is not, one is flirting with Pelagianism. The grace in the sacrament of penance is as gratuitous as the

grace in baptism; any other position than this verges on the heretical, and raises again the very complaints of the reformation theologians vis-à-vis this sacrament.

23. Cf. H. McSorley, "The Faith Necessary for the Sacrament of Penance: The Teaching of Luther and the Council of Trent," *Concilium,* 61 (1971) pp. 89–98; cf. also M. Gesteria Garza, op. cit., pp. 266–272.

24. Cf. J. Ramos-Regidor, op. cit., p. 213.

25. Adnès, op. cit., p. 184 states the theological position on secret confession to a priest in very clear terms: "El concilio no afirma, por tanto, que la confesión en secreto haya sido instituída por Cristo, ni que sea necesaria de derecho divino, áunque la considera manifiestamente como mas naturál que la confesión pública. Lo necesario de derecho divino es la confesión en cuanto tal. La modalidad de la confesión (pública or secreta) es de institución eclesiástica." These last few words are telling. Cf. also, Arendt, op. cit., pp. 297–330.

26. Cf. L. Ligier, "Pénitence et Eucharistie en Orient: théologie sur une interférence de prières et de rites," *Orientalia Christiana Periodica,* 29 (1963) pp. 5–78.

27. Cf. K. Rahner, "Gerecht und Sünder zugleich," *Geist und Leben* 36 (1963) pp. 434–443.

28. Cf. E.F. Latko, "Trent and Auricular Confession," *Franziskanische Studien,* 14 (1954) pp. 4–33; M. Manzelli, *La Confession dei peccati nella dottrina penitenziale del concilio di Trento* (Bergamo: Centro di studi ecumenici Giovanni XXIII, 1966); Z. Alszeghy–M. Flick, "La Dottrina tridentina sulla necessitá della confessione. Magistro e morale," *Atti del III Congresso nazionali dei moralisti* (Padua: 1970); J. Grundel, *Die Lehre von dem Umständen der menschlichen Handlung im Mittelalter* (Münster: Aschendorf, 1963); J. Ramos-Regidor, "Reconciliation in the Primitive Church," *Concilium,* 61 (1971) pp. 76–88; Ramos-Regidor refers to the many variations in the listing of sins, which had to be submitted to the *ordo paenitentiae,* in the patristic church. The public form of the penitential ritual was, he notes, exceptional in nature. Only a few Christians needed to submit to such a discipline, an indication that the sacrament of penance made sense only from the standpoint of serious and substantive breaks with God and with the church. The understanding of "mortal" sin, developed in the late medieval and counter-reformation periods, does not correspond to the "serious" sin to be submitted to public penance of the patristic church.

29. Cf. K. Osborne, "Why Confess to a Priest?" *Chicago Studies,* 14 (1975).

30. Cf. Ramos-Regidor, op. cit., pp. 216–223, in particular 218–223.

31. Cf. Luther, "The Babylonian Captivity of the Church," *Luther's Works,* 6, 543-548. Also, Luther, "Sermo de Paenitentia," *WA* 1, 323.
32. J. Calvin, *Institutes,* III, 4, 14.
33. Cf. Duval, op. cit., pp. 203-208; Adnès, op. cit., pp. 188-189. Adnès lists some of the major bibliographical material on this dispute.
34. F. Gil de las Heras, "Caracter judiciál de la absolución sacramentál según el Concilio de Trento," *Burgense: Collectanea Scientifica,* 3 (1962) p. 144.
35. Ramos-Regidor, op. cit., pp. 228-229.
36. Cf. K. Osborne, "Ecumenical Eucharist," *Journal of Ecumenical Studies,* 6 (1969) pp. 598-619, for a detailed analysis of this same issue, the full efficacy of Jesus' salvific act and the eucharist. The same conclusion applies to penance as it does to the eucharist.
37. On this subject, cf. Adnès, op. cit., pp. 190-192.
38. H. Vorgrimler, "Der Kampf des Christen mit der Sünde," op. cit., pp. 429-430. Vorgrimler cites favorably H. McSorley, "Der zum Busssakrament erforderte Glaube nach der Aufassung Luthers und des Tridentinums," *Concilium,* 7 (1971) pp. 43-48.
39. Poschmann, op. cit., p. 202.
40. H. Jedin, *A History of the Council of Trent,* v. II, pp. 239-316.
41. Jedin, op. cit., p. 248.
42. Cited in Jedin, op. cit., p. 285.
43. Cf. Osborne, *Sacramental Theology,* pp. 49-68.
44. McGrath, op. cit., pp. 85-86.
45. Cited by Jedin, op. cit., p. 310.

9. The Sacrament of Reconciliation, Justification and Vatican II

1. Cf. T. Zeldin, "The Conflict of Moralities: Confession, Sin and Pleasure in the Nineteenth Century," *Conflicts in French Society,* ed. T. Zeldin (London: G. Allen and Unwin, 1970), pp. 13-50.
2. Tavard, op. cit., pp. 80-94. Cf. also the analysis of Newman's *Lectures on Justification* by McGrath, op. cit., pp. 121-134. McGrath points out the many limitations inherent to Newman's discussion, but on pp. 132-133 he indicates the value (though negative) of the *via media* approach.
3. Dallen, op. cit., pp. 180-193.
4. Cf. Dallen, op. cit., pp. 190-193 for instances in both France and Holland, in which a communal form of penance was used even prior to Vatican II. It was certainly these liturgical efforts at renewal and the

forms of such renewal efforts which helped shape the eventual official form of the sacrament of penance, stemming from Vatican II.

5. *SC*, n. 72.

6. Ibid., n. 109.

7. Ibid., n. 35; cf. also ibid., n. 24.

8. Ibid., n. 26; cf. also ibid., n. 27.

9. Ibid., n. 34.

10. *LG*, n. 11.

11. *PO*, n. 5.

12. F. Sottocornola, *A Look at the New Rite of Penance* (Washington, D.C.: USCC, 1975) trans. T. Krosnicki, p. 3.

13. *National Bulletin on Liturgy,* Canadian Catholic Conference, 9 (1976) p. 13.

14. F. Sottocornola, "Commentarium: il nuovo 'Ordo Paenitentiae,'" *Notitiae,* 90 (1974) p. 66.

15. Cf. P. Jounel, "La Liturgie de la réconcilation," *La Maison-Dieu,* 117 (1974) p. 9.

16. Sottocornola, op. cit., p. 67. The comments from Sottocornola and Jounel are very helpful, since both men worked on the document and thus provide us with the unwritten background of many issues.

17. Cf. J.M.R. Tillard, "Pénitence et eucharistie," *La Maison-Dieu* 90 (1968) pp. 103–131; ibid., "The Bread and the Cup of Reconciliation," *Concilium* 61 (1971) pp. 38–54; L. Ligier, "Pénitence et Eucharistie en Orient," *Orientalia Christiana Periodica,* 29 (1963) pp. 5–78; ibid., "Dimension personelle et dimension communautaire de la pénitence en Orient," *La Maison-Dieu* 89 (1967) pp. 5–78; R.J. Kennedy, "Baptism, Eucharist and Penance: Theological and Liturgical Connections," *Reconciliation: The Continuing Agenda* (Collegeville, MN: Liturgical Press, 1987) pp. 43–52.

18. *National Bulletin on Liturgy,* loc. cit., p. 16. Cf. also D. Diederich, "The Church—Sin and Reconciliation," *The New Rite of Penance* (Pevely, Mo.: Federation of Diocesan Liturgical Commissions) pp. 8–11; J. Reedy, "Sin—Personal and Social," ibid., pp. 12–15.

19. Congregation for the Doctrine of the Faith, *Instruction on Christian Freedom and Liberation* (Washington, D.C.: USCC, 1986), n. 37.

20. Ibid., n. 38.

21. Sottocornola, *A Look at the New Rite of Penance,* pp. 10–11. Cf. also G. Diekmann, "Reconciliation Through the Prayer of the Community," *The Rite of Penance: Commentaries, Background and Directions* (Washington, D.C.: The Liturgical Conference, 1978) pp. 38–49.

22. For further discussion and bibliography on this issue of Jesus as the primordial sacrament and the church as a basic sacrament, cf. Os-

borne, *Sacramental Theology* (N.Y.: Paulist, 1988); P. Smith, *Teaching Sacraments* (Wilmington, Del.: Glazier, 1987) pp. 88–138.

23. Luther, *WA* 40, III, 352, 3.

24. G. Marron, *Kirche und Rechtfertigung* (Göttingen: Vandenhoeck & Ruprecht, 1969) p. 6: " 'Expressis verbis' enthalten die Texte des 2. Vaticanums nun allerdings so gut wie keine Aussage uber die Rechtfertigung."

25. O. Pesch, "Gottes Gnadenhandeln als Rechtfertigung des Menschen," *Mysterium Salutis* (Einsiedeln: Benziger, 1973), v. IV/2, p. 902.

26. E. Schillebeeckx, "The Tridentine Decree on Justification," *Concilium*, 1 (1965) p. 32.

27. *Sacrosanctum Oecumenicum Concilium Vaticanum II: Constitutiones, Decreta, Declarationes* (Vatican: Typis Polyglottis, 1966), p. 1188.

10. Post-Vatican II Theology and Unresolved Issues on Justification and the Sacrament of Reconciliation

1. "Sacramentum paenitentiae," *AAS* 64 (1972) pp. 510–514. An authorized English translation can be found in: *Penance and Reconciliation in the Church. Liturgy Documentary Series* n. 7 (Washington, D.C.: USCC, 1986), pp. 31–35. Also in ICEL, *Documents on the Liturgy, 1963–1979* (Collegeville, MN: The Liturgical Press, 1982) pp. 948–951.

2. *CIC*, 961, § 2.

3. "Sacramentum paenitentiae," loc. cit.

4. Cf. *AAS* 70 (1978) p. 330. In this allocution Paul VI began with some remarks on Jesus as reconciliation and the church as reconciliation. In doing this he rightly connects his statements on general absolution to both Jesus and to the church. He states (ibid.): "What is so important in the application of these norms is the general effectiveness of the basic ecclesial ministry of reconciliation in accordance with the intention of Christ the Savior." The reference to his previous remarks are found in a general audience given March 23, 1977. English translation in *Documents on the Liturgy*, 981–982. In the January 14, 1977 letter from the Sacred Congregation for the Doctrine of the Faith, *Penance and Reconciliation in the Church*, pp. 36–37, one reads: "The Pastoral Norms for General Absolution were developed to assist pastors in confronting those existing situations in the life of the Church which are attended by extraordinary circumstances. They are not intended . . . in the absence of such extraordinary circumstances." Since *Sacramentum paenitentiae* did not use the term "extraordinary," this evaluation seems to be an "extension" of the meaning of the document, not an interpretation inherent in the

document itself. *Sacramentum paenitentiae,* textually, does not allow for an interpretation involving the words "extraordinary" and "exceptional."

5. Eng. trans. *Penance and Reconciliation in the Church,* p. 41.

6. *AAS* 71 (1979) pp. 32–36. John Paul II contextualizes his remarks to these bishops by speaking first of the unity between bishops and pope, the unity in local dioceses, the unity which comes from preaching the gospel and celebrating the eucharist. This leads him to his references on (a) first confession and first eucharist, and (b) general absolution.

7. *AAS* 71 (1979) pp. 237–324; the reference to general absolution is found on p. 315. It is stated in most general terms. The reference, however, is contextualized by the entire encyclical, which deals with Jesus as source of all reconciliation and the church as a reconciling event.

8. *AAS* 76 (1984) reprinted in *Insegnamenti di Giovanni Paolo II,* v. 7, n. 2 (Rome: Libreria Editrice Vaticana, 1984) pp. 63–69.

9. *Insegnamenti di Giovanni Paolo II,* v, IX, n. 1 (1986) pp. 347–354, esp. 350–351.

10. Ibid., v. IX, n. 2 (1986) pp. 1161–1168, esp. 1165–1166.

11. On this subject of the church as a locus of reconciliation, cf. J. Lopresti, "The Church as Sinful Reconciler," *Reconciliation: The Continuing Agenda,* R.J. Kennedy, ed. (Collegeville: The Liturgical Press, 1987) pp. 1–13; also D. Donnelly, "Reconciliation and Community," ibid., pp. 34–42.

12. *Newsletter,* Bishops' Committee on the Liturgy, April 1975, v. 11, n. 4, p. 14. Cf. also E. O'Hara, "Penance and Canon Law," *Reconciliation: The Continuing Agenda,* pp. 238–253. The NCCB of the United States has recently spent a great deal of time on the issue of "a long time" (diu); important as this practical issue might be, the issue of how the forms of the new rite of penance express the mystery of salvation or justification is far more important.

13. Cf. *Penance and Reconciliation in the Church,* p. 37.

14. *AAS* 35 (1943). This comment of Pius XII is repeated by John Paul II in *Redemptor hominis.*

15. For a traditional author like S. González, "De Paenitentia," *Sacrae Theologiae Summa* (Madrid: BAC, 1962), v. IV, pp. 472–484, the issue "divine institution" for serious post-baptismal sins is carefully nuanced. That one must confess one's sinfulness (a genuine avowal of personal sin) can be found in the scriptures; that such an avowal must be integral, i.e. cover all one's sins, is also, according to González, found in scripture. Other more specified issues are not the focus of the *de iure divino* teaching.

16. John Paul II, *Reconciliation and Penance* (Washington, D.C.: USCC, 1984) pp. 56–64.

17. Ibid., pp. 57–58.

18. Cf. R. Brown, *The Epistles of John* (Garden City, N.Y.: Doubleday, 1982), pp. 615–617. The advantage of Brown's presentation lies in his exposition of all four views, with the many authors who subscribe to each.

19. John Paul II, ibid., p. 60. Cf. also D. Mongillo, "Peccato," *Dizionario Enciclopedico di Teologia Morale* (Milano: Ed. Paoline, 1987), ed. L. Rossi and A. Valsecchi, pp. 733–741, esp. 740–741.

20. Cf. *Conciliorum Oecumenicorum Decreta* (Herder: Freiburg i. Br., 1962), pp. 651, 656, 657. This is the same reference which is cited in the exhortation. Cf. also Arendt, op. cit.

21. John Paul II, ibid., pp. 61–62.

22. Cf. S. Dianich, "Opzione fondamentale," *Dizionario Enciclopedico di Teologia Morale,* pp. 694–705. Cf. also the study on conversion, W. Cieslak, "Reconciliation and Conversion in Pastoral Ministry: Problems and Possibilities," *Reconciliation: The Continuing Agenda,* pp. 190–205.

23. K. Rahner, "Theological Reflections on the Problem of Secularization," *Renewal of Religious Thought* (N.Y.: Herder and Herder, 1968) v. I, pp. 191–192.

24. Cf. J. Dallen, "Theological Foundations of Reconciliation," *Reconciliation: The Continuing Agenda,* pp. 14–33; also ibid., *The Reconciling Community,* pp. 265–269.

25. Pius X, "Quam singulari," *AAS,* 2 (1910) pp. 577–583.

26. *General Catechetical Directory;* cf. *AAS,* 64 (1972) pp. 97–176. The directory states on p. 174 that in explaining confession to children one should tell them that it is not only good and grace-giving, "immo per se et necessarium cum quis in grave peccatum inciderit."

27. Cf. *AAS* 65 (1973) p. 410; repeated in *AAS* 69 (1977) p. 427.

28. Cf. *AAS* 69 (1977) p. 402. There are other documents which do not have the same public weight; cf. the intervention of Cardinal Silvio Oddi, Prefect for the Congregation of the Clergy, presented at the Episcopal Synod in 1983, translated and printed in *Origins,* 13 (1983) pp. 373–376; cf. also the *National Catechetical Directory, Sharing the Light of Faith.*

29. L. Gaupin, " 'Let those who have faith not be hasty': Penance and Children," *Reconciliation: The Continuing Agenda,* pp. 219–238. Gaupin bases her historical research on E. Diebold, "Du Concile de Trente au Decret 'Quam Singulari,' " *Communion Solennelle et Profession de Foi,*

Lex Orandi 14 (1952) pp. 46–48; M. Sauvage, *Catéchèse et Laïcat* (Paris: Ligel, 1962); J.-C. D'Hotel, *Les Origines du Catéchesime Moderne* (Paris: Éditions Montaigne, 1967); W. Costello, "An Ecclesiastical Conference on 'Quam Singulari,' " *American Ecclesiastical Review,* 44 (1982).

30. Ibid., p. 225.
31. Ibid., p. 226.
32. Cf. J.H. Provost, "First Eucharist and First Penance, *The Jurist,* 43 (1983) pp. 450–453; Provost notes that the phrase in canon 914, "praemissa sacramentali confession," was a last minute addition and not thoroughly discussed by the committee. Cf. also Gaupin, op. cit., pp. 230–235 for a similar conclusion. This is echoed by E. O'Hara, op. cit., pp. 244–248; cf. N. Mette, "Children's Confession—A Plea for a Child-Centered Practice of Penance and Reconciliation," *Concilium* (Edinburgh, T. & T. Clark, 1987) pp. 64–73. Dallen, op. cit., p. 248 notes: "Though the RP ignores the controversy over first confession canon 914 mentions first communion prior to confession, seemingly requiring more of children than of adults, who are required to confess only when conscious of grave sins."
33. Cf. *Documents on the Liturgy,* p. 990.
34. Cf. K. Osborne, *Priesthood* (N.Y.: Paulist, 1989), pp. 307–342.
35. *Justification by Faith,* pp. 50–57.
36. McGrath, *Iustitia Dei,* v. II, pp. 170–191.
37. Tavard, op. cit., p. 110.
38. Heinz, op. cit., pp. 407–416.

Bibliography

SOURCE MATERIALS

Acta Synodalia Sacrosancti Concilii Oecumenici Vaticani II, Rome, Typis Polyglottis, 1962–1986.

Bishops' Committee on the Liturgy Newsletter. Washington, D.C., USCC, esp. 1974ff.

Codex Iuris Canonici, Vatican City, Libreria Editrice Vaticana, 1983; Eng. trans. *Code of Canon Law,* Washington, D.C., Canon Law Society of America, 1983.

Commentary on the Rite of Penance, Study Text IV, Washington, D.C., USCC, 1975.

Conciliorum Oecumenicorum Decreta, Herder, Freiburg i. Br., 1962.

Concilium Tridentinum. Görresgesselschaft, ed. Freiburg i. Br., Herder, 1919, 1938.

Councils and Ecclesiastical Documents Relating to Great Britain and Ireland, ed. A.W. Haddan and W. Stubbs, Oxford, Oxford Univ. Press, 1869, reprinted in 1964, 3 vols.

The Documents of Vatican II, A.P. Flannery, ed., Collegeville, Minn., The Liturgical Press, 1975.

Documents on the Liturgy, 1963–1979, ICEL, Collegeville, Minn., The Liturgical Press, 1982.

Emendations in the Liturgical Books Following Upon the New Code of Canon Law, ICEL, Washington, D.C., USCC, 1984.

Enchiridion Euchologicum Fontium Liturgicorum, Lodi, E. (ed), Rome, Edizioni Liturgiche, 1979.

Enchiridion Symbolorum, Definitionum et Declarationum, H. Denzinger, et al. eds. Freiburg i. Br., Herder, 1967.

General Absolution: Toward a Deeper Understanding, Chicago, Federation of Diocesan Liturgical Commissions, 1978.

Insegnamenti di Paolo VI, Vatican City, Tipographia poliglotta, 1963–1978.

Insegnamenti di Giovanni Paolo II, Vatican City, Libreria Editrice Vaticana, 1978ff.

National Bulletin on Liturgy: Reconciliation and Forgiveness, Ottawa, Canadian Catholic Conference, 1976.

National Catholic Directory, Sharing the Light of Faith, An Official Commentary, Washington, D.C., USCC, 1981.

The New Rite of Penance: Background Catechesis, Pevely, Mo., Federation of Diocesan Liturgical Commissions, 1974.

New Rite of Penance: Commentaries: v. I, *Understanding the Document,* ed. R. Keifer and F.R. McManus; v. II, *Implementing the Rite,* ed. E. McMahon-Jeep; v. III, *Background and Directions,* ed., N. Mitchell, Washington, D.C., The Liturgical Conference, 1978.

Penance and Reconciliation in the Mission of the Church, Washington, D.C., USCC, 1984.

Penance and Reconciliation in the Church Liturgy, Documentary Series, n. 7, Washington, D.C., USCC, 1982.

Sacred Congregation for the Clergy, *Directorium catechisticum generale,* 64, *AAS* (1972) 97–176. Eng. trans. General Catechetical Directory, Washington, D.C., USCC, 1971.

Sacred Congregation for Divine Worship, *Ritus paenitentiae,* Vatican City, Typis polyglottis, 1974; Eng. transl. in *The Rites,* N.Y., Pueblo, 1976.

Sacred Congregation for the Doctrine of the Faith, *Instructio: De quibusdam rationibus "Theologiae Liberationis,"* 76, *AAS* (1984) 876–909. Eng. transl. Vatican City, Typis polyglottis, 1984.

Sacred Congregation for the Doctrine of the Faith, *Instructio: De libertate christiana et liberatione,* 79, *AAS* (1987) 554–599; Eng. transl. *Christian Freedom and Liberation,* Washington, D.C., USCC, 1986.

Sacred Congregation for the Doctrine of the Faith. *Normae Pastorales: Sacramentum paenitentiae,* 64, *AAS* (1972) 510–514.

Sacred Congregation for the Discipline of the Sacraments and Sacred Congregation for the Clergy, *Declaratio: Sanctus, Pontifex,* 65, *AAS* (1973) 410.

Sacred Congregation for the Doctrine of the Faith, *Letter* (U.S.A.) commenting on the Pastoral Norms for General Absolution, Jan. 14, 1977; text in *Documents on the Liturgy,* 1963–1979, pp. 375–376.

Sacrosanctum Oecumenicum Concilium Vaticanum II: Constitutiones, Decreta, Declarationes, Vatican City, Typis Polyglottis, 1966.

BOOKS AND ARTICLES

Adams, K., "Die abendländische Kirchenbuße im Ausgang des christlichen Altertums, Kritische Bemerkungen," *Theologische Quartalschrift*, 109 (1928); reprinted in *Gesammelte Aufsätze zur Dogmengeschichte und Theologie der Gegenwart*, Augsburg, P. Haas, 1936, pp. 268–312.

——, *Die kirchliche Sündenvergebung nach dem hl. Augustin*, Paderborn, 1917.

Adnès, P., *La Penitencia*, Madrid, La Editorial Católica, 1981.

Albert the Great, *Opera Omnia: Commentarium in IV Sententiarum*, Paris, Vives, 1884.

Alexander of Hales, *Summa Theologica*, Quarrachi-Grottaferrata, Collegium S. Bonaventurae, 1924–1979.

Alzeghy, Z., *De paenitentia christiana*, Rome, Gregorian Univ. Press, 1962.

Alzeghy Z., and Flick, M., *Il sacramento della riconciliazione*, Turin, Marietti, 1976.

——, "La Dottrina tridentina sulla necessità dell confessione, *Magistero e morale*," Atti del III Congresso nazionali dei moralisti, Bologna, Edizioni Dehoniana (1970) 103–192.

Amann, E., "Pénitence," *Dictionnaire de théologie catholique*, Paris, Letouzey et Ané (1933) v. 12.

Anciaux, P., *La théologie du sacrement de pénitence au XIIe siècle*, Louvain, E. Nauwelaerts, 1949.

——, "Histoire de la discipline pénitentielle," *Problèmes du confesseur*, Paris, Éditions du Cerf, 1963, 53–80.

Anderson, H.G., Murphy, T.A., Burgess, J. (eds.), *Justification by Faith*, Minneapolis, Augsburg, 1985.

Anselm, *Opera Omnia*, ed. F.S. Schmitt, Stuttgart, Friedrich Fromann, 1968, 2 vols. Also, *L'oeuvre de S. Anselme de Cantorbery*, ed. M. Corbin, Éditions du Cerf, 1986–1989, 3 vols.

Arendt, H.-P., *Bußsakrament und Einzelbeichte*, Freiburg, Herder, 1981.

Auer, J., *Die Entwicklung der Gnadenlehre in der Hochscholastick*, Freiburg i Br., Herder, 1951.

——, "Textkritische Studien zur Gnadenlehre des Alexander von Hales," *Scholastik*, 15 (1940) 63–75.

Auer, J., and Ratzinger, J., *Kleine katholische Dogmatik: die Sakramente der Kirche*, v. VIII, Regensburg, Pustet, 1979.

Augustine, *Aurelii Augustini Opera, CCSL*, vv. 28 ff., Turnholt, Brepols, 1958.

Aulén, G., *Christus Victor*, N.Y., Macmillan, 1969, Eng. transl. A.G. Hebert.

The Baltimore Catechism, N.Y., Sadlier, revised ed. n. 2, 1941.

Baur, F.C., *Die christliche Lehre von der Versöhnung,* Tübingen, C.F. Osiander, 1838.

Bausch, W., *A New Look at the Sacraments,* Mystic, Conn., Twenty-Third Publications, 1983.

Benabarre, J.P., "La penitencia sacramental según J. Duns Escoto," *Verdad y Vida,* 31 (1973) 317–380.

Bieler, L., *The Life and Legend of St. Patrick: Problems of Modern Scholarship,* Dublin, Clonmore and Reynolds, 1949.

———, *The Works of St. Patrick,* Westminster, Md., Newman, 1953.

———, *The Irish Penitentials,* Dublin, The Dublin Institute for Advanced Studies, 1963.

Bolgar, R.R., *The Classical Heritage,* N.Y., Harper and Row, 1964.

Bonaventure, *Opera Omnia,* Quarrachi, Ad Claras Aquas, 1889ff.

Borgen, O.E., *John Wesley on the Sacraments,* Zürich, Gotthelf, 1972.

Bougerol, J.G., *Introduction à l'étude de Saint Bonaventure,* Tournai, Desclée, 1961; Eng. transl. by J. de Vinck, *Introduction to the Works of Bonaventure,* Paterson, N.J., St. Anthony's Guild Press, 1964.

Bourque, E., *Histoire de la Pénitence-Sacrement,* Quebec, Laval Univ. Press, 1947.

Braeckmans, L., *Confession et communion au Moyen Age et au Concile de Trent,* Gembloux, Duculot, 1971.

Brown, R., *The Gospel According to John,* Garden City, N.Y., Doubleday and Co., 1970.

———, *The Epistles of John,* Garden City, N.Y., Doubleday, 1982.

Calvin, J., *Institutes of the Christian Religion,* Philadelphia, Westminster, 1960, Eng. transl. F.L. Battles.

von Campenhausen, H. "The Ascetic Idea of Exile in Ancient and Medieval Monasticism," *Tradition and Life in the Church,* Philadelphia, Fortress, 1968, Eng. transl. A.V. Littledale, 231–251.

———, *Ecclesiastical Authority and Spiritual Power in the Church of the First Three Centuries,* Stanford, Ca., Stanford Univ. Press, 1969, Eng. transl. J.A. Baker.

Carlson, C.P., *Justification in Earlier Medieval Theology,* The Hague, Martinus Nijhoff, 1975.

Cavallera, F., "Le décret du concile de Trente sur la pénitence et l'extrême onction," *Bulletin de Littérature ecclésiastique,* 24 (1923) 277–297; 25 (1924) 127–143.

Charlesworth, J.H., *Jesus Within Judaism,* N.Y., Doubleday, 1988.

Cieslak, W., "Reconciliation and Conversion in Pastoral Ministry: Problems and Possibilities," *Reconciliation: The Continuing Agenda,*

Collegeville, Minn., The Liturgical Press, 1987, ed. R.J. Kennedy, 190–205.

Clarus, C., "An Ecclesiastical Conference on 'Quam Singulari'," *American Ecclesiastical Review,* 44 (1911) 81–85.

Clement of Alexandria, *Clemens Alexandrinus,* Berlin, Akademie Verlag, 1960–1985, ed. O. Stählin.

Collins, M., and Power, D. (eds), *The Fate of Confession,* Concilium, Edinburgh, T. & T. Clark, 1987.

Cooke, B., *Ministry to Word and Sacraments,* Philadelphia, Fortress, 1976.

Connolly, R.H., *Didascalia Apostolorum,* Oxford, Clarendon Press, 1929.

Conzelmann, H., et al., *Zur Bedeutung des Todes Jesu,* Gütersloh, Gerd Mohn, 1967.

Courtenay, W.J., "Necessity and Fredom in Anselm's Conception of God," *Analecta Anselmiana,* Frankfurt/Main, Minerva, 1975, 39–64.

CTSA, *The Renewal of the Sacrament of Penance* (Committee Report), Mahwah, N.J., The Catholic Theological Society of America, 1975.

Cyprian of Carthage, *Sanci Cypriani Episcopi Opera,* Turnholt, Brepols, 1972, ed. M. Bévenot.

Dallen, J., *The Reconciling Community: The Rite of Penance,* N.Y., Pueblo, 1986.

———, "Theological Foundations of Reconciliation," *Reconciliation: The Continuing Agenda,* Collegeville, MN., The Liturgical Press, 1987, ed. R.J. Kennedy, 14–33.

Davies, C.S.L., *Peace, Print and Protestantism,* London, Hart-Davis, MacGibbon, 1976.

Dettloff, W., *Die Entwicklung der Akzeptions-und Verdienstlehre von Duns Skotus bis Luther,* Münster, Aschendorff, 1963.

Dhanis, E., *Resurrexit: Actes du Symposium international sur la résurrection de Jésus, Rome, 1970,* Vatican City, Libreria Editrice Vaticana, 1974.

Dianich, S., "Opzione fondamentale," *Dizionario Enciclopedico di Teologia Morale,* Milan, Edizioni Paoline (1987) 694–705.

Diebold, E., "Du Concile de Trente au Decret 'Quam Singulari,'" *Communion Solennelle et Profession de Foi,* Lex Orandi, 14 (1952) Paris, Éditions du Cerf, 46–48.

Doyle, E., "John Duns Scotus and the Place of Christ," *Clergy Review,* 57 (1972) 667–675; 774–785; 860–868.

Duckett, E.S., *The Gateway to the Middle Ages: III Monasticism,* Ann Arbor, Mich., Univ. of Michigan Press, 1938; reprinted 1963.

Dudden, F. Homes, *The Life and Times of St. Ambrose,* Oxford, Clarendon Press, 1935, 2 vols.

Durwell, F.X., *La Résurrection de Jésus, Mystère de Salut,* Paris, Xavier
Mappus, 1950.

Duval, A., *Des Sacrements au concile de Trente,* Paris, Les Éditions du
Cerf, 1985.

Eno, R., "Some Patristic Views on the Relationship of Faith and Works
in Justification," *Recherches Augustiniennes,* Paris, Études Augustiniennes (1984) 3–27.

Entrich, M., *Albertus Magnus: Sein Leben und seine Bedeutung,* Graz,
Styria, 1982.

Favazza, J.A., *The Order of Penitents,* Collegeville, MN, The Liturgical
Press, 1988.

Favre, R., "Les condemnations avec anathème," *Bulletin de Litterature
Écclésiastique,* 47 (1946) 226–241; 48 (1947) 31–48.

Feltoe, C.L., *The Letters and Other Remains of Dionysius of Alexandria,*
Cambridge, Cambridge Univ. Press, 1904.

Fink, P. (ed), *Alternative Futures for Worship: Reconciliation.* Collegeville, Minn., The Liturgical Press, 1987.

Fitzmyer, J., "Pauline Theology," *The Jerome Biblical Commentary,*
Englewood Cliffs, N.J., Prentice-Hall (1968) 800–827.

Flanagan, N., *Friend Paul,* Wilmington, Del., Michael Glazier, 1986.

Franks, R.S., *A History of the Doctrine of the Work of Christ,* London,
Hodder and Stoughton, 1918.

Fransen, P., "Réflexions sur l'anathème au Concile de Trente," *Ephemerides theologicae lovanienses,* 29 (1953) 657–672.

Galtier, P., *L'Église et la rémission des péchés aux premiers siècles,* Paris,
Beaushesne, 1932.

———, *De Paenitentia: Tractatus dogmatico-historicus,* Rome, Gregorian Univ. Press, 1956.

———, "Comment on écarte la pénitence privée?" *Gregorianum* 21
(1940) 183–202.

———, "Les origenes de la pénitence irlandaise," *Recherches des
sciences religieuses,* 42 (1954) 58–85; 204–225.

———, *Aux origines du sacrement de pénitence,* Rome, Gregorian Univ.
Press, 1951.

Gaupin, L., "Let those who have faith not be hasty: Penance and Children," *Reconciliation: The Continuing Agenda,* Collegeville, MN.,
The Liturgical Press, 1987, ed. R.J. Kennedy, 219–238.

Gesteira-Garza, M., "El Sacramento de la Penitencia en Lutero hasta el
año 1521," *El Sacramento de la Penitencia,* Madrid, Aldecoa (1972)
251–302.

González, S., "De Paenitentia," *Sacrae Theologiae Summa*, v. IV, Madrid, BAC, 1962.

Gottler, J., *Der h. Thomas von Aquin und die vortridentinischen Thomisten über die Wirkingen des Bußsakraments*, Freiburg, i. Br., Herder, 1904.

Grensted, L.W., *A Short History of the Doctrine of the Atonement*, London, Longmans, Green and Co., 1920.

Gründel, J., *Die Lehre von dem Umständen der menschlichen Handlung im Mittelalter*, Münster, Aschendorf, 1963.

le Guillou, M.-J., "La Sacramentalité de l'Église," *La Maison-Dieu*, 93 (1968) 9–38.

Gula, R., *To Walk Together Again. The Sacrament of Reconciliation*, N.Y., Paulist, 1984.

Gy, P.-M., "Histoire liturgique du sacrement de pénitence," *La Maison-Dieu*, 56 (1958) 5–21.

———, "Les bases de la pénitence moderne," *La Maison-Dieu* 117 (1974) 63–85.

———, "Penance and Reconciliation," *The Church at Prayer*, vol. III, ed. A. Martimort, Collegeville, Minn., The Liturgical Press, 1988.

Hamm, B., *Promissio, pactum, ordinatio*, Tübingen, J.C.B. Mohr, 1977.

Haubst, R., "Anselms Satisfactionslehre einst und heute," *Analecta Anselmiana*, Frankfurt/Main, Minerva, 1975, 141–157.

Hellwig, M., *Sign of Reconciliation and Conversion, The Sacrament of Penance for Our Times*, Wilmington, Del., Michael Glazier, 1984.

Heinz, J., *Justification and Merit: Luther vs. Catholicism*, Berrien Springs, Mich., Andrews Univ. Press, 1984.

de las Heras, F. Gil., "Caracter judiciál de la absolución sacramentál según el Concilio de Trento, *Burgense*, 3 (1962) 117–175.

Hermas, *Hermas: Le Pasteur*, ed. R, Joly, Paris, Éditions du Cerf, 1968: text in Greek and French.

Heynck, V., "Zur Bußlehre des hl. Bonaventura," *Franziskanische Studien* 36, 1954, 1–82.

———, "Attritio sufficiens," *Franziskanische Studien*, 31 (1949) 76–134.

Hippolytus, *Hippolyte de Rome: La Tradition Apostolique d'après les anciennes versions*, ed. B. Botte, Paris, Éditions du Cerf, 1968.

D'Hotel, J.-C., *Les origines du catéchesime moderne*, Paris, Éditions Montaigne, 1967.

Hugh of St. Victor, *De Sacramentis fidei, PL*, 176.

Hughes, K., "The Celtic Church and the Papacy," *The English Church and the Papacy in the Middle Ages*, ed. C.H. Lawrence, London, Burns and Oates, 1965, 1–28.

Hughes, P.E., *Theology of the English Reformers,* London, Hodder and Stoughton, 1965.

Innocent I, *Epistula Inocentii Papae I ad Decentium Episcopum Eugubinum,* Turin, Tiposervizio, undated.

Jedin, H., *A History of the Council of Trent,* St. Louis, Mo., Herder Book Co., v. I, 1957; v. II, 1958, Eng. transl. E. Graf.

Jeremias, J., *New Testament Theology,* N.Y., Charles Scribners, 1971, Eng. transl. J. Bowden.

Jewell, J., *The Works of John Jewel, Bishop of Salisbury,* Cambridge, Univ. Press, ed. J. Ayre, 1845–1850, 4 vols.

John Duns Scotus, *Opera Omnia,* Vatican City, Scotus Commission, 1950–1982.

Joly, R., "La doctrine pénitentielle du Pasteur d'Hermas et l'exégèse récente," *Revue de l'histoire des religions,* 157 (1955) 32–49.

Jounel, P., "La Liturgie de la réconciliation," *La Maison-Dieu,* 117 (1974) 7–37.

Jungmann, J., *Die lateinischen Bußriten in ihrer geschichtlichen Entwicklung,* Innsbruck, Rauch, 1932.

Karpp, H., *Die Buße: Quellen zur Entstehung des altkirchlichen Bußwesens,* Zürich, EVZ Verlag, 1969: Greek and Latin texts with a German transl.

Kasper, W., *Jesus the Christ,* N.Y., Paulist, 1976, Eng. transl. V. Green.

Kelly, J.N.D., *Early Christian Doctrines,* San Francisco, Harper & Row, 1978, rev. ed.

Kennedy, R.J. (ed), *Reconciliation: The Continuing Agenda,* Collegeville, Minn., The Liturgical Press, 1987.

Krautwig, N., *Die Grundlagen der Bußlehre des J. Duns Skotus,* Freiburg i. Br., Herder, 1938.

Künneth, W., *The Theology of the Resurrection,* London, SCM, 1965, Eng. transl. J.W. Leitch.

Landgraf, A.M., *Dogmengeshichte der Frühscholastik,* Regensburg, Pustet, 1952–1956.

Lang, A., "Die Bedeutungswandel der Begriff 'fides' und 'haeresis' und die dogmatische Wertung der Konzilsentscheidungen von Vienne und Trient," *Münchener Theologische Zeitschrift,* 4 (1953) 133–146.

Latko, E.F., "Trent and Auricular Confession," *Franziskanische Studien,* 14 (1954) 4–33.

Lea, H.C., *A History of Auricular Confession and Indulgences in the Latin Church,* Philadelphia, Lea Bros. & Co., 1896.

Lecler, J., Holstein, H., Adnès, P., Lefebvre, C., *Trente,* Paris, Éditions de l'Orante, 1981.

Lehmann K., and Pannenberg, W. (eds.), *Lehrverurteilungen-kirchen-trennend? Rechtfertigung, Sakramente und Amt im Zeitalter der Reformation und heute*, Freiburg i. Br., Herder, 1986.

Lennerz, H., "Das Konzil von Trient und theologische Schulmeinungen," *Scholastik*, 4 (1929) 38–53.

——, "Notulae Tridentinae, Primum Anathema in Concilio Tridentino," *Gregorianum*, 27 (1946) 136–144.

Ligier, L., "Pénitence et Eucharistie en Orient; théologie sur une interférence de prières et de rites," *Orientalia Christiana Periodica*, 19 (1963) 5–78.

——, "Dimension personelle et dimension communautaire de la pénitence en Orient," *La Maison-Dieu*, 89 (1967) 155–187.

Lohse, B., "Die Privatbeichte bei Luther," *Arbeitstagung und Sitzung der Kommission für Gottesdienst und geistliches Leben des lutherischen Weltbundes*, Hannover, private printing, 1967.

Lonergan, B., *De Verbo Incarnato*, Rome, Gregorian Univ. Press, 1964.

Luther, M., *Werke*, Weimar, Herman Böhlaus and Herman Böhlhaus Nachfolger, 1883–1983; Eng. transl. *Luther's Works*, St. Louis, Mo., and Philadelphia, Fortress, 1958–1986, ed. J. Pelikan.

Lynch, K., "The Doctrine of Alexander of Hales on the Nature of Sacramental Grace," *Franciscan Studies*, 19, (1959) 334–383.

Macy, G., *The Theologies of the Eucharist in the Early Scholastic Period*, Oxford, Clarendon Press, 1984.

Manzelli, M., *La Confession dei peccati nella dottrina penitenziale del concilio di Trento*, Bergamo, Centro di studi ecumenici giovanni XXIII, 1966.

Marron, G., *Kirche und Rechtfertigung*, Göttingen, Vandenhoeck & Ruprecht, 1969.

Marthaler, B., *Original Justice and Sanctifying Grace in the Writings of St. Bonaventure*, Rome, Miscellanea Francescana, 1965.

Martinez, E., "The Interpretation of oi mathetai in Mt. XVIII," *Catholic Biblical Quarterly*, 23 (1961).

Martos, J., *Doors to the Sacred: A Historical Introduction to Sacraments in the Catholic Church*, N.Y., Doubleday, 1981.

Meinhold, P., "Entwicklung des Bußwesens und Handhabung der Beicht im Lutherischen Protestantismus, *Buße und Beichte*, Regensburg, Pustet, 1972.

Meyer, B.F., *The Early Christians*, Wilmington, Del., Michael Glazier, 1986.

Millenkamp, G., *Penance in Transition and Caesarius of Arles*, Rome, Gregorian Univ. Press, 1973.

Mongillo, D., "Peccato," *Dizionario Enciclopedico di Teologia Morale*, Milan Edizioni Paoline, 1987, 735–741.

Murphy-O'Connor, J., "Péche et communauté dan le Nouveau Testament," *Révue Biblique,* 74 (1967) 161–193.

McElrath, D., ed., *Franciscan Christology,* Olean, N.Y., St. Bonaventure University Press, 1980.

McGrath, A.E., *Justitia Dei: A History of the Christian Doctrine of Justification, v. I: From the beginnings to 1500,* London, Cambridge Univ. Press, 1986.

———, *Justitia Dei: A History of the Christian Doctrine of Justification, v. II, From 1500 to the present day,* London, Cambridge Univ. Press, 1986.

———, *The Intellectual Origins of the European Reformation,* Oxford, Basil Blackwell, 1987.

McNeill, J.T., and Gamer, Helena M., *Medieval Handbooks of Penance,* N.Y., Columbia Univ. Press, 1938.

McSorley, H., *Luther—Right or Wrong? An Ecumenical-Theological Study of Luther's Major Work, "The Bondage of the Will,"* N.Y., Newman, 1969.

———, "The Faith Necessary for the Sacrament of Penance: The Teaching of Luther and the Council of Trent," *Concilium* 61, 1971, 89–98.

Newman, J.H., *Lectures on the Doctrine of Justification,* Westminster, Md., Christian Classics, 1966.

Nicolau, M., *La reconciliación con Dios y con la Iglesia en la Biblia y en la Historia,* Madrid, 1977.

Nocent, A., *I Sacramenti: teologia e storia della celebrazione,* Genoa, Marietti, 1986.

Nyman, H., "Die Beichte im Luthertum des 17 und 18 Jahrhunderts, Orthodoxie und Pietismus," *Arbeitstagung und Sitzung,* Hannover, private printing, 1967.

Oakley, T.P., *English Penitential Discipline and Anglo-Saxon Law,* N.Y., Columbia Univ. Press, 1923.

Oberman, H., *The Harvest of Medieval Theology,* Cambridge, Mass., Harvard Univ. Press, 1963.

O'Brien, J.A., *The Faith of Millions,* Huntington, Ind., Our Sunday Visitor Press, 1938.

O'Day, R., *The Debate on the English Reformation,* London, Methuen, 1986.

Ohlmann, R., "St. Bonaventure and the Power of the Keys," *Franciscan Studies,* 6, 1956, 293–315.

Orsy, L., *The Evolving Church and the Sacrament of Penance,* Denville, N.J., Dimension Books, 1978.

Osborne, K., *Sacramental Theology,* N.Y., Paulist, 1988.

———, *The Christian Sacraments of Initiation,* N.Y., Paulist, 1987.

——, *Priesthood,* N.Y., Paulist, 1989.

——, "Why Confess to a Priest?" *Chicago Studies,* 14, 1975, 260–278.

——, "Ecumenical Eucharist," *Journal of Ecumenical Studies,* 6, 1969, 598–619.

Palmer, P., *Sacraments and Forgiveness,* Westminster, Md., Newman Press, 1959.

Pelikan, J., *The Christian Tradition: A History of the Development of Doctrine,* Chicago, Univ. of Chicago Press, 3. vols., 1971–1978.

Pesch, O., "Die Lehre vom 'Verdienst' als Problem für Theologie und Verkündigung," *Wahrheit und Verkündigung,* Munich, F. Schoningh, 1967.

——, "Gottes Gandenhandeln als Rechtfertigung des Menschen," *Mysterium Salutis,* Einsiedeln, Benziger, 1973, v. IV/2, 831–920.

Peter Abelard, *Ethics, PL,* 178; *Sic et Non,* critical ed. by B. Boyer and R. McKeon, Chicago, Chicago Univ. Press, 1977.

Peter Lombard, *Libri IV Sententiarum,* Quarrachi, Collegium S Bonaventurae, 1916; reprinted at Grottoferrata, 1971–1981.

Peter, K., "Auricular Confession and the Council of Trent," *The Jurist,* 28 (1968) 280–297.

Peter of Poitiers, *Sententiarum libri quinque, PL,* 211; *Compilatio praesens, CCSL,* v. 51, ed. J. Longère, Turnholt, Brepol, 1980.

Pianazzi, G., and Triacca, A. (eds.), *Sacramento della Penitenza,* Zurich Pas, 1974.

Pius X, "Quam Singulari," 2 *AAS* (1910) 577–583.

Pollard, A.F., *Henry VII,* N.Y., Harper, 1966.

Pope, H., *Saint Augustine of Hippo,* Westminster, Md., Newman Press, 1949.

Poschmann, B., *Buße und Letzte Ölung,* Freiburg i. Br., Herder, 1951. Eng. trans. F. Courtney, *Penance and the Anointing of the Sick,* N.Y., Herder and Herder, 1963.

——, *Kirchenbuße und "correptio secreta" bei Augustinus,* Braunsberg, Bender, 1923.

——, *Penitentia Secunda: Die Kirchliche Buße im ältesten Christentum bis Cyprian und Origenes,* Bonn, Peter Hanstein, 1940.

Portalié, E., *A Guide to the Thought of Saint Augustine,* Chicago, Henry Regnery Co., 1960.

Quasten, J., *Patrology* 3. vols. Westminster, Md. Newman Press, 1951–1960.

Provost, J.H., "First Eucharist and First Penance," *The Jurist,* 43, 1983, 450–453.

Rahner, K., "Salvation," *Sacramentum Mundi,* N.Y., Herder & Herder, 1970.

————, "Vergessene Wahrheiten über das Bußsakrament," *Schriften zur Theologie,* v. 2, Einsiedeln, Benziger, 1964, 143–183.

————, "Vom Sinn der häufigen Andachtsbeichte," *Schriften zur Theologie,* v. 3, Einsiedeln, Benziger, 1967, 211–225.

————, "Gerecht und Sünder zugleich," *Geist und Leben,* 36, 1963, 434–443.

————, "Theological Reflections on the Problem of Secularization," *Renewal of Religious Thought,* N.Y., Herder and Herder, 1968, v. I. 167–192.

Ramos-Regidor, J., *Il sacramento della penitenze,* Turin, Elle de Ci, 1974.

————, "Reconciliation in the Primitive Church and Its Lessons for Theology and Pastoral Practice Today," *Concilium,* 61, 1971, 76–88.

Rashdall, H., *The Idea of Atonement in Christian Theology,* London, Macmillan & Co., 1919.

Rigaux, B., " 'Lier et délier' Les Ministères de réconcilation dans l'Église des temps apostoliques," *La Maison-Dieu,* 117 (1974) 86–135.

Rivière, J., *Le Dogme de la Rédemption, Essai d'etude historique,* Paris, Lecoffre, 1905.

————, *Le dogme de la Rédemption, Études critiques et documents,* Louvain, Bureau de la revue, 1931.

————, *Le dogme de la Rédemption chez saint Augustine,* Paris, Gabalda, 1933.

————, *Le dogme de la Rédemption après saint Augustine,* Paris, Gabalda, 1933.

————, *Le Dogme de la Rédemption au debut du moyen-âge,* Paris, J. Vrin, 1934.

————, "Merite," *Dictionnaire de Theéologie Catholique.*

Rogers, E.F., *Peter Lombard and the Sacramental System,* Merrick, N.Y., Richwood Publishing Co., 1976.

Ryan, J., "The Early Irish Church and the See of Peter," *Medieval Studies Presented to Aubrey Gwynn,* Dublin, Colm O. Lochlainn, 1961.

————, *Irish Monasticism,* Dublin, Talbot Press, 1931.

Sanders, E.P., "The Search for Bedrock in the Jesus Material," *Proceedings of the Irish Biblical Association,* 7 (1983) 74–86.

Savage, M., *Catéchèse et Laïcat,* Paris, Ligel, 1962.

Schaefer, O., *Bibliographia de vita, operibus et doctrina Ioannis Duns Scotus,* Rome, Herder, 1955.

————, "Conspectus brevis bibliographiae scotisticae recentioris," *Acta Ordinis Fratrum Minorum,* 85, 1966.

Schillebeeckx, E., *Jesus, An Experiment in Christology,* N.Y., Seabury, 1979, Eng. transl. H. Hoskins.

———, "The Tridentine Decree on Justification," *Concilium* 1, 1965.

Schinzer, R., *Die doppelte Verdienstlehre des Spätmittelalters und Luthers reformatorische Entdeckung,* Munich, Chr. Kaiser, 1971.

Schleiermacher, F., *Der Christliche Glaube,* Berlin, Walter De Gruyter & Co., 1960, 2 vols.

Schoonenberg, P., "Der Mensch in der Sünde," *Mysterium Salutis,* Zürich, Benziger, 1976, v. 5.

Senior, D., *The Passion of Jesus in the Gospel of Matthew,* Wilmington, Del., Michael Glazier, 1985.

Sobrino, J., *Christology at the Crossroads,* N.Y., Orbis, 1982, Eng. transl. J. Drury.

———, *Jesús en América Latina,* San Salvador, UCA, 1982.

Sottocornola, F., "Commentarium: il nuovo 'Ordo paenitentiae'," *Notitiae* 90 (1974) 63–79.

———, *A Look at the New Rite of Penance,* Washington, D.C., USCC, 1975.

Stanley, D., *Christ's Resurrection in Pauline Soteriology,* Rome, Pontificio Instituto Biblico, 1961.

Stendahl, K., *Paul among the Jews and Gentiles and Other Essays,* Philadelphia, Fortress, 1976.

Tanquerey, A., *Manual of Dogmatic Theology,* N.Y., Desclée, 1959, 2 vols. Eng. transl. J. Byrnes.

Tappert, T.G., *Book of Concord,* Philadelphia, Fortress, 1959.

Tavard, G., *Justification: An Ecumenical Study,* N.Y., Paulist, 1983.

Teetaert, A., *La Confession aux laïques dans l'Église latine,* Paris, J. Gabalda, 1926.

Tegels, A., "The New Order or Rite of Penance," *Worship,* 48 (1974) 242–246.

Thomas Aquinas, *Opera Omnia,* ed. P. Busa, Stuttgart, Friedrich Fromann, 1980, 7 vols.

Tillard, J.M.R., "Pénitence et eucharistie," *La Maison-Dieu,* 90 (1968) 103–131.

———, "The Bread and the Cup of Reconciliation," *Concilium,* 61 (1971) 38–54.

Tyndale, W., *The Works of William Tyndale,* Appleford, The Sutton Courtenay Press, 1964.

Umberg, J.B., "Die Bewertung der Trienter Lehren durch Pius VI," *Scholastik,* 4 (1929) 402–409.

Vanneste, A., "La Théologie de la pénitence chez quelques Maitres Parisiens de la premiére moitié du XIIIe siècle," *Ephemerides theologicae lovanienses,* 28 (1952) 24–58.

Vogel, C., *La discipline pénitentielle en Gaule des origines à la fin du VIIe siècle,* Paris, Letouzey et Ané, 1952.

———, *Introduction aux sources de l'historire du culte chrétien au moyen âge,* Spoleto, Centro Italiano di Studi sull'Alto Medioevo, 1966. Engl. trans. *Medieval Liturgy: An Introduction to the Sources,* Washington, D.C., Pastoral Press, 1981, W.G. Storey and N.K. Rasmussen.

———, *Le pécheur et la pénitence au Moyen Age,* Paris, Ed. du Cerf, 1969.

Vorgrimler, H., "Der Kampf des Christen mit der Sünde," *Mysterium Salutis,* Einsiedeln, Benziger, 1976, v. V, 349–461.

———, *Buße und Krankensalbung,* Freiburg, Herder, 1978.

Watkins, O.D., *A History of Penance,* N.Y., Burt Franklin, 1961.

Wolter, A., *Duns Scotus on the Will and Morality,* Washington, D.C., The Catholic University of America Press, 1986.

Wolter, H., "The New Theology: Abelard, Peter Lombard, Gratian," *Handbook of Church History,* ed. H. Jedin, J. Dolan, N.Y., Herder and Herder, v. IV.

Yule, G., "Luther's Understanding of Justification by Grace Alone in Terms of Catholic Christology," *Luther, Theologian for Catholics and Protestants,* Edinburgh, T. & T. Clark, 1985.

Zeldin, T., "The Conflict of Moralities: Confession, Sin and Pleasure in the Nineteenth Century," *Conflicts in French Society,* London, G. Allen and Unwin, 1970.

Index of Authors

Biblical authors are not included. A few anonymous authors are cited by volume, e.g., *Didache.*

Adams, K., 263
Adnès, P., 172, 257, 258, 261, 262, 263, 269, 275, 276, 277
Agricola, J., 145
Alan of Lille, 130
Albert the Great, 91, 107, 110, 113, 114, 135, 269
d'Alès, A., 261, 262
Alexander II, 103
Alexander of Hales, 107, 110, 113, 114, 123, 125, 126, 135, 136, 268, 270
Alfaro, J., 134
Alger of Lüttich, 70, 111
Alszeghy, Z., 176, 200, 255, 276
Altaner, B., 261
Althaus, P., 48, 200
Amann, E., 267
Ambrose of Milan, 54, 63, 76, 80, 96, 164, 263
Ambrosiaster, 94, 264
Anciaux, P., 112, 200, 256, 267, 268
Anselm of Canterbury, 46, 96, 97, 98, 99, 101, 106, 107, 112, 114, 126, 127, 129, 266, 270
Anselm of Laon, 106
Anselm of Lucca, 103, 105
Antoninus, 158
Apostolic Constitutions, 72, 73, 90, 264
Arendt, H.-P., 176, 274, 276, 281
Aristides of Athens, 55
Athenegoras of Athens, 55
Auer, J., 267, 268, 271
Augustine of Canterbury, 84
Augustine of Hippo, 11, 27, 54, 61, 63, 69, 75, 76, 77, 81, 83, 95, 96, 101, 111, 118, 121, 129, 130, 132, 134, 141, 145, 148, 164, 186, 187, 194, 237, 263, 265, 266, 271
Aulén, G., 46, 107, 256, 260, 268
Aurelio of Rocca Contracta, 187

Baius, 134, 251
Baltimore Catechism, 40, 253, 259
Bancroft, R., 150
Bañez, D., 134, 199
Bardenhewer, O., 261
Barnabas, 53
Barth, K., 48